Global Sociology

Introducing Five Contemporary Societies

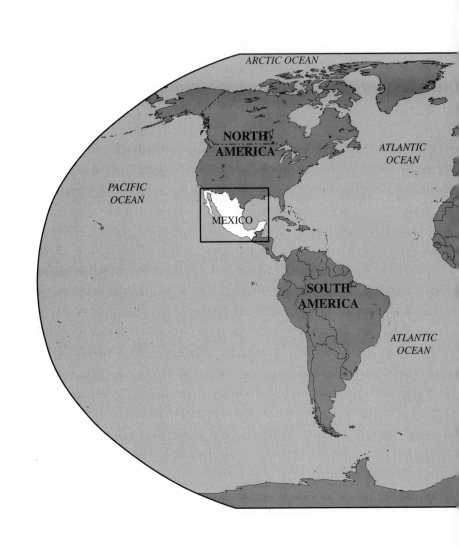

ARCTIC OCEAN

NORTH
AMERICA

ATLANTIC
OCEAN

PACIFIC
OCEAN

MEXICO

SOUTH
AMERICA

ATLANTIC
OCEAN

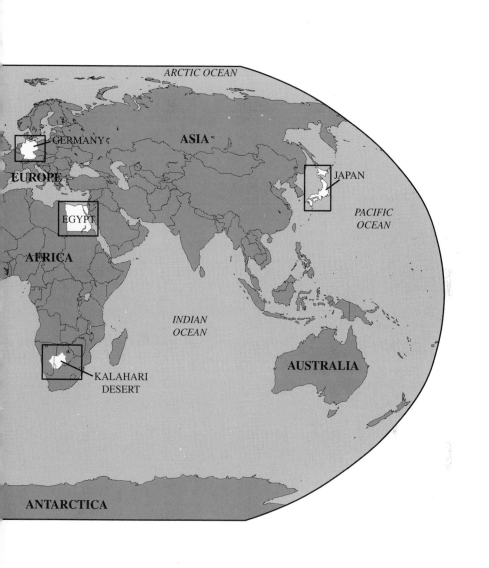

Global Sociology

Introducing Five Contemporary Societies

SECOND EDITION

Linda Schneider
Nassau Community College

Arnold Silverman
Nassau Community College

Boston   Burr Ridge, IL   Dubuque, IA   Madison, WI   New York
San Francisco   St. Louis
Bangkok   Bogotá   Caracas   Lisbon   London   Madrid
Mexico City   Milan   New Delhi   Seoul   Singapore   Sydney   Taipei   Toronto

McGraw-Hill Higher Education

A Division of The **McGraw-Hill** Companies

GLOBAL SOCIOLOGY: INTRODUCING FIVE
CONTEMPORARY SOCIETIES

This book is printed on acid-free paper.

1 2 3 4 5 6 7 8 9 0 FGR/FGR 9 0 9 8 7 6 5 4 3 2 1 0 9

ISBN 0-07-229430-2

Editorial director: *Phillip A. Butcher*
Sponsoring editor: *Sally Constable*
Developmental editor: *Katherine Blake*
Marketing manager: *Leslie A. Kraham*
Project manager: *Amy Hill*
Production supervisor: *Michael R. McCormick*
Designer: *Kiera Cunningham*
Cover photo: *R. M. Collins III/The Image Works*
Senior photo research coordinator: *Keri Johnson*
Photo research: *Connie Gardner*
Supplement coordinator: *Carol Bielski*
Compositor: *Shepherd Incorporated*
Typeface: *10.5/12 Times Roman*
Printer: *Quebecor Printing Book Group/Fairfield*

Library of Congress Cataloging-in-Publication Data

Schneider, Linda.
    Global sociology : introducing five contemporary societies / Linda
Schneider, Arnold Silverman. — 2nd ed.
        p.   cm.
    Includes bibliographical references and index.
    ISBN 0-07-229430-2 (pbk.)
    1. Sociology.   2. Sociology—Cross-cultural studies.
HM585.S36   2000
301—dc21   99-34826

http://www.mhhe.com

About the Authors

LINDA SCHNEIDER is Professor of Sociology at SUNY–Nassau Community College. She received her Ph. D. in sociology from Columbia University. Professor Schneider has for many years enjoyed teaching introductory sociology and has long been involved in activities related to undergraduate instruction. She has published in the ASA journal *Teaching Sociology*, and contributed to panels about teaching at conferences of the Eastern Sociological Society, the Community College Humanities Association, the Community College General Education Association, and the American Association of Community Colleges. Professor Schneider has directed several grants from the National Endowment for the Humanities, the Fund for the Improvement of Postsecondary Education, and the National Science Foundation for multidisciplinary and global curriculum development.

ARNOLD SILVERMAN is Professor of Sociology at SUNY–Nassau Community College. He received his Ph. D. in sociology from the University of Wisconsin, Madison. Professor Silverman has published widely, and his articles appear in *American Sociological Review, Built Environment, Contemporary Sociology, Social Service Review*, and elsewhere. He is the co-author of *Chosen Children*, a longitudinal study of American adopting families. Professor Silverman has also been active in efforts to improve the quality of undergraduate instruction. He co-directed a faculty development effort financed by the Fund for the Improvement of Postsecondary Education to encourage active learning in undergraduate teaching. He has been chair of the Eastern Sociological Society's Committee on Community Colleges, and he is currently the coordinator of Nassau Community College's Freshman Learning Communities program.

This book is dedicated to the peoples of Egypt, Germany, Mexico, and Japan, and the ¡Kung Bushmen, with whom we share a mutual human history and a common future.

Photo Credits

Contents

Chapter 4. Egypt: Faith, Gender, and Class   167

List of Tables and Figures

Introduction: To the Student

Global Sociology

Today, no one can afford to ignore the variety of the world's societies. If you go to work in the business world, it is very likely that in selling your products, or buying supplies, or managing your company's factories, you will need to deal with people from other societies. The better you understand cultures that differ from your own, the more likely it is that you will be successful. When you go on vacation or listen to music, you may come in contact with unfamiliar cultures. You will enjoy yourself more if you are comfortable with diversity. *Global Sociology* is a sociological introduction to the diversity of the world's societies.

Sociology has an important message for you: There are many ways to arrange human lives; many different kinds of families, economies, and governments; endlessly varied values, beliefs, attitudes, and customs. Until very recently in human history, most people lived quite isolated lives, seldom meeting people from other societies. People readily believed that their own way of life was the only way, or the best way, and that other societies were strange or evil. In today's global world, condemning other societies leads to misunderstanding and violence. The world's peoples need to learn about each other. We believe that the more you know about different ways of life, the more profoundly you will appreciate how much all humans have in common.

We chose five societies to include in this book:

Japan: A Conforming Culture

Mexico: Nation of Networks

The ¡Kung Bushmen: An Indigenous People of Southern Africa

Egypt: Faith, Gender, and Class

Germany: Social Institutions and Social Change in a Modern Western Society

It was hard to choose just five societies from all the hundreds in the world today. First of all, we chose societies from different parts of the world and different cultural traditions. One society in this book is in Asia, one in Latin America, one in Europe, and two in Africa, though one of these, Egypt, is culturally part of the Middle East. Japan and Germany are rich, industrialized nations. Mexico and Egypt are "developing" nations, struggling with poverty, and the ¡Kung Bushmen are not a nation at all.

We looked for societies very different from your own, to illustrate the range of the world's social diversity. Egypt is an Islamic society, where five times a day, the call to prayer penetrates every street and house. Many people pray at every call and strive to follow the laws of Islam. In Japan, people enjoy celebrating the holidays of many religions. At Christmas, Japanese people give each other presents and eat take-out fried chicken. Afterwards, they attend a ceremony in a Buddhist temple. But only 10 percent of Japanese people consider themselves religious.

The Germans and the ¡Kung Bushmen could not be more different peoples, but they have in common the experience of rapid social change. The ¡Kung Bushmen are one of the last peoples on earth who live by gathering wild food. They are now losing their land and their way of life, marking the end of a major chapter in the story of humanity. Since reunification, Germans have struggled to merge two very different societies, one capitalist and one socialist.

In Egypt and Mexico there are tremendous disparities between the rich and the poor. Rich Egyptians have made their country one of the world's largest importers of German luxury cars, but poor Egyptians, desperate for housing, have taken to living in cemeteries. Indian peasants in Chiapas, Mexico, took up arms against local landowners and the government, and their rebellion, which began in 1994, still continues.

Learning Sociology from Diversity

Learning about many different societies will help you deepen your understanding of sociological concepts. Sociology textbooks teach concepts like values, norms, roles, socialization, deviance, social stratification, modernization, etc. The five societies in this book were chosen to illustrate these and other important sociological concepts. When you understand how sociological concepts can be applied to differing societies, you will understand the concepts much better.

Let's take an example: the concept of social inequality. We have chosen societies for this book with very varied forms of social inequality. The ¡Kung Bushmen are an almost entirely egalitarian society: No one has any more possessions or any more power than anyone else. Learning about the ¡Kung will sharpen your ability to see inequalities in other societies, including your own. In Egypt, there are very sharp inequalities between men and women. In Japan, people pay close attention to status differences in age, gender, education, and occupation, but income inequalities are quite minimal. In Mexico, millions of people earn the minimum wage of under $4 a day, while the richest Mexicans have imported cars and air-conditioned houses and send their children to college abroad. When you learn about many different systems of social stratification, you will understand the concept better.

In order to help you understand what life is like in different societies, we have included in each chapter a number of *vignettes:* short, fictional sketches of individuals, their life situations, and their feelings. None of the characters in the vignettes are real people. We made them up, inspired by people we read about and people we met.

Learning through Comparison

Comparison and contrast are very powerful means of learning. The ¡Kung Bushmen spend all their lives in groups of 15 to 40 people, related by kinship. Imagine how hard it would be to teach them the concept of "bureaucracy." They have never waited in line at the Department of Motor Vehicles or filled out forms for registration at college. When you study the ¡Kung Bushmen, you will learn how new and unusual bureaucracies are in human experience.

Comparison has always been the essence of sociology. Sociologists know that when you are immersed in your own society, you take it for granted and assume that its ways are part of human nature, universal and unchanging. We most easily discover what our own society is like when we learn about a different society. As sociologists say, "the fish is the last to discover water."

Comparison is a wonderful means of applying concepts and theories and deepening your understanding of their meanings. Comparison is also a challenge to intolerance. Studying world societies shows us that there is no one right way to live, and that the most fundamental characteristic of "human nature" is our tremendous flexibility in creating diverse cultures.

Active Learning

Suppose you wanted to learn to play basketball and someone told you to listen to another person talk about the game, and then watch other people play it. You would be disgusted with this advice, because you know that in order to learn basketball, you must play the game yourself and then practice, practice, practice. If you have a coach or someone else to watch you and give you pointers, you will learn even faster.

Will you be surprised to hear that learning sociology (or any other college subject) works the same way? Just reading or hearing someone else present sociological ideas isn't enough. You must practice your own sociological reasoning, out loud and in writing and have others coach you in your work in order to learn the subject.

Global Sociology is designed so that you can practice applying sociological concepts to a descriptive "database" of information about five different societies. As you read this book, ask yourself: Can I talk about these societies using the language of sociology? Try to describe the values of each society, or the roles they expect men and women to play. Think about how family life is organized in each society, or what social groups are most important in peoples' lives. Questions at the end of each chapter will help you put your knowledge of sociology to active use.

One of the best ways of practicing sociological thinking is by making comparisons. We invite you to compare each of these societies to your own society: What similarities and what differences can you see? You can also compare the societies in this book with each other. In writing the book, we have been greatly tempted to make comparisons ourselves, but we have tried to discipline ourselves and stick to description. We wanted to leave the work and play of comparison to the students and instructors who use *Global Sociology*.

Preface: To the Instructor

We wrote this book to give students a broader context for understanding both sociology and their own societies. For several years both authors had assigned William Kephart's *Extraordinary Groups* when teaching introductory sociology. We liked Kephart's case study approach. Reading his descriptions of a variety of American religious groups, students were exposed to diverse cultures and social structures. Despite these advantages, we were unhappy confining our comparisons to religious sects. Linda's student Mike Godino put it nicely when he told us, "You know, introductory sociology is great. I'm learning about ways of life I never imagined, and it makes me see my own society so much more clearly by contrast. But I'm not sure I want to know this much about these little religious groups. Isn't there a book that does the same thing for different countries, important countries that we should understand?" Mike's comment crystallized our desire to extend the range of comparisons, and we searched around, but there wasn't such a book. There were ethnographies, but these were anthropological rather than sociological. Then there were "global" textbooks. We liked these texts, but we were looking for a supplement with in-depth case studies.

Finally we decided to write the book ourselves: *Global Sociology* is a softcover supplement to any standard sociology text, providing broad and comprehensive sociological description of five diverse contemporary societies. We aimed for wide geographic distribution: We chose one Asian society—Japan; one Latin American society—Mexico; one European society—Germany; and two African societies—Egypt and the ¡Kung Bushmen. Two of the societies are wealthy and industrial, and two are poor "developing" nations. For contrast, we included a nonnational society—the hunting and gathering ¡Kung Bushmen.

One of our concerns in writing *Global Sociology* has been to create a text that instructors can use without being specialists in the study of Japan, Mexico, Egypt, Germany, or the ¡Kung Bushmen. General knowledge and a sociologist's understanding of how societies work is ample background for using *Global Sociology*.

We are confident that you will see how *Global Sociology* can easily be introduced into your courses. Although it is interesting to read some of the more specialized studies we have recommended, it is by no means a requirement for the effective use of *Global Sociology*.

The five societies described here vary in many ways: in their definitions of male and female roles, in their degree of inequality, in the salience of religious values and norms in their cultures, and in their population dynamics. *Global Sociology* includes two different socialist societies, the former East Germany and Egypt, and it examines the post-socialist transformation of East Germany. The book also examines two different capitalist societies, West Germany and Japan, whose styles of capitalism contrast with that of the United States.

Global Sociology is structured so as to parallel the major sections of a standard sociology text. Each chapter is organized around basic sociological topics: culture, social structure and group life, socialization, deviance, social institutions, social stratification, and social change. Earlier chapters place more emphasis on topics usually introduced first in introductory sociology. Chapters on Japan, Mexico, and the ¡Kung Bushmen provide much discussion of culture, social structure, socialization, and deviance, though they include other topics too. Later chapters on Egypt and Germany touch more briefly on beginning concepts and emphasize social stratification, social institutions, and social change.

Global Sociology will help bring to life abstract textbook presentations of concepts with a wealth of vivid illustrations. Reading about Japanese greeting norms, or Mexican patronage politics, or the effects of population growth in Egypt, or East Germans' first encounters with capitalism, or how the ¡Kung Bushmen avoid conflict, students will see the universal relevance of sociological ideas. Questions posed at the end of each chapter lead students to make sociological comparisons and to apply sociological concepts to descriptive knowledge.

Comparison is one of the great strengths of sociology. By comparing other societies with their own, students learn about the range of social variation, and they learn what makes their own society distinctive. Reading *Global Sociology,* students will spontaneously make comparisons with their own society, and they can be encouraged to compare the diverse societies described in the book. To aid in this effort, the text provides a variety of tables, summarizing important comparative data for Japan, Mexico, Egypt, Germany, and the United States.

Although most of our students were born and raised in the United States, an increasing number are from countries as diverse as El Salvador, Haiti, Jamaica, Iran, China, Greece, and the former Soviet Union. It is exciting to see that these students can use *Global Sociology* to make meaningful comparisons with the societies and cultures they have been born and raised in. *Global Sociology* doesn't require that students carry the assumptions, insights, and values of an American childhood and schooling.

Learning about other societies helps all students become aware of their ethnocentrism and reach beyond it. Students develop a sense of attachment to the societies they study, even when some of what they read disturbs them. To help students use their imaginations in picturing unfamiliar societies, we have included fictional vignettes of individuals in each society. Vignettes help students make human connections across cultural divides.

We have found that reading *Global Sociology* heightens student interest in other societies. News from abroad becomes absorbing when students have a framework in which to place it. *Global Sociology* presents societies that are often in the news, and our own students have become alert to news coverage about the societies they study. When an economic crisis shook Japan and a revolutionary movement riveted Mexico, students brought in news clippings and compared Japanese, Mexican, and American responses to crises. When they read about Egypt, our students noticed for the first time that Muslims in their community and their college were observing Ramadan.

The Second Edition

World events move quickly. The second edition is revised to keep your students up to date. First of all, the statistical tables have been updated with the latest information available. We have searched out the best sources of world statistics on the Internet, and Web references are noted with the tables and in the bibliography. You and your students can continue to update data by using these sources. In many cases, Web sources will allow you to generate your own tables by selecting variables.

Global Sociology has been carefully revised for current events. There is new coverage of the social impact of Japan's economic crisis, and revised discussion of the status and roles of women in Japanese society. Analysis of Japanese society introduces new work on inequalities of class and power to give a more complete picture of current scholarly thinking about Japan today.

The chapter on Mexico contains new material on deviance, with discussion of the current crime wave and the effects of narcotics trafficking on Mexican society. We have updated and amplified coverage of political change in Mexico, discussing the rise of opposition parties and contested elections. There is more discussion of Mexico's place in the world economy and the effects of global economic crisis.

Chapter 4 on Egypt has been extensively revised, with a new section on deviance and more information about Islamic fundamentalism and revolutionary Islamic movements, in a world context. We have added coverage of women's rights and Islamic law and updated information on working women and on marriage in Egypt today.

The second edition contains more information about the current situation of the ¡Kung Bushmen in Namibia and Botswana and the impact of government policy, economic change, and foreign non-governmental organizations.

Ten years after reunification, Germany is a much-changed society. We have included a careful evaluation of just how far the social reunification of the two parts of Germany has progressed. In addition, the second edition discusses recent political change in Germany and the situation of Germany in a unifying Europe. There is more coverage of current controversies about guilt and remembrance, the Holocaust, and Germany's present treatment of immigrants.

Events, no doubt, will continue their rapid pace. We have tried to give you access to current news about the societies in this book, so it will be easy for you to keep up. Please use the Web guide in the Instructor's Manual that accompanies *Global Sociology*. It includes English-language newspaper Web sites for all five societies. We have carefully selected Web sites that are reputable and reliable, easy to access, and constantly updated. They should be a good source for news for you and your students.

We have enjoyed using *Global Sociology* with our students. We appreciate their sense of wonder as they confront diverse societies, and we are continually impressed with how much they learn about their own society when they study other societies. We hope you and your students will enjoy the book too.

Acknowledgments

We would like to acknowledge the help that so many people gave us throughout the writing of this book. First, we need to thank our students, whose response led us to this effort and who "field tested" earlier drafts of *Global Sociology*. Teresa Sala Imhof of McGraw-Hill offered the initial enthusiasm that led us to transform a good idea into a coherent proposal. Phil Butcher, also of McGraw-Hill, convinced us that our idea was both viable and appreciated by a potential publisher. Kathy Blake of McGraw-Hill did a great deal to expedite the development process through both editions of *Global Sociology*. Kathy helped us keep the entire project in perspective as we wrestled with the details of Egyptian population dynamics and Mexican credit cooperatives. Sally Constable, McGraw-Hill's sociology editor, and Leslie Kraham and Anne Sachs of McGraw-Hill's marketing department were continuously encouraging, insightful, and cooperative.

A panel of reviewers gave us useful insights and generously shared their knowledge of the societies described in *Global Sociology*. For the second edition, they include Michael Ball of the University of Wisconsin at Superior, Lee Frank of the Community College of Allegheny County, Kathleen Kalab of Western Kentucky University, Nelson Pichardo of the State University of New York at Albany, Sarah Soule of the University of Arizona, and David Wachtel of Lexington Community College (who thoughtfully included the comments of his students along with his own insights). Special thanks go to Jan AbuShakrah of Portland Community College and Jan Fiola of Moorhead State University. The comments of our reviewers from the first edition continued to be useful to us, especially those of Brenda Phillips of Texas Woman's University. Our reviewers' grasp of the teaching process has helped to make this book a more useful classroom document.

Gordon DeBlaey of Calvin College in Grand Rapids, Michigan was kind enough to offer us his insights based on the use of our text in his courses.

Our colleague Eric Wood graciously shared his insights and materials from his fieldwork among the ¡Kung Bushmen in Namibia. Louise Forsyth of Brooklyn Poly Prep contributed her thoughtful insights into the history and literature of the

Middle East and her good sense of what students needed to see and hear in a text dealing with Islamic cultures. Janet Abu-Lughod of the New School for Social Research and Lila Abu-Lughod of New York University helped us develop a broader and better understanding of contemporary Egypt. Their direction in terms of sources and ideas was invaluable.

Marilyn Rosenthal and Marcia Speigelman of Nassau Community College's library initiated us into the use of the Internet and its remarkable resources for an undertaking such as ours. Marilyn and her colleagues also worked hard to find the monographs, articles, and government documents so useful to our work. They were more than ably assisted by the staffs of the community libraries of Rochester, Vermont and Merrick, New York.

We owe a debt of thanks to our able student assistant Yongjoo Kwon, who photocopied endlessly, ran to the library and the mailroom, and helped us keep afloat in the sea of details that producing a text requires.

Finally, we recognize our debts to our respective spouses and children, who encouraged us and endured our preoccupation with researching and writing *Global Sociology*.

Linda Schneider
Arnold Silverman

Global Sociology

Introducing Five Contemporary Societies

JAPAN

To reach Japan from the United States or Canada you would fly across the North Pacific almost to the mainland of Asia. Air traffic to Tokyo is so busy you might need to fly to nearby Korea and take a shuttle. Rising from defeat in World War II, Japan has become the world's second largest economy.

LOCATION: Japan is located on the eastern edge of Asia, 200 miles from Korea and across the Sea of Japan from China and Russia. East of Japan lies the Pacific Ocean.

AREA: Japan consists of four large islands of Hokkaido, Honshu, Shikoku, and Kyushu (145,000 square miles or 420,000 square kilometers). Together they are the size of California or Germany. Honshu is the largest island and the site of Tokyo, the capital, and other large cities.

LAND: Japan is mountainous and rugged. Mt. Fuji, a dormant volcano, is 12,000 feet high. Less than 1 acre in 6 is flat; most of this is along the coasts where cities compete with farms for space. Almost half the population lives in three major metropolitan areas.

CLIMATE: Similar to the east coast of the United States. It is colder on Hokkaido and nearly subtropical in southern Kyushu. Japan receives 50 inches of rain a year, much of it falling as snow.

POPULATION: In 1995 there were 125 million people; in 2025 the population should be virtually the same. Japan's population is aging; 16 percent are over age 65.

INCOME: U.S. $36,658 per capita GNP in 1996.

EDUCATION: Japan has one of the highest average educational levels and the highest literacy rate in the world.

RELIGION: 75% combine Buddhism and Shinto, a unique Japanese religion; less than 2% are Christian.

MINORITIES: Korean Japanese, Ainu, Burakumin.

Japan: A Conforming Culture

INTRODUCTION

Of all the societies in this book, Japan is perhaps the one most widely known, and most surrounded by controversy. Especially in the United States, media coverage of Japan is constant. News articles, murder mysteries, plays, and movies take advantage of the public preoccupation with Japan as an economic rival. Much of the description of Japan is negative: The Japanese are portrayed as mindless drones; corrupt "crony capitalists" driving their country and perhaps the world economy to ruin; skilled copyists incapable of original, independent thought. But there is also a great deal of admiration for Japan. During Japan's economic boom years in the 1970s and '80s, many American studies examined the effectiveness of Japanese elementary education, Japanese corporate management and factory organization, and many Japanese practices were in fact adopted by western businesses. Also, thousands of westerners practice Japanese martial arts, or Japanese meditation techniques, and learn to admire ancient Japanese cultural traditions.

Will the real Japan please stand up? Spiritual culture? Stalled economy? Empire of conformity? Paradise of order, efficiency, and technology? Controversy about Japan and Japanese institutions will doubtless continue, but there are some strikingly important aspects of Japanese society you should know about in order to understand Japan's rise to economic power and world importance.

A Sense of "Peoplehood"

The Japanese believe that you cannot understand their society unless you know that they are a unique people, physically and mentally different from all the rest of the world's peoples. Tradition holds that the Japanese people are a single family, all descended from a common ancestor, the sun goddess Amaterasu. Many Japanese people believe that their society's economic success, low crime rate, and high level of education are the result of its people's distinct racial stock.

But Japanese racial identity is in reality a social belief, not a physical fact. Anthropologists tell us that the Japanese people are part of the Mongoloid group of peoples, which includes the Koreans and the Han Chinese. There is some variety, too, in the appearance of the Japanese people—different shades of skin color, and hair and eyes ranging from black to brown reflect a heritage of Polynesian, Chinese, and East Asian ancestry. And while they believe that Koreans are physically distinctive, the Japanese are unable to identify Japanese-born Koreans by their appearance (Tasker, pp. 15–16, 34; Feiler, p. 135).

Although it is not a physical fact, the Japanese sense of "peoplehood" has a firm social foundation. Japan, like most other societies, is inhabited by people whose ancestors came from many places. Japan is a chain of islands, about 200 miles off the coast of Korea. The most ancient people to arrive in Japan were the Ainu, a distinctive race which dates back thousands of years into prehistory. After the Ainu, other peoples came to Japan from southern and northern Asia. But it is important to know that there has been no significant immigration into Japan for more than a thousand years. For all that time, the peoples of Japan mingled, until they developed the world's most racially and culturally unified society. There are in fact some minority groups in Japan (which we will examine later), but they are few and small in size. The Japanese sense of distinctiveness is reinforced by language: Unlike the rest of the world's major languages, Japanese is spoken by only one ethnic group, and by relatively few foreigners.

While the Japanese people are not the separate race they believe themselves to be, they are indeed an unusually homogeneous people, much more so than the people of other societies. Their sense of peoplehood has given them unique advantages that other societies don't have. They are able to merge the concepts of racial and national identity, and their acute sense of distinctiveness, carefully cultivated by Japan's leaders, helps foster an unusually strong feeling of group solidarity and national purpose in Japanese society.

"An Island Nation"

"Japan is an island nation," schoolchildren are repeatedly told, "surrounded by seas and enemies, so we must depend on each other." Though their country is perceived by others as a giant power in the global economy, the Japanese people share a sense of national vulnerability. Many Japanese think of their country as small, even weak, unprotected from assault by outside forces. They are acutely aware that Japan, though self-sufficient up to the twentieth century, is now highly dependent on the world economy, more so than any other major power. Japan has no oil, almost no raw materials, and must import much of its meat and grain. Since the land is very mountainous, only a small portion is suitable for agriculture, and almost the entire population is squeezed into only one-fifth of the total area. The Japanese play down their early twentieth-century history as an aggressive imperial power, which invaded China and other Asian nations and provoked the United States to war (Tasker, pp. 8–10; Feiler, pp. 88, 141).

JAPAN'S HISTORY

The Japanese sense of vulnerability to external powers, with its accompanying feeling of loyalty and obligation to the nation, is not of recent origin. Japan's history can best be understood as a sequence of eras in which the nation alternately isolated itself from, or eagerly absorbed, foreign influences. Geography gave

Japan a choice about its relation to the outside world. Two hundred miles of stormy seas protected the country from invasion by foreign forces, but permitted contact with the great mainland Asian cultures through travel and trade. In the modern era, Japan was one of the last Asian cultures to face western colonizers, and had the opportunity to study the effects of western domination elsewhere.

Contact with China

The first great turning point in Japanese history happened over a thousand years ago, in the seventh century. Japan was at that time a tribal society in which people lived by gardening and fishing, without cities, with only a weak national government and a ruling family whose importance was largely symbolic. But early in the seventh century, a prince of the ruling family, Prince Shotoku, began to import cultural practices from China, at that time the world's most advanced nation. Prince Shotoku began by importing Chinese Buddhism and Buddhist art. For the next three centuries, Japan's rulers continued to study China and adopt Chinese institutions, arts, and technology, deliberately "improving" Japanese society. Japan adopted China's courtly manners and arts, its centralized government and elaborate bureaucracy, its tax system, and its system of writing. The Japanese even built elaborate Chinese-style capital cities, remarkable in a society which previously had lacked even towns! But it is important to understand that then, and later, all of Japan's foreign borrowings were voluntary. Japan never was conquered and colonized by another country. In fact, after the ninth century, Japan retreated into isolation and slowly digested all its borrowed Chinese culture, blending it with native ways, and finally producing a new, distinctly Japanese culture (Reischauer, 1977, pp. 41–51).

The Tokugawa Era

By the sixteenth century Japan was enjoying a period of commercial growth and artistic expression. It was a relatively open time when individual self-development flourished. When Portuguese missionaries and traders reached Japan, they were greeted with curiosity and interest. In the next 100 years, more than 300,000 Japanese were converted to Christianity. But then Japan's rulers decided things had gone too far and forced thousands of Japanese Christians to renounce their religion or face execution. By 1638, they had completely sealed off Japan from the outside world. Laws forbade the Japanese from building ocean-going ships or traveling abroad, and only a few foreign traders—Koreans, Chinese, and Dutch— were allowed to enter Japan. Japan became a much more closed, hierarchical society. During two centuries of isolation (known as the Tokugawa Era, 1635–1853, after the leading line of shoguns, or rulers of the period) Japan was peaceful and stable. Important changes took place, though, including the development of a class of entrepreneurs, the rise of a centralized government, and the forging of a strong sense of national identity. A few Japanese scholars read Dutch books and kept up with news of the scientific and political revolutions taking place in the West (Christopher, pp. 47–48; Schooler, pp. 32–36).

The Meiji Restoration

Japan's second contact with the West had a very different outcome. By the mid-nineteenth century, western powers had colonized Africa, India, and much of Southeast Asia, forcing trade concessions upon China as well. Finally, in 1853, under Commodore Perry, the American Navy forced Japan to open its ports to American ships and sign a series of trade treaties. Fear of subjection to foreign powers brought on a national crisis in Japan. In 1868, rebel provincial rulers, backed by reform-minded middle- and low-ranking *samurai* (members of Japan's hereditary warrior caste) seized power from the shoguns. Their rule was called the *Meiji Restoration,* because they claimed to restore power to the emperor, the hereditary monarch. In fact, however, they ruled in his stead. During the nineteenth century European empires were taking control all over Asia, Africa, and Latin America. Only the Japanese took radical defensive action against colonization. The Meiji rulers successfully argued that the only way Japan could enjoy equality with western powers was to modernize and adopt western technology. Under Meiji leadership Japan was able to deliberately bring about its own modernization and fend off European colonization.

The Meiji government in effect went shopping for new institutions, finding a model for its navy in Britain, its army in France, its universities in America, and its constitution in Germany (Tasker, p. 21). Meiji rulers created a new government bureaucracy, based on European models and staffed by a new university-educated civil service. They adopted a modern court system and public school system. Meiji Japan promoted economic modernization, making peasants owners of the land they farmed, and encouraging modern agriculture, based on American models. The government created western-style banks, railroads, and ports, and developed mining, steel, and weapons production, and silk manufacture. They sent students abroad to learn western skills and hired western experts to come to Japan. And all of this was done by the end of the nineteenth century!

Japan also emulated the imperial ambitions of western countries, both to demonstrate its military strength to the West and to build an empire of its own. In 1894–1895, Japan defeated China in a war for control of Korea, and in 1904–1905, it fought again for Korea, this time against Russia, gaining Korea and several other possessions in its victory. By World War I, Japan was a major colonial power, the equal of western powers. Militarism intensified in Japan during the difficult years of the 1920s and 1930s. Imperial ambitions once again led Japan into war with China, a war which dragged on and finally escalated into the Pacific theater of World War II. Japan's defeat opened a new chapter in its westernization and economic development.

The Occupation Reforms

Japan was utterly devastated by the war, and its people were demoralized and disillusioned with militarism. They were open to change and new ideas. And the American occupying forces, in their self-confident, well-meaning American way, were eager to make over Japanese society. General Douglas MacArthur, acting as supreme commander for the allied powers, dismantled Japan's military, reformed its government and constitution, broke up its industrial monopolies, and redistributed land ownership. MacArthur's reforms were radical, giving individuals rights beyond what is guaranteed in the U.S. Constitution, including equal rights for women, the right of labor to bargain collectively, and the right of all individuals to an equal education. As we will see, in the years since the occupation, Japan has strengthened the reforms that were compatible with its culture and ignored the rest. A new combination of western institutions and Japanese centralized government, created with Japanese-style drive, brought about Japan's postwar "economic miracle."

JAPANESE CULTURE

In its long history, Japan has three times adopted foreign institutions and practices. Today, Japan looks more and more like modern western industrial societies, with its sprawling cities, skyscrapers, traffic jams, global corporations, automated factories, and parliamentary government. Some American and European observers think that Japan is becoming completely westernized and indistinguishable from modern industrial societies in Europe and North America. The Japanese themselves say that isn't so: They say they adopted western technologies and institutions, but not western values and beliefs. In Japan, you can still hear an old slogan from the Meiji Era, "*wakon yosai*" (Japanese spirit and western knowledge), and Japanese people will tell you that the foreign models they adopt are transformed by the addition of a "Japanese heart" (Tasker, p. 21; Feiler, pp. 36–37).

You can understand *wakon yosai* better with the aid of sociology. Sociologists divide the culture of every society into two parts: **material** and **nonmaterial culture.** Material culture consists of things: houses, clothing, machines, art objects, tools, technologies, and so forth. Nonmaterial culture is abstract; it can't be touched. It includes values, beliefs, language, symbols, and norms and sanctions. Japan's material culture is indeed being rapidly westernized. Japanese people used to live in distinctive houses made of wood and paper, with *tatami* mat floors and special family altars; they wore *kimonos* and *obis* (wrapped robes tied with sashes), and slept on *futons* unrolled on the floor at night. Nowadays, most Japanese people live in western-style apartments in concrete apartment houses, filled with televisions, CD players, and video games, just like houses in New York, or Paris, or Berlin. They wear jeans and T-shirts, or suits and ties, like people anywhere in the western world.

But Japan's nonmaterial culture has changed much more slowly and remains much more distinctly Japanese. In fact, as a result, many important Japanese institutions, which are borrowed from the West, like parliamentary government and corporate business organization, actually function very differently in Japan than they do in the West. Japanese culture differs from western culture in many important ways. First of all, Japan has much less internal diversity than most western cultures. Distinctively Japanese values and norms, beliefs, and forms of symbolic expression are very widely shared in Japanese society.

It is Saturday night and the whole family is eating dinner together. Many Japanese fathers work late every weekday night and eat dinner with their families only on weekends. In this picture, the food and chopsticks are Japanese, but family members, like other Japanese people, are wearing western clothing. Japanese homes are small by western standards and this dining room is crowded with a large television, mementos, and furniture.

Cultural Integration

Sociologists believe that one important way societies differ from each other is in their degree of **cultural integration.** Some societies have highly integrated cultures: Norms and values are consistent throughout the society and the different elements of culture and social structure "fit together" well: Institutions are organized in ways that seem to reflect the society's values, and living up to one norm seldom automatically puts a person in violation of another. Most highly integrated cultures are small, isolated, preindustrial societies like the ¡Kung Bushmen. It is rare that a large, modern, industrial society will exhibit a high degree of cultural integration. Most modern industrial societies are internally diverse: People in urban and rural areas have different lifestyles and interpret their cultures differently; various social classes, ethnic groups, and subcultures may subscribe to differing values and norms; and because of rapid social change, new norms and values may develop and clash with the old. For all these reasons, in most modern societies, culture is internally inconsistent and contradictory and people often disagree about the proper way to live one's life and behave toward others.

People in Japan hear constantly that their society is special, like no other. They are told that the Japanese are like one family; that everyone works together to help their country, and that each person shares the same values and the same culture. There are many books written to explain the uniqueness of Japan both to the Japanese and to others. This literature claims that Japan is unlike other industrial societies because it is an integrated culture. In Japan people take pride in the homogeneity of their society. They agree about norms and values and they agree that conformity to the norms is very important so that society can function smoothly and harmoniously. In Japan one hears often that low crime rates, low divorce rates, and high levels of economic equality show how well Japanese society works (Sugimoto, p. 4).

Reading about the uniqueness of Japan, it would not be hard for one to imagine that Japanese society has been designed by a **functionalist** sociologist! Like functionalist theorists, the Japanese stress the importance of order and consensus in their society, they carefully examine how every part of society contributes to the smooth functioning of the whole, and they emphasize that individuals should subordinate their personal desires to common goals.

Are you looking around skeptically now and thinking Japan is too perfect to be believed? Is Japan really so homogeneous and conforming? If you visit Japan, you might quickly concur. Less than 4 percent of the Japanese population can be classed as members of minority groups, and very few of these are racial minorities. So if you visit a Japanese city you will not see the kind of racial and ethnic diversity that you would encounter in Los Angeles or Toronto or London. You won't see any great diversity in dress either. Businessmen dress very conservatively; they never even exchange their white shirts for blue shirts or striped ones. Sales clerks in department stores wear uniforms and so do all the workers and managers in factories. Adult women usually dress quite conservatively too; they wear skirts and avoid bright colors. Subway riders wait in two neat rows for the train doors to open and even the vegetables for sale in markets are beautifully marshalled in rows of carefully tied bunches.

But when you got to know Japan better you would realize that some diversity exists; not nearly as much as in the United States or Canada, but more than at first meets the eye. Sociologist Yoshio Sugimoto points out that there is some regional diversity in Japan. Also, in Japan as in other societies, the rural way of life differs somewhat from city ways. But the principle source of diversity in Japan today is generational. Young people are definitely different from their elders. They are more influenced by the global consumer culture, buying the latest in rock music and trendy clothes from many countries. Unlike older Japanese, they never experienced the tragic years of World War II and the terrible poverty which followed. They are children of affluence, less devoted to hard work and duty than their parents, and more interested in leisure, self-development, and fun (Sugimoto, pp. 56–57, 65–73). But while their attitudes may be different from their parents', young Japanese are well aware of their society's dominant values. School authorities, employers, government officials, parents, television personalities, and journalists speak with one voice about the values that make Japan special.

The Value of Harmony

Japan has a large population relative to its land mass, and most Japanese people live crowded together in an urban corridor squeezed along the eastern edge of the

Japanese islands. The Japanese believe that crowding has taught them to place a very high value on public harmony and avoidance of conflict. There is little crime, so you needn't lock your car or fear being mugged, and couples can safely walk in the park at midnight. It would be very rare to see people arguing in public or come upon a fight outside a bar. Japanese norms require people to be willing to apologize and humble themselves. So after a car accident the drivers will jump out and apologize and bow to each other. In the Japanese version of the fairy tale Little Red Riding Hood, the wolf apologizes, the grandmother is saved and forgives him, and they all sit down together to tea. As you can imagine, lawsuits are uncommon in Japan; people are more likely to avoid confrontation and reach informal compromises. But lest you get the idea that the Japanese are inhumanly perfect, you should understand that people must work very hard to maintain public harmony and order. Japanese people get insulted or angry just like anyone else, but in their society values and norms forcefully promote self-control and the avoidance of direct personal confrontation.

The idea of two people openly expressing disagreement fills Japanese people with horror. In business or personal life, people are expected to avoid committing themselves to hard and fast positions; they try not to acknowledge or clarify their disagreements. Instead, Japanese people proceed by cautiously feeling each other out, making ambiguous statements, and using nonverbal clues to figure out what others prefer, aiming for compromise without revelation of conflict.

Decisions in Japanese corporations are usually made after a long process of consultations, often through the circulation of memos, typically written by middle-ranking associates, and usually vaguely phrased. Each reader puts his seal on the document and may add comments to it. The memo is gradually revised as the members of the staff edge toward agreement. By the end, everyone is familiar with the problem under discussion, but no one stakes out a clear position from which they might have to retreat, and there are no clear winners and losers. There is one tremendous advantage to this procedure: Once a decision is reached there is no losing minority, licking its wounds and grudging support. On the other hand, decision making is slow and cumbersome, and in a crisis, like an earthquake or a financial panic, Japanese institutions are infuriatingly slow to respond (Smith, pp. 54–55).

Another way the Japanese avoid conflict is by use of a "go-between," a neutral person who literally goes between two parties when there is some matter to be worked out. Go-betweens are frequently used in Japan in negotiating marriages. With a go-between, one need not turn down a potential bride or groom to her or his face, avoiding open disagreement and embarrassment.

The Value of Fitting In

Achieving smooth, harmonious relationships among group members may seem a very desirable goal, particularly to anyone who has endured a workplace or family filled with discord, or a city full of crime and conflict. But group harmony in Japan has its price: It is achieved by constant care and individual self-discipline. In Japanese society, the group comes first. For most people, being alone, outside the web of group life, is unthinkable. In the Japanese view, it is only in groups that people can develop as individuals, experience the pleasures of human feeling, and enjoy a sense of secure interdependence with others.

Why do Japanese people consider group life so important? One significant reason is that the Japanese find their identities in groups. One's self-esteem is fed by being selected to join a group, and, if asked to identify themselves, people offer their group affiliations. Thus, a Japanese "salaryman" asked his profession is unlikely to answer, "I am a programmer." Rather, "I work for SONY" will be offered and a stranger might respectfully refer to him personally as "Sony-san" ("Mr. Sony").[1]

Of course there are individualists in Japan: brilliant entrepreneurs who start billion-dollar companies alone, iconoclastic artists and writers. But they are not celebrated in Japanese society. They are not cultural idols and children don't look up to them and imitate them. Popular legends attach instead to the loyal company man, the salaryman, who puts his company first, despite his personal wishes and problems. Novels, television series, and movies portray him.

Maintaining Relationships

In Japanese society, people value being part of a group, and they work at getting along. But life in Japanese groups takes a great deal of time and work, because of the emphasis placed on avoidance of conflict. Self-assertion, overtly disagreeing with others, making demands, or even clearly stating one's wishes, all look like threats to group harmony and are out of the question. Such behavior is downright frightening to the Japanese. In relating to others, it is far preferable to express your feelings and wishes indirectly.

In Japan people try not to call attention to themselves. This *enryo* or "reserve" restrains people from giving opinions, expressing desires, or even making choices if they are offered. But how can a group function, if no one can express individual wishes? Because of *enryo,* it is of fundamental importance that people are highly sensitive to the unspoken wishes of others. The Japanese value *ninjo,* which means compassion, sympathy, rapport, or "fellow feeling." A good person strives to empathize—to understand the feelings of others and the situational difficulties others may be experiencing. In Japan if something bad happens to you—if someone close to you dies, or your mate leaves you, or you fail your exams, your friends will rally round. They will keep you company and bring you food and try to distract you from your troubles. But they will never say "you must feel terrible about . . ." or even "do you want to talk about. . . ." That would seem terribly crude. In Japan your friends support you by showing you they understand, but people don't believe that expressing feelings directly is especially useful or healing.

In ordinary Japanese life a good host knows a guest well enough to anticipate what food will be pleasing, and sets it before the guest so no choices are required. Good guests eat what they are given so as not to cause embarrassment by implying that the host has misunderstood their desires. If you make your wishes known, it is an insult to others: It implies that you believe the other person is too insensitive to

---

[1]*Sarariman* is the Japanese form of the English "salaryman." It is used to describe managers who are, almost without exception, men. Women work in business as "office ladies"—secretaries. There is no gender-neutral language in Japan (like "businessperson") to describe employees, because men and women play sharply different workplace roles.

perceive them. For example, the worst thing a husband can say about his wife is "I have to ask for what I want." Members of Japanese groups also expect other group members to anticipate their unexpressed desires (Smith, pp. 57–58).

How do the Japanese manage to do this? For one thing, spending a lot of time together helps. People who are in constant contact, in informal as well as formal situations, come to understand each other intuitively. Also, the Japanese place great emphasis on nonverbal communication. Because of *enryo,* people's words are not a good guide to their feelings. From childhood, people practice observing others' behavior for tiny hints in body language, tone of voice, the timing of silences. Just as children in many cultures can read their parents' disapproval in a glance or body posture, so members of Japanese groups come to read each other. In fact, a person who insists on explicit rational explanation is called a "reason freak" and is considered immature (Smith, p. 58).

The Value of Perseverance

Japanese contains many words, used constantly, that tell people to endure, or persevere, bear, accept, or accommodate. Children must endure after-school cram classes and long nights of study to pass their high school and college entrance exams. Principals tell their students that school is "life's first big battle," and they must put their all into it. Businessmen must endure after-hours parties with clients, even if they would rather be home sleeping or spending time with their families. Even a person lugging a heavy suitcase up a street in Japan can count on others to call out encouragingly, "go on, *gambatte* (keep going), you can do it."

Perseverance is linked to another Japanese value, dedication or *seishin.* People judge others by how hard they try, how hard they work at whatever task or role is their lot. They are willing to make excuses for poor work, as long as great effort went into it, while good work produced without effort does not impress them. *Seishin* literally means "spirit"; it means the spiritual development that results from effort, discipline, and self-control. It doesn't matter what the task is: It can be studying for exams, paving a road, or learning the tea ceremony; if you persevere in working at it and try to do it perfectly, you will become a better person and people will respect you (Bayley, pp. 118–119).

The Value of Duty

Doing one's duty, or *giri* in Japanese, particularly one's public duty to nation, company, community, or school, is a traditional Japanese value. We can certainly see it in the duties of the various castes in Tokugawa times, most famously in the samurai's duty to loyally serve his lord. And of course duty was a prime virtue in Japan's militaristic period before and through World War II. Today, when a young person leaves school and takes their first job they become *shakaihin*—a "public person" (Roberson, p. 293). Duty to family, and particularly to one's parents, is also a traditional Japanese value, but in Japanese society public *giri* comes first, before private obligations. Even today, a Japanese employee will not take time off from work to attend a child's graduation, or even to take his mother to the hospital. Though it is painful, everyone acknowledges that work, one's public duty, must come first. There is a Japanese folk saying which points up this harsh truth: "You can't be there when your father dies."

At the same time, a person who overconforms, who is too fussy about duty, is seen as "hard." As sociologist David Bayley puts it, "a moral person embodies both *giri* and *ninjo* (compassion). Giri without ninjo lacks warmth; ninjo without giri lacks principles" (Bayley, p. 106). People in Japan must struggle to balance the two.

Nowadays, many Japanese are less dedicated to *giri* as an abstract principle. Survey data reveals that in 1993 only 4 percent of Japanese respondents said that they would like best "to live life devoted entirely to society without thought of self." In 1940 30 percent had chosen that option. (The option most frequently chosen in 1993—40 percent—was "to do what you find interesting, regardless of money or honor") (Sugimoto, p. 70). Duty today appears more personal, as something you owe other people with whom you are interacting in order to spare them discomfort and show them respect. In fact, Japanese people picture their society as a web of individuals linked together by ties of *giri*. When another person does something for you—whether it is a friend who gives you a gift, or your boss who takes you out to dinner—it is your *giri* to pay it back appropriately. You may reciprocate with a gift for your friend and you may pay your boss back by working hard to make the group's quota.

Japanese Norms

Being Japanese requires self-control. Not only must you restrain the expression of your feelings, you must devote enormous effort to behaving properly in all situations. "Good form," compliance with very strict and specific norms of good conduct, matters greatly. Good intentions, or "having one's heart in the right place," don't count. Whether it is addressing an envelope or wrapping a gift, whether it is bowing to greet an individual or drinking at a party, there is only one correct way to behave in a particular situation. And there are very few all-purpose norms to rely on: Japanese norms tend to be **particularistic** (pertaining to a specific situation), rather than **universalistic** (good in all situations). This means there are no general norms—like "honesty is the best policy," or "just be yourself," to guide you in unfamiliar situations. Japanese people learn to be very tuned in to the behavior, dress, and language of others, so as to understand how they should behave. They find strange groups and new social situations anxiety-provoking, because the norms are unknown and one might unwittingly fail to conform. Westerners sometimes regard Japanese people as insincere, or even dishonest, because they see them behaving very differently in different social situations (for example, deferential and reserved in one situation, aggressive or joking in another). To a Japanese person, the western expectation of consistent individual behavior seems immature and foolish: The wise person matches his or her behavior to the requirements of the situation.

Situational Norms

In every society, norms are **situational:** They prescribe expected behavior in a particular situation. The Japanese are unusually conscious of how norms vary depending on the social situation. They place special emphasis on the difference between two fundamentally different kinds of situations, *omote* and *ura*. *Omote* is the surface, or front of an object, the official, public face of a person, event, or social institution; *ura* is its back, its reverse or private side. In Japan it is outward compliance to social norms that counts. People accept your conventionalized *omote* behavior at face value; they know your private feelings may not match it, and you can expect them to intuit your real feelings and have unspoken compassion for you. While standards for *omote* behavior are rigorous, and appearances are highly valued, they are not expected to correspond to realities (Tasker, pp. 67–71). So that salaryman working so late at night may not be doing it out of dedication and loyalty; he may just be afraid to be seen as letting his work team down. But that's OK as long as he acts dedicated. Private feelings and behavior are never condemned as "bad," inappropriate, neurotic, and so on, as long as they remain in their place. Private feelings are accepted as only human, and outward behavior alone is judged.

Ura is the private side of life, the situations in which people are with close friends or family and can be relaxed, informal, and spontaneous and express their emotions. Women friends or male co-workers spending the weekend together at an inn will put on *yukata,* the cotton robes the hotel supplies and drink and eat in a private room, after relaxing together in the hotel's hot tub. Children are controlled and orderly in the classroom, but are given frequent playground breaks when they are left to their own devices and play wildly and noisily. People are not "free" of norms in the world of *ura,* but the norms are different: They allow more spontaneous self-expression (Bachnik, p. 166).

Religion and Japanese Culture

In some societies (like Egypt) religion is of major importance and norms and values are closely linked to religious belief. Some people think that it is only when people are religious that values and norms are taken seriously. This is not the case in Japan. Though most people carefully conform to the society's norms, very few Japanese people consider themselves religious believers and few are observant of religious practices. But, although formal religion has little influence, Japan has an interesting religious heritage which in a very general sense infuses its culture.

There are many religious traditions in Japan: Shinto, Buddhism, Confucianism, Taoism, and Christianity, as well as a number of more modern religious sects usually referred to as the New Religions. Except for a very small number of people (less than 2 percent) who are practicing Christians, most Japanese don't feel they must choose a single religious identity from this heritage. Instead, they practice a kind of folk religion, observing Shinto, Buddhist, and Christian holidays, having Buddhist funerals, and weddings that combine elements of Shinto and Christian rituals, and choosing lucky days by the Taoist calendar.

Shintoism is the most ancient Japanese religion; its tradition extends back to Japan's prehistoric past. Shinto reveres nature in the form of *kami,* deities that embody natural objects, like trees, mountains, the sun, and animals, and represent the life force. *Kami* are everywhere and they are worshiped at Shinto shrines where people ask for their blessings (Earhart, pp. 16–17). No one really takes the Shinto *kami* literally today, but Shinto is a lively part of Japanese folklore and shrines and shrine festivals figure in folk religion. Shinto does have one real influence on Japanese values: It survives in a love of nature, which is a deep current in Japanese culture and is expressed in poetry, landscape painting, and traditions of pottery, landscaping, and architecture that stress subtle, natural materials.

Buddhism, a religion that began in India, came to Japan by way of China in the sixth century A.D. In Japan it is both a monastic tradition and a family religion that honors family ancestors and offers the possibility of salvation and an afterlife in a Buddhist paradise. For almost a thousand years, Buddhism was a very important part of Japanese culture and society, until, in the sixteenth century, Japan's Tokugawa revolution attacked Buddhism as the religion of the old political system and substituted a new emphasis on Confucianism (Reischauer, 1988, pp. 206–207). Today Buddhism permeates Japanese values in a very subtle way: The Japanese belief in perfectionism, the idea of improving one's spirituality through dedication to any task, no matter how humble, is deeply Buddhist. It is notable that in Buddhism (and Shinto), it is the family, not the individual, that is the basic unit of religious participation. People participate in religious rites as family members and maintain family altars and objects of ancestor worship in the home. Traditional religions helped shape Japan's dominant group consciousness (Earhart, pp. 69–71).

Confucianism is not a religion in the same sense that Buddhism, Shinto, or Christianity are religions. It is a philosophical tradition, named for Confucius, its originator in China in the fifth century B.C. Confucianism became prominent in China in the twelfth century A.D., as a rational, ethical system with strict norms, stressing loyalty to the ruler, obedience toward one's father, and proper behavior. Confucianism has no priests, no temples, no religious rituals. From the sixteenth century to the late nineteenth century, Confucianism was very important in Japan, shaping values in a lasting way. You can see its influence today in the Japanese stress on loyalty and obedience, and in the importance of education, hard work, and doing one's duty to family, employers, and the nation (Reischauer, 1988, pp. 203–204).

Christianity came to Japan in the sixteenth century and it spread rapidly before being suppressed by the Tokugawa rulers. When Christianity was permitted again in the late nineteenth century, Protestant and Catholic missionaries entered Japan, but found only small numbers of converts. Today, however, Christian culture has come to Japan as part of a larger western influence, and most Japanese people celebrate Christmas, know Bible stories, and respect Christian values, though they are not themselves Christians (Reischauer, 1988, pp. 212–213).

Japanese people today who feel a strong need for religious faith generally turn to the New Religions, popular religious movements, the best-known of which are *Soka Gakkai,* and *Tenrikyo,* which combine ideas and rituals from Shinto, Buddhism, Taoism, and sometimes Christianity. The New Religions offer their members help in solving personal problems through faith and religious observance, and perhaps even more important, they offer close-knit communities, with festivities, rallies, study groups, and leadership hierarchies. *Aum Shinrikyo,* the group implicated in the 1995 poison gas attacks in Tokyo's subways, was completely atypical of the New Religions in its violence and doomsday predictions, but representative in its intense community life (Inoue, pp. 220–228).

SOCIAL STRUCTURE AND GROUP LIFE

In Japan group life comes first. People think of themselves primarily as members of groups, and only secondarily as individuals. Japanese sociologists consider this **group consciousness** or **group identification** a traditional part of Japanese culture.[2] Over the course of the twentieth century, different groups have risen to preeminence in Japanese life, but group identification remains the basic pattern. In prewar Japan, when most people lived in rural villages, the *ie,* or household, was the primary social unit. The *ie* was a family—and more—a "house," with its property, perhaps its family business, and its good name, passed on down the generations. The *ie* was headed by its eldest male, who had authority over all the members of his household, and controlled their collective finances. Ideally, his household consisted of his wife and their eldest son and his wife, the eldest son of that marriage and his family, on down the family line. Younger sons formed multigenerational households of their own, regarded as branches of the ancestral *ie.*

The *ie* was an all-encompassing group affiliation: Within it the Japanese raised their children, made a living, held religious worship, and satisfied their needs for companionship (Fukutake, pp. 25–28). The obligation of the individual to the *ie* was the basic fact of social life, and filial piety, or respect and obedience toward one's parents, was the ruling value. People's relationships with their parents were much more important than their relationships with their spouses.

Up to the start of World War II, people in Japan lived out their lives "embedded" in their *ie* and in their village or neighborhood (Fukutake, p. 214). Villages were small, consisting of not more than 100 *ie,* and they were closed, self-sufficient communities, within which most people spent their entire lives. Villages were self-governing units, responsible as a whole for collecting taxes imposed on the village, not its households. The households of a village worked together in the fields, or in maintaining the village irrigation system. They helped each other build and repair houses and hold weddings and funerals. Ties between superiors and subordinates were emphasized in the village as well as in the *ie,* since wealthier, landowning families and their tenants and laborers were in constant interaction (Fukutake, pp. 33–39).

Group Life in Modern Japan

The old-fashioned *ie* and village community are disappearing in Japan today. Since World War II, the size of Japanese households has gotten smaller and smaller. In the 1990s, Japan had the world's third lowest birthrate, with Japanese women bearing an average of only 1.46 children each. As a result, the size of the average household numbered only about three people. In Japan today 61 percent of people live in a nuclear family. Because nearly three-quarters of elderly people live with their children (especially their eldest sons), 30 percent of Japanese still live in extended families. Only 8 percent live in single-person households, but the figure is rising as Japanese men and women postpone marriage into their late

[2]See, for example, Nakane, pp. 1–22; or for a recent discussion, Kuwayama, pp. 121–151.

twenties and venture to live independently. Fifteen percent of women between the ages of twenty and twenty-four now live alone (Sugimoto, pp. 73, 163; United Nations, Demographic Yearbook, 1995, pp. 650, 950, 952). (See Table 1.1.)

The modern nuclear family is a much less dominating group than the traditional *ie*. Typically, the husband has less authority than the old head of household and he almost always works outside the home, often quite far away. Long commutes and many hours of work result in fathers spending less time with their children. Salarymen, whose long hours are legendary, must return home after their children are asleep and leave home before the children awaken in the morning. Mothers and children are close, but children typically spend long hours at school and after-school activities. Husbands and wives usually have different friends and don't socialize as a couple. Their leisure activities and even their vacations are spent separately (Fukutake, pp. 123–126).

Postwar industrialization has also broken up the village community. After the war, massive migration from the countryside to cities emptied the villages, as young Japanese searched for industrial jobs. Today, most Japanese, even those in rural areas, commute long distances to work, so few people both live and work in the same community. People are less involved in local community life, and less concerned about what their neighbors think of them, especially in big cities (Fukutake, pp. 134–136).

Many western sociologists expected Japan to follow a pattern observed in Europe and North America: When societies industrialize, people spend less time in **primary groups** (small, personal, face-to-face groups) like families and villages, and more time in **secondary groups** (large, relatively impersonal, goal-oriented organizations) like cities and corporations. Then, group membership becomes less important in people's lives and they begin to think of themselves as individuals and to value their liberty to make individual choices. Away from the close supervision of family and neighbors, people feel freer to defy social norms. In western societies industrialization has meant more individual freedom, but less social order. This is an important observation, worth pondering. Ask yourself—is there too little freedom in your society? Is there too much? Is there too little order, or too much?

TABLE 1.1. Persons Per Household (1986–1993):
Egyptians and Mexicans are more likely to live in large
households than Japanese or Germans.

Country	Percent of Population in One-Person Households	Percent of Population in Households of 2–4 Persons	Percent of Population in Households of 5–7 Persons	Percent of Population in Households of 8 or More Persons
Egypt	1	25	64	24
Mexico	1	28	71	27
Japan	8	61	31	2
Germany	14	71	15	Not Available
USA	9	68	14	Not Available

Source: 1995 Demographic Yearbook, United Nations, New York, 1997

Japan is fascinating to sociologists because there the social consequences of industrialization have been different than in the West. When Japan became a modern, industrialized nation, the *ie* and the community became much less important. But individualism didn't take their place. Instead, Japan has been remarkably successful in creating new primary groups within the secondary groups of school and company, so much so that these new groups have become the focus of Japanese life.

Group Life in School

School dominates the lives of Japanese children. They have long school days and short summer vacations and they attend school on Saturday mornings. The authority of the school extends outward into the community and the home. Teachers make home visits, and each elementary school child has a little notebook in which the teacher writes notes to the child's mother and the mother replies. When police see children behaving improperly, they call their principal as well as their parents.

In elementary and junior high school, Japanese children are taught to see themselves first and foremost as members of their homeroom class, or *kumi*. (The word *kumi* is old: Originally it meant a band of samurai warriors.) Starting in first grade, children spend nine years together in the same *kumi*. In elementary school, they stay with each teacher for two years. Each *kumi* of about forty to forty-five children is encouraged to think of its classroom as the children's own collective home. They arrange and rearrange its furniture, bring in plants and flowers from home, and each day the *kumi* and teacher completely clean the room—scrubbing the desks and floors, washing windows, cleaning blackboards and erasers. Each *kumi* also takes a turn cleaning the school halls and toilets, the teachers' rooms, and the street outside the school. The *kumi* eats lunch in its own room, and even in junior high school, teachers for different subjects move from classroom to classroom, while the students stay in their own room. On the playground, members of a *kumi* play on the same team, competing with other *kumi* in their grade.

Teachers divide *kumi* into smaller groups, called *han,* which are like study or work groups, but they stay together for quite a long time. Each *han* elects a leader or *han-cho,* whose job it is to lead the group into harmonious decision making, by patiently eliciting a consensus (Duke, pp. 25–29). Japanese elementary and junior high schools do not practice ability grouping and, typically, children from both rich and poor families attend the same school. The emphasis is on keeping the whole class moving through the work at the same pace, with the more able students helping their slower *han*-mates. *Hans* compete against each other in the classroom.

Keiko's Story: The Han

Keiko is nervous as she arrives in her fifth-grade classroom. Today her han *must present its report on the Tokugawa Era. They've been working on it in school and for the past two days they have met after school at Yukichi's house to practice making the oral presentation. Keiko is afraid she will make a mistake and let her* han *down. She hardly hears the music over the loudspeaker that signals the official start of the school day, and she follows the* kumi *through the prescribed exercises without even noticing. But her teacher, walking up and down the rows, does notice. "Keiko seems distracted; not concentrating," she writes in her little notebook.*

It's lunchtime in Mitaka Middle School. Dressed in their informal exercise clothes, these students eat lunch in their classrooms and good-naturedly clown for the camera. After lunch they will change back to formal uniforms and return to the restrained formal behavior expected for lessons.

After the presentation, Keiko is giddy with relief. They did well! The teacher gives Keiko's han *gold stars for preparation and presentation. They are the only* han *with no demerits! Today Keiko's* han *has its turn to serve lunch and she gaily wraps herself in the white apron and puts on the surgical mask. She and her* han-*mates haul the heavy pots and bins of rice, stew, and salad up to the classroom from the school kitchen and dish them out. The whole* kumi *chants together the phrases that begin a meal, then breaks out in laughter and conversation while the students eat. Keiko is particularly animated. She has done her part in supporting her* han.

Working and playing so closely together, members of a *kumi* come to know each other intimately and think of themselves as a group. Children work hard, not to please the teacher, but to avoid letting down their *han*-mates. Habits of group loyalty, a preference for uniformity, and the learned skill of building a group consensus through patient negotiation prepare children for the all-important work groups of Japanese adult life (Feiler, pp. 99–102; Leestma, p. 3).

But as much as group life in school illustrates the strength and importance of group life in Japan, it also illustrates its dark underside. It was American sociologist William Graham Sumner (1840–1910) who long ago articulated the principle that the more closely people identify as a group and the stronger their **in-group** feelings, the more hostility they direct toward **out-groups,** or people outside the group. We see this in Japanese schools in the practice of *ijime,* or bullying, usually after school or during free play, when children single out one child who is different in some way (perhaps Korean, or foreign-born, or poorer or richer than the others) and subject him (it is usually a boy) to ceaseless torment. They tease him, make fun of him, kick and punch, sometimes extort money or pressure him to commit petty theft. The Japanese are ashamed of *ijime,* but even though they are disturbed about it they seem unable to prevent it. Sometimes teachers ignore bullying or even abet it. Every year there are several reports of suicides of 12- or 13-year old children who are victims of *ijime.* Bullying shows us that as much as the Japanese value harmony, it is harmony within the group that matters; hostility towards outsiders, towards those who are different, is tolerated. Is it possible that bullying those who are different is essential to maintaining the tight cohesion of Japanese school groups? (Pollack, Dec. 18, 1994, p. 20; Sugimoto, pp. 127–128).

The Work Group

Following World War II, as Japanese industry expanded, and drew in an ever-larger workforce from the farms and villages, Japanese companies encouraged their workers to see the company as their family. They invented a new focus for group identity in modern Japanese life. Large corporations hired their employees right out of high school or college. Promised lifetime employment and guaranteed promotion, employees spent their whole working lives in one company, advancing in step with those hired in their year. Company housing, company sports teams and recreation complexes, cafeterias, health clinics, and company discount stores re-created the all-absorbing village within the company. Today, while only a minority of Japan's labor force is employed by large corporations, their organization has set the tone for Japanese work life. Government employees, as well as employees in smaller companies look to work for a sense of community. They find it in the work group, or "section," of the office or factory.

Hiroshi's Story: The "Section"

When the bullet train suddenly slowed, Hiroshi glanced out the window and saw beside the track the village where he had been born. Staring, Hiroshi thought about how different his life was now from his village childhood. He spotted his family's old house—a large wooden structure with its own courtyard and small garden—where he had lived with his parents, brother and sisters, and grandparents. Hiroshi looked down into the quiet streets of the town where he had spent his days at play, even as a 2-year-old, watched by his brother.

Now Hiroshi lives in an apartment house outside Tokyo. He is home so little that he doesn't even know his neighbors and his children never play outside. They hurry from school to lessons to homework indoors. Really, his office is now the focus of his life. Hiroshi knows his family wants him at home, but he feels that he has to give his all to his job. He doesn't do it to get a raise, or even a promotion; he just wants to do a good job.

Every morning the nine men of his section assemble, greet each other, and drink their first cups of tea together. Takeshi has become a close friend: He really knows what is in Hiroshi's heart. But all the men are important to him. That year when Hiroshi's mother was dying so painfully, they knew how he felt without his having to explain. They took over most of his duties at work and took him out after work, making sure he ate and gently distracting him with stories and songs. Kenji-san had introduced Hiroshi's son to his niece, and they were soon to be married. Mr. Fuji, the department chief looked after them all, and was now arranging a marriage for Masao, the only unmarried man in the section. After work, and before the long commute home, the section and its chief usually go out together to a local bar, to drink and chat more informally. Hiroshi enjoys the monthly evening parties paid for by the company, and the twice-yearly weekend retreats when the whole section goes away together to a country inn. His real home, he thinks, is at the office with his office "family."

SOCIALIZATION

Japan is a demanding society: It asks of individuals a high level of conformity with very detailed norms, and it demands self-discipline in subordinating individual needs to the requirements of the group. Most people do conform. The Japanese pride themselves on how orderly their society is. Most people embrace Japanese values, identify with their roles, and do what is expected of them. Foreigners often wonder how Japanese society achieves such a high level of conformity.

One good answer is that conformity is carefully taught in Japan. Japanese people learn the beliefs and role expectations of their culture and learn to play their roles properly through the process sociologists call **socialization.** While all societies and social groups socialize their members, in some cases the process is haphazard and disorganized and people may be largely unaware that socialization is taking place. In Japan, socialization is highly consistent, explicit, and carefully planned.

Studying Japan provides a wonderful opportunity to understand the process of socialization, how socialization actually takes place, because the Japanese carry out socialization so thoughtfully. First of all, Japanese groups give their members a tremendous amount of **explicit instruction.** Then they provide many opportunities to **practice** proper behavior, often through repeated drill. **Ceremonies** mark transitions to new roles and alert people to the need for changed behavior. **Role models** are often provided to help people learn roles. Finally, the Japanese are highly skilled in **framing** situations in such a way as to ease, some would say manipulate, people into proper role performance. We can examine these processes of socialization in action in Japanese schools and businesses.

Socialization through Instruction

Since the beginning of the postwar Japanese economic boom, Japanese companies have treated worker socialization with extreme seriousness. Training courses for new workers often last for several weeks, and include socialization in the values and norms of company life as well as technical instruction. Many large companies maintain training centers in rural areas where new and old workers are brought periodically for intensive retreats, featuring motivational workshops and lectures on ethics. Large companies maintain an in-house staff of trainers, who create company slogans and chants, inspirational comic books and poems, and conduct training sessions (Chapman, pp. 132–134).

One of the most striking characteristics of socialization in Japanese society is that people in positions of authority don't hesitate to tell trainees exactly what is expected of them. They tell them formally, repeatedly, and in very great detail. Then they provide many opportunities for practice. In school and at work, people are constantly exhorted by signs, slogans, and maxims. Posters on classroom walls exhort: "Let us not run in the corridors," "Let us keep our school toilets clean." Students select these goals and then hold self-criticism sessions in which they decide whether they have met the goal, and if not, what should be done next. A recent comic book distributed by The Fuji Bank urges new employees to be like "Ultraman," the superhero who performs all his exploits in just three minutes; they are to get up three minutes earlier, limit phone calls to three minutes, study new technology every day for three minutes, and so forth (Kristof, August 17, 1997, pp. 40–43; Chapman, p. 133).

Socialization through Practice

It is the Japanese way to follow instruction with repeated drill. Perseverance and drill are assumed to be necessary to learn anything properly. Japanese mothers teach little children how to speak politely by repeating over and over again the proper forms of address. Schoolchildren through junior high school are drilled in proper bowing, formal greeting, sitting and standing (all together), answering their teachers (immediately and loudly), and arranging their desktops for study (in a set format). Reading, singing, and exercising in unison foster a sense of group cohesion. A teacher, preparing eighth graders for a class trip, arranges chairs on the floor of the gym in the shape of a bus, and for hours students practice getting in and out of the seats in orderly fashion (Hendry, p. 102; Sugimoto, pp. 123–124; Feiler, p. 264; Leestma, p. 27).

When Mazda opened its first U.S. auto plant in 1985, employees were given a training program lasting ten to twelve weeks, time the company considered necessary to communicate to American workers the values and expectations of a Japanese company. Training included a week of work on "interpersonal relations" using group discussions with a trainer, videotapes of "correct" and "incorrect" ways to interact, workbooks and role-playing exercises. For example, in one workshop trainees practiced the proper way to tell a co-worker that his body odor was offensive. (Incidentally, some of the Americans hated the training and dropped out, but many loved it. They said that the new techniques for relating to others transformed their home lives.) (See Fucini and Fucini, pp. 71–74.)

Ceremonies Support Socialization

Initiation ceremonies, marking the transition to new roles, are an effective part of Japanese socialization. Ceremonies help people learn to recognize that they are in a new stage of life, with new roles and norms. Carefully staged ceremonies are an important part of children's progress through school. Interestingly, the Japanese place more emphasis on ceremonies that mark the beginning of different stages of education, than on graduation ceremonies. Corporations also often provide elaborate welcome ceremonies for new recruits (described by one observer as "a cross between a coming-of-age ceremony and initiation into an American fraternity"). Starting in the 1950s, companies devised rituals in which cohorts of new employees, and in some cases their parents too, were first greeted and lectured by company officials in welcome ceremonies at the factory, then escorted on several days of touring and partying (Chapman, p. 131).

Role Models Aid Socialization

The Japanese believe in providing role models to help people learn expected behavior. Mothers and teachers consciously "model" correct behavior for children. Nursery school teachers wash their hands and brush their teeth alongside their charges, and elementary school teachers eat lunch with their students and work alongside the students during the regular daily cleaning period. At home and at school older children are urged to set good examples for younger ones, and take pride in their roles as "elder brother" or "elder sister" (Hendry, p. 149). The elder child as role model is a recurrent pattern in Japanese society. Corporations appoint "elder brothers" to instruct new recruits in proper behavior; and in business, government, and even in organized crime, younger men seek out "mentors" to guide their progress.

Framing Opportunities for Socialization

Sociologist Erving Goffman used the term **framing** to convey the way people structure interaction symbolically, through gestures, the use of props, the physical arrangement of rooms, or spoken cues (Goffman, pp. 22–30). If you are Japanese, from infancy through adulthood you find yourself in situations framed in such a way as to emphasize group consciousness and dependence on the group. This is actually a form of socialization, though it is much more indirect than instruction or drill.

Socialization to dependence on the group begins at birth, according to Takeo Doi, a famous Japanese psychiatrist. Care of infants is based on the assumption that babies should experience as little anxiety as possible. Caregivers try to anticipate the baby's needs and satisfy them before crying and fretfulness signal a problem. Cribs are placed beside adult beds, and children are never put in their cribs to fall asleep alone; they are sung to sleep before being laid down. Use of babysitters is highly unusual, and mothers and babies enjoy a constant physical closeness. The Japanese also avoid playpens, preferring instead that the child be protected by the constant close attention of an adult. Mothers' all-embracing, unconditional love and support results in bonds of tremendous emotional closeness with their children, argues Doi, and a taste for dependency that is expressed in adult group life. Children learn implicitly that if you conform, and do what others expect of you, then people will be kind and considerate, and they will gratify your wishes without your having to ask (Hendry, pp. 18–25, 97, 116; Christopher, pp. 68–70; Doi, p. 20).

Framing Interaction in School

Life in Japanese elementary schools is framed in such a way as to stress the similarity of all children, and the importance of the group. Teachers seldom address children individually, or overtly recognize differences in individual ability, and they minimize situations in which children compete individually with each other. Instead, each *han* is held responsible collectively for the progress of all its members. Also, teachers do not discipline individual students in Japanese schools. Rather, if a class or an individual is unruly, the teacher will turn to that day's assigned monitor and request him or her to restore order. The classroom situation is structured in such a way as to emphasize group participation, group loyalty, and the responsibility of the individual to the class. In this situation, students experience no conflict between loyalty to their friends and conformity with school norms (Feiler, pp. 30, 100–102; Leestma, pp. 3, 27).

Kiyoshi's Story: The Team

Kiyoshi's high school baseball team was a world of its own. When he joined it as a freshman, they practiced every day. The freshmen had to wear special headbands and chant while the senior team played. They had to come early to set up the field. One day Kiyoshi was late to practice. As soon as he saw Kiyoshi, the coach stopped all the playing and chanting. He called the freshmen out on the field and every man had to do 100 push-ups while the whole team watched. Kiyoshi was so ashamed! He apologized to each freshman teammate for putting him through so much pain and embarrassment. He never came late again. But there were times when other freshmen did something wrong, and then the whole freshman squad would do push-ups or sprints. Somehow, enduring this punishment together made them brothers.

Teachers are well aware of the importance of framing opportunities for socialization. For example, Bruce Feiler describes a seventh-grade class trip to Tokyo's Disneyland framed in such a way as to encourage students' dependency on their *han*. Students were required to stay with their *han* during the visit. In each *han*, one member was assigned to carry the money, one to wear the watch, one to take the photos, and one to take notes. "The management of this trip," Feiler explained, "revealed the skill with which Japanese schools transfer abstract goals into concrete educational practices" (Feiler, p. 266).

Schools also frame interaction with dress norms. As they move through their day, from formal classroom activities to informal recreation, lunch, and cleanup, elementary and junior high school children repeatedly change their clothes, from regular uniforms and slippers to warm-up suits and outdoor sneakers. Changes in clothing help children learn to distinguish between the private, relaxed parts of life and more public, formal settings.

Framing Interaction in the Office

When young people graduate from school and move on to the world of work, they again enter situations framed to encourage group identification. Japanese offices are physically arranged in such a way as to make it very difficult to behave individualistically, but easy to become part of the group. Offices are huge undivided areas, with the desks of each "section" grouped together. Within a section, desks are arranged in facing rows, all touching, so as to form one huge tabletop,

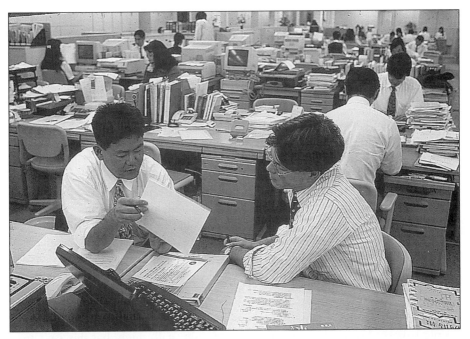

An American (in the striped shirt) visits a Japanese office. Here, coworkers can all see and hear one another, and it is easy for them to exchange information informally. Secretaries and managers work in the same room. Are offices in your society arranged like this, or are there separate rooms for managers and partitioned cubicles for other workers?

with the section chief's desk perpendicular across the end. Among the eight or nine section members, every conversation is a group affair; every memo can be read by all. Even telephones are shared. Only one desk stands alone in a Japanese office: the director's (Feiler, pp. 19–20, 28). Like mothers, Japanese section heads are kind and attentive to their subordinates, listening to their personal problems, taking them out after work, helping them arrange marriages. In gratitude, employees devote themselves to their work beyond formal job requirements and call their company *uchi* (our house or home) (Sugimoto, pp. 21–22, 91).

DEVIANCE IN A DEMANDING SOCIETY

Japan is a demanding society; there is strong pressure to conform to very detailed, explicit norms. Socialization is extensive. Families, schools, and businesses work hard to make sure their members learn their roles and play them properly. Under these circumstances, would you expect there to be very little, or a great deal of **deviant behavior** in Japan? Deviance is universal: Every society establishes norms and in every society people defy socialization and group pressure; they violate norms, incurring disapproval and some sort of punishment. But in some societies there is a great deal more deviance than in others. In some societies crime rates are high, teenagers drink and take drugs, and many people engage in sexual behavior that scandalizes others. This is not the case in Japan. Although it doesn't take much to violate social norms in Japan, there is, in fact, very little deviance.

Low Levels of Deviance

Crime rates are exceptionally low in Japan. With a population one-half the size of the United States, Japan has fewer robberies in a year than take place in two days in the United States; fewer rapes than in one week. In a recent year, there were 805 homicides in all of Japan, compared to 26,254 in the United States. Thirty-eight of the homicides in Japan were committed with handguns, while more than 16,000 killings were done with handguns in the United States. Handguns are outlawed in Japan, except for sports use. There are only forty-nine legal handguns in the whole country and they are registered with the police and must be kept at the shooting range. There are about 425,000 rifles and air guns in Japan, held by people who have passed exams and rigorous licensing procedures, repeated every three years. (Compare this to the estimated 200 million guns owned by individuals in the United States.) More minor crimes are also uncommon. There is little drug use in Japan, and no graffiti or litter on the streets. Traffic laws are obeyed, and despite the importance of bars in Japanese culture, there is almost no drunk driving. Many people believe that suicide rates in Japan are unusually high, but this isn't true. Suicide rates are similar to those in other industrialized countries, like Germany and the United States (Tasker, pp. 71, 73; Kristof, p. 8). (See Table 1.2.)

The Yakuza

There is some crime in Japan, but it is a particularly orderly sort of crime. Criminal activity is financed and organized by the *Yakuza,* Japan's organized crime syndicates. There are few individual criminals. Approximately 90,000 Yakuza members are organized into three main syndicates and 3,000 groups, running prostitution, pornography, gambling, drugs, extortion, and labor rackets, and taking in billions of dollars a year. The Yakuza also engage in violence on behalf of legitimate authorities who wish to avoid the use of violence themselves. They have bro-

TABLE 1.2. Murders and Suicides per Year:
The rate of murder is far higher in the United States and Mexico
than in Egypt, Germany, and Japan.

	Total Number of Suicides	Number of Suicides Among Every Million People	Total Number of Murders	Number of Murders Among Every Million People
Egypt	22	less than 1	241	5
Mexico	2,246	25	16,560	185
Germany	12,690	156	966	12
Japan	20,516	165	805	6
USA	30,810	122	26,254	104

Source: 1994 Demographic Yearbook, United Nations, New York, 1996.

ken strikes, silenced dissenters, evicted tenants from valuable real estate, and halted the work of lone criminals. The Yakuza have worked for corporations, the ruling Liberal Democratic Party, the American CIA, and the police.

But it is somewhat deceptive to speak of the Yakuza as "organized crime." They enjoy a legitimacy and acceptance in Japanese society very different from their American counterparts. The Yakuza is accepted as a public presence in Japan: Their offices publicly display gang insignia on the door, like an insurance office or loan company. Members wear gang badges, like the company pins Japanese salarymen wear. People who join the Yakuza become part of a social group like others in Japan—one that stresses group identity and conformity to group norms (Wildeman, unpublished material; Tasker, p. 78; Sterngold, 1992, pp. A1, A6).

Japanese Style Deviance

By now you may be asking, isn't there any deviant behavior in Japan? There is some, of course, but it may not seem like very major deviance to you. The bullying that goes on in middle school is of course deviant behavior and is very distressing to the Japanese. "School refusal" is another form of youth deviance that is on the increase. Children who suffer from "school phobia" refuse to go to school and stay home in their own rooms, speaking to no one, seemingly as a kind of protest against pressures to conform at school. Young women who travel on Japan's crowded trains complain about men who grope them, but police generally ignore such molestation. "Controversial kissing" is another form of deviance. Middle-aged Japanese are scandalized by young people who kiss and touch in public (Sugimoto, pp. 128–129; Tanikawa, pp. 39, 41).

Many Japanese are disturbed by new attitudes among teenagers and young adults. Since the Japanese are enthusiastic poll-takers, it is widely known that many young people say they are not very interested in dedicating their lives to work or to a single lifelong job. Many say they are more interested in leisure and fun, in travel or outdoor activity, in privacy and comfort. However, so far these deviant attitudes have not been expressed in widespread deviant behavior. "Dropouts" can be found in Japan, but they are rare.

Hideo's Story: The Drop-out

It all began with "tea hair." In his first year of high school, Hideo sang in his friend's rock band, and for one special performance they all tinted their hair reddish brown—"tea hair." The school administration went crazy. They called all their parents to school and made them dye their hair dark again. Somehow that changed things permanently for Hideo. The son of a government bureaucrat, Hideo had always done well in school and attended an academic high school. His parents expected him to go to Tokyo University and enter a government career. Hideo horrified them by refusing to take the college entrance exams. He had always fooled around with computers and he taught himself programming, so he was able to get short-term computer jobs with foreign companies. After a year or two he found an apartment down by the docks and moved out; it wasn't clear whether his parents were more embarrassed or relieved. Now he sleeps until 1:00 or 2:00 PM every day, watches television, and acts as a grip for his friends in a rock band. When he works, it's during the night at home or at company offices. He has dyed his hair red and wears an earring.

Making a Scene

There is some behavior, often tolerated in other societies, that is seen as major deviance in Japan. One such behavior is deliberately creating conflict, usually in the context of a social protest. People do this by addressing superiors disrespectfully, by making public denunciations, by slamming doors, or actually pushing and hitting. Such behavior is profoundly shocking. People who start a conflict in Japan have a certain advantage, because their opponents are likely to try to avoid conflict, even if it means making concessions. In the end, though, nobody wins, because all parties are seen as having brought shame to their group by allowing the social harmony to be shattered (Pharr, pp. 143–144).

Public and Private Deviance

One reason why there is so little deviance in Japan is that a lot of behavior condemned as deviant in other societies is acceptable in Japan, as long as it remains private. The paired concepts of *omote* and *ura* are fundamental to Japanese life. Japanese society requires outward conformity in a person's *omote* or public life, but behind the scenes, on the *ura* side, Japan is very accepting. It is characteristic of Japanese culture that no human behavior, and no person, is considered intrinsically bad, or sick, or evil: What matters is that you keep your behavior appropriate to the social situation. The world of *ura* may be seen as a safety valve for Japanese society. In *ura* social settings people can express individualism and rebellion and let off steam that builds up in the pressure cooker of Japan's conformist public life.

Drinking is one such release. Alcohol plays an important role in Japanese life. Most drinking takes place in groups, in bars or restaurants. Levels of habitual alcohol consumption that would be labelled alcoholism in other societies are not seen as deviant in Japan. Drinking together, business associates or co-workers are able to ease the tensions of formal, *omote* relations. Often groups in bars engage in *karaoke* singing, taking turns singing into a microphone to a taped accompaniment. A TV screen shows the words of the song, with accompanying pictures. Laughing and singing together, participants are relieved of the need to make conversation (Sugimoto, p. 227).

Similarly, it is common for the whole staff of a work section, including the boss (and sometimes the female workers), to go out drinking together after work. Drunk, the boss may make a fool of himself, singing and crying, but the next day in the office, when he is once again his proper, formal self, no one's respect for him will be in the least diminished. Employees, under cover of "drunkenness," may complain to the boss openly about their treatment, but the next day no one will "remember" that it happened.

Hostesses in bars offer their male guests flirtation and flattery. Nearby, men can visit Japan's "soaplands," baths where massages and other sexual attentions are available for purchase. Sexually explicit stripper shows even feature (illegal) "open stage" events, in which a member of the audience joins the stripper in public sexual acts. Until they were closed down, "no-panties waitress" coffee shops, with glass or mirrored floors, offered the option of looking without touching (Condon, pp. 76, 82, 247; Bornoff, pp. 263–272, 295–296, 312–322). The women who work in such establishments may preserve an *omote* public life in distant apartments where they raise their children with propriety. Pornography is also ubiquitous. Pornographic comic books, often filled with violence, are sold in vending machines and porn videos are shown in bars (Tasker, pp. 111, 113–114).

Japanese society is matter-of-fact about sex—in its proper *ura* place. While a husband would never kiss his wife goodbye in public at the train station, nevertheless Japan is dotted with conspicuous "love hotels"—fantastically decorated as castles, or pirate ships, or chalets—which rent rooms by the hour, and these hotels are much used by young people, adulterous couples, and even married pairs looking for privacy. In the past, the world of bars and sex was just for men, but increasingly, women and girls participate too. Teenaged girls look cute and innocent in their school uniforms, going about in giggling groups, but behind the scenes two-thirds of the girls engage in sex by age 15 (White, pp. 170–189). Some teenaged girls go further, working on telephone sex lines or even as prostitutes. The schoolgirl look is considered the last frontier in illicit sexual appeal, so girls are much in demand (White, pp. 170–189).

Emiko's Story: The Housewife

Outwardly, Emiko is an exemplary wife and mother. She defers to her husband in public, keeps her sidewalk immaculate, takes care of her husband's father who lives with them, and goes regularly to PTA meetings. But when her daughter reached middle school she found she had time on her hands and took a part-time job as a cashier in a local grocery. Emiko manages the family finances and her husband never asks about the money she earns. So now Emiko has a little money to go out with her girlfriends. They go to karaoke boxes together (these are private karaoke parlors separate from bars), and they've become big fans of the dance troupe Takarazuka. They travel long distances to see this all-female group perform, and they cheer the lead dancers who play the male roles. Now they've found a new and expensive amusement—male "hostess" bars, where an all-female clientele is entertained by male hosts who flirt and dance, accept gifts, and perhaps—she's not sure—give sexual favors. Emiko's husband doesn't know about any of her nights out with the girls and Emiko says its nothing to worry about—her husband ought to hear about her friend Yuko who has a secret job as a stripper!

Deviance and Stigma

Another kind of behavior strongly condemned as deviant in Japan is adopting a deviant identity. **Primary deviance,** that is, deviant acts, is much more readily forgiven than is **secondary deviance,** or the adoption of deviant statuses. When Japanese people adopt a deviant identity—one that proclaims their difference from other Japanese—they are strongly **stigmatized** or publicly labeled as different and deviant. For example, homosexual sex acts are not seen as perverted or sinful in Japan, but people who announce that they are gay scandalize others and they bring shame on their family members who will experience difficulty getting jobs and finding spouses. Having AIDS is a matter of the deepest shame, and many AIDS sufferers move to Hawaii before their symptoms show so as to spare their families from ostracism. Even people with disabilities occupy a deviant status in Japan. People in wheelchairs are almost never seen in public and, indeed, there are no wheelchair ramps or other accommodations for them (Sesser, pp. 62–63). We can say that in a very real way being seen to be different is deviant in Japan. Even talk-ing about people who are different is offensive.

Effective Social Controls

Why is there so little truly deviant behavior in Japanese society? One explanation lies in the effectiveness of **social controls.** Thorough socialization to strict stan-dards is followed by constant supervision and effective **social sanctions.** In every society sanctions are the muscle behind social control. Social sanctions reward those who conform and play their roles well, and punish those who fail to shape up. In Japanese society there are a variety of **positive sanctions** that are real incen-tives, coupled with **negative sanctions** that people very much wish to avoid. You could say that in Japanese society people are managed very effectively. The Japan-ese themselves say, "The nail that sticks up gets pounded down."

With great consistency and regularity, the reward for role conformity in Japan-ese society is inclusion in the warm and pleasant life of the group. Those who fail to play their roles correctly face exclusion: misbehaving children are excluded from family activities, or left standing alone outside the classroom or playground, ignored by teachers. A mother may say, "If you keep doing that, the garbage col-lectors will come and take you away," or she may punish extremely serious of-fenses by locking the child out of the house (Lebra, 1984, p. 149).

Ridicule is also a common sanction, and children are actually encouraged to make fun of a child who fails to conform. Mothers commonly censure misbehav-ior by telling children, "If you do that, people will laugh at you." Children come to fear ridicule, and this fear continues into adult life as an important social pressure to conform (Hendry, pp. 106–108, 114–115).

In Japanese corporations social sanctions back up all the slogans and chants and exhortations to work hard and be loyal to the company. Those who work for big companies are looked up to by others; their sons are sought out in marriage. They find it easier to get a home mortgage. Company expense accounts fund visits to bars and nightclubs and golf club memberships. Once past his twenties, a man who leaves his company pays a heavy price. Not only does he lose company bene-fits, but he loses his friends at work. If he finds a new job (and most companies won't hire a man they label as disloyal for leaving his company), he finds it hard to make new friends among men who have worked together for years. Positive and negative sanctions ensure that it pays for a corporate employee to act loyal, even if he or she doesn't feel loyal (Chapman, pp. 137–139).

Criminal sanctions in Japan are a serious matter. With crime rates so low, Japan actually has a very small prison population—only 37 people out of every 100,000 people are in prison, compared to 519 per 100,000 in the United States, and 80 per 100,000 in Germany. Jail sentences are relatively short, but harsh. Pris-oners are often kept in isolation and not even allowed to talk to each other. There are no gangs in Japanese prisons, or any prison rapes or assaults. Also, Japanese people are ashamed to have relatives in jail. They seldom visit them and often re-fuse to accept them back home once they are released (Kristof, pp. 1, 8).

Surveillance

Japanese society is unusual in the sureness with which negative sanctions follow deviance. You can be certain that if you violate norms in Japan, someone will notice and will definitely take action, and you will surely pay a price. Strict norms are enforced through constant supervision. Some schools organize regular after-school patrols of the neighborhood by parents and teachers (to watch students, not to protect them from others, since all neighborhoods are quite safe). School dress codes are extremely detailed and exacting, specifying, for example, the width of trouser legs and the distance from the floor of cuffs and skirt hems. Teachers and principals check uniforms every day. They punish and embarrass offenders and confiscate nonconforming garments. Teenagers try to bend the rules, but about the most they can manage is to sew a bright lining inside a jacket pocket. Police will actually take a teenager into custody for smoking, an act considered seriously delinquent, then call both parents and the school guidance counselor to the police station (Feiler, pp. 171, 233; Leestma, p. 46).

Adults too find their behavior constantly scrutinized, with deviant acts reported to the higher-status members of their social groups. Bruce Feiler, an American who taught in Japan, has written of his surprise at the tightness of Japanese social controls. Feiler used a bicycle to travel around his town, and late at night when there was no other traffic he saw no need to stop for red lights. But someone observed him and called the board of education, which called his principal, and Feiler found himself rebuked by his supervisor (Feiler, p. 25). An adult man, arrested in a police sweep of an illegal stripper show or "massage parlor," can expect police to call both his wife and his boss. Publicly humiliated, his job lost and career ruined, such a man is a vivid lesson to all of the dangers of deviance.

Surveillance is constantly carried out by the police, organized in a national network of 15,000 police boxes, most manned 24 hours a day. Police take an active approach to surveillance, visiting each household in their district yearly, and discreetly keeping track of the private lives of all district residents (Tasker, p. 73).

"Friendly Authoritarianism"

Yoshio Sugimoto calls the Japanese system of sanctions "friendly authoritarianism," because authority figures in Japan are usually warm and caring. They help people and give them rewards and people come to trust them. But people also know that if they don't conform, these same authorities can be very harsh. Police, for example. are very polite and helpful. They lend people umbrellas when it rains and they lend money to people who have lost their wallets or are short trainfare (and people almost always return the umbrellas and pay back the money) (Sugimoto, pp. 245–258; Kristof, June 4, 1995). Police often decide not to prosecute for minor offenses, but only if the suspect writes out a sincere apology. The same police, however, are given great leeway in searching and questioning people. They can hold suspects without a formal hearing for up to twenty-one days, and often subject them to long interrogations and pressure to confess. Evidence obtained illegally is admissible in court (Kristof, May 14, 1995, p. 8).

SOCIAL INEQUALITY IN JAPAN:
CLASS, STATUS, AND POWER

Inequality is universal; it can be found in every society, but that doesn't make all societies similar. Actually societies differ quite a lot, both in how much inequality they contain and what forms these inequalities take. Max Weber's classic discussion of social stratification is useful for understanding the varieties of social inequality in Japan. Weber said that there are three basic aspects of inequality: class, status, and power. **Class** has to do with the wealth and income people enjoy as the result of their property or job. **Status** refers to prestige. It is the cultural dimension of inequality, because it results from the way a culture views different groups of people—men and women, ethnic or racial groups, people in different occupations, people from particular families. Weber defined **power** as the ability to make people do what you want, even against their will. In every society, some individuals and groups have more power than others.

In Japan class inequalities make people uncomfortable. The Japanese don't want to have great inequalities of wealth or income in their society and they have made great efforts to minimize them. At the same time, Japanese people are undisturbed by sharp inequalities of status and power. Men and women occupy quite unequal statuses in Japanese society, and Japan also has several very small minority groups of quite low status. Power in Japan is closely held in the hands of a small elite of government bureaucrats and big business leaders.

A History of Change

For most of its history (up until the Meiji Restoration), Japan was a society of hereditary status rankings: It was a **caste society.** Everyone was born into their parents' caste, as aristocrat, samurai, commoner, or (those in the most menial occupations) outcaste. Caste was destiny: Everyone had to live and marry within the caste, no matter what his or her talents might be, and there were rules regulating what members of different castes and subcastes were permitted to do and wear. Especially during the Tokugawa period (1635–1853), caste divisions were very carefully enforced (Reischauer, 1977, p. 158).

Meiji Inequality

Then, in one of Japan's most remarkable self-transformations, the Meiji government declared that "the four orders are equal" and legal distinctions between the castes were officially discarded (Fukutake, pp. 27–28). Remarkably, most caste distinctions faded into the background after they were legally abolished. The emperor and his famility are the only nobility recognized in Japan today, and while descendants of samurai are proud of their ancestors, people don't try to marry within the samurai caste. The only exception is the descendants of the outcastes, the *burakumin:* Those still identifiable face a persistent, though unacknowledged prejudice (Reischauer, 1977, pp. 159–160).

But inequality by no means disappeared from Meiji Japan, rather, it changed its character. In the early twentieth century, class inequalities grew as Japan industrialized. Rural land was concentrated in the hands of a wealthy landlord class, while the growing industrial economy quickly came to be dominated by the *zaibatsu*—the small number of vastly powerful, family-owned business conglomerates with close ties to government and the military (Chapman, p. 198).

Postwar Equality

But the story is far from over for, remarkably, World War II ushered in yet another era of Japanese social stratification. Defeat destroyed Japan's industry and left nearly everyone poor. Many inequalities were leveled by the American Occupation reforms, which broke up the landlords' estates and distributed the land to the peasants, dismantled the great *zaibatsu* empires and purged their executives as war collaborators. Occupation authorities instituted progressive income taxes and (briefly) supported labor unions. Building on Occupation reforms, radical Japanese rebuilt Japan on egalitarian foundations (Chapman, p. 198).

Contracts between labor and management followed the principle of equal pay for equal work, regardless of the education, skill, or status of the employees. Unions aimed for a "livelihood wage" for all, and there was little difference in the pay received by blue- and white-collar employees. New schools, shaped by the Occupation authorities, and by teachers' socialist unions, tried to create equal opportunity through education. Teachers told their students that everyone had equal ability; hard work and perseverance were what counted for success. Schools did no IQ testing or ability grouping, so each elementary school class was a cross section of the community. Those in high positions tended to disguise their wealth. Executives avoided conspicuous luxury in dress or housing and took buses and trains like their employees (Chapman, p. 199).

In the postwar years the Japanese came to believe that class inequalities of wealth, income, and opportunity are unfair and should be minimized and this belief persists today. But it is very important to understand that the Japanese accept other inequalities. They take status inequalities for granted and make no attempt to diminish them. Even today, women and minority groups in Japan experience unequal treatment which is rarely challenged. In fact, status inequalities pervade personal life in Japan and are the basis of everyday interaction.

Personal Status Inequalities in Japanese Groups

If you visit Japan, or even perhaps if you go to an authentic Japanese restaurant in a big city in Europe or America, you may well see a "section," a group of co-workers out for dinner or drinks. Observe them unobtrusively so you will not be rude: The group will probably be all male, but they are of different ages and their clothing indicates varied statuses—the older, well-dressed section chief, his employees of various ages and statuses, and possibly even the limousine driver, more informally dressed or in uniform. Japanese people find it natural to belong to close-knit groups

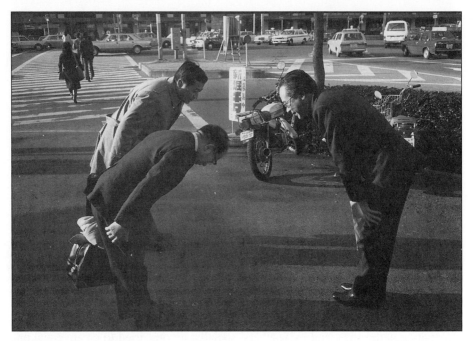

Businessmen meet and bow in a traditional greeting that is very much a part of Japanese life today. An employee of a small company will bow lower than one working for Toyota. A new employee at Toyota bows lower than the senior Toyota manager he meets. Who bows lowest when a senior official of a small firm meets a junior representative of Toyota? Everyday politeness in Japan requires that you solve such problems quickly.

of people who are status unequals. Don't picture this unequal status as a hierarchy like the military, where orders flow down from a pinnacle at the top. There are, of course, institutional hierarchies in Japan, but more distinctively, Japanese hierarchy is personal: It pervades the relationships among individuals.

Japanese people are always keenly aware of their status relative to others. In a group of strangers they quickly assess relative status. The most obvious status difference is that of **gender.** Gender inequalities are of fundamental importance in Japan. Women are assumed to be of lower status than men. They defer to men and serve them. It is extremely rare to find a woman in a position in which she supervises and gives orders to men. In fact, the few Japanese women who are business owners tend to surround themselves with female employees.

In a group that is all men or all women, like a group of women at a flower-arranging class, people hasten to find out how old each member is, so that everyone will know where they are ranked by **age.** In big companies, male office workers are hired in age cohorts right after high school or college and they advance together as a group. Even an exceptionally talented worker will not be promoted ahead of his age cohort. It is only at the age of 55 or 60 when most of the cohort retires that some will be promoted into upper management. By this method companies ensure that older men need never take orders from younger men.

Judging relative status is further complicated by the importance of **job title.** A group of young businessmen, meeting for the first time, eagerly proffer their business cards to each other, almost before saying a word. They do this because Japanese cards contain vital information: More prominently than a person's name, they tell his title and what organization he works for. Once occupational statuses are clearly established, Japanese men feel more comfortable: They know how to treat each other as unequals. In Japan, when you meet another person, you must be able to assess whether your status is higher or lower than theirs. Then you will be able to judge what role you should play: how low you should bow in greeting or taking leave of them, and what words you should use in addressing them. You must be able to switch smoothly from one role to another as you interact with people in different statuses. This social knowledge is explicitly recognized and taught to children in Japan (Bachnik, pp. 155–199, 164).

Language and Status

Status hierarchy is structured into the Japanese language in such a way that you literally cannot speak to other people without knowing their status compared to yours. A very important part of Japanese is *keigo,* or "respect language." Japanese provides almost no vocabulary for use with a status equal. Every time you speak to another person, the language forces you to decide what level of formality to choose in your verbs and pronouns, depending on the status, age, gender, and intimacy of you, your listener, and anyone else you refer to. A question addressed to a woman, your younger brother, or your subordinate at work will be phrased in very different words than the same request to a man, your boss, or your father. Women always use the more polite speech forms, especially to men, but even to each other (Smith, pp. 74–77; Christopher, p. 40).

Japanese children learn early to sort out relative status, because *keigo* is employed even within the family. You cannot address any relative senior to you by either his or her personal name or a personal pronoun. So a child always addresses an elder sibling, parent, grandparent, and so forth, by a kin status name [for example, *onisan* ("elder brother")] and is, in turn, addressed by her or his personal name, even if there are only two children. A wife calls her husband by a kin name (typically, father or daddy), but her husband addresses her by her personal name. Outside the family, except when addressing children or people who have been friends since childhood, Japanese people call each other by status names. You call your neighbor *okusan* (Mrs. Lady of the Household), your teacher *sensei,* the government official *kyokucho-san* (Mr. Bureau Chief). Everyone of higher status than you is addressed with the suffix *san* added to her or his status name, or with great formality, *sama* (Hendry, p. 86; Reischauer, 1977, p. 163).

The most fascinating example of the problem of language and status in Japan occurs in television talk shows. All sorts of specialists—professors, authors, officials, and so on—speak on Japanese TV. Each speaker faces a heterogeneous audience; some viewers are of higher status than the speaker, and some lower. How are they to speak to this group, without giving offense or undercutting their own dignity? This dilemma is solved by the role of the *kikite,* "the listener," a young, clearly lower-status woman, to whom the speaker ostensibly addresses all remarks (Rudolph, p. 8).

Unequal Dependencies

People of unequal status address each other differently and they also expect different behavior from each other. Generally, lower-status people show deference, respect, and loyalty to higher-status people. Politeness is very important. In a group, older people walk first. In an office, or at formal meetings or parties, people are seated in order of status, and it is a common sight to find people jammed up at the door, deferring to each other and trying to sort out the correct seating. If people of higher status, or people you don't know well, come to your house, you will treat them with great deference, seating them in the best spot in the best room, and serving them special food and drink on the best dishes, and choosing topics of conversation they will enjoy (Bachnik, pp. 160–162).

But those in higher statuses also owe much to the people below them. They are expected to act their age, or live up to their positions. Acting like "one of the boys" or "like a kid" is felt to be extremely unbecoming and embarrassing. Higher-status people are expected to treat those below them with parental kindness. A common relationship in Japan, particularly in business, is that of mentor and protégé, in which an older, higher-status man helps his younger protégé, not only in business, but in his personal life, advising him and commonly acting as his go-between in arranging a marriage. The protégé relies upon, and positively enjoys, his dependence on his mentor.[3] Takeo Doi, 1977, provided the classic description of the pleasure the Japanese often take in relations of dependence.

Status Inequality Based on Gender

The deepest inequality in Japanese society is based on status. Gender inequality, the subordination of women to men, is built into Japanese institutions, shaping family life, education, and the economy. There is little public objection to gender inequality in Japan. Almost everyone assumes that the purpose of a woman's life is to serve others, especially her children and her husband.

Women in Japanese History

Centuries ago, early in Japanese history, women apparently held a higher status. After marriage, a man became part of his wife's family. The ancient Japanese religion worshiped a goddess, Amaterasu, from whom the royal family still claims descent. There were even a number of powerful empresses from the third through the eighth centuries A.D. (Condon, pp. 2–3).

Japanese society changed, however, between the sixth and eighth centuries when Chinese culture was so enthusiastically imported. Confucian belief in the inferiority of women was also adopted. Women were told it was their duty and their fate to be humble and self-sacrificing, to obey first their fathers, then their fathers-in-law and their husbands, then their sons. In public, they shuffled three steps be-

---

[3]In the rare female-owned Japanese businesses, female executives play this mentor role in relation to their female employees.

hind their husbands. Especially during the conservative Tokugawa period (1635–1853), the subordination of women was strongly enforced. Women could own no property, and their husbands could divorce them readily for failure to produce sons, or even for quarreling with their mothers-in-law. Women who committed adultery could be punished by death (Condon, pp. 3, 20, 181).

The reforms of the Meiji Restoration gave a small boost to women's status. Girls were allowed an elementary education, and a few girls' high schools were established. Women were granted the right to divorce their husbands. This period also saw the first stirrings of feminism in Japan. But it was not until after World War II that any major changes in the status of women took place. Immediately after the war, American Occupation authorities imposed legal reforms guaranteeing women new rights, including the right to vote, the right to attend universities, and the right to marry by "mutual consent." Industrialization and urbanization liberated women from the *ie* and from the necessity of arranged marriage. With longer lives and fewer children, more women were drawn into the paid labor force. But while women were less oppressed after World War II than they had been before, they remained very much subordinated to men (Condon, pp. 23, 181).

Women's Status Today

Analysts disagree about the extent of women's subordination in Japan today. Some observers argue that Japanese women are still fundamentally unequal to men, in status, power, and wealth. Journalist Jane Condon contends that Japanese women now walk not three steps but "half a step behind" their men (p. 1). It is accepted by both sexes that women are fundamentally different from, and inferior to, men. Their role in life is seen as a supporting one, their duty to devote themselves to the care of children, old people, and husbands; to be patient and "endure" and put their own needs last.

Women defer to men; they giggle behind their hands, act shy, cute, and submissive, and lower their eyes. They are taught to listen and quietly observe men to interpret men's feelings and anticipate their needs. When women do speak, they are expected to have small, high voices and to use the forms of "respect speech" that express hesitation. At home and at work, women are the backup support, providing graceful personal service, but excluded from public life and institutional power. The feminist movement in Japan is tiny, and has little influence.

But while women are certainly subordinate in the public realm of life, "off-stage" at home they exercise considerable power. Japanese wives are in charge of family budgets and, with their husbands away at work so much, they are the emotional center of family life. Many psychologists and anthropologists claim that Japanese women manipulate their husbands and children by playing the role of the martyr. Feeling guilt for inflicting suffering on their wives and mothers, Japanese men and children spontaneously strive to please them. Other analysts depict Japanese men as dependent on their wives, both physically and psychologically. Anthropologist Takie Sugiyama Lebra describes the traditional wife as offering her husband so much "around the body care" that he cannot even find his socks without her (Kato, pp. 184–185; Lebra, 1984, p. 133).

An all-female festival group carries a *mikoshi,* or sacred palanquin, in a neighborhood temple festival. Their dress is traditional, but the role is not; until recently only men carried Shinto gods in processions.

Shoko's Story: Modern Marriage

Shoko Sato was born in 1957 in a small city near Kyoto. She graduated high school and began working in the office of a big local construction company. She enjoyed working very much. Her department chief was very kind to her and he allowed her an unusual amount of responsibility for organizing the paperwork on contracts. When she was 24 Shoko married Taichi. The match was semi-arranged. She knew Taichi from high school and from neighborhood temple festivals. When Taichi's boss, who knew her father, suggested the marriage, they found themselves very drawn to each other. Shoko wanted to continue working after she married, so she felt terribly frustrated and confused when her boss immediately began to talk about a party for her "retirement" when he learned of the engagement. It was too embarrassing to try to explain that she had imagined she could keep working, and she didn't want to suggest that he hadn't understood her. So Shoko went along. Anyway, her first child was born just a year after the marriage, and Shoko firmly believed that she should fully devote herself to her children.

While Shoko plunged into the world of babies and mothers, she was still in some ways disappointed in her marriage. The romance she and her husband Taichi had enjoyed during their engagement seemed to vanish in the face of his obligation to work long hours and travel frequently for his company. Shoko made his breakfast every morning, and waited up for him at night until he returned at ten or eleven, since he didn't carry a key to the apartment. At any rate, she wanted to give him dinner and run his bath for him and lay out his clothes for the morning. Taichi turned his paycheck over to her and she arranged the family finances. They moved several times and each time Shoko found the new apartment, since her husband was too busy at work to join her. Raising her children was a great joy to Shoko. At every milestone, like starting first grade, or graduating junior high school, she relived her own happy childhood and strove to make her children's as secure and loving as her own. Shoko became active in the PTA and kept up her friendships with several women she had known ever since junior high school. Now, helping her son and daughter with their homework and driving them to lessons take a lot of her time. She works on the yearly festival of their local shrine and studies flower arranging in the town cultural center. Last year she began working part-time for a nearby bank. Shoko feels her life is full, but she doesn't really know her husband very well any more.

Gender Segregation

One thing is clear about Japanese adult men and women: Their roles are highly segregated. They lead separate lives. The word "wife" in Japanese literally means "inside person" (Condon, p. 1). It is the wife's role to be in charge of the home and children. The husband is the "outside man," who goes out into the world, relieved of all worries at home. He is sometimes referred to as a "boarder," so uninvolved is he in household matters. In a real way, the primary ties in the family are those between mothers and children. Women are expected to live through their children, taking pride in their successes and blaming themselves for failures. Childcare and housework are demanding jobs in Japan. Mothers are expected to teach their children to read at home, before they enter kindergarten, and to spend hours a day helping their children with homework. Apartments are very small and few women have cars, so they must shop for groceries every day. Automatic clothes dryers are rare in Japan and women are expected to hang their wash out to dry on the balcony or in the backyard. A very significant obligation for women is care of the elderly. They are expected to care for their husband's parents, and often their own as well.

Women and Work

It is also clear that in terms of paid work, Japanese women are unequal to men. Their job opportunities are much more constricted and their earnings less. In Japanese society everyone is expected to marry, and almost everyone does. Adulthood doesn't really start until marriage, so single people in their late twenties or early thirties are considered peculiar. By then, one should definitely have found a mate. Between high school or college graduation and marriage, women are expected to work outside the home. But when their first child is born, usually within a year of marriage, three-quarters of women leave work. They begin working again, on a part-time basis, once their last child has begun school. (See Table 1.3.)

Young Women and Work. Young women find they have few job alternatives. The jobs available to them keep them dependent, separated from and subordinated to men, usually without prospect of promotion. Unmarried women work in offices, in factories, and in retail stores. A job traditionally considered highly desirable for young women is "office lady" (called OL), especially with a prestigious company. OLs are selected for looks, since their duties are minimal: They do photocopying and filing, make tea, and tidy up. They are really a corporate status symbol, employed to be decorative and act as hostesses for business guests. Newly hired OLs

TABLE 1.3. Working Women 1970–1996:
Half of all Japanese women work, but they bring home only a third of all income.

	Percentage of Women in the Adult Labor Force****		Women's Income as a Percent of All Income
	1970*	1996**	1994*
Egypt	***	22	25
Germany	39	47	35
Japan	39	50	34
Mexico	19	37	25
USA	37	59	41

Sources:
*   United Nations Human Development Database, 1997
**   United Nations Statistical Division, Statistics and Indicators on the World's Women *http://www.un.org/Depts/unsd/gender*
***   Data not available
****Adult Labor force is defined here as those 15 years old and older.

are trained in bowing, greeting phone callers correctly, and offering tea. They are expected to live with their parents, and most companies will not hire girls who don't live at home, unless they live in the company dormitories provided for some female factory workers (Tasker, pp. 102–103; Condon, p. 194). (See Table 4.1, p. 189.) Jobs like OL offer some rewards to young women: They aren't very demanding and the pay is quite good for a person who lives at home, so unmarried women have money and unparalleled freedom to travel and go out and go shopping. Recently young women have been prolonging this pleasant period by postponing marriage a few more years (Itoi and Powell, pp. 38–39). But almost all young women marry and marriage remains women's primary job.

Most women say they wouldn't want a man's job if they could have one; that they don't envy men all the long hours and social pressure and anxiety. However, there are some young women now who want managerial or professional promotion-track jobs, and the big companies have responded to their demands by creating a new employment track for female employees who want a career. But these women must work overtime, be willing to transfer to distant offices, and work through their childbearing years, just like men. Very few women have been hired in the career track. Only university graduates are eligible and only 21 percent of female high school graduates go to a university.[4] Of that 21 percent, only 1 percent take career track jobs (Sugimoto, pp. 145–147). Sometimes women can find promotion-track jobs with foreign companies or in the very few female-owned companies. But overall, very few women in Japan hold high-ranking jobs. Of the 27,000 companies listed on the Tokyo stock exchange, only 12 are headed by women and 10 of those are family businesses. There are only 58 women in the top four levels of the Japanese bureaucracy (out of 5,573 such employees) (Condon, p. 276; Sugimoto, p. 147). (See Table 5.3, p. 266.)

[4]It is much more common for female high school graduates to take a 2-year degree at a junior college. Ninety percent of junior college students are women (Condon, p. 119).

Working Mothers. Powerful forces are at work in Japan today, changing women's roles and values. But there are equally powerful counteracting forces, absorbing change and quieting protest. New demographic and economic trends have had the combined impact of drawing married women into the workforce. The average 40-year-old woman today in Japan has no small children at home, but has another 40 years of life ahead of her. For women, middle age has become a period of crisis. Divorce rates are highest, and increasing most rapidly, among women in their 40s and 50s. Many women who find they don't have enough to do turn to paid work, both for meaningful occupation and to help pay rising family expenses.

Since 1977, more employed women have been married than single, and 40 percent of the workforce is female (Condon, pp. 219, 263; Sugimoto, p. 142). But married women work on terms even more disadvantageous than do single women. Accommodating the needs of their families, most married women find unskilled work with flexible hours near home in supermarkets, fast-food shops, department stores, and small factories (Condon, p. 194; Tasker, p. 103). Under the pressure of economic competition, more and more Japanese companies now hire a small core of men for full-time, lifetime security jobs, and then accommodate the ups and downs of the business cycle with part-timers, often women.

Women and Social Change

Japanese women are still seen primarily as wives and mothers and it is as wives and mothers that they are registering their strongest rebellion against their roles. Women are postponing marriage, prolonging that pleasurable time after leaving school and before marrying when they are relatively independent and have jobs and money of their own. While 90 percent of all Japanese marry by the age of 40, young women are postponing marriage more and more; from age 25 closer and closer to age 30, which is still seen as the latest possible age for having a first child. Japanese men complain about their difficulty in finding wives. Farmers and fishermen find it particularly hard to persuade women to live in rural areas and in the same house with their in-laws. Marriage bureaus do a big business in arranging marriages for Japanese men with Chinese, Taiwanese, and Filipino women (Jolivet, pp. 40, 146–147).

Politicians in Japan are very worried about the falling birthrate. In the 1980s, Japanese women were bearing an average of 1.57 children each, and by the 1990s, the rate had fallen to 1.46. That is considerably below **replacement level** of about 2.1, so if the birthrate doesn't rise, Japan's population will begin to decrease in size. Officials fear that at current rates, Japan will have the oldest population in the world by the twenty-first century. Problems in funding pensions and problems in finding enough employees will result (Jolivet, p. 1). It appears that Japanese women are staging a kind of silent rebellion against their limited work roles, against their subordination within the family, and against their isolation in the home. If the Japanese are unwilling to allow significant immigration, they may have to find a way to make male and female roles more equal, so women can do more meaningful work outside their homes and men can participate in rearing their children and can spend time with their wives.

Status Inequality and Minority Groups

Japan is a very homogeneous society; few groups differ racially, ethnically, or socially from the majority of the population, and these groups are very small. At most, 4 to 5 million people out of the total population of 120 million could be classified as members of **minority groups,** groups which are seen as inferior and are treated unequally by the **majority** population. It may seem strange to you that even though Japanese minorities differ very little from other Japanese, they are nonetheless treated with distaste and face considerable discrimination (Reischauer, 1977, pp. 32–33; Tasker, pp. 23–24).

The Ainu

The oldest Japanese minority is descended from the Ainu, the ancient race that inhabited Japan before Asian settlers arrived more than a thousand years ago. The Asians pushed the Ainu north into the less desirable, wintry islands at the top of Japan. They also intermarried with the Ainu, so that today many of the Ainu have been absorbed into the majority population. About 24,000 Ainu still live as a distinct group. They are poorer than other Japanese and are looked down upon. Today, the Ainu are becoming more conscious of themselves as a minority group. They are writing down their aboriginal language before it disappears, and have come to identify themselves with the aboriginal peoples of Alaska and northern Canada with whom they believe they are racially linked, and whose experience with settlers they see as similar to their own (Reischauer, 1977, pp. 32–33; Tasker, pp. 23–24).

Ethnic Japanese

About 700,000 people of Korean background live in Japan. Most of them come from families brought to Japan as cheap labor during the period when Japan annexed Korea in the aggression which led up to World War II. Even those Koreans who were born in Japan and speak only Japanese are not granted citizenship and face discrimination by employers (Reischauer, 1977, pp. 32–35; Tasker, pp. 23–24; Sugimoto, pp. 177–184).

An interesting new minority in Japan is the growing community of approximately 150,000 people of Japanese descent who were born in Brazil and Peru. Faced with a shortage of unskilled workers, and fearful of illegal immigration from other Asian countries, the Japanese government decided to welcome Japanese of foreign descent whose ancestors had emigrated in the past. Japanese Brazilians and Peruvians, many of them skilled and educated, have come to Japan seeking escape from their countries' troubled economies. In Japan they take factory jobs, often living in company dormitories and working 14-hour days. These new immigrants are "racially" identical to the Japanese, but culturally they are different. They speak and laugh loudly and embrace in public, and hold street festivals with salsa and samba music. The Latin Americans face discrimination in Japan: they are treated fearfully in restaurants and stores and often exploited by labor contractors. "The Japanese treat us like some kind of inferior race," said one Brazilian immigrant (Weisman, p. 1).

The Burakumin

Not all Japanese minority groups are racial or ethnic minorities. The *burakumin* are Japanese, but they are rejected nonetheless. They are the descendants of Japan's ancient "outcastes," those who did dirty jobs (like butchering or leatherwork) considered offensive by others. The *burakumin* today are physically and culturally indistinguishable from other Japanese. Only their family names and sometimes the neighborhoods where they live mark them for discrimination and distaste. Estimates of the number of *burakumin* today range from 1.2 million to 3 million, no more than 2 percent of the population (Pharr, p. 76).

Burakumin faced the most intense discrimination during the Tokugawa period when they were required to live in separate villages, and to defer to majority Japanese in an exaggerated way, for example, by rushing away or lying facedown on the ground when they met a majority group member. They were forbidden to enter temples, shrines, and festivals. When the caste system was abolished during the Meiji period, *burakumin* became legally free of restrictions. But, in fact, discrimination continued. The Ministry of Justice itself referred to *burakumin* as "the lowliest of all people, almost like animals," and they continued to be excluded from temples and public baths (Pharr, pp. 76–77).

Today, *burakumin* face discrimination in employment and marriage. It is common practice in Japan for families to hire a "marriage detective" to research the background of a prospective spouse whose family is not known to them. Marriages are canceled when the family is traced to a *burakumin* village. The same thing happens when employers research the family background of new hires. "Buraku place-name registers" are (illegally) sold in Japan. As a result of this discrimination, *burakumin* have lower incomes and less education than majority Japanese; they follow more insecure occupations, and have higher crime rates than other Japanese, and this feeds the contempt in which they are held, perpetuating their disadvantage (Pharr, pp. 77–79).

Since World War II there have been several active "*burakumin* liberation groups" with large memberships, which do research and carry out protest activities. In 1969 several major cities passed *burakumin* affirmative action policies, designed to improve the school performance of *burakumin* children, through remedial classes and counseling. These measures have often had the unintended consequence of calling attention to the children's *burakumin* background and low status, and exposing them to bullying. Other measures were devised to prevent majority Japanese from withdrawing their children from schools with a large *burakumin* population. *Burakumin* have been so excluded and isolated from majority society that it has been relatively easy for them to develop a strong sense of group identity and to organize protests (Pharr, pp. 85–88).

Class Inequality in Japan

Class inequalities in Japan are much less noticeable than are status inequalities. Traveling in Japan, you will look in vain for rundown, crime-ridden neighborhoods with abandoned buildings, decaying schools, and corner drug dealers. Nor will you find gated suburbs filled with huge homes, with private pools and gyms. Only 1.2 percent of the Japanese population receives any welfare payments, and the number of people who are homeless alcoholic men, petty criminals, able-bodied but permanently unemployed dropouts is very small (Fukutake, p. 158). In survey after survey, about 90 percent of Japanese identify themselves as middle class, reflecting their lack of consciousness of class inequalities. It is also true that to an unusual degree people of different classes mix socially. In city neighborhoods modern luxury towers have been built in the midst of old tumbledown houses, and since almost all residents send their children to neighborhood public elementary schools, children from different class backgrounds become friends. Also, school uniforms mask class differences.

In addition, cultural differences among Japanese people of different social classes are minimal: There are no class accents, and styles of dress, leisure pursuits, even the newspapers and magazines people read, vary very little along class lines. Japanese people spend a lot of time in association with those higher or lower in class position than themselves in the typical hierarchical relationships, and in the close group associations of school and office. They spend little time in groups which bring together those of one class or status. Even Japanese unions are distinctive in this respect, joining both blue- and white-collar workers of a particular enterprise.

Income, Occupation, and Social Class

People in Japan don't like to acknowledge the existence of class inequalities in their society. People value equality and they try to maintain an *omote* depiction of Japan as a very egalitarian society. For example, official government information on income distribution still uses data from 1979 when equality of incomes was at a high. Let us try to puzzle out just how much class inequality there really is in Japan.

According to Yoshio Sugimoto, about 10 percent of Japanese are part of an upper-middle class of university-educated managers and professionals. They have income more than twice the national average and they have some wealth—fancy cars, stocks and bonds, costly memberships in sports clubs. They can afford expensive sports like golf and sailing, and attend theater and concerts. At the other end of the income spectrum is a much larger working class—as much as 30 percent of Japanese who have completed only junior high or high school. They are manual workers and farmers and their incomes are only about half the national average.

Most Japanese fall somewhere between the richest 10 percent and the poorest 30 percent, and for this large population class differences are blurred. Many "salarymen" and professionals have university degrees and prestigious jobs, but their incomes are only in the middle range. Blue-collar employees of big corporations earn less, but not a great deal less. Many self-employed workers—owners of small businesses and skilled tradesmen like plumbers and electricians—earn more on average than the salarymen, though they enjoy less prestige (Sugimoto, pp. 37–39).

Within Japanese corporations, there is unusual equality of incomes. The average corporate department head is paid approximately three times what the lowest-

TABLE 1.4. Purchasing Power Distribution:
Buying power is more equally distributed among Japanese and Germans
than among Americans.

	Average Yearly Purchasing Power Per Person in the Poorest 20% of the Population 1980–1994	Average Yearly Purchasing Power Per Person in the Richest 20% of the Population 1980–1994	Ratio of the Purchasing Power of the Richest 20% of the Population to the Poorest 20% 1980–1994
Egypt	$1,653	$7,809	4.72
Mexico	$1,437	$19,383	13.49
Germany	$6,594	$37,963	5.76
Japan	$8,987	$38,738	4.31
USA	$5,800	$51,705	8.91

Source: Human Development Database 1997, United Nations, New York, 1998

paid employee receives. Company presidents average six to seven times the pay of newly hired recruits. (By contrast, in the United States and Europe, executive pay averages 30 to 40 times starting employee pay.) In late 1988, Japanese company presidents averaged $240,000 per year in salary and bonuses, about 10 percent of average American CEO pay. Similar pay differentials prevail in Japanese government offices. Without high incomes, Japanese executives are unable to accumulate great wealth. High inheritance taxes and heavy taxes on high incomes also make it difficult to pass on any wealth amassed (Chapman, p. 200).

Table 1.4 displays differences in income distribution in five societies. In the United States, those in the poorest 20 percent of the population have an average per person spending power of $5,800 a year. In Japan, the comparable figure is $8,987, so the poor are much better off in Japan. The richest 20 percent have $51,705 apiece to spend in the United States and only $38,738 in Japan. You can see that inequalities between the richest fifth of the population and the poorest fifth are only half as great in Japan as in the United States.

Social Mobility and Class Inequality

Because the Japanese are uncomfortable with class inequalities, they support an educational system that puts tremendous effort into making sure that children from all classes start out equal in a competition to achieve success through education. All public schools in Japan are centrally controlled by the Ministry of Education, and it is ministry policy to make sure that all elementary and junior high schools are of uniform quality. There are no budget disparities between primary schools in rich and poor communities in Japan. All have the same facilities, and teachers get the same high salaries in every school. (Teaching is a prestigious career in Japan and a very competitive field to enter.) Teachers are even rotated from school to school every five years to ensure that all children have the same quality of instruction. This system works to provide greater upward mobility for poor children than exists in most other industrialized nations. One in three children from the poorest 20 percent of Japanese families ends up attending a university, an unusually large percentage.

To a remarkable degree, Japanese society is a **meritocracy,** a social system in which one's place in the social stratification system is based solely on merit, or achievement, not on inherited advantage (or disadvantage). Education is the heart of Japan's meritocracy, which makes sense in a modern, technological society where education is the gateway to jobs. In Japan, academic excellence and high scores on achievement tests are the ticket to high-status jobs. But take careful note: An educational meritocracy may be fair, but it doesn't make life easy for children. A child's school performance, at an early age, has a lifelong impact, and there are very few second chances. As a result, competition is fierce and childhood is a serious time. From junior high school on, children are occupied with preparation for exams. They put in long hours of study, and competitive pressure compels many to attend cram schools, called *juku,* for many hours after school and on Saturdays. The purpose of cram schools is just to prepare students for the exams. It's like attending school twice every day.

The Japanese educational system is set up to give children from different classes equal opportunities. Note, however, that it doesn't give girls the same opportunities as boys. Though girls and boys start off equal in elementary school, girls tend not to go to universities and not to go into high-paid, prestigious career jobs. Furthermore, while the Japanese are working on it, their educational system hasn't yet succeeded in giving *burakumin* equal opportunities either.

Competition for Success

High school entrance exams are a conspicuous moment of truth in the lives of Japanese children. High schools are not all equal; they are ranked in prestige, the higher-status schools serving as feeders for the most prestigious universities. Almost everyone goes to some high school, but only students with good school records are permitted even to take the tests for the most prestigious schools. At the end of high school they must again take very difficult, competitive exams for admission to college. But then those who excel can gain admission to prestigious "national" universities, practically guaranteeing access to higher-paid, high-status jobs. As many as three-quarters of the people hired for upper-level civil service jobs and almost half the company presidents in Japan are graduates of prestigious Tokyo University. Many companies don't even bother to recruit employees outside a few select universities.

Whether they attend college or not, students' high school performance is crucial. For students who go into the labor market after high school, job placement depends on school performance: Close coordination between employers and schools results in all hiring being done through the school. In fact, direct contact between employers and students is forbidden. Schools have the power to decide which student will get which job, offering each graduate only one job, with decisions based on grades, attendance, and behavior. Students who have failed to conform find themselves left with temporary, low-paid work (Leestma, p. 58).

Class Inequality Increases

Despite postwar egalitarian institutions and beliefs, inequalities of income, wealth, and opportunity have increased in the last two decades in Japan. In the "bubble economy" of the 1980s, those who happened to own land or stock found themselves suddenly rich and speculators amassed fortunes. Old values of frugality and restraint gave way to a burst of conspicuous consumption. Expensive western goods—designer-label clothes, foreign cars, and art works—became fashionable and credit cards were introduced. Corporate executives lived lavishly at company expense, enjoying headquarters in palatial office towers, and sometimes even company apartments. Limousines took them to expensive restaurants, bars, and golf clubs, all paid for out of corporate expense accounts. The luxurious corporate lifestyle was emulated by the newly rich, and by young women and middle-aged couples who spent their earnings on consumer goods, rejecting traditional habits of saving (Chapman, pp. 174, 190–194).

At the same time, a new generation of wealthy Japanese inherited advantages from their wealthy parents. Doctors inherited their fathers' practices, and the children of politicians took over their fathers' seats in the Diet and their carefully nurtured political support groups (Chapman, p. 203).

Most Japanese disapproved of these new economic disparities. Perhaps that is why the public registered little concern over the crash and depression of the 1990s, when real estate prices fell as much as 90 percent, the stock market crashed, and expense account living was cut back drastically. But the recession of the 90s also increased inequality between two kinds of employees: A minority (less than a quarter of full-time workers) continued to enjoy lifetime security, high wages, and guaranteed promotions in their jobs with major corporations. At the same time an increasing percentage of workers, especially women, were much less well off: They worked full-time for smaller companies at lower wages; or they worked in the rapidly expanding force of part-time workers, often putting in as much as 35 to 40 hours a week, but at low wages and without security, benefits, or union membership. Part-time workers are not even counted in unemployment statistics.

Inequalities in Education

Most importantly, inequalities appeared and sharpened in the educational system, so much so that many Japanese began to characterize it as "unfair" and to resent the relentless emphasis on passing tests as the sine qua non for success in adult life. What happened was that in the boom years of the 80s well-off families began to pour their new-found wealth into helping their children succeed in school. They sent them to expensive *juku* (after-school cram schools) and, even more important, they sent their children to private junior high and high schools, schools with special relationships with the most prestigious colleges. In 1992 a Japanese television special revealed that at Tokyo University, the top university, half of the students were graduates of the 20 top high schools in Japan and 18 of those high schools were private schools. Many expensive private high schools started their own junior highs so their students wouldn't have to take the grueling high school exams (Sugimoto, pp. 117–119; Sanger, 1991, p. 4). Education became more expensive too. *Jukus* are expensive and while fees for public high schools and universities remained moderate, tuition at private schools rose. People in Japan don't fully appreciate that their society still has less class inequality than most other industrialized societies; what they see is increasing inequality and they find it very offensive.

Inequalities of Power in Japan Today

In the late 1990s, American officials became convinced that Japan held the key to pulling all of Asia out of its sudden economic collapse, if only it would revive its own lagging economy. Americans looked around for decision makers who could change Japanese economic and fiscal policies and introduce free-market reforms. "Wait a minute," the Americans seemed to say, "isn't anybody in charge here?"

Formally and officially, Japan is a western-style parliamentary democracy. After Japan's defeat in World War II, democracy was imposed by the American occupying forces. Occupation authorities created a legislature (the Diet) with an upper and a lower house, political parties, a prime minister, and a liberal constitution guaranteeing free speech, universal suffrage, labor's right to organize, and the rule of law. In theory, the people govern by electing representatives who make laws implemented by the bureaucracy. Japan's economy was also remade to resemble western ideals. The Occupation destroyed Japan's powerful family-owned conglomerates (the *zaibatsu*) hoping to encourage a free-enterprise economy in which economic power also would be widely and equally distributed among a great many small companies.

Government and Business: Western Structures, Japanese Spirit

Japanese society did not turn out the way Occupation forces intended. After the Occupation, the Japanese retained the American preference for separation of powers, so no one branch of government could dominate. They retained and exaggerated the choice of a weak executive who cannot make decisions alone, and a weak military excluded from political power. To the American formula they added a very Japanese preference for cooperation over confrontation, for behind-the-scenes compromise over public debate. Though Japan today has a legislature, political parties, labor unions, and stockholders, these western institutions function in a distinctly Japanese fashion. As they say, it is a case of *wakon yosai,* western forms transformed by Japanese spirit. Parliamentary structures are actually the *omote* face of Japanese power. In reality, power is concentrated in the hands of a small elite, a partnership among government bureaucrats, legislators, and industrialists. Most powerholders are not elected, and power is exercised almost entirely behind the scenes.

The Bureaucracy

In Japan's tripartite power structure, commonly called the "iron triangle," the government bureaucracy stands at the top, coordinating its power with that of business leaders and elected officials. Bureaucrats today, who work in the various government ministries like the famous MITI (the Ministry of International Trade and Industry) and the Ministry of Finance, actually draft the legislation that is brought to the floor of the Diet. According to Atsushi Ueda, "we might go so far as to say that a Diet session is a kind of ceremonial performance, to give people inside and outside Japan the impression that decisions are being made democratically" (Ueda, p. 129). Then after passage, the bureaucracy implements laws and policies it has developed and sent to the legislature. But bureaucratic power extends further, because the bureaucracy doesn't simply mechanically apply the law; it exercises what is known as "administrative guidance," flexibility in enforcing regulations.

The bureaucracy was the guiding hand behind Japan's fabulously successful post–World War II economic growth. In each important industry, MITI selected a few strong companies and encouraged them to compete with each other for market shares and profits, while sheltering them from foreign competition. The bureaucracy supplied capital to companies they supported and denied it to others. Bureaucrats rather than individual companies decided which types of foreign technology would be imported and manufactured in Japan. They decided where to send Japanese products for export and taught companies how to produce for export.

The Ministries Manage the Economy

Ministries like MITI are not like western regulatory agencies, which have a somewhat adversarial relationship with the industries they are regulating. A Japanese ministry is like a mother hen incubating her chicks under her cozy wings. Japan is sometimes termed a system of **state capitalism,** because while businesses are privately owned, the government directs the economy. Government bureaucrats help businesses make money and business helps the government increase Japan's power and prestige. State capitalism is different from **free-market capitalism** in which the government is expected to keep its hands off business and let businesses make their own decisions. It is also different from **communism** in which the government not only runs the economy, but owns all the businesses too, and making a profit is not a permissible goal.

Who are Japan's powerful bureaucrats? They are an elite group, but not a hereditary elite. Young people who attend Japan's top universities may enter the bureaucracy, and it is considered very prestigious, very respected work. There is no sense in Japan that bureaucrats are corrupt, or incompetent, or wasting the taxpayers' money. The Japanese have trusted their bureaucrats because they don't use their power to enrich themselves or favor their families. Because Japan's educational system provides opportunities for upward mobility to children of every class, the bureaucracy is open to talent. It is staffed by people from all class backgrounds who have succeeded by excelling in school. People see bureaucrats as society's best and brightest. They see them as apolitical: Bureaucrats are not allied to any political parties (Ueda, pp. 130, 134–137). Up to now, the Japanese have accepted bureaucratic power because it is traditional in their society and because they agree with the goals of the ministries: economic growth, increased market share abroad, the protection of Japanese businesses, and restraint on the growth of inequality. However, in the late 1990s there was a crisis of public confidence in the bureaucracy. Faced with a stubborn economic recession at home and sharpened competition from the global economy, the ministries stumbled and couldn't seem to get the Japanese economy moving again.

Businesses and Bureaucrats

Businesses cultivate their relationships with bureaucrats. In a way it is difficult to decide whether bureaucrats are the masters or the servants of business, since all their efforts are aimed at maximizing the long-run expansion of industry. For example, until the scandals of 1998, every bank designated a number of young employees to spend all their time developing relationships with bureaucrats at the Ministry of Finance. They "dropped in" at Ministry offices and they entertained Ministry officials at bars and restaurants, getting tips about new policies, scheduled bank inspections, anything that might help their bank. Sometimes they sent birthday gifts to the bureaucrats' wives. When these young *MOF-tans* (ministry handlers) moved on to other assignments in the bank, they took their connections with them. In the 90s, as it became clear that the Ministry of Finance had protected banks from the consequences of their bad loans, the Japanese public became much more cynical about relationships between businessmen and bureaucrats, and business entertainment spending, formerly accepted as a normal part of business, came to be seen as a form of bribery. Banks abolished their *MOF-tans* and some ministry officials were even arrested for taking bribes (WuDunn, Oct. 29, 1995, p. E14; Mar. 17, 1998; January 27, 1998, pp. D1, D12; May 19, 1998, p. A4).

Business Organization

Today, business in Japan is far different from the thousands of competing small firms Occupation authorities envisioned. Japanese business is big business and it is highly organized to coordinate economic activity. Industries are organized by sector: auto manufacturers in one association, iron and steel companies in another, their industrywide organizations setting unwritten rules for business operations, and successfully pressuring members to comply. *Keidanren,* the federation of industrial organizations, brings together officials and chairmen of the boards of all the industrial associations.

But this is only the beginning of business organization. Most large corporations also belong to conglomerates: There are six giant ones which date to the early postwar years, and a number of newer, smaller ones. Conglomerates organize companies from many industries around a bank, also bringing in real estate, insurance, and trading firms. Conglomerates are united both by interlocking directorates and by joint stock ownership. It is customary for 60 to 70 percent of all shares in Japanese companies to be held by other companies in their conglomerate. These shares are never traded: Held off the market they link the companies of a conglomerate together and make outsider takeovers of companies impossible. Organization goes further: Each member of a conglomerate heads a *keiretsu,* a hierarchy of subsidiaries, suppliers, distributors, and subcontractors. Small enterprises produce for firms higher up in their *keiretsu,* both protected from the market and dependent on the larger companies (van Wolferen, 1989, pp. 34, 46–47).

In Japan, this is called "the convoy system": Strong companies (the big ships) protect and help weak companies (the little ships) with which they sail, often at the bidding of the ministries, so all survive. In the financial crisis of the 90s, strong banks held up the weak ones, and that meant that banks which had made too many bad loans were not permitted to fail and the whole economy was burdened by an unresolved banking crisis. Of course, it also meant that bank employees' jobs were protected, and the businesses that couldn't keep up payments on their loans were protected too. Even within a company, protecting managers and workers, customers, and vendors takes precedence over maximizing profits for the shareholders (Safire, p. 16; Kristof, July 15, 1997, pp. A1, A6).

The Elected Government

The official institutions of Japanese power, that is, the legislature, the political parties, the prime minister, the cabinet, and the electorate, are probably the weakest partner in Japan's ruling triumvirate. This was especially true after 1993 when the long domination of the Liberal Democratic Party (the LDP) began to weaken, without other strong parties emerging.

For forty years, the LDP held power and dominated Japanese politics, running what was essentially a single-party system. The LDP was a vote-getting machine and politicians treated politics as the business of getting elected. The legislature seldom legislated. The prime minister was often a relative unknown installed by behind-the-scenes kingmakers and had very limited power; and the cabinet served a merely ceremonial function, automatically approving policies developed by the bureaucrats. Over the decades, the party itself became divided into cliques, loyal to different leaders, but not distinguished by different ideologies or programs (van Wolferen, 1989, pp. 45, 110). This political system rewarded politicians for patience, loyalty, and obedience to their faction, not for dynamic leadership or assertiveness or vision. Factions gave out cabinet positions on the seniority system, based on a faction member's number of terms in the legislature. It resulted in prime ministers and cabinet ministers who were elderly, affable, and good at holding long meetings to reach consensus. In the economic crisis of the 90s, younger Japanese and western leaders chafed with frustration at the weakness of Japanese elected officials (Kristof, July 14, 1998, pp. A1, A8; July 15, 1998, p. A10; July 20, 1998, p. A6; Hagitani, p. 7).

So what do Japanese politicians really do? What power do they have? Politicians are mostly engaged in what Americans call "pork barrel politics"—securing government funding for their constituents in exchange for political support (Kristof, July 5, 1998, p. A4; Ogawa, p. 4). Politicians play the role of go-between linking citizens with business and bureaucrats and helping all three groups informally trade favors and influence with each other. The politics of the construction industry illustrates this relationship. The Ministry of Construction controls licenses for the entire industry and it has a huge budget to spend on government construction. Politicians, especially those from rural districts, use their contacts in the ministry to get construction projects approved for their home districts. Then the communities that elected them benefit from jobs and local spending. Local construction companies are big contributors to political campaign funds, and they are rewarded with contracts. Then politicians reward retired construction ministry bureaucrats by helping them gain election to the Diet (the legislature), reinforcing the connections between politicians and the ministry (van Wolferen, 1989, pp. 114–120).

Seiichi's Story: The Heir

With regret, Seiichi Kawashima admits to himself that his graduation from the University of Tokyo is approaching. College has been fun; it has been the most relaxed period in Seiichi's life, but now the pressure is on again. His father has made it clear that he expects

Seiichi to go on to the University of Tokyo law school to prepare for a career in politics. Seiichi's father wants to retire from the lower house of the Diet, and he wants Seiichi to run for and "inherit" his seat.

Seiichi cannot help but be aware that he is the child of two of the oldest governing families in Japan. If nothing else, the busy matchmakers bring the point home to him. Though his father emphasizes that Seiichi may not even think of marriage until he finishes his law degree, Seiichi knows the matchmakers are already calling his father with the names of the daughters of important politicians, successful businessmen, and top bureaucrats. His mother keeps mentioning the daughter of a top bureaucrat in the Ministry of Construction. Her brother is married to Seiichi's cousin. "Life is so predictable," Seiichi complains.

SOCIAL CHANGE AND THE FUTURE

It is hard to assess just how much Japan is changing, culturally and institutionally. American journalists eagerly record every hint of American and European influence: When the Japanese play soccer, buy L. L. Bean clothes, or embrace Disneyworld, you will be sure to read about it in American newspapers. But Japanese culture is still tremendously durable. The Japanese still prize effort, self-discipline, duty, conformity, and harmony. How much real change is taking place?

The Growth Consensus

Certainly there are some signs of change. For 40 years after the Occupation, the Japanese were in agreement about their society's goals and the means to use to achieve their goals. Business, government, and the Japanese people agreed that industrial expansion was their nation's goal: everything was geared to it. Starting in the 1950s, companies competed fiercely, not for profits but for market shares. Business executives took the long view, pouring revenues into capital reinvestment, always aiming for long-term growth, not short-term profits. The ministries used their power to lure business into growing sectors and advancing technologies and helped companies secure foreign markets.

Japanese workers and consumers supported this "growth consensus" because they benefited. Wages doubled and redoubled. Companies promised job security and rising wages in exchange for worker loyalty, and once-radical unions were declawed. The Japanese "embraced the drama of business growth," making business their national identity (Chapman, pp. 120–121). People looked up to big companies and business life became glamorous. The "salaryman" going to work became a kind of warrior, headed into battle, with the nation cheering him on.

The Economic Crisis

At the end of the twentieth century economic crisis is breaking down both the "growth consensus" and Japanese confidence. The roots of the crisis are fairly clear. The problem started in the prosperous 1980s when individuals and companies flush with cash bought real estate and stocks and drove up prices spectacularly. Tokyo land and buildings became the most expensive in the world. Brokers joked that if they could sell the imperial palace grounds in the middle of Tokyo, the property would be worth more than all of Los Angeles. Then in the early 90s real estate prices started to fall rapidly, by as much as 90 percent in some cases (so the apartment you bought for 10 million yen was soon worth only one million). No one wanted to buy real estate, anticipating further drops in prices, and soon property owners began defaulting on their mortgages. That put the banks in danger of failing. By 1998 the banks were limping along, saddled with $600 billion in bad loans, so they didn't have much money to make further loans. When companies were unable to borrow, the crisis spread beyond the banks to the rest of the economy. The stock market crashed and the value of the yen fell in relation to the dollar, and the economy stumbled into recession—consumers bought less and company sales fell and unemployment rose. Crises like this are characteristic of capitalist economies and they happen in many societies. The United States had a very similar crisis in the 1980s.

The Economic Crisis and the World Economy

However, the world economy is now so interconnected that a crisis in one country, particularly one like Japan, the world's second largest economy, rumbles like an earthquake through many other countries. This was particularly true in the late 90s, when a dangerous currency crisis had brought the rest of Asia into a serious economic depression. So the United States and international financial institutions like the World Bank began to pressure Japan to take action to bring its stalled economy back to life. They gave Japan the same advice they had given Russia and Mexico and Great Britain and Germany: You're part of the world economy now and to compete you must make your society a free-market system. You must deregulate; make the government stop interfering in business. Let the weak fail; let unprofitable banks and businesses go under. Let companies fire their excess employees and cut wages. Don't let banks and companies hide their debts; require "transparency" so investors can make rational decisions. Then profitability will be restored and the economy will expand again.

American advisors and politicians have taken a certain amount of satisfaction in the Japanese crisis. They believe it shows that Japanese-style state capitalism cannot succeed; that no country can restrict the free play of the market and that American capitalism is really the only way to run an economy. The Japanese feel depressed about the crisis, because they see that the respect with which their society is viewed is at stake. Japanese politicians have all called for deregulating the economy, cutting taxes and restructuring banks, but they have taken little action. Now the Japanese public is disgusted with elected officials, both for verbally embracing the American model, and at the same time, for failing to end the recession. As a result, the LDP's already insecure hold on power has been weakened, but no party or politician has stepped into the vacuum with an alternative the Japanese can feel proud of.

Capitalism, Japanese Style

The Japanese have not wanted to follow the American model, and for a good reason. A free-market system runs counter to a very fundamental part of Japanese culture: the web of *giri*, of obligation, that makes companies refuse to fire inefficient employees, preferring to cut everyone's bonuses a little instead, and makes banks lend more money to debtors rather than calling in loans and forcing debtors into bankruptcy. Because of *giri* consumers buy overpriced rice or appliances from neighborhood stores rather than going to discount chains, and the government refuses to allow discount chains. *Giri* makes companies pay seniority wages instead of merit-based wages. When you pull up to a Japanese gas station, three white-gloved attendants rush out and fill your tank and wash your windows and check your oil. And in gratitude, you return again, even though the gas is expensive there. All this mutual protection has limited the impact of the decade-long recession on the Japanese people. The unemployment rate at the bottom of the recession was about the same as the unemployment rate in the United States at the top of its economic boom (Kristof, April 21, 1998; July 15, 1997).

The Crisis and the Future

Nevertheless, the recession deepens and the Japanese feel gloomy and threatened. They fear that they will have to accept the free-market prescription in order to make their economy competitive in world markets. But they also fear that deregulation will bring unwelcome, very un-Japanese changes to their society. They fear that cooperation and a sense of national community and duty to each other will suffer, and that inequality, crime, and unemployment will increase (Kristof, April, 21, 1998, July 15, 1997).

Will Japan give way in the end and institute free-market reforms? Will such institutional change really fundamentally transform Japanese culture? Will the bureaucrats instead find a distinctively Japanese way out of the recession? Caution is in order when anticipating change in Japanese society. Japanese institutions of power have been very flexible in the past. Time and again, they have instituted radical changes in Japan, in response to a foreign threat, and each time Japanese society has found some way to absorb and adapt the changes and keep its distinctive culture. It may well happen again.

Thinking Sociologically

1. When you read Chapter 1, were you ethnocentric in your reaction to the Japanese?
2. Using a highlighter pen, go through pages 7 to 15 of Chapter 1. Highlight descriptions of Japanese values in blue and descriptions of norms in yellow. Are you confident you understand the difference between values and norms?
3. When some large American luxury cars were recently put on display in Tokyo, many Japanese shoppers said they wouldn't want to purchase them. "I would get a lot of attention if I drove that car," one woman said. Using what you now know about Japanese society, decide what kinds of cars you would choose to export to Japan if you were making this decision for an American auto company.
4. What are some Japanese values that contrast sharply with values in your own society?
5. What social groups are most important in the lives of the Japanese? What groups are most important in your life, in your society?
6. How are offices in your society physically arranged? (Are the desks separated, or all touching, as in Japan? Are there cubicles? Separate offices with doors?) Are offices in

your society similar to Japanese offices or different? What kinds of interaction and attitudes does office arrangement in your society encourage?

7. Turn to Table 1.2 (p. 26) and compare the homicide rates in Japan and in the United States. Thinking sociologically, can you explain what causes the tremendous difference in these rates?

8. Are there any similarities in the roles of women in Japanese society and in your society? What differences are there?

9. Compare the educational system in your society with the educational system in Japan. Which system is more of a meritocracy?

For Further Reading

BAYLEY, DAVID H., *Forces of Order: Policing Modern Japan.* Berkeley: University of California Press, 1991.

BUMILLER, ELIZABETH, *The Secrets of Mariko: A Year in the Life of a Japanese Woman and Her Family.* New York: Times Books, Random House, 1995.

FEILER, BRUCE S., *Learning to Bow: An American Teacher in a Japanese School.* New York: Ticknor & Fields, 1991.

FUCINI, JOSEPH J., and SUZY FUCINI, *Working for the Japanese: Inside Mazda's American Auto Plant.* New York: Macmillan, Free Press, 1990.

HENDRY, JOY, *Marriage in a Changing Japan: Community and Society.* New York: St. Martin's Press, 1981.

IWAO, SUMIKO, *The Japanese Woman: Traditional Image and Changing Reality.* New York: Free Press, 1993.

JOLIVET, MURIEL, *Japan: The Childless Society?: The Crisis of Motherhood.* London and New York: Routledge, 1997.

LO, JEANNIE, *Office Ladies, Factory Women: Life and Work at a Japanese Company.* Armonk, NY: M. E. Sharp, 1990.

PHARR, SUSAN J., *Losing Face: Status Politics in Japan.* University of California Press, 1990.

SUGIMOTO, YOSHIO, *An Introduction to Japanese Society.* Cambridge: Cambridge University Press, 1997.

WASWO, ANN, *Modern Japanese Society: 1868–1994.* Oxford: Oxford University Press, 1994.

WHITE, MERRY, *The Material Child: Coming of Age in Japan and America.* New York: Free Press, 1993.

Bibliography

BACHNIK, JANE, "Kejime, Defining a Shifting Self in Multiple Organizational Modes," in Nancy R. Rosenberger, ed., *Japanese Sense of Self.* Cambridge: Cambridge University Press, 1994.

BAYLEY, DAVID H., "The Forces of Order in Japan and in the United States," in Gregg Lee Carter, ed., *Empirical Approaches to Sociology.* New York: Macmillan, 1994, pp. 101–119.

BENEDICT, RUTH, *The Chrysanthemum and the Sword.* Boston: Houghton Mifflin, 1946.

BORNOFF, NICHOLAS, *Pink Samurai: Love, Marriage and Sex in Contemporary Japan.* New York: Simon & Schuster Pocket Books, 1991.

BROOK, JAMES, "Jobs Lure Japanese-Brazilians to Old World," *The New York Times,* Aug. 13, 1992, p. A5.

BURUMA, IAN, *The Wages of Guilt: Memories of War in Germany and Japan.* New York: Farrar, Straus & Giroux, 1994.

CHAPMAN, WILLIAM, *Inventing Japan: The Making of a Postwar Civilization.* Englewood Cliffs, NJ: Prentice-Hall, 1991.

CHRISTOPHER, ROBERT C., *The Japanese Mind: The Goliath Explained.* New York: Simon & Schuster, 1983.

CONDON, JANE, *A Half Step Behind: Japanese Women of the Eighties.* New York: Dodd, Mead, 1985.

DOI, TAKEO, *The Anatomy of Dependence.* Tokyo: Kodansha, 1977.

DUKE, BENJAMIN, *The Japanese School.* New York: Praeger, 1986.

EARHART, H. BYRON, *Religions of Japan.* San Francisco: Harper & Row, 1984.

FEILER, BRUCE S., *Learning to Bow: An American Teacher in a Japanese School.* New York: Ticknor & Fields, 1991.

FUCINI, JOSEPH J., and SUZY FUCINI, *Working for the Japanese: Inside Mazda's American Auto Plant.* New York: Macmillan, Free Press, 1990.

FUKUTAKE, TADASHI, *Japanese Society Today,* 2d ed. Tokyo: University of Tokyo Press, 1981.

GOFFMAN, ERVING, *The Presentation of Self in Everyday Life.* New York: Doubleday, 1959.

HAGITANI, JUN, "New Politics: Factions Obsolete," *Asahi Evening News,* July 18, 1998.

HENDRY, JOY, *Marriage in a Changing Japan: Community and Society.* New York: St. Martin's Press, 1981.

INOUE, SHOICHI, "Religions Old and New," in Atsushi Ueda, ed., *The Electric Geisha: Exploring Japan's Popular Culture.* Tokyo: Kodansha International, 1994, pp. 220–228.

ISHIDA, HIROSHI, *Social Mobility in Contemporary Japan.* Stanford, CA: Stanford University Press, 1993.

ISHIDA, TAKESHI, *Japanese Political Culture: Change and Continuity.* New Brunswick, NJ: Transaction Books, 1983.

IWAO, SUMIKO, *The Japanese Woman: Traditional Image and Changing Reality.* New York: Free Press, 1993.

JOLIVET, MURIEL, *Japan: The Childless Society? The Crisis of Motherhood.* London and New York: Routledge, 1997.

KATO, RYOKO, "Japanese Women: Subordination or Domination," in James Curtis and Lorne Tepperman, eds., *Haves and Have-Nots: An International Reader on Social Inequality.* Englewood Cliffs, NJ: Prentice-Hall, 1994.

KRISTOF, NICHOLAS D., "Japanese Say No to Crime: Tough Methods, at a Price," *The New York Times,* May 14, 1995, pp. 1, 8.

———, "A Neighborly Style of Police State," *The New York Times,* June 4, 1995, p. E5.

———, "Real Capitalism Breaks Japan's Old Rules," *The New York Times,* July 15, 1997, pp. A1, A8.

———, "Where Children Rule," *The New York Times Magazine,* Aug. 17, 1997, pp. 40–44.

———, "Shops Closing, Japan Still Asks, 'What Crisis'?" *The New York Times,* Apr. 21, 1998, pp. A1, A6.

———, "Japan Voters Send Message: No Change," *The New York Times,* July 5, 1998, p. A4.

———, "Jockeying Begins for Post in Japan," *The New York Times,* July 14, 1998, pp. A1, A8.

———, "Who Will Lead Japan," *The New York Times,* July 15, 1998, p. A10.

———, "A Man With a Plan? Japanese Prefer Premiers," *The New York Times,* July 20, 1998, p. A6.

KUWAYAMA, TAKAMI, "The Reference Other Orientation," in Nancy L. Rosenberger, ed., *Japanese Sense of Self.* Cambridge: Cambridge University Press, 1994, pp. 121–151.

LEBRA, TAKIE SUGIYAMA, *Japanese Women: Constraint and Fulfillment.* Honolulu: University of Hawaii Press, 1984.

———, ed., *Japanese Social Organization.* Honolulu: University of Hawaii Press, 1992.

LEESTMA, ROBERT, *Japanese Education Today.* U.S. Department of Education, Washington, DC: Government Printing Office, 1987.

LO, JEANNIE, *Office Ladies, Factory Women: Life and Work at a Japanese Company.* Armonk, NY: M. E. Sharpe, 1990.

NAKANE, CHIE, *Japanese Society.* Berkeley: University of California Press, 1970.

OGAWA, AKIO, "Public Works Opposed, But System Hard to Break," *Asahi Evening News,* July 19, 1998.

PHARR, SUSAN J., *Losing Face: Status Politics in Japan.* Berkeley: University of California Press, 1990.

POLLACK, ANDREW, "Suicides by Bullied Students Stir Japanese Furor," *The New York Times,* Dec. 18, 1994, p. 20.

REISCHAUER, EDWIN O., *The Japanese.* Cambridge, MA: Harvard University Press, 1977.

———, *The Japanese Today: Change and Continuity.* Cambridge, MA: Harvard University Press, 1988.

ROBERSON, JAMES E., "Becoming Shakaijin: Working-class Reproduction in Japan," *Ethnology,* vol. 34, no. 4 (Fall, 1995): pp. 293–314.

ROHLEN, THOMAS P., *Japan's High Schools.* Berkeley: University of California Press, 1983.

ROSENBERGER, NANCY R., ed., *Japanese Sense of Self.* Cambridge: Cambridge University Press, 1994.

RUDOLPH, ELLEN, "On Language," *The New York Times Magazine,* Sept. 1, 1992, p. 8.

SAFIRE, WILLIAM, "Ratcheting Up the Periscope," *The New York Times Magazine,* July 21, 1998, p. 16.

SANGER, DAVID E., "Best College Money Can Buy" (Can It Be Bought?)," *The New York Times,* June 24, 1991, p. 4.

SCHOOLER, CAMI, "History, Social Structure and Individualism: A Cross-cultural Perspective on Japan," *International Journal of Comparative Sociology,* vol. 39, no. 1 (Feb., 1998): pp. 32–52.

SESSER, STAN, "Hidden Death," *The New Yorker,* Nov. 14, 1994, pp. 62–89.

SMITH, ROBERT J., *Japanese Society: Tradition, Self and the Social Order.* Cambridge: Cambridge University Press, 1983.

STERNGOLD, JAMES, "Mob and Politics Intersect, Fueling Cynicism in Japan," *The New York Times,* Oct. 21, 1992, pp. A1, A6.

———, "Fear of Phrases," *The New York Times,* Dec. 18, 1994, pp. E1, E6.

SUGIMOTO, YOSHIO, *An Introduction to Japanese Society.* Cambridge: Cambridge University Press, 1997.

TANIKAWA, MIKI, "Japan's Young Couples Discover the Kiss," *The New York Times,* May 28, 1995, p. 39.

TASKER, PETER, *The Japanese: Portrait of a Nation.* New York: Penguin Books, New American Library, 1987.

TOBIN, JOSEPH, "Japanese Preschools and the Pedagogy of Selfhood," in Nancy R. Rosenberger, ed., *Japanese Sense of Self.* Cambridge: Cambridge University Press, 1994.

UEDA, ATSUSHI, "How Bureaucrats Manage Society," in Atsushi Ueda, ed., *The Electric Geisha: Exploring Japan's Popular Culture.* Tokyo: Kodansha International, 1994, pp. 127–138.

UNITED NATIONS, *1994 Demographic Yearbook,* United Nations, New York, 1996.

UNITED NATIONS, *1995 Demographic Yearbook,* United Nations, New York, 1997.

UNITED NATIONS, *Human Development Database,* United Nations, New York, 1998.

————, Statistical Division, Statistics and Indicators on the World's Women, http://www.un.org/Depts/unsd/gender.

VAN WOLFEREN, KAREL, *The Enigma of Japanese Power: People and Politics in a Stateless Nation.* New York: Knopf, 1989.

————, "Japan's Non-Revolution," *Foreign Affairs,* Vol. 72, No. 4, Sept–Oct. 1993, pp. 54–65.

WASWO, ANN, *Modern Japanese Society, 1868–1994.* Oxford: Oxford University Press, 1996.

WEISMAN, STEVEN R., "In Japan, Bias Is an Obstacle Even for the Ethnic Japanese," *The New York Times,* Nov. 13, 1991, pp. A1, A10.

WHITE, MERRY, *The Material Child: Coming of Age in Japan and America.* New York: Free Press, 1993.

WILDEMAN, JOHN, "Crime and Crime Control in Modern Japan," unpublished material.

WUDUNN, SHERYL, "The Japan Bank Alarm," *The New York Times,* Oct. 29, 1995, p. E14.

————, "Two Top Japanese Bank Inspectors Arrested and Accused in Bribery," *The New York Times,* Jan. 27, 1998, pp. D1, D7.

————, "A No Pan Shabu Shabu Scandal in the Ministry of Finance," *The New York Times,* Mar. 17, 1998.

————, "Like the Geisha, the Good-Time Bar Is Endangered," *The New York Times,* May 19, 1998, p. A4.

MEXICO

You can fly to Mexico from New York in five hours, from London in ten, or you can walk across a border bridge from Texas in five minutes. You will find yourself in a society created from two clashing cultures: the Native American culture of Mexico and the Spanish culture of the European conquerors.

LOCATION: Mexico is a North American country, just south of the American states of Texas, New Mexico, Arizona, and California. Mexico is bordered on the east by the Gulf of Mexico and on the west by the Pacific. To the south Mexico borders Guatemala and Belize.

AREA: One-fifth the size of the United States or Canada, Mexico (756,000 square miles or 2,128,600 square kilometers) is four times the size of Germany.

LAND: A rugged, mountainous country. Mexico City, the country's capital, is several thousand feet above sea level.

CLIMATE: Hot, humid, and tropical in the south; arid and desertlike in the north. Temperatures cool as one climbs higher. The year alternates between rainy and dry seasons.

POPULATION: 2000: 99 million people. 21.6 million people live in the capital. The population is relatively young. 36 percent of the people are under age 15.

INCOME: U.S. $3,554 GDP per person per year in 1996. 23 percent live in absolute poverty.

EDUCATION: 87 percent of adult women and 92 percent of adult men are literate.

RELIGION: 93 percent are Roman Catholic; 3 percent are Protestant.

MINORITIES: 7 million people (8 percent of the population) belong to indigenous Indian groups, including the Nahua, the Zapotec, the Maya, the Totonac, the Mixtec, and many smaller populations.

CHAPTER 2

_____

Mexico: Nation of Networks

INTRODUCTION

Visitors to Teotihuacán, the ancient Indo-American ruins 25 miles northeast of Mexico City, come upon richly carved walls, crammed with intricate patterns, picked out in sharp relief by the bright sunlight of the mountains. These stone carvings might well symbolize Mexico itself, a diverse society marked by strong social and cultural contrasts. There are really many Mexicos: urban and rural, rich and poor, European and Indo-American.

Mexico City is a twenty-first century megacity (Kandell, p. 8): It points the way to the problems of urbanization increasingly visible all over the world. Twenty million people live crowded into Mexico City's high, mountain-ringed valley: in apartment towers, leafy middle-class suburbs, and squatter shantytowns. They jam its highways, buses, subways, and markets, their cars spewing out a toxic haze of air pollution, their accumulating sewage and garbage a constant hazard. But in Mexico's rural hinterlands, village life proceeds at a very different pace. Though most villages now have electricity and roads, the modern world is distant. People grow the food they eat, often without machinery, and build their own houses; some wear traditional Indian dress. In the most remote villages, paths, not streets, link the houses; there are seldom any newspapers, and perhaps not even a telephone.

Even in Mexico City, the rich and the poor live so differently they might inhabit different societies. A rich teenager may drive an imported car, live in his family's air-conditioned house, wear European designer clothes, and dance at a club built to look as much as possible like one in New York or Los Angeles. The family's maid will probably travel four hours a day on packed buses and trains, returning at night to a one-room shanty with a bare light bulb (wired illegally to a city streetlight), a single mattress, and no refrigerator or running water.

Walk around Mexico City and you will see simultaneously the contrasting layers of Mexican history. At the famous Plaza of the Three Cultures, ancient Indian, colonial Spanish, and modern western cultures stand side by side. In this place where the Aztecs actually fought and lost their last battle against the Spanish, archeological excavation has uncovered ancient Aztec pyramids and carvings. Next to the ancient ruins you will see the sixteenth-century colonial church of Santiago Tlatelolco, built from the very stones of the defeated Aztec city. The plaza is completed by the modern architecture of the Ministry of Foreign Affairs building (Nolen, p. xix; Kandell, p. 524).

61

For Mexicans, the Plaza of the Three Cultures represents their uneasy heritage of cultural diversity. The sixteenth-century Spanish conquistadors tried to obliterate Indian culture, but did not succeed. Through Mexico's tempestuous history, Indian and Spanish cultures became interwoven. Now a new element has been added to Mexico's diversity: the culture of the modern "global village," with its glass office towers, TV soap operas, and ubiquitous fast food.

Understanding Mexico: The Conflict Perspective

Just as Japanese society appears constructed to illustrate the **structural-functionalist perspective** in sociology, so Mexican society seems to call for analysis with the **conflict perspective.** When we examine Mexico we see all sorts of divisions and disagreements within the society. Diverse groups struggle for control of scarce resources and justify their claims with conflicting worldviews. Those who hold power use it to dominate others and to protect their own privileges. Disagreement about values is common. A conflict theorist, looking at Mexico's long history, would contend that conflict and value **dissensus** (disagreement, the opposite of consensus) are the normal condition of society, and any period of order is really a period of domination by one or another ruling group.

MEXICAN HISTORY

In order to better understand both the conflict perspective and Mexican society, you must first know something about Mexico's dramatic history. Mexicans themselves believe that their history holds the key to their character, and they relish its romance and extravagance. In every period in Mexican history, different groups struggled to control society so as to benefit themselves. Mexico's history is easy to understand, because it is divided by dramatic events into three clearly marked periods: the pre-Columbian, the colonial, and the modern.

The Pre-Columbian Period (c. 300 B.C.–A.D. 1519)

The earliest period of Mexican history was the longest: this was the pre-Columbian period (c. 300 B.C.–A.D. 1519) when the great Maya and Aztec and other Indo-American empires ruled Central America. By the first century B.C., there were great civilizations in Mexico, the equal of anything in Europe. The Indo-Americans built large cities, developed sophisticated systems of writing and mathematics, kept astronomy records, and built monumental works of architecture. These empires also fought frequent wars to subjugate neighboring peoples and make them pay **tribute** (goods which conquered people had to pay to their conquerors) and also to take captives who were made into slaves or sacrificed to the gods (Rudolph, pp. 5–8; Ruiz, pp. 18–20).

The Aztecs

The last Indo-American empire was that of the Aztecs, who rose to power in the fourteenth century. Dedicated to conquest, the Aztecs glorified fighting and bravery. Nobles ruled and merchants enjoyed a relatively high status, but commoners, conquered people, and slaves labored hard to build the gleaming pyramids, roads, and aqueducts of their capital, Tenochtitlán (site of today's Mexico City). The Aztecs exacted more and more tribute from subject peoples to make their gorgeous feathered cloaks and jewelry, and the resentment and hatred of the conquered peoples grew. The Aztecs' religion reflected their fascination with conquest and destruction. The sun and earth, they believed, were periodically destroyed and renewed. There had been four previous "suns" and their own epoch was the time of the "fifth sun," soon to be destroyed in its turn (Ruiz, p. 24; Rudolph, p. 14; Kandell, pp. 49–54).

The Conquest

The pre-Columbian period in Mexico ended in a new episode of struggle and domination in 1519, the year of the Spanish Conquest. Aztec religion predicted the next periodic destruction of the world in the year 1519. Legend held that at that time the white-skinned Quetzalcoátl (god of the earlier Toltec people) would return from the sea and take back his empire from the Aztecs and their god, Huitzilopochtli. The prophecy proved uncannily accurate, since in 1519 Aztec society was indeed destroyed—but at the hands of the Spanish *conquistadors,* led by Hernán Cortés.

The Spaniards. At the time of the Conquest, Spanish society had much in common with Aztec society: Both were shaped by war and religion. The most important force in Spain was the *Reconquista,* the politico-military "crusade" to recapture all of Spain from the Muslims or "Moors" who had ruled it for seven centuries. Under the leadership of Ferdinand and Isabella, Granada, the last bastion of the Moors, was reconquered in 1492. The crusader mentality glorified war and looked down upon agriculture and manufacture, which it associated with the Moors, and also looked down on finance, associated with the despised Jews (expelled from Spain in 1492). Spanish warriors found it proper to live off the labor of those they conquered, the crown rewarding them with land grants and "infidel" serfs.

Cortés and Moctezuma. Hernán Cortés was the very model of a conquistador, thirsting for adventure, greedy for gold, aggressive, brave, and ruthless. He was a brilliant strategist, able to switch gears instantly and turn misfortune to advantage. In 1519, at the age of 33, Cortés assembled 11 ships, 500 soldiers, 100 sailors, 200 Cuban Indians, weapons, and 16 horses and sailed from Cuba for the Yucatán (the southeastern coast of Mexico).

Once arrived in Mexico, Cortés quickly learned of the ruling power, the Aztecs and their current king Moctezuma in their capital, Technochtitlán. Chosen as king in 1503, Moctezuma was an unstable monarch, at times arrogant, but often paralyzed by depression and terror at the prophesied next destruction. The coincidence of Cortés' arrival from the sea in 1519 was extraordinary, and apparently unbalanced Moctezuma completely. Cortés' invading force was tiny, compared to the military might of the Aztecs. Three special weaknesses made the Conquest possible. First was the power of ideas: Belief in the coming end of their world undercut Aztec resistance. Second, the Aztecs had made many, many enemies among neighboring peoples, who gladly joined Cortés, swelling his army from 500 to 10,000. It was not really Cortés who conquered the Aztecs, but the Aztecs' Indian enemies. Finally, if any European force really mattered, it was an army of European germs: smallpox—absent in the Americas—which arrived with the Spanish and ravaged Tenochtitlán.

The Colonial Period (1519–1810)

The Conquest ushered in 300 years of colonial rule in Mexico, now christened New Spain. Mexico's native peoples were inclined at first to see the Spanish as just the next in a long series of conquerors, but in many ways the Spanish empire was harsher and more destructive than any previous Indo-American rule.

The Spaniards wanted wealth from Mexico, gold or silver, ideally, but also sugar, indigo (a valuable dye), cattle, or wheat for export. They were not much interested in settling Mexico. The Spaniards in Mexico wanted to become rich and they wanted to do so by using Indian labor to extract the wealth of the land. The Spanish monarchy had similar ambitions: The king and queen hoped to tax Mexico's exports. The colonizers in Mexico had another goal too: They wanted to save souls and to convert the Indians to Catholicism and stamp out the worship of pagan gods.

A Genocidal Beginning

Spanish rule turned out to be much more disastrous for the native Mexicans than Cortés' Indian allies could ever have imagined. First of all, Spanish rule began with a tragedy—a "biological catastrophe"—a terrible plague of Old World diseases to which the Indo-Americans had no immunities. Measles and influenza, minor diseases in Europe, became killers in Mexico (as everywhere in the New World). Smallpox became epidemic. Demographers estimate a population of 25 million in central Mexico at the time of the Conquest; by 1650, only 1 million native Mexicans survived there (Kandell, p. 149; Wolf, p. 195). Disease wiped out families, villages, ruling classes, and whole cultures.

The Hacienda System

Without an abundant Indian labor force, Spanish colonizers' plans for wealth were frustrated. It took them until the seventeenth century to work out a sustainable system for colonizing Mexico: the *hacienda system*. The *hacienda* was an estate or plantation on which Indians were forced into a kind of slavery. Spanish colonizers helped themselves to the best land, and then offered to employ the now-landless Indians. They tricked the Indians into debt by giving them advances on their wages until they owed so much money they could never finish working off the debt. *Haciendas* were land-hungry: the more Indian land they could take, the more Indians they could force into dependence. They also imported some black slaves (Wolf, pp. 203–208; Ruiz, pp. 81, 102–103; Rudolph, p. 23).

The society the Spanish created in Mexico was highly race-conscious and racially stratified. Every person had an official racial classification: white, followed by *casta* (mixed white and Indian), with Indian and black at the bottom. People had different rights based on their race.

The Modern Period (1810–Present)

The modern period in Mexico began with the War of Independence, which freed Mexico from Spanish rule. Much of the modern period has been characterized by a high level of conflict between different groups. From 1810 until the early twentieth century, Mexico was in an almost constant state of upheaval as the different strata of Mexican society fought for justice, recognition, equality, or power. Every group had grievances: The wealthy colonists wanted more political independence, the middle class wanted greater economic opportunities, and the poor and the Indians wanted land, food, jobs, and an end to slavery and to tribute payments.

After declaring independence from Spain in 1824, rural guerrilla bands, royalists, and republicans fell to fighting each other. The next 50 years were marked by government instability and corruption and a succession of coups by generals. There were 42 different governments between 1821 and 1855 (Kandell, p. 319). During this period of disintegration, Mexico lost Texas to the United States, lost the Mexican-American War, and suffered a French invasion and occupation. Finally, a new middle class emerged as the ruling elite. They looked toward Europe and sought to remake Mexico according to the ideals of the French and American Revolutions, as a capitalist republic. Mexico abolished slavery, established constitutional government on the American model, and guaranteed freedom of religion, but these paper reforms had little practical effect.

Order and Revolution

Order was finally imposed by a brilliant politician, Porfirio Díaz, whose eight terms of office as president, between 1876 and 1911 are known as the Porfiriate. Díaz advocated "order and progress" and threw all his tremendous power into modernizing the economy, securing international recognition, and attracting foreign investment. He built railroads and ports, extended electric and telephone service, modernized Mexico City, strengthened mining and agriculture, began oil exploration, and balanced the national budget. Díaz was ruthless in his exercise of power. He executed rival generals, massacred rebellious Indians, held fraudulent elections, and censored the press. The wealthy enjoyed a golden age during the Porfiriate, but the misery of the poor intensified, paving the way for Mexico's next great upheaval.

Mexico's revolution, begun in 1910, was one of the great early twentieth-century revolutions, like the Russian Revolution. The Mexican Revolution spoke for workers and peasants whose living and working conditions had steadily worsened in the late nineteenth century. The revolution rejected Europe as a model, asserted an Indian identity for Mexico, and committed the government to providing security for peasants and workers by redistributing land and income.

Middle-class liberals who wanted democracy started the revolution, but it blazed into violent struggle as it attracted those who had suffered most under the Porfiriate. Peasants and Indians, led by the famous Emiliano Zapata and by Pancho Villa, waged guerrilla struggles to take back land from the *haciendas*. Fighting continued for almost two decades, with every region convulsed by conflict between rival armies. A radical constitution promulgated in 1917 stipulated restoration of all Indian lands and national ownership of all natural resources, guaranteed free public education, an eight-hour workday, equal pay for equal work, and the right to organize and strike. Amid the prevailing disorder, most of these provisions were not put into practice for years, if ever (Fuentes, *The Buried Mirror,* pp. 299–306).

Revolutionary Change

It was not until the 1930s, and the presidency of Lázaro Cárdenas that the government finally made good on its promises to retrieve for the Indians lands stolen by the *haciendas.* Cárdenas redistributed 46 million acres of land. Two-thirds of Mexican farmers received land, mostly through the creation of *ejidos*—landholdings given to villages to be held in common and assigned by the village for individual use—on the traditional Indian model. (Later, in the 1950s and 1960s, the government redistributed more land through *ejidos.*) Cárdenas also nationalized the whole oil industry (mostly foreign-owned), another enormously popular action.

Finally, poor rural Mexicans saw some improvements in their lives. Schools, roads, electricity, and hospitals began to reach the countryside. The number of people dependent on *haciendas* decreased. Now it became possible for the government to move from revolutionary change to the consolidation of power. Those who had benefited from reform were readily rallied as supporters of the government: *Ejidos,* trade unions, and government workers were all organized into subsidiary units of the Institutional Revolutionary Party, the PRI. The party has dominated Mexican politics down to the present, making Mexican politics orderly, channeling benefits to organized peasants and workers, but also substituting one-party rule for democracy.

The Age of NAFTA

In the last decades of the twentieth century, Mexico has once again returned to the outlook of the middle-class modernizers like Porfirio Díaz. In the 1990s, Presidents Carlos Salinas de Gortari and Ernesto Zedillo opened Mexico to free trade and foreign investment, assuring Mexicans that the best way to achieve a better life was to become part of the global capitalist "free-market" economy. President Salinas signed the North American Free Trade Agreement (NAFTA), making Mexico, the United States, and Canada free-trade partners. The Mexican government also committed itself to the policies of the International Monetary Fund, accepting the Fund's "structural adjustment program," which required higher interest rates, less government spending, and higher prices, as the condition of international loans. But joining the world economy proved to have its dangers as well as its rewards. Mexico's economic growth was interrupted by two world financial crises, the "peso crisis" of 1995, when international investors fled Mexico, and the world financial crisis of 1998, touched off by financial failures in Asia and Russia. By the late 90s, the Mexican economy was a "free market" success story: Economic production was growing at an impressive rate. But not all Mexicans were benefitting. Prices and interest rates rose, poverty and unemployment increased, while at the same time the government cut spending on social welfare programs. When world oil prices plummeted in the late 90s, that made things even harder for Mexico, because oil revenues fund a big part of the government's budget.

Today Mexicans see their country beset by political as well as economic problems, as the government's ability to maintain law and order wavers. In poverty-stricken Chiapas state in southern Mexico, the Zapatista Liberation Army, a revolutionary movement, demands land for peasants, justice, and political democracy. In Mexico City and the border states, crime rates have skyrocketed, as cross-border drug trafficking thrives. Police corruption both feeds the crime wave and makes it very difficult for the government to satisfy voters' demands that the government impose order. The PRI's virtual domination of Mexico's government is challenged by two active opposition parties—the leftist Party of the Democratic Revolution (PRD) and the pro-business National Action Party (PAN). Both opposition parties have elected state governors, city mayors, and representatives to the national legislature. While Mexicans welcome a more competitive, democratic party system, they also fear increasing disorder and unpredictability in Mexican life.

MEXICAN CULTURE

Every era of Mexican history has left its own ambiguous cultural legacy. Spanish colonialism remade Mexico, but it didn't make it into a "New Spain." Nor did the revolution make Mexico an egalitarian democracy. A distinctive society developed, in which Indo-American, Spanish, western European, American, socialist, and Catholic influences were adapted and combined.

Mexicans debate the effects of Spanish colonialism on their society. In one view, Spanish and Indo-American cultures blended in Mexico. The Spanish colonizers tried their best to destroy Aztec civilization—its religion, cities, government, army, and system of social stratification—and to substitute their own church, Spanish law, and the *hacienda* system. They succeeded in eliminating Aztec institutions, but were less successful in destroying Indo-American culture. Instead, similarities between the two cultures facilitated blending: Both cultures were warlike, hierarchical, and religious. Their family structures and norms were similar. Celia Falicov argues that "today the Spanish and Indian heritages are so fused that it is difficult to separate them" (Falicov, p. 135).

Some analysts (like Mexican writer Octavio Paz) have seen the colonial legacy as much more destructive. Paz argued that the experience of conquest and colonial domination caused lasting damage to the Mexican psyche. Mexicans, he contended, saw their origins in a historical act of violation and wished to deny both their Spanish and their Indian origins. Some contemporary socialists argue that today Mexico continues to be enmeshed in economic colonialism, distorting its development to serve the needs of multinational corporations, while unemployment, poverty, and undernourishment increase. In this view, relations of economic dependency are deeply embedded in Mexican society, shaping its political system as well as its economy (Paz, pp. 86–87; Barkin, pp. 11–22, 93–95).

Other Mexicans identify with their country's revolutionary tradition. Mexicans still see the revolutionary murals of Diego Rivera, and they faithfully remember

President Lázaro Cárdenas. "Subcommandante Marcos," leader of the Zapatista rebels, aligns himself with Mexico's historic revolutionaries. All these figures have stressed Mexico's heritage of resistance, rather than dependence—resistance to Spanish colonialism, to the *hacienda* system, to undemocratic government. The legacies of cultural blending, of colonial domination, and of resistance can all be seen in Mexico's religious heritage.

Catholicism in Mexican Culture

The most enduring legacy of the Conquest was Catholicism. Mexico became, and remains, a Catholic country. Colonial churches and images of Catholic saints are seen everywhere. Catholicism is so much a part of Mexico that it is as multisided and contradictory as Mexican culture itself.

Catholicism arrived with the Conquest. Spanish friars immediately set about converting the conquered Indians. In Mexico City, one friar, Pedro de Gante, baptized Indians at the rate of 14,000 per day. Many writers have wondered why the work of conversion was so successful. In some measure, force was responsible: The Catholic Church drove out the old priests, destroyed the idols and temples, ended human sacrifice, and burned sacred books. Indians who refused to accept the new religion were sometimes tortured or whipped. But the Catholic clergy also offered genuine concern and care for the Indians and sometimes defended them against abusive colonial practices. Probably most important, the Church declared Indians to have immortal souls, to be human. In a dehumanizing colonialism, the Church offered Indians hope for justice.

In some ways too, Catholicism offered the Indians a way to continue their religious traditions after their own gods had failed. Colonial Mexico, like Aztec Mexico, was a society permeated by religious faith and ritual. There were similarities between Catholicism and Indo-American religions, so it was not difficult to join them. The Indians looked on the Catholic saints as an array of gods, similar to their own. They were familiar with rituals of baptism, confession, and communion, enacted in their own religion too. The cross was even familiar to the Maya, though their cross emerged from a base of carved snakes and represented the god of fertility.

In fact, the Indians adapted Catholicism to meet their own needs for religious grace and human respect. Nowhere is this clearer than in the legend of the Virgin of Guadalupe, still today the patron saint of Mexicans. The story tells that in 1531, the Virgin Mary appeared before a humble Indian man at Tepeyac, just north of Mexico City, at the site of a temple to Tonantzin, the Aztec mother of gods. Miraculously her image appeared on his cloak, and lo! she was a dark-skinned Mary. Worship of the Virgin of Guadalupe spread rapidly in Mexico, and after initial opposition the friars accepted her, implicitly conceding the full humanity of the Indians (Wolf, pp. 165–175; Ruiz, pp. 66–70).

Catholicism in Mexico (as elsewhere in Latin America) absorbed and became joined to deep Indo-American religious feeling. As Carlos Fuentes, the famous Mexican novelist, describes it, there is "a deep sense of the sacred and recognition that the world is holy." Shrines and altars, incense and flowers, religious ceremonies and processions make Catholicism in Mexico "a sensuous, tactile religion" (Fuentes, Mar. 30, 1992, p. 410).

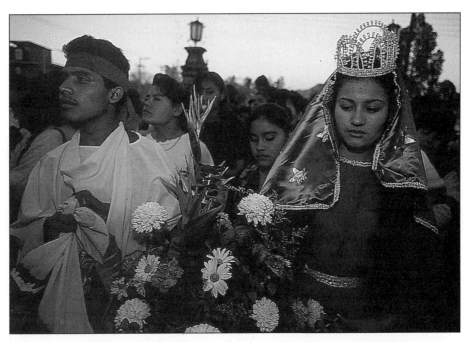

Dressed as the Virgin of Guadalupe, in her characteristic silver-starred cape and crown, a young woman walks at the front of a procession to celebrate the feast day of the Virgin, patron saint of this northern Mexican town.

Popular Religion

Everywhere that it has gone in the world, the Catholic Church has adapted to local practices of folk religion, and Mexico is no exception. Mexican Catholicism has absorbed local *fiestas* (festivals) and local Indo-American saints. All over Mexico, villages celebrate the saint's days of their patron saints with brass bands and processions, bright costumes, special masses, colorful decorations of the church and town, fireworks, bullfights, sports contests, food, drink, and dancing, and street sales of fruits, candy, and toys. Some *fiestas,* like Holy Week, Christmas, and the Festival of Our Lady of Guadalupe are national holidays.

El Día de Los Muertos. Probably the most famous of Mexico's *fiestas* is El Día de Los Muertos (The Day of the Dead). By an odd coincidence, both the Spanish and the Aztecs commemorated the dead on November 2, and this holiday fuses the two celebrations (as well as the Christian All Saints Day, November 1).

Weeks before November 2, candy vendors begin selling skulls of white sugar, decorated with sequins, ribbons, and foil, with first names on their foreheads. People buy skulls with the names of their dead relatives and set them on homemade altars, along with statues of saints, ears of corn, fruit, candy, foods the dead especially liked, soda, liquor and cigarettes, incense and candles. People give each other gifts of cookies shaped like skeletons, or chocolate skulls, or sugar coffins (Braganti and Devine, p. 156; Nolen pp. 48–49).

Before midnight on November 1, Mexicans spread a path of flower petals from their doors to the altar, and settle down to await a visit from the dead. The next day, they jam the roads to the cemeteries, to bring flowers and candles and perhaps a toy for a dead child, and to clean up grave sites. There is a party atmosphere, as people picnic and chat with graveside neighbors. Afterward, at home, they feast on the food which the dead have enjoyed in spirit (Reavis, pp. 194–198).

The Saints. Every village in Mexico adopts a patron saint who watches over villagers. If you visit a village church, you will see a statue or doll representing the saint at a special altar. People pray to their patron saint and ask for miracles, often cures for illness, or good harvests. The saint of San Juan Jaltepac, for example, is a 3-foot-tall plaster statue of the Virgin of Candelaria. In Zapopan, the tiny doll-like Our Lady of Zapopan, covered in jewels, is said to protect against floods (Oster, p. 200; Reavis, pp. 200–203). People often devote part of the main room of their house, or a special separate room to a home altar where they light candles, hang religious pictures, and spend time in prayer.

> ### Doña Ana's Story: The Believer
> *Doña Ana is a woman in her fifties who works as a maid for a middle-class family. Every night she takes the subway and two buses and returns to her family in Colonia Caultepac at the northern edge of Mexico City, where she lives with her husband, daughter, and granddaughter. When her granddaughter fell ill with hepatitis, the doctors at the clinic said they weren't sure they could save her. Doña Ana prayed to the Virgin of Candelaria. A special room in her house contains an altar: a shelf covered with a lace tablecloth, decorated with marigolds and a picture of the saint. Doña Ana burned candles to the Virgin and prayed every night. When her granddaughter recovered, Doña Ana cried with joy. She felt bad that she couldn't go to the Virgin's own church in San Juan Jaltepac to thank the saint. So Doña Ana saved her money and the next year, on the Virgin's own saint's day, she made the long trip to her village, bringing the saint flowers and candles. Doña Ana's foolish son José laughed at her, but she felt she did the right thing and that there could be no better use for her precious savings.*

Religion and Politics

Catholicism has long played an active, but contradictory role in Mexican politics. In the beginning, the Church worked hand in hand with the conquistadores, but even then, some clerics, like Fray Bartolomé de las Casas criticized the treatment of the Indians and spoke movingly on their behalf. Many leaders of the fight for independence were clerics like Miguel Hidalgo, but the Church, itself a huge and wealthy landowner, was seen as part of Spanish colonialism by the independence fighters. The Revolution too was anti-Church, and the Constitution of 1917 made the Catholic Church subject to civil authority and forbade clerics from teaching in primary schools or even wearing their religious robes in public.

Today, the relationship between Catholicism and politics is also contradictory. In the 1960s and 1970s many Mexican clergy were attracted to **liberation theology.** Even today, religious leaders like Bishop Samuel Ruiz, head of the Roman Catholic diocese in Chiapas, argue that the Church must take an active role in seeking justice and a better life for the poor. But other priests and members of the

Church hierarchy appointed by Pope John Paul II are much more conservative. The opposition party PAN, which has a considerable following in northern Mexico, is pro-free market and antigovernment and has a big following among conservative Catholics (Preston, May 28, 1997, p. A4; June 16, 1998, p. A4).

A Culture of Opposites

Mexicans tend to see the world divided into two opposite realms: the "City of God"—the world of the sacred, of religion, home, and loyal friends—and it's opposite, the "City of Man"—the public world of power struggle, appearances, and dishonesty. It could certainly be argued that Mexicans' colonial experience contributed to their dualistic view of the world. In colonial times, the public world was indeed a hostile, exploitative place for Indo-Americans. Developing a strong, protective family life was a healthy response.

Family and home represent loyalty, trust, and warmth to Mexicans. The family is "a fortress against the misery of the outside world" (Goodwin, pp. 3, 6). It is "the hearth, the sustaining warmth" (Fuentes, Mar. 30, 1992, p. 410). Today, Mexicans who can afford it build high, solid walls around their homes, sometimes topped with broken glass. The mother is seen as the caring heart of the family, taking pleasure in serving her children and treasuring the loyalty they return. While respect for the father may keep him a somewhat remote figure, siblings are often very close, even in adulthood. For men, a small group of old friends may form another inner world of trust in which they freely let down their defenses and express their feelings, especially in the forgiving setting of a drinking party. In the popular mystery novels of Paco Taibo, for example, the hero is always rescued in a crisis by his drinking buddies or his sister and brother.

Negotiating the Public Realm

In contrast to the inner world of family and friends, the outer world is perceived as a dangerous, treacherous, corrupt place. Business, government, the police, unions, schools, towns, and neighbors are not to be trusted. Social relations in the public world require watchfulness. Outside the family, Mexicans hide their feelings and fears behind "masks of formality" (Riding, p. 10). Like actors, they practice what symbolic interactionist Erving Goffman called **role distance,** self-consciously playing a role fit for a situation, but not identifying with the role. Formal language, empty phrases, false promises, and even lies allow Mexicans to meet role expectations without risking their real selves. Goffman would say that for Mexicans the world outside the family is a **front region** where people play their roles carefully and engage in **impression management** to try to control how others see them, while at home in the **back region** they relax their guard.

Respect and Dignity

In the public world Mexicans try to attain and keep respect and dignity. *Respeto* in Spanish has a different meaning than does the corresponding word "respect" in English. In English, when one person "respects" another, it has a connotation of individuals acknowledging their essential equality. In Mexico, *respeto* is more like deference: it means that one person acknowledges the high status of another. Mexicans agree that people ought to be respected by others of lower status, by younger people and children, and that men ought to be respected by women.

Respect allows people to preserve their *dignidad.* Mexicans attach greater importance to honesty and the preservation of their dignity than they do to individual achievement. People will proudly depict themselves and their families as "poor but honest" (Falicov, p. 138).

Norms of Public Formality

Interaction in the dangerous outer world is smoothed by norms of public conduct which help people show respect to one another and avoid unwanted provocation. Alan Riding points out that even in the dreadful Mexico City traffic jams, drivers are usually polite and rarely honk their horns. They may get angry and want to shout at others, but they are restrained by their distrust of potentially hostile strangers (Riding, p. 10). Mexicans also make heavy use of honorific titles to show respect. New acquaintances met at a party are addressed as *señor, señora,* and *señorita.* In business, people address managers with titles like director, doctor, *ingeniero* (engineer), or *licienciado* (someone who has a higher education degree).

Many Mexican folkways involve showing respect to others and allowing them to protect their dignity. Men reassure each other with rituals of physical contact. The *abrazo,* an embrace demonstrating friendship, always follows the same pattern: a handshake, a hug, two backslaps, another handshake, and a shoulder slap. Recoiling from the *abrazo* would be highly insulting, as would failing to say a formal goodbye when departing, or evidencing dislike for the food someone has served you. Showing respect is important in little gestures too. It is insulting to place money on the counter, rather than in the cashier's hand, and you would never toss a key to someone. If you bribe a policeman, or tip a maid, you tuck the money into their pocket or apron, so they needn't humble themselves by acknowledging it (Riding, p. 10; Braganti and Devine, pp. 139–155).

In the formal public world, appearances matter a great deal. Men try to impress each other with their importance. Being late to an appointment makes you appear a busy man; buying drinks a prosperous one. Poor neighborhoods bristle with TV antennas, though there may be no TVs inside the houses (Goodwin, p. 4).

Gender Dualities

One of the most famous pairs of opposites in Mexican culture is the pair of strongly differentiated **role ideals** for men and women: the *macho* (more or less, "the real man") and the mother. These gender dualities are traditional in Mexican culture and Mexicans are fond of depicting these roles in film and fiction and social commentary. Whether people actually play these roles, or believe they should play them, is another story. We must discuss Mexican gender roles carefully so as not to mistake cultural stereotypes for reality.

In Mexican culture, women and men are often depicted as deeply and tragically different from each other. Women, as mothers, belong to the City of God, set apart in the protected and protecting home. Motherhood is a sacred value in Mexico, and through motherhood, women become spiritual creatures, submissive, long-suffering, and patient, offering unconditional love and care to their families. The treasured national symbol of the mother is the Virgin of Guadalupe, the miraculous Mexican Virgin Mary, the virtuous, humble mother who looks after her suffering Mexican children. Men, in contrast, are depicted as belonging to the City of Man. They live in the dangerous public world where they must guard their honor, protect their families, and battle for respect. Every man's life is an adventure story, a quest for recognition in a corrupt society. The *macho* is courageous and capable of violence and it is understood that he is sexually active.

Mexico's famous essayist Octavio Paz described these gender dualities so forcefully in his 1950 book, *The Labyrinth of Solitude,* that his work helped to confirm the ideals, even though he wrote about them critically. "The ideal of manliness," Paz wrote, "is never to 'crack,' never to back down. Those who 'open themselves up' are cowards." And, "Manliness is judged according to one's invulnerability to enemy arms or the impacts of the outside world." Paz also wrote about both "the myth of the long-suffering Mexican woman," and "the image of the *mala mujer*—the 'bad woman.'" "She is not passive like the 'self-denying mother,' the 'waiting sweetheart,'. . . the *mala* is hard and impious and independent like the *macho*" (Paz, pp. 29–31, 38–39).

Changing Roles?

At the beginning of the twenty-first century, do these stereotypes still have power in Mexican culture? Do people accept these role ideals and try to play them in their own lives? Did they ever? Mexico's gender dualities are contested terrain: Everyone knows them, but not everyone accepts them, and not everyone who accepts them actually plays them in real life. Feminists today remind us that Mexican women have long been neither martyrs nor whores. They fought alongside men in the revolution, worked in factories, and participated in Mexican public life. Though they did not gain the right to vote in national elections until 1953, women have since become deputies and senators, occupied seats on the Supreme Court, and held high positions in the Institutional Revolutionary Party, the ruling party, known as the PRI. In 1982, Rosario Ibarra de Piedra was the first woman to run for President of Mexico and another woman, Cecilia Soto, ran in 1994. In the 90s dozens of women ran for state and federal office, though few were elected. Less than 10 percent of the members of the legislature are women. Perhaps more significantly, women have played important political roles as neighborhood and union organizers. (Ruiz, pp. 425, 449; DePalma, Aug. 20, 1994, p. 3; Crossette, p. A14).

More and more Mexican women today are working outside their homes, and more are heading their own households, because of separation, divorce, or migration. It is clear that Mexican men are playing new roles too. In his 1996 book, *The Meaning of Macho: Being a Man in Mexico City,* Matthew C. Guttman found Mexican men playing more companionate roles in their marriages, spending time at home with their wives and even discussing childcare. He could find no case among ordinary working Mexicans of the legendary philandering *macho,* supporting a mistress on the side. Robert Fox and Pedro Solis Camacho found Mexican men as involved in childcare as their American counterparts (Fox and Camacho, pp. 489–495).

Dora and Inés Discuss Men

Dora rushed eagerly up to her cousin Inés at the birthday party. Six years older, Inés had always been the older sister Dora never had, loving and wise, better than a best friend. "He's just wonderful!" Dora exclaimed; "so handsome and strong and silent. I want to marry him. He'll just fold me in his arms and take care of me all my life." "Sure, when he bothers to come home, and he's not drunk, and he doesn't beat you up," retorted Inés. "No, he's not like that," protested Dora. "He only drinks when he's out with his friends, and he would never hit a woman. He's so brave; I believe he really can defend his wife and family. Oh, Roberto," she sighed.

"Stick up for yourself," replied Inés. "I certainly don't want a man like that. I want a man who can talk to me; who'll stay home and be part of the family and be part of his childrens' lives. I want a man who will help me out at home so I can work and have a life of my own." "I don't want a life of my own," Dora sniffed. "I just want to be a wife and mother and stay home and take care of my family." "Just wait," Inés warned, "you'll see."

Individualism and Familism

Mexicans have been characterized both as **individualistic** and as **familistic** (that is, as putting the family before the individual). In the public world, Mexicans are individualistic: they see no reason to trust any institution that may demand their loyalty. They admire the matador or the boxer more than the team player in soccer or basketball. Mexicans personalize their history, telling it as a story about heroes and villains like Cortés, Zapata, Porfirio Díaz, and Lázaro Cárdenas. Successful politicians are never simply party functionaries; by force of personality they build a following of their own (Wolf, pp. 238–239; Riding, p. 5). Mexicans are clearly individualistic when compared with the Japanese or with Egyptians.

Mexican individualism makes sense as a legacy of colonialism. The Spanish conquerors purposely shattered Indo-American communities, evicting peasants from their land. During the colonial period a large population of displaced Mexicans roamed the country. They were landless Indians and people of mixed blood who had no official status and no legal rights. They traveled from place to place and job to job, living by their wits. Survival depended on adaptability, improvisation, and the ability to assume roles, and manipulate people, markets, and situations.

But Mexicans are also familistic: They are intensely loyal to their families and pride themselves on their willingness to put their families first. It is not uncommon for Mexicans to sacrifice opportunities for individual advance or enrichment in order to remain near their parents, or support their widowed sisters or other relatives. Mexicans see their status in society as an attribute of their families, not an individual quality.

In further contrast, those Mexicans who still live in traditional Indian communities are group-oriented, not individualistic or familistic. Anthropologist Eric Wolf makes a clear contrast: Where the modern Mexican is rootless and individualistic, he says, Indians are rooted in their community. They cling to their group and their customs. Urban Mexicans value personal power and the ability to manipulate others, but Indians value collective control of land and avoid the accumulation of individual power (Wolf, pp. 238–240).

Cynicism and Fatalism

Mexicans' distrust of the public world makes them cynical, and in a way, fatalistic. They don't trust the government to make rational decisions and they are skeptical of government promises to solve social problems through legislation and government action. Mexicans believe it would be foolish to make business decisions or career plans based on government forecasts and foolish to plan too far ahead. If you save now for retirement, the banks could fail, inflation could skyrocket; it makes more sense to spend your money now on a house that will last, or a business that will generate income.

Also, Mexicans are cynical about the idea of "progress," about the value of modern science and technology. When things go wrong—when corrupt governments disregard the Constitution; when modern technology pollutes the countryside—Mexicans are cynically unsurprised. If the bus fails to arrive, if the store is out of what you need, people shrug and cynically say "*ni modo*" (literally "no way," but with the connotation, "that's life"). They are likely to tell you that people always make mistakes; that something inevitably goes wrong, even with the best intentions. They cite the old proverb "There is no evil that does not come from good."

Anticipating your cynicism, Mexicans minimize their own accomplishments. A Mexican who is ambitious says, "*tengo ilusiónes*" ("I have illusions"). He calls his ambition a weakness, and if you call him ambitious, it is a criticism. It is more acceptable to praise a person for their good qualities—their strength, bravery, intelligence, or skill, than their accomplishments. People usually attribute a person's success to luck (Reavis, pp. 289–293).

SOCIAL STRUCTURE AND GROUP LIFE

Sociologists often find it useful to distinguish between **culture** and **social structure.** So far, we have been discussing Mexican culture: Mexicans' distinctive norms and customs, their particular beliefs, attitudes, and values. When we are introduced to an unfamiliar society, we notice culture first. Sometimes it seems exotic: Other peoples' religion, their holidays, food, art, and music may be noticeably different from our own. It takes longer to notice social structure, but it is equally important. Put most broadly, culture always involves meaning, while social structure describes how people organize their social lives. Every society is built out of **status positions,** like "student," "woman," or "employee," linked together in a **status system,** together with **roles** and **norms.** The resulting social structures may be small—like a nuclear family built of three statuses: mother, father, child—or they may be large and complex, like a corporation or university. Three distinctive types of social structures are found in all societies: **social networks, groups,** and **social institutions.**

Social Networks in Mexican Society

People in every society are members of networks. Networks are webs of relationships that connect each person to other people, and through them to yet others.

People have family networks, and networks of friends, neighbors, co-workers, and so forth, and sometimes these networks interlock. You may find a job, or an apartment, or meet your spouse-to-be through your networks.

Networks are of enormous importance in Mexican society. Mexicans place great value on family loyalty, and as we have seen, they are distrustful of public institutions and nonrelatives. There is nothing in Mexican life equivalent, for example, to the importance of the company and the school in the lives of the Japanese. This leaves Mexicans with a problem: Everyone needs relationships beyond the family, particularly in modern cities where one cannot count on being surrounded by relatives.

Compadrazgo and Personal Networks

Mexicans create relations of trust beyond the family by developing personal networks. One way they do this is by adapting the traditional Latin American practice of *compadrazgo* or godparenthood. It is customary for important occasions in a child's life, like baptism, confirmation, marriage, or even nonreligious events like graduation, or a first haircut, to be marked by the appointment of godparents, or "sponsors." A child then has many sets of godparents and the relationship between parents and their children's godparents is a special one. *Compadres,* as they are called, might be equals like neighbors, friends, or co-workers. Often people seek as *compadres* those of greater wealth or power, like bosses or local politicians. *Compadres* have a special relationship: They treat each other with formality and respect. The don't drink together or discuss personal matters. Because of this mutual respect, *compadres* can turn to each other for favors, like a loan of money. *Compadrazgo* creates personal networks, but not necessarily social groups, because each person's *compadres* are different, and one individual's *compadres* may not all know each other (Goodwin, pp. 8–9; Falicov, pp. 142–143).

Patronage

Mexicans also may construct networks by seeking out **patron-client relationships. Patronage** is a special kind of relationship between unequals; between a **patron,** a person with power of some kind, and a **client,** a person who gives the patron loyalty and perhaps something else of value in exchange for the patron's protection and help. Traditionally, in rural villages, people sought out the local elite as *compadres,* to establish a kind of protected relationship with them. Nowadays, ordinary people are likely to become clients (or dependents) of patrons (or bosses) in other ways: by joining a political party, or community organization, or by becoming a follower of a local boss who controls access to stalls in a market or unionized jobs. Clients owe patrons loyalty, sometimes votes, and often payments of one kind or another. Patrons will often lend money in time of need, attend the client's saints' day celebrations, or even find ways to register a favored client in the national social security system (Selby, Murphy, and Lorenzen, p. 121; Cross, pp. 123–127, 151–153).

Reciprocity Networks

Through kinship, friendship, *compadrazgo,* and patronage, ordinary Mexicans create what they call *redes de seguridad* (literally, "security networks"), or, as anthropologist Larissa Lomnitz terms them, **reciprocity networks.** Members of such networks are linked by exchange: They help each other find work; they lend each other food, money, pots and pans, even clothing. They visit back and forth and watch each other's children. They care for each other when ill, and in a crisis, they take in each other's children, for a day, or even for years. Economists used to talk of reciprocity as a mode of exchange found only in traditional societies (like the ¡Kung Bushmen) and absent in modern industrial societies, except for minor practices like Christmas gift giving. Lomnitz argues that reciprocity remains an important pattern in complex, modern societies, existing alongside exchange of goods for money: "the enduring importance of social connections and influence peddling in societies as different as Mexico, the United States, and the Soviet Union attests to the fact that reciprocity as an economic force is today very much alive" (Lomnitz, p. 4).

A good example of a Mexican reciprocity network is a *tanda,* an informal, rotating credit arrangement. The members of a *tanda* are usually close relatives, neighbors, or co-workers who join together to help each other save and who must trust each other to continue contributing (Lomnitz, pp. 88–89).

Rosa's Story: The Tanda

Rosa, Carmen's daughter, is desperate to get married and leave home, but there is no money. She has only a slim hope. Next month is Rosa's turn for the tanda. *She and Carmen and their two neighbors and two cousins each contribute 5 pesos weekly to the* tanda, *and then every month a different person gets to take the whole 120 pesos. When they began the* tanda *they drew lots to establish the order and now it is Rosa's turn. Her great plan is to use the money as a down payment on a sewing machine. With the machine, she figures that she and Héctor, her fiancé, will be able to afford to marry. They can live with Héctor's family, and she can sew piecework at home.*

Social Groups in Mexican Society: The Household

Groups are more highly structured than networks. Group members occupy statuses and play roles that are special to the group, and have some kind of group culture: shared values and norms, perhaps group folkways, and even some special way of talking. Finally, group members interact regularly and they see themselves as a group, drawing a boundary between those who are members and those who are outsiders. Most people belong to many social groups: families, friendship groups, work groups, teams, clubs, and other organizations.

The social group of greatest importance to most Mexicans is the household, the group of people with whom they live. For poor urban Mexicans, it is household sharing and reciprocity that enables them to get along, to feed and clothe their families. In the majority of cases, the members of a household form one **nuclear family** (a family composed of two parents and their children), but it is considered desirable for households to shelter an **extended family** (several nuclear units linked by kinship), and, in fact, extended family households tend to be better off economically. Households may also include more distant relatives, godchildren, or even friends or neighbors.

Most urban Mexicans live in a detached house on a small plot of land (a *solar*). Ideally, they want a brick house with a wall to close the household off from the street. In this small domain, the household sets about *defendiendose,* or "looking after themselves" (Selby, Murphy, and Lorenzen, pp. 70, 89). Many households are productive units, a functioning part of the economy. Households often raise animals for their own consumption or for sale; they sometimes open tiny workshops that produce textiles, carpentry, upholstery, or custom ironwork; or sidewalk businesses that do auto and truck repair or customize trucks. Sometimes household members take in washing or run sidewalk stands or rudimentary stores, selling fruit or milk, beer, crackers, and candy (Selby, Murphy, and Lorenzen, p. 71).

The Gómez' Story: The Household

The Gómez household, consisting of fourteen people, lives in Ciudad Nezahuacóyotl, the huge working-class neighborhood east of Mexico City. Their solar contains a series of rooms grouped in a U-shape around a central patio. Here live three related nuclear families and two individuals, linked to the household by kinship. There is Don Ramón, the head of the household, his wife Consuela, their two teenage children, and a 5-year-old godchild, who all share the main room. Don Ramón's older son and his family live in another room, and a younger son and his family live in a third room. Both daughters-in-law have orphaned younger siblings living with them too. When each son married, the whole family worked together to build a new room. The children of all three families are raised by everybody in the household, and the women go out together to shop and visit church. They borrow food, money, and other items from each other.

Many facilities in the solar are shared by the whole household. There is a small pen for pigs, rabbits, and chickens, and a privy. Also, there is a woodstove, a barrel for water, which all share in refilling, and laundry tubs used by all. Consuela and her two daughters-in-law help support the household by taking in laundry. The two teenagers carry the laundry for Consuela when she collects and delivers it, and the two young mothers wash the clothes at home. The married sons work in the same factory and the older helped the younger get a job. Sometimes, when the factory is busy, they are able to get Don Ramón hired too. Each nuclear family keeps its separate finances, but the two married sons give their father a weekly allowance in exchange for the use of his solar. Don Ramón says that they all "stick up for themselves and keep going." (See Selby, Murphy, and Lorenzen, p. 70, and Lomnitz, pp. 112–114, for descriptions of similar households.)

SOCIAL INSTITUTIONS

The Gómez household is a social group, but it also illustrates a third aspect of social structure. It shows us some of the characteristics of the Mexican family, a major Mexican **social institution.** While social groups are concrete units of real people, social institutions are patterns of behavior. Sociologists use the term **social institution** when they need to discuss how clusters of social groups and organizations, statuses and roles, and associated norms and values operate to serve some important need in social life. In modern societies there are five major social institutions: the family, political institutions, the economy, educational institutions, and religious institutions, each performing functions that are vital to the continued existence of the society. Each of these institutions can be organized in a variety of ways, as you have seen in this book; but in each society, social institutions are long-lasting and widely accepted. Often, people don't even imagine different ways of organizing their society's institutions, and when institutions do change (see Chapter 5, Germany), they find it difficult to adjust.

Mexican Social Institutions: The Family

Families in all societies do similar things for society (that is, they perform basic functions), though they do them in different ways. Families regulate sexual activity, supervising their members to be sure they conform to sexual norms. Families are in charge of reproduction to keep the society going, and they socialize the children they produce. Also families provide physical care and protection for their members. They also provide emotional support and caring. When sociologists discuss "the family," they are talking about a cultural ideal: how families are supposed to work in a given society. The ideal may or may not coincide with what things are actually like in any given family group.

The Mexican family fulfills these universal functions in a distinctive way. The structures and the values, norms, beliefs, and attitudes that permeate family life are characteristically Mexican or Latin American. According to Selby, Murphy, and Lorenzen, "it is difficult to overemphasize the importance of the nuclear family in Mexico, for it truly is the emotional center of the psychological and social life of all Mexicans" (p. 98). Ordinary Mexicans don't go downtown to shop, or eat out in restaurants, or go to clubs or concerts or sports events. Their lives revolve around home and work; family TV watching, family celebrations, visits among relatives and neighbors, and for men, going out drinking with close friends. Although Mexican families are typically large, only the well-to-do in Mexico live in houses with many bedrooms. Ordinary Mexicans will even rebuild the interiors of houses to make fewer bedrooms and more shared common space for family work and socializing (Selby, Murphy, and Lorenzen, pp. 22, 26, 98).

Practically everyone in Mexico lives in a family-based household, and almost all of these are headed by a man who is the principal wage earner. In 1990, 17 percent of households were female-headed (compared to 36 percent in the United States in 1990). Mexicans tend to marry young (51 percent of Mexican women aged 20 to 24 are married), and stay married. In Mexico there are only five divorces yearly per hundred marriages. Almost no one lives alone (only 1 percent of Mexicans lived in one-person households in 1990) and indeed it is almost unthinkable to do so, and very inconvenient too, since Mexican society assumes the presence of children or servants in every household, to run errands, stand in line to pay bills (since the mails are so unreliable), or carry messages (since so many people lack telephones). The average household size in Mexico is still rather large: five persons (compared to 2.6 in the United States), because most adults have children living in the house with them, and often grandchildren as well. Seventy-one percent of Mexicans live in households of five or more, and 27 percent live in households of eight or more. (United Nations, "Statistics and Indicators on the World's Women," http://www.un.org/Depts/unsd/gender/1-3dev.htm; Selby, Murphy, and Lorenzen, pp. 53, 91, 99.) (See Table 1.1, p. 17 and Table 4.1, p. 189.)

Family Structure

In Mexico the ideal nuclear family is part of an extended family network and the household willingly expands to include grandparents, uncles, aunts or cousins, related children who are orphans or children of divorced parents, or relatives who

FIGURE 2.1. Patterns of Marriage and Divorce, 1986–1996

	ǃKUNG: Early marriages and many divorces	MEXICO: Early marriages and few divorces
Percent of all women 15–24 who have ever married *	100%	51%
Divorces each year for every hundred marriages **	49 ***	5
	GERMANY: Later marriages and many divorces	JAPAN: Later marriages and few divorces
Percent of all women 15–24 who have ever married	16%	15%
Divorces each year for every hundred marriages **	39	25

Source: *** *The Dobe ǃKung,* Richard B. Lee, Harcourt Brace, 1984, pages 83–85
   ** *Demographic Yearbook,* United Nations, 1995, pages 542–544, 559–561
   *International Data Base, United States Census, http://www.census.gov/ipc/www/idbsprd.html

are single, widowed, or divorced. People feel close to their third and fourth cousins. Extended family members rely on each other to take care of children, help with money, or provide friendship and support. People live in families at every stage of their lives and families demand loyalty. "What you have to do," an informant told Selby, "is care for your family, so your family will care for you" (Falicov, p. 138; Selby, Murphy, and Lorenzen, p. 5).

Families are also hierarchical: The old have authority over the young, and men have authority over women, at every stage of the life cycle. People are expected to remain loyal to their family of origin throughout their lives. Indeed, ideally, married sons and their families will share households with their parents, and married daughters often do so as well. Married sons and daughters who live separately will try to live nearby and visit often, and sons will contribute money to their parents' household. According to Falicov, family values stress proximity, cohesiveness, respect for parental authority, and cooperation. Confrontation and competition are discouraged, and individual autonomy and individual achievement are not emphasized (Falicov, p. 138).

Roles in the Mexican Family

Role expectations for husbands and wives stress complementarity. Ideally, the husband is hard-working and continuously employed. He disciplines and controls the family. The husband hands over his wages to his wife, who manages the household. It is her task to maintain the home, physically and emotionally. She creates an emotional shelter, a refuge for her family, where they can recover from the stresses of life in the public world outside. Taking care of everyone is the mother's task: She sustains and nurtures and serves her family.

Traditionally, the roles parents play in relation to their children are considered much more important than the roles they play toward each other as spouses. They don't expect much romantic intimacy or friendly companionship, but rather respect, consideration, and control of anger. As Falicov explains, "it is thought that *el amor de madre* (motherly love) is a much greater force than wifely love" and "a Mexican woman feels more challenged to perform as a mother than as a wife, companion or sexual partner" (Falicov, pp. 140, 149). In fact, since Mexican families are large, and adult children remain close, husbands and wives rarely live without children and are able to transfer their early involvement in raising their children to a lasting relationship with their grandchildren.

Children are expected to respect and obey their parents, but they wouldn't think of being friends with them. Ideally, children put the family's needs before their own. When they see their parents working so hard to maintain the family, they feel tremendous gratitude and a sense of protectiveness toward their mother. They are eager to help by working with their parents, or if they obtain paid work, by contributing their wages. Selby, Murphy, and Lorenzen estimate that by the time working children are 20, they will have paid back their parents all the expenses entailed in raising them. When adult children live with their parents, or regularly give them money, parents soon realize a net gain in the financial calculus of childrearing (Selby, Murphy, and Lorenzen, p. 55).

Siblings are expected to have very close ties throughout their lives. Brothers and sisters and cousins are encouraged to play together, and it is not unusual for Mexican children to have few friends who are not relatives. Older siblings are usually given some authority over younger ones and these age hierarchies may continue into adult life. Adult brothers and sisters may quarrel and carry grudges, but they seldom break off relations with each other, because family celebrations or crises reunite them.

Changing Families and Changing Roles

The institution of the family is changing in Mexico today, and gender roles are changing along with it. Two changes are leading the trend: People are having fewer children and more women are working outside their homes. Obviously these two big changes are related in complex ways. Both changes may be a response to Mexico's economic crisis, as families try to make ends meet. But it is also true that when women have fewer children they are freer to work, and conversely, when women work, they are likely to have fewer children. In 1967, Mexican women bore an average of 6.8 children in their lifetimes. By 1980, it had fallen to 4.6, and by 1999, this **total fertility rate** was down to 2.8. Falling fertility rates are reflected in smaller household sizes. Nevertheless, many Mexicans continue to live in large households; a quarter of the population lives in households of eight or more and people continue to see large households as desirable (U.S. Bureau of the Census, International Data Base, http://www.census.gov/cgi-bin/ipc/idbsprd). (See Table 1.1, p. 17.)

More Mexican women are working for wages outside their homes—as maids, in factories, in small shops and markets, in agriculture and in family enterprises. The *maquiladoras* (foreign-owned assembly plants) concentrated along the border, but found elsewhere in Mexico as well, employ workers who are mostly female and young—aged 16–24. In 1996, 37.4 percent of Mexican women were in the labor force, a tremendous change from 1950, when the corresponding figure was only 8 percent. (See Table 1.3, p. 40.)

At this point you may be asking yourself, have women in Mexico become more "liberated"? That's a hard question to answer because it involves how people act and how they feel, not just whether or not they work or how many children they have. Many Mexican women would prefer not to work. They work out of necessity, to feed their families, at jobs that are menial and badly paid. After all, if you had to leave your children and your house to work at cleaning someone else's house and caring for their children, wouldn't you prefer not to work? Increasingly, Mexican women work a "double day," working for wages all day outside their homes, then grocery shopping, cooking, cleaning, and caring for their own children. The poorest women, who have no refrigerators, must shop for food every day and also must fill and carry containers of water from the nearest public tap. Many commute two hours each way besides! In contrast, being a housewife in Mexico is a desirable and honorable job. It is still seen by many as a woman's highest calling and it carries another sort of prestige as well. A woman who can afford to be a housewife tells the world that her husband (and/or sons) makes enough money to support the family without her working (Isaac, pp. 125–130).

At the same time, when women work and leave their homes for the public world, there is something liberating about it, especially when they work in factories or other situations where there are many female employees. Women talk together, they give each other advice, and they develop a broader social perspective on their lives. Some move on to union or political activism. Women who run their own businesses, even as laundresses or market stall proprietors, feel a sense of pride in their business skills and in what they have built up. Also, when women bring home some of their family's income, it does have an effect on roles within the family: "Breadwinners" have a say in making decisions.

It is also becoming more acceptable for the husbands of working women to "help out" at home. Both men and women speak of it as "helping out." The belief that the home is primarily the woman's responsibility is unchanged in Mexico. But when men "help," especially with childcare, they learn how much work it is, and it makes them think differently about how many children they want and whether use of contraceptives is acceptable to them.

Mexican Political Institutions: The "Official" Party

Every society develops some means to maintain order, protect the members of the society from outside threats, control crime, and resolve conflicts among different groups. All modern societies have separate political institutions which exist to serve these functions: governments, political parties, the military, and legal institutions.

Mexico's political institutions are in transition. A well-organized, effective, but undemocratic system is opening up under pressure from new political parties. There is more democracy in Mexico today, but less order. For 70 years, the PRI (the Institutional Revolutionary Party) has been Mexico's "official" political party.

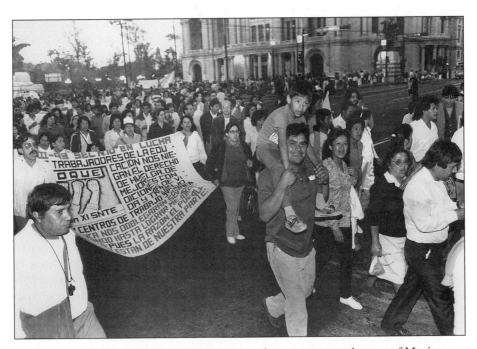

Teachers demonstrate in Mexico City. Demonstrations are very much a part of Mexican life. Political parades and rallies are held by those who oppose national government policies and by the PRI, the traditional governing party, to show its popular support. Women are frequently part of demonstrations. This reflects their long history of activity in Mexico's unions, political parties, and revolutionary movements.

Since 1929 every president has come from its ranks and almost every governor and lesser official. The party has been a permanent institution that dominates the government and touches most peoples' lives on a daily basis. It is much more than a vote-getting organization that gears up at election time. The PRI has dominated the Mexican parliament and the lives of ordinary Mexicans through its affiliated labor unions, peasant groups, student groups, and urban community organizations. Participation in the PRI has been the only real route to political power and, in most cases, even economic advance. The distinction between party and government has been blurred in Mexico.

According to political scientists Wayne A. Cornelius and Ann L. Craig, Mexico has had "a highly centralized political system," in which the president dominates the government. Mexico's political institutions are part free and part authoritarian. The government is not rigidly repressive, and it strives to include a broad range of interest groups, but political competition between opposing parties is very limited. The PRI government has kept benefits restricted to its own supporters, manipulated the mass media, and kept decision making centralized in the federal government and in the hands of the president and his cabinet (Cornelius and Craig, pp. 23–31). When opposition parties took control of the lower house of Mexico's congress in 1997, newly elected members looked forward to drafting legislation in committees.

They discovered that the huge congressional building didn't even have committee meeting rooms! In the past, committees had existed on paper, but had never met. All legislation was actually drafted by the president's office and was sent to the committee chair with a "committee report" already attached! (De Palma, Aug. 30, 1998, p. 12).

The PRI and Order

Until very recently Mexico was really a **single-party system.** All the diverse groups—workers and businessmen, peasants and soldiers, rival politicians and their followers—that might have supported opposed parties became organized factions under the umbrella of a single party. The party became the **patron** of them all, giving each something that it wanted, and in exchange, all the **clients** acknowledged the supremacy of the party and accepted its choice of president. Every president since 1929 has served out his term of office—an extraordinary record.

One reason why the PRI has been so successful is that it is firmly based in Mexican culture and social structure. The party is a hierarchical network of patron–client relationships, based on personal favors, gratitude, and personal loyalty. Sociologists and political scientists call this way of running a government **patronage politics.** Patronage politics is highly developed in Mexico, but it is found in many, many other societies too.

Don Miguel's Story: The Patron

Don Miguel is a PRI jefe (or boss). He is the president of the Citizens Action Committee of Colonia "Lázaro Cárdenas," a newly settled colonia populare (or squatter neighborhood) on the outskirts of Oaxaca. Five years ago, Don Miguel got involved with his neighbors in order to build a much-needed school. To his own astonishment, he found he had a talent for organizing and leading people. With Don Miguel as president, the Citizens Action Committee collected signatures on petitions, visited the mayor's office, and searched for every possible personal connection to officials of the city government. Demonstrations in front of city hall finally culminated in a memorable visit by the mayor to the colonia, when he promised to provide sewer service.

By the time the bulldozers arrived, Don Miguel found he had a new profession. Residents of the colonia came to him with all sorts of problems: this one's brother needed a job; that one's son was brilliant, but needed a scholarship; that one's mother was senile and kept wandering off and getting lost. As he got to know the officials at city hall better, Don Miguel found he could get help for some of his neighbors. They looked up to him as a kind of protector, a patron, and they willingly gave 5 pesos a month per family to finance the Citizens Action Committee. In turn, Don Miguel felt grateful and loyal to the mayor and the other PRI officials for their help. When they asked him to bring his people to a campaign rally in Oaxaca to cheer the mayor and the PRI, he was glad to do it, and his neighbors were happy to come to show their gratitude and loyalty to him. The PRI even served them all a free lunch when they arrived.

Although the citizens of Lázaro Cárdenas know, in an abstract way, that the city is obliged to provide sewer service, they haven't demanded it with a feeling of entitlement. Rather, they believe that it is their personal relationship with a patron, Don Miguel, and his relationship with his patron, the mayor, which made the sewers possible.

A Successful Institution

The PRI's success has been based on its ability to deliver real benefits to Mexican workers and peasants in exchange for their political loyalties. It was President Lázaro Cárdenas, remembered with gratitude to this day, who organized Mexican peasants into their own federations within the PRI and actually put into practice the constitutional guarantee of land for any Mexican family that would farm it themselves. Between 1934 and 1940 Cárdenas redistributed 46 million acres of land, formerly held in large estates, creating more than 180,000 *ejidos* (tracts of land held communally by villages, which could be inherited but not sold), farmed by 750,000 families. Cárdenas formed confederations of peasants, workers, white-collar workers, and small businessmen, under the umbrella of the PRI. These groups made the PRI a powerful machine for gathering votes and channeling benefits (Riding, pp. 53–55).

Peasants received land and vital loans from state banks to buy seeds and equipment. Workers unionized by party affiliates received wage increases, some benefits, and also access to jobs in industries newly taken over by the state, like the railroads, the oil industry, and, as time went by, thousands of smaller state companies as well. Public funds invested in rural development—road construction, power lines, health clinics, and schools—yielded benefits for peasants and also jobs for manual workers, teachers, health care workers, and government bureaucrats.

Social Mobility and the PRI. Ambitious Mexicans often thanked the PRI for providing them with opportunities for **upward social mobility** (that is, movement to a higher social rank or position). Like a good patron, the PRI "sponsored" the rise of politically talented individuals up the ladder of power. It was possible to become active in your local union or *ejido* or student group and then, supported by the power of the organization you controlled, to be tapped by the party for higher positions. Sociologists call this pattern of improving your social position **sponsored mobility.** In this way, some people who came from quite poor origins ended up in congress or in high government positions (Riding, p. 75). At the same time, the PRI created networks that linked together potentially opposed groups, granting benefits to each and absorbing into itself the natural leadership of each group.

What Price Stability?

If you are thinking that this political system sounds too good to be true, you are right. There is a substantial downside to a one-party patronage machine, a downside that worries more and more Mexicans. Because, for all practical purposes, the PRI and the Mexican government have been identical, certain kinds of abuses of power can more readily occur.

Co-optation and Repression. Faced with any new organization, like a newly settled community, or a new union, the PRI/Mexican government has followed a consistent policy. When local authorities judge the new group and its leaders willing to play the game, the organization is **co-opted**—that is, it is given some benefits, allowed to achieve some of its goals in return for becoming a loyal part of the PRI. Leaders can be co-opted personally with recognition and paid positions. But organizations with interests and goals that conflict with those of the PRI, or organizations bent on achieving power independent of the PRI, are ruthlessly repressed. Because the PRI and the government are identical, it is an easy matter for the party to call out soldiers to bulldoze the too-independent shantytown, or police to crush the too-radical union. Mexicans long suspected that the PRI also used its power to alter election returns, minimizing the votes gained by opposition parties.

Lack of Democracy. In theory, the PRI gives representation to all groups, through its subsidiary organizations. But in fact, this system is a far cry from representative democracy. Power is held by a hierarchy of bosses: union chiefs, or local leaders who are appointed by those above. Election is a mere formality. Even the president is essentially appointed (by his outgoing predecessor); the election just legitimates his selection. Basically, Mexican elected officials are accountable to the patrons who appointed them, not the people they represent (Cornelius and Craig, p. 25).

Corruption. The practice of patronage, combined with the *sexenio,* the single six-year presidential term of office, has fostered corruption in Mexico. Every high-level politician has his following of loyal clients, who have helped him rise. When a politician is selected to be the next president, his patronage network has struck it rich. Every client can expect a government job, or perhaps a government contract, an import license, sewers and streetlights for the community, or other government funds, a portion of which will find their way into the private wealth of the client. But the largesse will last only six years, after which another politician and other clients will take over. The temptation to line one's pockets as fast as possible usually proves irresistible. Corruption filters down to lower civil servants, police, judges, businesspeople, and the media.

Police corruption is probably most notorious. To become a police officer in Mexico City, you don't take an exam or train at a police academy. You must know someone in the PRI and then you will have to buy your job with a payment to the bureaucrat in charge of hiring, or to someone to whom he owes a favor. The job itself is hardly worth having, since the pay is absurdly low. It is valuable only as an opportunity for corruption, for *la mordida* ("the little bite"), as police payoffs are called. In Mexico you can expect to be stopped for tiny, or imaginary infractions of the traffic laws, but the police officer will be happy to "pay your ticket for you" if you give him the fine. The police officer must pay a bigger bribe for a better corner, so he must also take more "little bites" from motorists. Police are also paid off by drug dealers and prostitution operators. They must be "tipped" before they will investigate a crime, and small criminals can buy their way out of charges. Like police officers, judges are poorly paid. Some simply give the decision to the party that makes the biggest payoff (Riding, p. 117).

In business it is difficult to accomplish anything without kickbacks and payoffs to suppliers, government bureaucrats, or union officials. Many union leaders use their power primarily to obtain the largest possible payoff in return for not striking. And union bosses often fill jobs by selling them to the highest bidder. Newspaper reporters, paid very low wages, make a living by accepting a monthly "retainer" from the government agency, industry, or criminal operation they are assigned to cover (Riding, pp. 123–124, 126).

Challenges to the PRI

The PRI is beleaguered today. It still dominates Mexican government because of the institutional power it wields, built up over the past 70 years, but challenges abound. In the north, the PAN (the National Action Party) attacks the whole idea of patronage politics. PAN attracts small business owners and conservative Catholics to its advocacy of shrinking government, expanding private enterprise, and cleaning up corruption. PAN supporters believe in competition and self-reliance and they are willing to do without the favors and benefits of a patronage system. In an unprecedented upset for the PRI, which had always controlled all Mexican governorships, PAN governors have been elected in six northern states. The PRD (the Party of the Democratic Revolution) is another opposition party, more popular in southern Mexico, where it speaks for the impoverished Indians and poor city dwellers. Cuahtémoc Cárdenas leads the PRD and his very name tells a story to Mexican voters. Cuahtémoc Cárdenas is the son of Lázaro Cárdenas, named by his father for Cuahtémoc, the last king of the Aztecs who heroically led the last Aztec warriors before their defeat by the Spanish. Cuahtémoc Cárdenas broke with the PRI in 1988 and ran for president against Carlos Salinas. It is widely believed that he would have won the 1988 election for president had the PRI not falsified the results. In 1997 Cárdenas was elected mayor of Mexico City, in two firsts for the nation: the first elected (rather than appointed) mayor of the capital, and the first time in seventy years that the Mexican capital has not had a PRI mayor. At the same time, the lower house of congress was captured by the opposition as well (Dillon, Aug. 3, 1998, p. A7; Preston, July 2, 1997, pp. A1, A8; Berman, p. 51).

It is not easy to explain why the PRI has loosened its iron grip on power. The strength of the opposition has had some effect, as has international pressure for fair and free elections. One must understand as well the effect of economic liberalization. As the governing PRI has privatized the economy, selling off government-owned industries and welcoming foreign-owned assembly plants, the party has lost patronage opportunities. The old way of holding power through patronage has become less effective and new American-educated PRI leaders like Ernesto Zedillo are trying to transform their party into an American-style electoral party, holding primaries, competing through policy debates, and advertising and reaching voters as individuals, as consumers, rather than as members of PRI organizations. The PRI has taken a political gamble, and perhaps the gamble will pay off. In 1998 the PRI retook the governships of four states, after a campaign largely fought with TV ads (Dillon, Nov. 10, 1998, p. A7).

Power and Deviance

What is very clear is that the PRI's lessening authoritarian control has coincided with a massive crime wave. Mexicans long tolerated the pervasive corruption that was so much a part of PRI rule. But Mexico's old-fashioned corruption, while it violated **ideal norms** of honesty, was governed by **real norms** that everyone could rely upon. There were limits to how far the police would go in extracting bribes and limits to how much presidents would enrich themselves and their friends. While there was corruption, Mexico felt like a safe place and people travelled and went about their business without fear. Now it appears that the old normative limits have been discarded. Violent crime seems out of control to Mexicans and they are furiously demanding government action.

In Mexico City reported murders rose 50 percent between 1990 and 1995 and there were six times as many robberies in 1998 as in 1973. Assaults almost doubled between 1993 and 1997. When Mexico City's government announced a war on crime in 1998, the rate of violent crimes immediately rose 25 percent. And these statistics understate the problem, because many, perhaps most crimes are now never reported because victims fear that police will demand bribes or even prove to be accomplices of the criminals. People don't see much point in going to the police. According to official statistics, only 5 percent of all reported crimes are ever investigated and even when it comes to violent crimes, 94 percent are never solved or prosecuted. Ordinary citizens have lost confidence in the police and in the power of the government to maintain order. Criminals see that they run little risk of being apprehended (Dillon, 6/28/98, WK4; Preston, 11/7/97, A1, A6, 11/17/98, p. A3). It's no wonder that Mexicans are upset; sociologists tell us that two of the primary functions of government are to maintain order and control crime. In Mexico City, Cuahtémoc Cárdenas, newly elected as mayor, promised to restore "a state of law." It was a bold promise, a clear response to public demands, but it is not clear that Cárdenas has the power to make good on his pledge (Berman, p. 53).

Mexicans are particularly alarmed by the increasing number of bold public holdups and the surge in kidnappings for ransom. In one case, a Mexican diplomat returned from Europe lost everything when the moving van carrying her possessions was hijacked on a major street in Mexico City, apparently with the help of the police. A hidden video camera captured a mugger in a subway station handing a just-stolen wallet to police officers who took the cash for themselves and handed the credit cards to the mugger. Robbers hold up drivers at red lights, or masquerade as taxi drivers and then take their victims around all the cash machines in town, emptying their accounts. Armed robbers even walked right into the Chamber of Deputies (the congress) and seized the staff payroll. Kidnappings for ransom take place at the rate of one a day, many in Mexico City. One kidnapper, since captured, sent a severed ear to each victim's family to increase the pressure to ransom the captive (Preston, Preston, De Palma, 8/19/98, A2).

Explaining the Rise in Crime

There is no single explanation for the crime wave accepted by all Mexican experts, and it may indeed be too early for anyone to come up with a definitive explanation. It is possible, however, to say that the sudden rise in crime rates in the late 1990s in Mexico is causally related to three linked problems: the economic crisis, the political crisis, and the vast increase in drug trafficking in Mexico.

The current economic crisis, which started in 1995, has brought a major drop in real wages, an increase in unemployment, and a widening gap between rich and poor. Up until 1995, crime was something that happened in poor neighborhoods, but the economic crisis coincided with the new wave of kidnappings and assaults on middle class and rich Mexicans. Mexican criminologist Rafael Ruiz Harrell, has charted the relationship between crime and economic crisis between 1930 and the present and finds a clear association, with crime declining as long as real wages rose (Dillon, 6/28/98, WK1).

So is the crime wave simply the result of economic crisis? Many Mexicans disagree and argue that the government must bear much of the blame. Criminologist Ernesto López Portillo contends that as opposition parties have loosened the PRI's stranglehold on power, the PRI has lost its ability to deter criminals. The old PRI controlled organized crime, favoring one crime syndicate over another in exchange for kickbacks and it kept crime within certain limits. Many Mexicans believe that the Mexican government today has simply lost control over criminal deviance (Dillon, 6/28/98, WK1).

Crime and Drugs

It may be, though, that in significant degree the Mexican government has not simply failed to control criminals; it has actually joined them in the lucrative drug trade. Have you ever lived in a neighborhood or a city or country where illegal drug dealing was big business? If so, you will understand how much drug trafficking increases crime; how it brings in its wake murders and kidnappings among dealers, hold-ups and thefts by drug addicts, and corruption of the police. All this and more took place in Mexico in the 1990s, as Mexico became a major route for the transport of cocaine from Colombia to the United States. Cocaine trafficking involves huge amounts of money—billions and billions of dollars yearly in Mexico—and as a result police and judicial corruption has ballooned out of control. When Mexican drug smugglers bring Colombian cocaine into the United States, they take half the shipment as their fee. Out of those billions of dollars they pay off everyone involved: the airport workers who illegally refuel the planes, the airport official who turns a blind eye to unrecorded landings and takeoffs, the border guards who allow smugglers' trucks to go through, the drug police who ignore the guards, and the judges who dismiss cases against traffickers brought in by other police. There are competing drug gangs and they pay off officials and police to support their gang against other gangs and to look away from gang murders. People higher in the Mexican government take their own cuts from the traffickers and from those lower down. Drugs that fail to make it across the border are sold in Mexico, so drug use is rising, especially crack cocaine use by young people in the poorest communities (Thompson, Jan. 11, 1999, p. A4).

In 1997 Mexico's newly appointed Attorney General fired all 2,300 of the country's narcotics police and prosecutors, rehiring only those who passed lie-detector tests. Three-quarters failed (Dillon, 12/22/97, pp. A1, A12). In 1998 the governor of the State of Morelos, Jorge Carillo Olea, a prominent member of the PRI, was forced to resign when a police commander, caught dumping the body of a man killed under torture, turned state's evidence and explained how state police had turned the state into an operating base for drug traffickers (Dillon, 5/13/98, p. A10). In May 1998, the United States charged three major Mexican banks and 26 bankers with laundering drug money (Van Natte, 5/19/98, p. A6; Preston,

5/20/98, p. A6). Later that year, the jailed former head of Mexico's national police testified that he collected $1,500 for every kilo of cocaine that he permitted to move through the country (Golden, 7/15/98, pp. A1, A6). The most scandalous evidence concerns Raúl Salinas de Gortari, brother of Carlos Salinas de Gortari, who was president of Mexico from 1988 to 1994. Swiss investigators have uncovered $132 million in drug bribes hidden by Raúl Salinas in Swiss bank accounts. Many Mexicans speculate that several hundred million dollars more remain hidden in accounts in other countries (Golden, 8/4/98, pp. A1, A8).

News in Mexico has a kind of hall-of-mirrors quality, because so often things are not what they seem. A man arrested for murder is suddenly released and then as suddenly abducted and murdered, and Mexicans speculate about what drug gangs and what corrupt officials were involved. Political assassinations turn out to be cocaine-gang assassinations. Cynical Mexicans argue that the government cannot afford to clean up the drug trade because it is the only activity that keeps the Mexican economy afloat, and without it Mexicans would be much worse off economically and much angrier. Perhaps one reason narcotics trafficking has taken such deep hold in Mexico is that so many people are poor and desperate and see themselves getting poorer.

SOCIAL INEQUALITY

What do sociologists mean when they say that a given society has deep inequalities, or that another is relatively egalitarian? How do we judge the extent of inequality in a society or compare the amount of inequality in different societies? In every society there are scarce resources that are distributed unequally: Some people receive more and others less. Sociologists usually point to three categories of scarce goods: **power, prestige,** and **wealth.** Then, in examining any society, they ask who, which groups or categories of people, have more or less power, prestige, or wealth.

In every society there is some degree of inequality between men and women. (We call this **gender inequality.**) We have seen how in Mexican society women are often economically dependent on men and defer to their husbands and fathers. In Mexican society (and in many other societies) there are also **racial inequalities** in which some races (or ethnic groups) enjoy higher status than others, more wealth, and more power over other races. Finally, in Mexico, as in many other societies, we can distinguish distinct groups or **strata** (layers) of the population whose access to power, prestige, and wealth differs because they start out with different economic resources. We call these groups **social classes** and this kind of inequality **class inequality.**

Class Inequality in Mexican Society

Is there a great deal of class inequality in Mexican society? Is there more or less than in other societies? In trying to answer these questions, we can start with two relatively simple comparisons. First, we can ask, do most people in this society make pretty much the same amount of money? Are there just a handful of rich people and a sprinkling of poor people, with everyone else clustered in the middle? Or are people spread out over the whole range of incomes? Second, we can ask, how big is that range from the richest to the poorest? Do the richest people receive double the share of total income that the poorest receive? Ten times as much? One hundred times as much? These are questions about **income distribution.**

According to these measures, Mexico is quite an unequal society: There are many poor people and they are very poor indeed, both **relatively,** compared to very rich Mexicans, and **absolutely,** in terms of the absolute minimum necessary for human survival. Except for African countries, the gap between rich and poor is larger in Mexico than in all but six countries in the world. Real wages today have fallen below their 1981 level and 22 million Mexicans live in extreme poverty (De Palma, "Income Gulf in Mexico Grows and So Do Protests," 7/20/96, p. 3).

Income Distribution

Sociologist James W. Russell calculates that Mexico's upper class is tiny—making up less than 1 percent of the population. The middle class, including well-off small business owners, privileged bureaucrats, managers, and well-paid professionals, is very small, encompassing only 16.5 percent of the workforce and their families. All other Mexicans, a group which includes farmers and farm workers, blue-collar workers, and most self-employed people, make up a huge 83 percent of the labor force and their families. Approximately half of this majority lives in poverty (Russell, p. 69).

We can learn a lot about the extent of inequality in a society by looking at income distribution by "income fifths," or **quintiles.** This calculation adds up all the income everyone receives, then divides up all the households into five equal size groups: the 20 percent who are the top income earners, the 20 percent who are the bottom income earners, and the three-fifths in the middle.

In Mexico in 1992 the richest income fifth received 55.3 percent of total income earned, and the poorest fifth received only 4.1 percent. That means the richest fifth received 13 ½ times as much income as the poorest fifth. Compare this to Egypt (in 1991) where the richest fifth received only 4.7 times as much of total income as the poorest fifth; or Germany where the richest fifth received 7 times as much; and the United States, where the richest fifth received 9 times as much (see Fig. 2.2, p. 92).

Social Classes and Standards of Living

Income distribution figures will make more sense if you know how much money rich people and poor people earn, or at least what their money will buy them. The official minimum wage in Mexico is $3.42 per day, or approximately $100 per month (and $1,200 per year), a wage typical for unskilled workers in the city or countryside, but one that leaves them very, very poor. Earnings of approximately $800 a month (or $9,600 a year) put you squarely in the middle class. Only 8 percent of Mexicans earn that much money. Rich Mexicans receive a great deal more income: Russell estimates that $60,000 a year puts you in the Mexican upper class, a level that fewer than 1 percent of Mexicans can attain (Russell, pp. 78–79). (See Table 1.4, p. 45.)

FIGURE 2.2. Patterns of Income Inequality, 1979–1992

	JAPAN: A rich country with more income equality	EGYPT: A poor country with more income equality
Average income per person (per capita GNP)	$22,110	$3,820
For every hundred dollars the poorest 20% of the people take home, the richest 20% take home	$430	$470
	USA: A rich country with less income equality	MEXICO: A poor country with less income equality
Average income per person (per capita GNP)	$26,980	$6,400
For every hundred dollars the poorest 20% of the people take home, the richest 20% take home	$890	$1,350

Source: The State in a Changing World, Oxford University Press, 1998, pp. 214–215, 222–223.

People with similar incomes and about the same amount of wealth often resemble each other in many aspects of their lives. Their income enables them to buy one or another standard of living, and they also develop shared values, norms, and customs. They live in the same neighborhoods, send their children to the same schools, and usually marry each other as well. We call these groups **social classes.** In Mexico the various social classes live apart from each other and follow very different ways of life.

The Upper-Class Way of Life

Upper-class Mexicans have sufficient money to live like the wealthy of rich western societies, with cars, vacations abroad, designer clothes, and investments in foreign real estate. They think of themselves as an elite group, setting standards for their society (Rudolph, pp. 115–116).

Eduardo's Story: The Industrialist

Eduardo Sandoval's Lexus leaves the driveway of his home in the exclusive Polanco district of Mexico City, the gates closing behind him. While Eduardo argues over the telephone with his father, Geraldo, his driver, pilots the car through traffic, the air conditioner blasting. Eduardo wants to accept a big partnership offer from a Japanese company. They want to contract with Eduardo's food processing company to produce frozen specialty vegetables for the American market. Eduardo likes the offer. He thinks they need to reposition the company in the new free-market NAFTA era. His father Juan, who started the business, and runs it together with Eduardo, is opposed. Juan says his company has always produced for the Mexican market and Mexicans have been good to the Sandoval family. Juan worries that competing in an unrestricted international market could hurt the company as easily as help it.

Eduardo's wife doesn't work. She is at home, completing preparations for next week's holiday trip. The Sandovals and their teenage daughter plan to fly to Vail, Colorado, to stay in the vacation home they own there. Their son, who is attending college at Stanford, will fly in to join them so the whole family can ski together.

Traditionally, there are three somewhat overlapping sectors of the Mexican upper class, which are distinct, but linked through kinship and social interaction.

The Industrial Elite. Business fortunes in Mexico are often held by extended families, like the Garza Sada family fortune begun in the 1890s when the family founded Cervecería Cuautémoc, today Mexico's largest brewery. Descendants have invested in chemicals, oil, steel, banking, insurance, and finance. Families like the Garza Sadas intermarry with each other. They give relatives jobs in various family-controlled businesses, and form alliances with other family business groups (Rudolph, pp. 116–117).

The Landowning Elite. Another group of wealthy people in Mexico are rural large landowners. They are the owners of the (mostly northwestern) large estates of good, irrigated land used to grow winter vegetables for export to the United States. Large landowners make enough money to invest in the most modern farm technology: irrigation systems, farm machinery, fertilizers, herbicides, and pesticides. Many have also invested in commerce, industry, and banking, forming alliances with Mexico's industrial elite (Rudolph, pp. 117, 124–125).

The Political Elite. Politics is the most conspicuous route to wealth in Mexico. It is almost expected that elected officials and the networks of clients they bring with them into office will spend their six-year terms skimming government budgets and accumulating payoffs. As long ago as the 1960s, research revealed that the average senior official "finished his term with two or three houses, two or three automobiles, a ranch and the equivalent of U.S. $100,000 in cash." (Rudolph, p. 118). Today, with drug money, the sums elected officials accumulate are staggering. Raúl Salinas' $132 million is one example, and he was only the President's brother! Former President Salinas lives now in Ireland and the south of France and no one knows how much money he has.

The Middle-Class Way of Life

Middle class in Mexico is an elusive term. Some people, like teachers, have professions usually considered middle-class, but in Mexico they are paid so little that in terms of their income they are poor. Other Mexicans own businesses, but their businesses are so small that they have no employees and their earnings don't keep them out of poverty. More than half the Mexican middle class earn less than $10,000 a year. At these wages it is hard to afford goods produced for the world market, like cars and TVs, which cost as much in Mexico as they do in the United States. But lower-middle-class families may still employ cheap household help. Often they are better off than their income indicates: Many civil servants (and some unionized workers) enjoy government benefits like subsidized housing, pensions, free medical care, even coupons to exchange for food. Such families are part of the richest fifth: better off than the other 80 percent of all Mexicans.

Prosperous business owners, the top managers of Mexico's small number of big businesses, top bureaucrats, and well-off professionals make up the Mexican upper middle class. Though they earn less than $60,000 a year, they can afford a suburban middle-class life similar to that of their counterparts in the United States. Their children go to private schools and universities and are taught to be conscious of proper language and manners (Rudolph, p. 113).

Bernardo and Francesca's Story: The Family Business

Francesca Guzmán leaves the office early to take her two children to the dentist. She drives the family Ford up the hill to their home in a new suburb of Mérida. The house has four bedrooms and two baths, a modern kitchen, a stereo, and a two-car garage. When she thinks of how hard her mother worked in the fields all her life, she is very grateful for her luxurious life. But Francesca has one regret: She always wanted a big, noisy, lively family, like the one she grew up in. She could still have more children, but Francesca knows that in today's world, her children will need college education, even graduate school, and she and her husband Bernardo have decided to limit the size of their family so they can afford the best education for their children.

Also, Francesca recognizes that she is needed in the factory, where she runs the office. Bernardo and Francesca have built up the custom ironwork business, growing along with the city of Mérida. However, as Francesca would be the first to point out, they couldn't have done it without Bernardo's older brother, the accountant, who lent them the capital to get started and found them contacts through his business connections. Francesca and Bernardo are proud of what they have accomplished: They have a thriving business, a new home, with a maid and a cook; they take vacations at the beach, support Francesca's mother, and pay for her youngest sister's tuition at the university. They hope to send their own children to college in the United States.

The Lower-Class Way of Life

You have to admire the resourcefulness, tenacity, and hard work with which **lower-class** families struggle to put together sufficient income to survive. There is no "safety net" to fall back upon: no welfare, no unemployment insurance, no social security pensions. People can rely only upon their families and their networks of patrons and friends.

If a family has more than one adult wage earner, a favored strategy is for one person to find a job for wages—in a factory, as a bus driver, or even a teacher. Such jobs often pay no more than one minimum wage, but they are desirable if they carry health benefits, pension, and access to other government subsidies. Other family members look for work in the **informal sector,** where there is a chance of earning more, but no benefits. (See Hellman, especially pp. 220–221, for discussion of "survival strategies.")

The Informal Sector. One important difference between Mexico (and other "developing" nations) and the "developed" industrial nations is that many Mexicans lack "formal" paying jobs in business or government. Many are "informally" self-employed in tiny businesses which usually have no employees or employ other family members working without wages. These businesses have no official licenses and pay no fees or taxes. Russell estimates that more than a quarter of the Mexican labor force is self-employed in this way. Often people work for wages when they can, but if they are laid off they hustle work until they can find employment again. Many peddle goods or services from place to place (Russell, p. 59; Castells and Portes, pp. 11–37).

There are few chain stores or chain restaurants in Mexico, but lots of "Mom and Pop" groceries and cafés. Outdoor markets are crowded with stalls selling fruit and candy, cooked food, appliances, new and used clothing, and anything else you might want. In sidewalk workshops people make and sell shoes; they print stationery and business cards; they sew dresses. On a busy street or square you can buy a song from a mariachi band, have your shoes shined, hire a child to watch your car, or watch a sword swallower or fire-eater who hopes for your tip. In Mexico City, 2500 people work as garbage pickers, sorting through the city's huge garbage dump for recyclable materials to sell. (Incidentally, most of these "informal sector" occupations can't be adopted casually. The market or the street corner or the dump has its boss, and you must pay him or her for your spot. You will become his client and he will try to provide you some protection from shakedowns by police and competition from other peddlers.) Struggling for a livelihood, poor Mexicans find every possible niche in the economy. You can see how tempting jobs in the drug trade would be to impoverished Mexicans, but remember that people from every class—from the poorest, unemployed workers to the highest judge—get involved with narcotics trafficking.

Absolute Poverty. The bottom line for Mexican families is that if they cannot somehow earn enough for necessities, they will simply have to do without. If they cannot afford rent, they will live in a shack in a squatter settlement, without electricity, running water, or sewage pipes. In 1989 52 percent of Mexicans had no running water or toilets in their house. It is usual for the families of an apartment building or a squatter neighborhood to share a single water tap which runs continually. Often there is a rotating schedule for filling each family's containers at the tap: today your turn may come at 3 A.M. (Hellman, p. 15). Less money frequently means less food: 20 percent of Mexicans eat no eggs or meat; 40 percent never have milk. In the poorest Mexican states 80 to 90 percent of the population doesn't eat eggs, meat, or milk (Hellman, p. 15). When you learn about the poorest Mexicans, the term **life chances** really becomes vivid. Lack of food results in malnutrition for children and mothers, weakening their health. The poorest Mexicans also lack access to good medical care, which results in high infant mortality rates. (See Table 2.1, p. 96.)

The Way of Life of the Rural Poor

So far, we have been describing the lives of poor people in urban areas, but actually more than half of Mexico's poor families live in the countryside. A quarter of Mexicans depend on agriculture for a living (compared to less than 3 percent in the United States). The southern agricultural states of Chiapas, Oaxaca, Campeche, Yucatán, and Quintana Roo are the poorest in the nation. (See Table 2.2, p. 96.)

TABLE 2.1. Death and Hunger 1990–1995:
The poverty of Mexicans and Egyptians is reflected in frequent infant deaths
and the chronic hunger of mothers and children.

	Infant Deaths for Every Thousand Live Births	Malnourished Children (Per 100 Children under 5)	Malnourished Mothers (Per 100 Mothers Giving Birth)
Egypt	67	25	10.4
Mexico	36	13	12
USA	8.8	6.3	6.9
Japan	4.3	3	5.7
Germany	6.3	Data not available	6

Source: World Health Organization, http://who.int/whosis/hfa, 1996

TABLE 2.2. Men and Women Working in Agriculture and Their Families:
The number of Mexicans and Egyptians working the land has increased.
At the same time the agricultural populations of Egypt and Mexico
have decreased as a percent of their total population.

	Men and Women Working in Agriculture and Their Families 1950	Agricultural Families as a Percent of the Total Population 1950	Men and Women Working in Agriculture and Their Families 2000	Agricultural Families as a Percent of the Total Population 2000
Egypt	15,400,000	71%	24,900,000	37%
Germany	15,800,000	23	2,100,000	3
Japan	39,400,000	47	5,100,000	4
Mexico	17,500,000	63	23,500,000	24
USA	21,700,000	14	6,200,000	2

Source: Food and Agriculture Organization, On Line FAOSTAT Database http://apps.fao.org

Félipe's Story: The Peasant

Félipe Vásquez is starting to feel desperate about his future. He is only 23, but he has already tried three different ways of earning a living. Félipe's parents in the tiny ejido of Santa Maria Tepayac in the State of Chiapas had been making a bare living raising coffee beans on their five acres, which they sell to the government warehouse in San Cristóbal de las Casas. When he was younger, Félipe assumed he too would make a life working on the ejido. But then, in 1989, when the government turned the coffee business over to the private sector, coffee prices plummeted. The price they offered his parents for their coffee crop was laughable: Their whole harvest brought in just $300, less than a dollar a day. Félipe went to stay with a cousin in San Cristóbal to look for paid work to help his parents, but all he could get was occasional day labor, at the minimum wage. At that rate, he could hardly help his parents, let alone marry his fiancée Juana.

This *colonia populare*, or squatter settlement, is located in Tijuana, close to Mexico's border with the United States. Like half of all Mexicans, the residents have built their houses themselves, in this case out of cast-off industrial byproducts—used plywood and surplus sheet metal. Assembly plants provide jobs for the inhabitants of the *colonia*, but little else. As you can see, the roads are unpaved. There is no sewage system and no running water.

So when he was 20 Félipe went to the United States with his cousin who had been there before. He worked in California harvesting vegetables. He was actually able to save money to send home to his parents, but he hated the life. People treated the Mexican laborers like animals! And the wealth and luxury he saw around him electrified him. At home everyone was poor. He had no idea such wealth existed in the world. After three years he went back home, afraid Juana would tire of waiting and marry someone else. He found his village and the whole state in an uproar. Some of the men were calling themselves "Zapatistas." They had dug up their old rifles and forced out the Velasco de Leóns, the biggest landowners around, taking over their good, fertile land for the ejido. Félipe could scarcely restrain himself from joining them. That land once belonged to his people and the government had never acted on their claims. If they had the land back, he could marry Juana and they could live decently. But his father was furious and shouted at him that the rebels would bring death and destruction upon them all. (See DePalma, Feb. 2, 1994, p. 2, for discussion of coffee producers.)

A third of the people living in poverty in rural areas work their own farms or *ejido* plots. They produce most of the food they consume: corn tortillas and beans and possibly eggs, chicken, and pork. Any surplus they sell for cash. A small percentage of households (3.2 percent) are really living outside the modern money economy: the value of what they grow for their own use exceeds their money income. Two-thirds of the rural poor have no land. They work for the large landowners, increasingly as seasonally employed migrants, moving around the country from harvest to harvest, living in shacks in the fields, and often paid less than the minimum wage (Russell, pp. 71, 79; Rudolph, pp. 125–126).

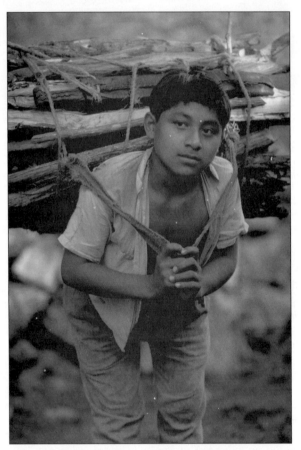

The extreme poverty of rural Mexico forces many Mexicans to migrate to the cities or to the United States. Those who remain exploit themselves and their environment to survive. The cutting of forests for firewood has left the land open to erosion, making it even more difficult to make a bare living by farming. This young man lives in the Yucatán, not far from the resorts of Cozumel and Cancun.

Historically, rural Mexicans have tried to improve their lives through political action, supporting the Mexican Revolution and then petitioning the government to create or expand *ejidos*. Though the government was obligated under Article 27 of the Constitution to redistribute land to any Mexican who would work it, after Lázaro Cárdenas, government enthusiasm for this commitment weakened greatly. *Ejidos* were created on the poorest land: steep, rocky, and dry. Although it was forbidden to sell *ejido* land, many peasants found their only alternative was to enter into arrangements with landowners in which they lost control of their land and had to work it as employees. Many found that as the fertility of their land decreased, and their families grew, they could no longer make a living off the land.

Population Growth and Rural Poverty

The problems of poor, rural Mexicans have been exacerbated by rapid population growth. Stagnant for centuries, Mexican population growth took off after World War II. There were approximately 28 million Mexicans in 1950, 35 million in 1960, and 70 million in 1980. Population growth is slowing now; there were 99 million Mexicans in 2000.

As population grew, rural Mexicans found themselves with limited alternatives. Poor families didn't have enough land to divide among all their children. As a result, the number of landless peasants who had to work for wages also grew. Large-scale commercial farming created some jobs, but it also damaged the land by pouring unregulated pesticides and other chemicals over it and by draining rivers and groundwater for irrigation. When peasants tried to remain on their own land, they often caused environmental damage too, by clearing more and more of the infertile common lands, formerly considered unsuitable for farming. In poverty-stricken Chiapas, so much of the rainforest has been cleared that the border with forested Guatemala is visible from space. Overall, rural population in Mexico has increased about 30 percent since 1940. The percentage would be higher, were it not for the fact that so many rural Mexicans have left the countryside and moved to the cities or across the border to the United States. (See Table 2.3, p. 100.)

Migration and Emigration

Since the 1940s, rural Mexicans have been flocking to the cities in search of work. Fifty years ago, 57 percent of Mexicans lived in rural areas and 43 percent lived in towns and cities. Today, only 26 percent live in the countryside and 74 percent live in urban areas. Mexico City's population is now twenty times greater than it was in 1950; approximately 20 million people are living today in and around the capital. (See Table 2.4, p. 100 and also see Table 4.3, p. 198).

Millions of Mexicans from both rural and urban areas have moved even further, emigrating temporarily or permanently to the United States. In 1942 the United States and Mexico established the Bracero Program which formalized what Mexicans had been doing all along—crossing the border to do seasonal agricultural work in the United States. Under the Bracero Program thousands of Mexicans filled wartime labor shortages, picking vegetables and fruit, especially in California, Oregon, and Washington, moving north with the harvest. When the program was terminated in 1964, Mexicans continued to migrate north, often seasonally, returning

TABLE 2.3. Total Population Growth 1950–2000:
Mexico and Egypt have tripled their populations in 50 years.

	Total Population, 1950	Total Population, 2000 (estimated)	For Every 100 People in 1950, Today (2000) There Are:
Egypt	21,800,000	68,100,000	310
Germany	68,400,000	82,700,000	120
Japan	83,600,000	126,400,000	150
Mexico	27,700,000	98,900,000	360
USA	157,800,000	277,800,000	180

Source: Food and Agriculture Organization, On Line FAOSTAT Database http://apps.fao.org

TABLE 2.4. Urban Population Growth, 1950–2000:
Mexico and Japan are significantly more urban today than they were 50 years ago.

	Urban Population, 1950	Urban Population as a Percent of the Total, 1950	Urban Population, 2000	Urban Population as a Percent of the Total, 2000
Egypt	6,800,000	31	31,300,000	46
Germany	49,200,000	72	72,400,000	88
Japan	42,100,000	50	99,700,000	79
Mexico	11,800,000	43	73,600,000	74
USA	101,200,000	64	214,500,000	77

Source: Food and Agriculture Organization, On Line FAOSTAT Database http://apps.fao.org

home in time for spring planting. For those who crossed illegally, there was a whole border industry of guides, called *coyotes,* who charged a fee to see an immigrant safely across to the United States and often into the hands of a crew boss who transported the immigrant to his or her first job.

By the 1990s, emigration patterns had changed somewhat. The U.S. government no longer welcomed Mexican immigrants. The border was militarized, fenced and patrolled by agents of the Immigration and Naturalization Service. It became harder for Mexicans to make repeated short stays, so immigration became more permanent. The "amnesty" offered to illegal immigrants as part of the Immigration Reform and Control Act of 1986 helped as many as 3 million Mexicans become American citizens and make their homes permanently in the United States.

Mexicans in the United States. Today, the Mexican government estimates that there are 10 million Mexicans living in the United States, about 10 percent of Mexico's population. Perhaps two and a half million of these are "undocumented," that is, they have no immigration documents and would be arrested and deported if found by the INS. The United States Census Bureau counted 6,679,000 people who were born in Mexico living in the United States in 1996 and reported that 1,838,000 Mexican immigrants arrived between 1990 and 1996. Three-quarters of all Mexicans in the United States live in seven states: the border states of California, Texas, and Arizona, nearby Colorado, and also Illinois, Georgia, and New York (Dillon, Dec. 7, 1998, p. A3; US Current Population Survey Report).

Its not hard to understand how Mexicans came to be concentrated in so few states. Sociologists call the process **chain migration.** Mexicans, like other immigrants before and since, use their social networks when they immigrate. They go where a brother, cousin, or neighbor has already settled and can put them up while they look for work, or help them find a job. Sometimes many Mexicans from a particular village or city will be found living in one American town. For example, at least 3,000 Mexicans have settled in Poughkeepsie, New York, a Hudson River mill city north of New York City. Hundreds of them are from one small Mexican village, San Agustín Yatareni, outside the city of Oaxaca. At some times of the year, a quarter of the adult men from San Agustín are in Poughkeepsie (Berger, Jan. 7, 1999, pp. B1, B8).

Mexicans in the United States work as migrant farmworkers, as laborers—in lawncare crews, in restaurants and construction. Some work in factories or as maids. Even at minimum wages, they can make many times more than Mexican wages. They send at least $2 billion a year home to Mexico, helping their families buy seeds and fertilizer, building materials to improve their house, a sewing machine to start a business, or tuition to send a sibling or child to school. Immigrants also join together to improve their villages in Mexico, paying for construction work on the village church or school, for electric lines or water pipes (Dillon, Jan. 7, 1998, p. A3; Payne, p. 69). (See Table 4.5, p. 211.)

Racial Inequality in Mexican Society

Mexico is a racially diverse society, and it began as a **caste** society: one in which everyone was racially classified at birth and race determined people's rights and obligations. Modern Mexico has explicitly rejected caste structures. Race consciousness has been greatly reduced, but there are still racial inequalities.

Race and Class in Colonial Mexico

Colonial Mexico was a society of vast inequalities, in which a person's status was set mostly by race, but also by wealth. Most basically, there was a three-level pyramid, with whites at the top, followed by *castas* (mixed bloods) in the middle, and Indians at the bottom, with blacks (originally brought to Mexico as slaves) even below them.

Whites, while they dominated colonial society, were never more than a tiny minority of the Mexican population. In 1570 there were approximately 7,000 Spaniards and 3½ million Indians. In fact, during the whole three centuries of colonial rule, no more than about 300,000 Spaniards ever came to Mexico. The *conquistadors* took Indian mistresses as soon as they arrived, fathering the growing *casta* population. By 1810 Indians were approximately 60 percent of the population, and people of mixed race nearly 40 percent (Ruiz, p. 85; Kandell, p. 213).

The colonial administration, highly race-conscious, tried to classify and regulate Mexico's varied people. A person born of Indian and white parents was a *mestizo;* someone of mixed black and white ancestry, a *mulato.* A person classified as Indian was entitled to a share in village communal lands, but couldn't own land as an individual. A person of African and Indian parents could not be enslaved, but had no rights to communal lands. Every racial category had a different legal standing.

But as time went on, *criollos* (whites born in Mexico) mixed with *mestizos,* with Indians who had left their communities, and with the descendants of African slaves. People came to call all poor urban dwellers *mestizos,* so the word became social, rather than racial in meaning. Today, a person stops being an Indian and becomes a *mestizo* through a social change of identity, by adopting the Spanish language and western dress.

The Revolution and Mexican Identity

After the 1910 revolution, Mexican intellectuals embarked on a period of intense soul-searching about their national identity. They rejected the idea that Mexico should try to be like a European country, and began to find value in their Indian past. A very influential essay by José Vasconcelos (1882–1959), *La Raza Cósmica* (*The Cosmic Race*) praised Mexico's mixed-race character as a crowning achievement in world history, forging from the world's four races (whites, blacks, Asians, and Indians) a new "fifth race" (Russell, p. 172). The revolutionary murals of Diego Rivera depict Mexicans as proud brown-skinned people, and a plaque at Tlatelolco Plaza proclaims: "On August 13, 1521, heroically defended by Cuauhtémoc, Tlatelolco fell into the hands of Hernán Cortés. It was neither a triumph nor a defeat: it was the powerful birth of the mestizo nation that is Mexico today" (quoted in Riding, p. 3).

Race in Mexico Today

In Mexico today school textbooks and politicians proudly depict the *mestizo* as the ideal Mexican. The PRI reminds Mexicans that it is the party of the Revolution, still carrying the banner of a multi-racial Mexico. Mexican society doesn't force people to choose between polar racial identities: Anyone can adopt a *mestizo* identity. In its official census, the Mexican government does not ask people to classify themselves by race, a practice it says is racist. No data is collected on the percentages of Mexicans of different races and their residences, occupations, incomes, education, and so forth. Indians are recognized as a culturally distinctive group, but blacks, who are viewed as culturally identical to other Mexicans, are not recognized as a minority group (Russell, p. 95).[1] In general, in Mexico, as in other Latin American societies, skin color is viewed as an individual rather than a group attribute. Individuals may be lighter- or darker-skinned. Even within a family, one sister may be described as "white" and another as "black" without their feeling they belong to different racial groups.

---

[1]Sociologists have had to estimate the percentage of Mexicans of different races. Russell suggests that Mexico's population is now 79 percent *mestizo,* 15 percent Indian, 5 percent white, and less than 1 percent black or Asian (p. 95).

But while government policies have minimized race consciousness in Mexico, racial inequalities persist. The government's refusal to collect data about race makes it hard to document racial inequalities that obviously exist. There is a strong association between skin color and status, and skin color and wealth. Whiteness is admired: *la güera* ("the blonde") is the ideal of feminine beauty, seen in advertisements, on television, and in the movies. Light skin and European features are associated with wealth and success; government officials and corporation executives look European. Dark skin is associated with Indians, with poverty, ignorance, and dirt. To call a person an *Indio* (Indian) is an insult. Cuauhtémoc Cárdenas, opposition candidate in the 1988 and 1994 presidential elections, was the first candidate to be seen in decades with dark skin and Indian features.

Indian Minority Groups. While Mexico collects no statistics about people who are racially Indian, data is available about people who speak Indian languages. In 1990 the Mexican census recorded about 7 million people (or 8 percent of the population) who spoke 55 different Indian languages and dialects. The largest language groups were the Zapotec (512,000 speakers) living in Oaxaca and neighboring Guerrero and Puebla, the Maya of the Yucatán (with 740,000 speakers), the Totonac of Puebla and Veracruz (with 256,000 speakers), the Mixtec, living chiefly in the State of Oaxaca (with 230,000 speakers), and the Nahua, Mexico's largest indigenous group, of 1,687,000 members, speaking the language of the ancient Aztecs (Grimes, http://www.sil.org/ethnologue/countries/Mexi.html).

Indians are much more likely than non-Indians to live in rural areas, and they are more likely than other Mexicans to be self-employed peasant farmers. They are also much poorer than other Mexicans. Of Indians living in Indian counties 77 percent earn less than the minimum wage (compared to 27 percent of all Mexicans). Their median monthly income is only $30. Half live in houses without electricity, 90 percent have no indoor plumbing, and 45 percent are illiterate (Russell, pp. 125–128).

Rural Indians are much more likely than non-Indians to use their land for subsistence farming, growing their own food and minimizing their involvement in the modern money economy. While they would like to be better off economically, they greatly value their land, and their ability to maintain a traditional identity in an Indian community. They would be glad to have more land and better land, but they are reluctant to sell or leave their land for wages elsewhere (Russell, pp. 129–130).

SOCIAL CHANGE AND MEXICO'S FUTURE

Mexico is now in the midst of serious political and economic change. It is not clear what the outcome will be, either for the continued dominance of the PRI, or for the economy and the impoverished Mexican majority. Current changes have their roots in the crises of the 1970s and early 1980s. So to understand social change in Mexico today, you must know something about events of the past 20 years. Then you will see that political change and economic change have been closely linked in Mexico and that possibilities for the future are constrained by the world economy and by problems of poverty and corruption.

Protectionism and the Crisis of the 1980s

For 40 years, starting in the 1940s, **protectionism** and the power of the PRI went hand in hand. Protectionism, or "import substitution," was a development strategy in which the Mexican government used high tariffs and import licenses to keep out foreign goods. This helped Mexican industries grow and sell their goods at home. The government gave new companies loans and tax exemptions and it restricted the number of companies competing in any one industry—all to help the domestic economy grow (Hellman, p. 8). The government itself became a major industrialist and employer, operating railroads, the oil industry, telephone service, and thousands of smaller companies. Business owners and employees who benefited from these policies, and all Mexicans who saw their standard of living rise in what was called the "Mexican miracle" of successful industrialization, felt grateful to the PRI.

Protectionist policies were very successful for thirty years, but they began to run up against their limits by the end of the 1960s. It was easy to produce simple goods, like beer or shoes, locally, at affordable prices, but substituting Mexican-made televisions or computers for imported ones was more difficult and expensive. So economic growth slowed down. It slowed for another reason too: Lack of competition led to growing inefficiencies. Industries protected by tariffs, government regulations, or corruption were not driven by international competition to stay lean: They used old machinery, or old methods, or more workers than they needed, and the quality of their products deteriorated. People in other countries bought fewer Mexican products and by the mid-1970s, more money was leaving Mexico than was coming in from exports (Selby, Murphy, and Lorenzen, p. 65). As the economy slowed, the PRI found itself in a bind: Government revenues decreased, so the PRI had less to spend on benefits (like roads, schools, hospitals, and other public works that created jobs) to be channeled down to party supporters. Just when economic slowdown made Mexicans demand more government help, the PRI could afford less!

The Oil Boom and Bust

But then a miraculous thing happened: vast new reserves of oil were discovered in Mexico. Gleefully the PRI and the Mexican people saw before them a bonanza, a resource that would bring in endless revenues from sales abroad. The government borrowed freely from foreign banks to set up the oil industry, and it borrowed more for other spending to keep Mexicans happy while the oil industry was starting up. In the early 1970s, oil poured revenues into government coffers, and government spending in every area soared.

Then, in 1982 oil prices plummeted worldwide and Mexico found itself in a debt crisis. There was insufficient revenue to pay the interest on loans. The International Monetary Fund required, as a condition of refinancing Mexico's foreign debt, that the government embark on an austerity program, cutting state spending in every area. Without loans and subsidies, companies collapsed and at least 800,000 jobs were lost, at the same time that government social spending was cut. Inflation rose and the standard of living of most Mexicans fell drastically, as real wages dropped 40 percent in just five years (Hellman, pp. 8–9). Now the PRI was in trouble again. People were suffering the worst economic crisis in many decades and the party could not increase government spending to help. To ordinary Mexicans it looked like the PRI wanted to keep them in line, without giving them any benefits. People became cynical about the PRI and its organizations, and about politics in general.

The New "Free-Market" Mexico

After 1982, continuation of the old protectionist economy was impossible. But the PRI needed to find a new way to rescue Mexico from economic crisis in order to remain in power. PRI leaders found their new strategy in the **"neoliberal"** policy of **free-market development.** This has meant opening the Mexican economy to the world market, getting rid of tariffs designed to protect Mexican manufacturers and price controls designed to prevent inflation, selling off government-owned companies to private investors, and reducing government involvement in both economic regulation and social welfare. Signing NAFTA (the North American Free Trade Agreement) in 1993 was part of this development strategy. Salinas and other young PRI leaders were schooled in **neoliberal** economics in U.S. universities, but in any case this policy was the orthodoxy of the 1980s and 1990s, triumphant as Soviet socialism collapsed. A free-market orientation would have been demanded by international banks and development agencies even if Mexico's leaders had not advocated it.

President Carlos Salinas and President Ernesto Zedillo after him created new "free-market" economic institutions for Mexico. They offered foreign (mainly U.S.) companies favorable conditions for locating factories in Mexico, ended the government's old commitment to protect peasant farms, and, after the 1995 peso devaluation, they adopted the International Monetary Fund's "structural adjustment program" (cutting government spending, raising taxes and prices, and restricting credit) as the condition of bailout loans (Ramirez, p. 8; Otero, pp. 320–321).

NAFTA

NAFTA is probably the best-known part of Mexico's new free-market economy. NAFTA (the North American Free Trade Agreement) is a trade treaty that links Mexico with its two wealthy northern neighbors, the United States and Canada. NAFTA removed trade barriers so that goods and money could move more freely across borders. NAFTA's advocates argued that freer trade would help all three nations. Mexico would benefit from increased foreign investment, both in Mexican companies and in factories built by foreign companies. That would create more jobs and improve Mexico's trade balance by increasing the amount of Mexican goods imported into the United States and Canada (Burgoon, p. 2). It is clear that NAFTA has resulted in increased foreign investment in Mexico, but there is a great deal of dispute about whether this investment has helped or harmed the country. NAFTA certainly made it easier for narcotics traffickers to move cocaine and money back and forth across the border. Just as clearly, NAFTA helped support the boom in manufacturing along the U.S.–Mexican border.

Maquiladoras

Foreign assembly plants are known in Mexico as *maquiladoras*. Most are owned by U.S.-based multinational firms which send partly finished materials to Mexico for assembly into finished goods. Almost all *maquiladoras* are clustered near the United States–Mexico border so that the materials for clothes or electronics can be sent to Mexico one day and returned to the United States as finished goods on the next. *Maquiladoras* come to Mexico for cheap wages. The average daily wage of *maquiladora* workers (mostly women) in 1998 was $5.00, down from $6.80 in 1992 (Clark; Russell, p. 95). As an additional incentive to build assembly plants the Mexican government made the border a free-trade zone where foreign corporations can operate without taxation. The United States cooperates by charging customs duty only on the amount spent on wages in Mexico, not on the value added to the company's products at the *maquiladora*. Big companies like GE, Zenith, RCA, and General Motors, as well as many smaller businesses, have set up *maquiladoras* in Mexico (Russell, p. 189). While the *maquiladora* program was first begun in the 1960s, its greatest growth has been in the 1980s and 1990s (Russell, p. 195).

Maquiladoras now employ at least 750,000 Mexicans, working in over 2,500 factories (Burgoon, pp. 2–3). *Maquiladoras* exist because Mexicans are so desperate for jobs that they are willing to move to often-desolate border areas, accept low wages, long hours, and frequently unsafe working conditions, just to have a job. *Maquiladora* workers usually live in shantytowns, with unpaved streets, and without running water or sewage systems, because they can't afford to pay rent. Prices on the Mexican side of the border aren't much lower than in the United States, so $5.00 a day won't go far. Most workers in the assembly plants are women in their teens and twenties, some as young as 13 or 14 (Clark, p. 2).

Free-Market Agriculture

During the 1980s, Mexico privatized most of the 1,155 businesses the government once ran. Privatization was part of the neoliberal free-market development policy. Once government-owned businesses were privatized, President Carlos Salinas turned his attention to agriculture. Salinas undertook the most radical changes in Mexican agriculture since the revolution. His purpose was modernization: to replace the inefficient subsistence farmer with modern "agribusiness"—big farm companies, often multinationals—to grow food for export to the world market.

The most radical of Salinas' reforms was the revocation of Article 27 of the Constitution, the article that had promised land to any Mexican who would work it himself, and had protected small farmers by prohibiting the sale of *ejidos*. (If *ejidos* were salable, the old reasoning went, then bad harvests or debt would force peasants to sell them.) The Mexican government had dragged its feet on creation of new *ejidos* for decades. But actually stating categorically that the old *ejido* policy was abolished was a revolutionary step. The *ejido* was a "sacred" symbol of Mexico's commitment to its Indian heritage and to peasants. Many Mexicans who would never benefit from its provisions felt attached to the revolutionary hopes embodied in Article 27.

There has been revolutionary change in Mexican agriculture in the past two decades. More food is being produced, much of it on large, modern farms, many owned by foreign companies. Mexican agriculture now produces more food for export and more grain to feed animals, but production of food for domestic consumption has fallen. Mexico is in the seemingly contradictory situation of no longer being self-sufficient in food, even while foodstuffs are a major export. Rural Mexicans especially (like many people in other third world countries that export food) are eating less and eating worse and experiencing more unemployment (Barkin, pp. 11, 16–22, 28–32; Klein-Robbenhaar, pp. 1–14).

Agricultural modernization has given rise to several practical problems. Agribusiness uses machines and chemicals; it needs far fewer workers than peasant subsistence agriculture. Where will displaced peasants go? Most peasants live in the impoverished south. Will they migrate all the way to the north and take jobs in *maquiladoras?* Will they cross the border, irritating the United States? Will they flock to other Mexican cities where people already lack jobs? Will they stay in the countryside and be content to live on whatever government welfare benefits are made available?

The Crises of the 1990s

Advocates of free-market development have promised Mexicans that the new policies will make Mexico a "first world nation," like the United States, Japan, and the European industrial countries. This promise holds a powerful appeal for Mexicans who know how well people live in the United States, because they have been there or have seen it on TV. The problem is that while free-market modernization may benefit all Mexicans in the long run, in the short run it benefits only large businesses, many of them foreign, and reduces the standard of living of almost all Mexicans. Neoliberals in the PRI have gambled: They have bet that they can make free-market economics produce benefits for many Mexicans before popular discontent overtakes them and forces them from power.

Economic Crises

So far, it doesn't look like their gamble has paid off. Since the adoption of NAFTA in 1993, Mexico has been hit by two economic crises. The first crisis began in December 1994, just as Ernesto Zedillo took office as President. His predecessor, Carlos Salinas, had encouraged foreign investment in Mexican businesses and government bonds, as part of his free-trade development program. The government had actually become increasingly dependent on foreign investments and foreign loans for dollars to balance Mexican imports. But when Mexico became more involved in the world economy, it became more vulnerable to change and crisis in international markets. In December 1994, foreign investors suddenly panicked. They sold their bonds and Mexico found itself with insufficient cash reserves of dollars. The government had to devalue the peso—to set a new, lower, value for pesos in exchange for dollars. After a $50 billion international loan bailout, Mexico's economy seemed to recover quickly. Economic growth resumed, the stock market set records, the peso gained value, and interest rates fell. But for most Mexicans, the effects of the "peso crisis" were long-lasting and severe.

Mexicans found their wages worth less and the price of basic goods much higher. Gasoline prices increased by a third, electricity by 20 percent. The prices of milk and oil and eggs rose sharply. At least 500,000 people lost their jobs, as businesses, lacking customers, collapsed. The value of everyone's wages fell by more than 30 percent. Inflation rose to 42 percent yearly. Even though Mexico's economy was actually much sounder than it had been in 1982, for ordinary people it was 1982 all over again (De Palma, July 16, 1995, pp. F1, F11).

Then, before most Mexicans were able to see any real gains from economic growth, the country was hit by a second international financial crisis in 1998. This crisis really demonstrated the risks of being part of a global economy, because Mexico's economy was essentially sound. Nevertheless, international investors, made jittery by the Asian financial crisis, panicked when the Russian ruble collapsed. Investors pulled their money out of all developing economies and Mexico found itself in a crisis once again, with the value of the peso falling, interest rates rising, and a capital shortage crippling business. Real wages fell again and unemployment rose. Mexico's crisis was made worse by falling oil prices, since oil sales make up a big part of government revenues. Mexicans began to lose faith in their government's ability to pull off a free-market economic miracle. In one survey, 79 percent of respondents said they thought the country was on the wrong track economically (De Palma, Aug. 12, 1997, p. A3; Dillon, Sept. 2, 1998, p. A13).

Mexico's Government: A Crisis of Legitimacy

In Mexico the government and the PRI have long been one and the same. When people lose faith in the government's policies, where do they turn? Mexico's problems have undermined people's trust in the government. This is what Max Weber called a crisis of **legitimacy.** Weber drew a distinction between **power** and **authority.** Power, he said, is just the ability to make people do what you want, even without their consent. If you force them against their will, that is called **coercion.** But when people believe in the right of those who have power to make decisions for others, that is called **legitimacy.** The Mexican government is suffering from a crisis of legitimacy, because many people are asking whether the government plays by the rules, whether it has the right to govern.

The Zapatista Rebels

In 1994, just months before presidential elections, an unknown peasant revolutionary movement in the state of Chiapas (calling itself the Zapatista National Liberation Army) took Mexico by surprise. They seized the state's major city, San Cristóbal de las Casas, and several other villages and towns, installing their own governments, courts, and jails. In the weeks that followed the initial armed attack, peasants in at least a dozen other towns seized their town halls and demanded the removal of local (PRI-selected) authorities. By 1998 Zapatistas ran parallel governments in 33 different villages. Sympathetic protesters held rallies in Mexico City and other cities to support the Zapatistas's demands for honest elections, re-

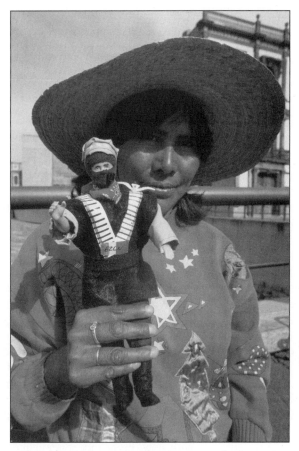

Dolls representing Subcommandante Marcos, the masked spokesman for the Zapatista rebels in Mexico's southern states, sell briskly in cosmopolitan Mexico City. For many Mexicans, the Zapatistas are a symbol of opposition to a government that has become increasingly corrupt and indifferent to the suffering of poor and middle class Mexicans.

distribution of land, better treatment of Indians, and government development aid (Golden, Feb. 9, 1994, pp. A1, A9).

The Indian Zapatistas reminded Mexicans of their revolutionary heritage and their national hero, Emiliano Zapata, peasant leader of the 1910 revolution. The Zapatista's masked leader "Subcommandante Marcos" captured Mexicans' affections with his clever manifestos and good humor. He was treated as a celebrity and "Marcos" dolls became the latest hot toy. To avoid alienating voters, Mexico's government agreed to "negotiate" with the Zapatistas, instead of moving against them militarily. But peace talks collapsed in 1996 and since then state and federal governments have been using troops and paramilitary forces to attack Zapatista

villages. The governor of Chiapas declared the Zapatista towns illegal and promised to "eradicate" them. But Zapatista leaders replied that "the federal and state
governments aren't legitimate because they weren't chosen by the people." When
45 Zapatista supporters were massacred in the village of Chenalhó in December
1997 by a paramilitary force allied with the government, the PRI fell further in
public opinion (Wager and Schulz, p. 11; *The New York Times,* Aug. 3, 1998,
p. A22; Preston, May 17, 1998, p. 14; Fisher, Dec. 25, 1997, p. A8).

Electoral Challenges

In a democracy, the legitimacy of the government rests on elections, on public
belief that elections are free and fair and that an official or party that loses an election will follow the law by leaving office and making way for the victor. The legitimacy of Mexico's government is undercut by widespread belief that the PRI has manipulated elections and used force in place of law. It was widely believed that the
PRI cheated in the 1988 election of Carlos Salinas. Before the 1994 election, only
30 percent of Mexicans said they expected an honest election (Riding, p. A17).

In the 1994 presidential election and in state and local elections since then, it
has been critical to the legitimacy of the PRI government that it convince Mexicans to trust their country's electoral system. The government publicized new procedures designed to guarantee the honesty of elections and accepted opposition
party poll watchers and foreign observers. Also, the PRI made a major new
pledge: It promised to share power with any opposition party candidates who were
elected. So far, it appears the PRI has followed through on this pledge to a remarkable degree. It allowed the election of PAN mayors and a governor in northern
states, and of opposition legislators as well. Once in office, President Ernesto
Zedillo continued to share power. He was the first president to invite opposition
legislators to breakfast and lunch. He fired the entire PRI-appointed Supreme
Court and replaced the justices with new, more independent judges. Zedillo appointed the first-ever attorney general from an opposition party. He gave the Mexican legislature more real power and allowed opposition legislators to head congressional committees. Impeachment proceedings were begun against two PRI
governors accused of electoral fraud (De Palma, Aug. 30, 1998, p. 12). Indeed,
PAN and PRD governors have been elected in many states, Cuahtémoc Cárdenas
has been elected major of Mexico City, and opposition parties now control the
lower house of parliament.

Abjuring electoral fraud, the PRI has set about transforming itself into an effective political party, adopting modern vote-getting techniques. The party has
spent millions on advertising and it adopted primaries in some state elections to
reassure voters that elections were not fixed. The PRI flooded Mexican TV with
party ads. It also set up a new government program, the National Solidarity Program, a $3.8 billion per year antipoverty initiative that provides water pipes, elec-
tricity, scholarships, and other benefits to poor communities (especially those in
Zapatista territory), and it has not hesitated to remind voters that the PRI mandated
the largesse. The combination of electoral reform and big spending has definitely
worked for the PRI, which has even regained some governorships. A few years
ago, Mexicans were convinced the PRI would lose in the presidential elections in
2000; now no one is willing to rule out a PRI victory.

A Corruption Crisis

The greatest challenge to PRI legitimacy today is not the economic crisis or the Zapatistas or the growth of opposition parties; it is the growing perception that the PRI is corrupt, that the party has allied itself with drug traffickers, permitted corruption and illegal violence by Mexico's police and military, and that party members have enriched themselves in total disregard of the rule of law. The scandals stemming from Carlos Salinas' presidency will probably last through Ernesto Zedillo's entire presidency. It now appears clear that in 1988, the Salinas campaign received money directly from a Colombian drug cartel, and that Salinas' brother Raúl was given vast sums of money by drug traffickers—perhaps as much as $500 million—who sought the compliance of his brother's administration. Also Raúl Salinas was convicted of the 1994 assassination of a PRI official, José Francisco Ruiz Massieu. In 1998 the governor of the state of Morelos, a prominent PRI politician, was forced to resign amid charges of corruption and association with narcotics traffickers. Police, prosecutors, judges, and special anti-narcotics police squads have all been linked to the drug cartels and discovered taking bribes and kidnapping and assassinating members of rival gangs. No doubt new scandals and new charges are surfacing in Mexico now as you read this chapter.

To its credit, the Zedillo government has permitted investigation of corruption, drug cartel links, and assassinations. These investigations are unprecedented: Never before has a PRI president allowed prosecution of PRI leaders, and especially not at such a high level. "This is a landmark in Mexican history. . . . The lid has been blown off the system," said one American expert, Professor Richard Craig of Kent State University (quoted in Sánchez, p. A12; Golden, Mar. 7, 1995, p. A3).

The Future

Now, more than ever, Zedillo and the PRI and all Mexicans face a terrible dilemma. Will PRI officials be able to bring the promised benefits of a free-market economy to the majority of Mexicans? In the midst of the current financial crisis, their promise to make Mexico a "first-world nation" seems a bitter joke to poor Mexicans.

Further, will the PRI be willing and able to move from one-party patronage politics to multi-party democracy? Will the Mexican government be able to establish its own legitimate authority separate from the identity of the PRI? Will the government be able to win back the loyalty of rebellious, impoverished Indians in southern Mexico? Will it be able to clean up corruption among its elected officials and in its police and judiciary? Will it prove possible to establish any police system safe from corruption by drug money? Both the wealthy industrialized nations of the world and the "developing" third world are watching to see if Mexico's new economic and political strategies will work.

Thinking Sociologically

1. Describe some norms that are important in Mexican culture.
2. Are there any similarities in the roles men are expected to play in Mexican society and in Japanese society? What differences are there?

3. Explain what is meant by the term *reciprocity network,* using examples from Chapter 2. Do people in your society form reciprocity networks? Can you give an example of a reciprocity network from your own experience?

4. Compare the Gómez family household in Mexico (p. 78) with the Sato family household in Japan (pp. 38–39). Which of these does your own household resemble more?

5. Can you explain what political patronage is and how it works? Can you find an example of political patronage in your own society?

6. Look up the most recent data you can find on income distribution by quintiles in your society. Is your society more like Mexico or more like Japan in its degree of inequality?

7. Does the social category of "mixed race" exist in your society, as it does in Mexico, or does everyone have to be classified as belonging to one race or another? Which way of thinking about race would you prefer?

8. Refer to Figure 2.1 (p. 80) and compare the rates of divorce in Mexico and in the United States. Use Chapter 2 and your introductory sociology textbook to help you explain why the divorce rate is so much higher in the United States than in Mexico.

9. What are some of the problems that have caused a "legitimacy crisis" for the Mexican government? Do people in your own society question the legitimacy of the government?

For Further Reading

BARKIN, DAVID, *Distorted Development: Mexico and the World Economy.* Boulder, CO: Westview Press, 1990.

GUILLERMOPRIETO, ALMA, *The Heart That Bleeds: Latin America Now.* New York: Knopf, 1994.

HELLMAN, JUDITH ALDER, *Mexican Lives: Conversations on the Future of Mexico.* New York: New Press, 1994.

KATZENBERGER, ELAINE, *First World, Ha Ha Ha! The Zapatista Challenge.* San Francisco: City Lights Books, 1995.

KRAUSE, ENRIQUE, *Mexico: Biography of Power.* New York: HarperCollins Pubs., 1997.

OSTER, PATRICK, *The Mexicans: A Personal Portrait of a People.* New York: Morrow, 1989.

PAZ, OCTAVIO, *The Labyrinth of Solitude.* New York: Grove Press, 1961.

REAVIS, DICK J., *Conversations with Moctezuma: The Soul of Modern Mexico.* New York: Quill, Morrow, 1990.

SELBY, HENRY A., ARTHUR D. MURPHY, and STEPHEN A. LORENZEN, *The Mexican Urban Household: Organized for Self-Defense.* Austin: University of Texas Press, 1990.

Bibliography

ALARCÓN, NORMA, "Chicana Feminist Literature: A Re-Vision through Malintzin/ or Malintzin: Putting Flesh Back on the Object," in Cheríe Moraga and Gloria Anzaldua, eds., *This Bridge Called My Back: Writing by Radical Women of Color.* New York: Kitchen Table Press, 1983, pp. 182–189.

BARKIN, DAVID, *Distorted Development: Mexico and the World Economy.* Boulder, CO: Westview Press, 1990.

BERGER, JOSEPH, "Detective's Kindness Helps Awaken City," *The New York Times,* Jan. 7, 1999, pp. B1, B8.

BERMAN, PAUL, "Labyrinth of Solitude," *The New York Times Magazine,* Aug. 2, 1998, pp. 50–73.

BLEA, IRENE I., *La Chicana and the Intersection of Race, Class and Gender.* Westport, CT: Praeger, 1992.

BRAGANTI, NANCY, and ELIZABETH DEVINE, *The Travelers' Guide to Latin American Customs and Manners.* New York: St. Martin's Press, 1989.

BURGOON, BRIAN, "The Job-Eating Villain: Is It NAFTA or Mexico's Currency Crisis?" *Dollars and Sense* (July–August, 1996), pp. 12–20.

CASTELLS, MANUEL, and ALEJANDRO PORTES, "World Underneath: The Origins, Dynamics, and Effects of the Informal Economy," in Alejandro Portes, Manual Castells, and Lauren A. Benton, eds., *The Informal Economy.* Baltimore: Johns Hopkins University Press, 1989, pp. 11–37.

CLARK, CAROL, "NAFTA's Effects on Mexico Are Grim," *Greensboro News and Record,* May 31, 1998.

CORNELIUS, WAYNE A., and ANN L. CRAIG, *The Mexican Political System in Transition.*La Jolla, CA: Center for U.S.–Mexican Studies, University of California, San Diego, 1991.

CROSS, JOHN C., *Informal Politics: Street Vendors and the State in Mexico City.* Stanford: Stanford University Press, 1998.

CROSSETTE, BARBARA, "Albright Makes Her U.N. Post a Focal Point," *The New York Times,* Nov. 25, 1994, pp. A1, A14.

DEPALMA, ANTHONY, "In Mexico's Poor South, Coffee Now Blights Lives," *The New York Times,* Feb. 2, 1994, p. 2.

———, "Rage Builds in Chiapas Village Where Land Is Life," *The New York Times,* Feb. 27, 1994, p. 10.

———, "Mexican Women Progress, Slowly," *The New York Times,* Aug. 20, 1994, p. 3.

———, "After the Fall, Two Faces of Mexico's Economy," *The New York Times,* July 16, 1995, pp. F1, F11.

———, "Income Gulf in Mexico Grows and So Do Protests," *The New York Times,* July 20, 1996, p. 3.

———, "Mexico's Recovery Just Bypasses the Poor," *The New York Times,* Aug. 12, 1997, p. A3.

———, "Mexico Says It Has Kidnapper Who Cut Wealthy Victims' Ears," *The New York Times,* Aug. 19, 1998, p. A2.

———, "Mexico's Rookie Deputies Hope for Better Season," *The New York Times,* Aug. 30, 1998, p. 12.

DILLON, SAM, "Stemming Drugs and Graft Is Mexican's Daunting Task," *The New York Times,* Dec. 22, 1997, pp. A1, A12.

———, "With Drugs and Gangs Rife, Mexican Governor Resigns," *The New York Times,* May 13, 1998, p. A10.

———, "Mexico Can't Fathom Its Rising Crime," *The New York Times,* June 28, 1998, pp. WK1, WK4.

———, "Mexico's Radical New Politics: Top Party May Adopt Primaries," *The New York Times,* Jul. 22, 1998, pp. A1, A10.

———, "Governing Party Seems to Hold Pivotal Mexican Statehouse," *The New York Times,* Aug. 3, 1998, p. A4.

———, "Zedillo Tells Mexicans Painful Economic Policies Are Farsighted," *The New York Times,* Sept. 2, 1998, p. A13.

———, "PRI Reverses Fortunes and Wins Crucial Mexican Governorships," *The New York Times,* Nov. 10, 1998, p. A7.

———, "Mexico Weighs Voting by Its Emigrants in U.S.," *The New York Times,* Dec. 7, 1998, p. A3.

DOMINGUEZ, JORGE L., and JAMES A. MCCANN, *Democratizing Mexico: Public Opinion and Electoral Choices.* Baltimore: Johns Hopkins University Press, 1996.

FALICOV, CELIA JAES, "Mexican Families," in Marian McGoldrick, John K. Pearce, and Joseph Giordano, eds., *Ethnicity and Family Therapy.* New York: Guildford Press, 1982, pp. 134–163.

FAOSTAT Database, http://apps.fao.org.

FISHER, IAN, "In Mexican Village, Signs of Death Hang Heavy," *The New York Times,* Dec. 25, 1997, p. A8.

FOX, ROBERT A., and PEDRO SOLIS CAMARA, "Parenting of Young Children by Fathers in Mexico and the United States," *Journal of Social Psychology,* Vol. 137, no. 4 (August, 1997), pp. 489–495.

FUENTES, CARLOS, *The Buried Mirror.* Boston: Houghton Mifflin, 1992.

———, "The Mirror of the Other," *The Nation,* Mar. 30, 1992, pp. 408–411.

GOLDEN, TIM, " 'Awakened' Peasant Farmers Overrunning Mexican Towns," *The New York Times,* Feb. 9, 1994, pp. A1, A9.

———, "Mexican Conflict Heats Up, with Peasants Seizing Land," *The New York Times,* Mar. 14, 1994, p. 2.

———, "Mexican Is Charged with Cover-Up in Brother's Slaying," *The New York Times,* Mar. 7, 1995, p. A3.

———, "In Breakthrough, Mexican Official Testifies in Texas," *The New York Times,* Jul. 15, 1998, pp. A1, A6.

———, "Tracing Money, Swiss Outdo U.S. On Mexican Drug Corruption Case," *The New York Times,* Aug. 4, 1998, pp. A1, A8.

———, "Elite Mexican Drug Officers Said To Be Tied To Traffickers," *The New York Times,* Sept. 16, 1998, pp. A1, A10.

———, "Saying Salinas Aided Traffickers, Swiss Seize $90 Million," *The New York Times,* Oct. 21, 1998, p. A3.

GOODWIN, PAUL, ed., *Global Studies: Latin America.* Guilford, CT: Dushkin Publishing Group, 1991.

GRIMES, BARBARA, ed., Ethnologue. Dallas, Texas: Summer Institute of Linguistics, Inc., 1996. http://www.sil.org/ethnologue/countries/Mexi.html.

GUILLERMOPRIETO, ALMA, *The Heart That Bleeds: Latin America Now.* New York: Knopf, 1994.

GUTMANN, MATTHEW C. *The Meaning of Macho: Being A Man in Mexico City.* Berkeley: University of California Press, 1996.

HELLMAN, JUDITH ALDER, *Mexican Lives: Conversations on the Future of Mexico.* New York: New Press, 1994.

ISAAC, CLAUDIA B., "Class Stratification and Cooperative Production Among Rural Women in Central Mexico," *Latin American Research Review,* Vol. 30, no. 2, 1995, pp. 123–150.

KANDELL, JONATHAN, *La Capital: The Biography of Mexico City.* New York: Random House, 1988.

KLEIN-ROBBENHAAR, JOHN F., "Agro-Industry and the Environment: The Case of Mexico in the 1990s," *Agricultural History,* Vol. 69, no. 3 (Summer, 1995), pp. 395–419.

KRAUSE, ENRIQUE, *Mexico: Biography of Power.* New York: HarperCollins Publishers, 1997.

LEWIS, OSCAR, *Five Families: Mexican Case Studies in the Culture of Poverty.* New York: Wiley, 1959.

———, *Tepoztlán, Village in Mexico.* New York: Holt, Rinehart & Winston, 1960.

LOMNITZ, LARISSA, *Networks and Marginality: Life in a Mexican Shantytown.* New York: Academic Press, 1977.

MADISON, D. SOYINI, *The Woman That I Am.* New York: St. Martin's Press, 1994.

MIDDLEBROOK, KEVIN, *The Paradox of Revolution: Labor, the State, and Authoritarianism in Mexico.* Baltimore: Johns Hopkins University Press, 1995.

MORRIS, STEPHEN D., *Corruption and Politics in Contemporary Mexico.* Tuscaloosa: University of Alabama Press, 1991.

MURPHY, ARTHUR D., and ALEX STEPNICK, *Social Inequality in Oaxaca.* Philadelphia: Temple University Press, 1991.

THE NEW YORK TIMES, "Traffickers Reportedly Donated to Mexicans," Aug. 3, 1998, p. A22.

NOLEN, BARBARA, ed., *Mexico Is People: Land of Three Cultures.* New York: Scribner's, 1973.

OSTER, PATRICK, *The Mexicans: A Personal Portrait of a People.* New York: Morrow, 1989.

OTERO, GERALDO, "Mexico's Political Future(s) in a Globalizing World Economy," *The Canadian Review of Sociology and Anthropology,* Vol. 32, no. 3 (August, 1995), pp. 315–338.

PAYNE, DOUGLAS, "Mexico and Its Discontents," *Harper's Magazine,* April, 1995, pp. 68–74.

PAZ, OCTAVIO, *The Labyrinth of Solitude: Life and Thought in Mexico.* New York: Grove Press, 1961.

PRESTON, JULIA, "1 Blunt Bishop. Pope Steps In. Now There Are Two," *The New York Times,* May 28, 1997, p. A4.

———, "Voters in Mexico Venting Outrage at Ruling Party," *The New York Times,* July 2, 1997, pp. A1, A8.

———, "In Mexico City's War On Crime, Citizens Are Armed and Angry," *The New York Times,* Nov. 7, 1997, pp. A1, A6.

———, "In Mexico City Elected Major Opens New Political Era," *The New York Times,* Dec. 6, 1997, p. A3.

———, "Mexico Sees Both Carrot and Stick Fail in Chiapas," *The New York Times,* May 17, 1998, p. 14.

———, "Mexicans Belittle Drug-Money Sting," *The New York Times,* May 20, 1998, p. A6.

———, "Helmet Instead of Miter for the Bishop of Chiapas," *The New York Times,* May 28, 1998, p. A4.

———, "Under Siege, Zapatistas Keep Their Profile Low," *The New York Times,* Oct. 17, 1998, p. A4.

———, "In Defiance of Reforms, Crime Rises in Mexico City," *The New York Times,* Nov. 17, 1998, p. A3.

RAMIREZ, MICHAEL D., "The Latest IMF-Sponsored Stabilization Pregram: Does It Represent a Long-Term Solution for Mexico's Economy?" *Journal of InterAmerican Studies and World Affairs,* Vol. 38, no. 4 (Winter, 1996), pp. 129–149.

RAMOS, SAMUEL, *Profile of Man and Culture in Mexico,* trans., Peter G. Earle. 1934. Reprint. Austin: University of Texas Press, 1972.

REAVIS, DICK J., *Conversations with Moctezuma: The Soul of Modern Mexico.* New York: Quill, Morrow, 1990.

RIDING, ALAN, *Distant Neighbors: A Portrait of the Mexicans.* New York: Knopf, 1985.

RUDOLPH, JAMES A., ed., *Mexico: A Country Study* (Area Handbook Series). Washington, DC: U.S. Government Printing Office, 1985.

RUIZ, RAMON EDUARDO, *Triumphs and Tragedy: A History of the Mexican People.* New York: Norton, 1992.

———, *On the Rim of Mexico: Encounters of the Rich and Poor.* Westview Press, 1998.

RUSSELL, JAMES W., *After the Fifth Sun: Class and Race in North America.* Englewood Cliffs, NJ: Prentice-Hall, 1994.

SÁNCHEZ, RAY, "Drug Graft Seen in 'Old Mexico,' " *Newsday,* Mar. 13, 1995, pp. A7, A12.

Selby, Henry A., Arthur D. Murphy, and Stephen A. Lorenzen, *The Mexican Urban Household: Organized for Self-Defense.* Austin: University of Texas Press, 1990.

Thompson, Ginger, "Cocaine Doesn't Just 'Transit': Some of It Seeps," *The New York Times,* Jan. 11, 1999, p. A4.

United Nations, Statistics and Indicators on the World's Women, http://www.un.org/Depts/unsd/gender/1-3dev.htm.

U.S. Bureau of the Census, U.S. Current Population Survey Report—The Foreign Born Population: 1996. http://www/census.gov/population/www/socdemo/foreign96.html.

——, International Data Base, http://www.census.gov/cgi-bin/ipc/idsprd.

Van Natte, Don, Jr., "U.S. Indicts 26 Mexican Bankers in Laundering of Drug Funds," *The New York Times,* May 19, 1998, p. A6.

Wager, Stephen J. and Donald E. Schulz, "Civil-Military Relations in Mexico: the Zapatista Revolt and Its Implications," *Journal of Interamerican Studies and World Affairs,* Vol. 37, no. 1 (Spring, 1995), pp. 1–42.

Wolf, Eric, *Sons of the Shaking Earth.* Chicago: University of Chicago Press, 1959.

World Bank, *World Development Report, 1993: Investing in Health.* New York: Oxford University Press, 1993.

World Health Organization, http://who.int/whosis/hfa.1996.

THE KALAHARI DESERT:
LAND OF THE ¡KUNG BUSHMEN

To get to the Kalahari Desert you would fly to the southern tip of Africa, probably to Johannesburg, South Africa—a long day's flight from Toronto or Los Angeles. From there, a local airline will take you north to the edge of the Kalahari. Then you will need to hire a jeep and a guide to reach the ¡Kung.

LOCATION: The Kalahari Desert stretches across much of Botswana. It dips south into South Africa and occupies a small area of Namibia on the west.

AREA: The Kalahari Desert is the size of New Jersey or Wales (8,000 square miles; 23,200 square kilometers).

LAND: It is a dry, sandy plain 4,000 feet high. Scattered trees, a few hills, and mostly dry riverbeds punctuate the rolling grassland.

CLIMATE: Temperatures go as high as 120° F in the summer and as low as 10° F in winter. There is less than 10 inches of rain yearly in most areas.

PEOPLE: There are approximately 30,000 ¡Kung Bushmen today in Namibia and Botswana and as many as 90,000 people speaking various Bushman languages in all of southern Africa.

CHAPTER 3

The ǀKung Bushmen:
An Indigenous People
of Southern Africa

INTRODUCTION

The ǀKung Bushmen are a people sharply different from all the other groups in this book. For centuries, and probably for thousands of years, they have been a **hunting and gathering** (or **foraging**) people who live in small bands of ten to fifty people and gather wild plant foods and hunt game. Systematically moving among food and water sources, the ǀKung are **nomadic:** they make no permanent homes, and carry with them their few possessions. They have no rulers, no schools, no money, no written language, no police, no hospitals, and no inequalities of wealth or privilege. The ǀKung occupied the Kalahari Desert long before black people from southeastern Africa or whites from Europe arrived. Archeologists have found evidence of people like the ǀKung living in this region as long ago as 11,000 years before the present and occupying the area without interruption ever since (Tobias, pp. 4, 30–31).

> *Bumping along sand tracks in the Kalahari Desert in dry season, you will not see the ǀKung Bushman camp until your jeep is almost upon it: a circle of shelters roughly built of sticks and grasses, facing inward toward a cleared area, and almost invisible in the surrounding landscape of dry brush. The full band of perhaps 20 individuals gathers around their campfires. You see small people with yellowish-brown skins, partially clothed in animal hides, blending readily into their environment.*
>
> *It is dusk and they are blowing their fires into flames to cook the evening meal. Women are sorting through their day's collection of wild foods: nuts of the mongongo tree, tsama melons, water-bearing roots, perhaps birds' eggs or a snake, or in a wetter season, wild onions, leafy greens, tsin beans, or baobab fruit. The men have killed a small antelope and they are distributing the meat among their relatives. You may hear many voices: Men tell the story of their hunt, women report on the tracks they have seen while out gathering; people gossip, tease, and joke. You hear the children's games, played to a rhythm of clapping and singing. The ǀKung come forward to meet you, carefully leaving their weapons—their small bows with the lethal poison-coated arrows—behind. They will doubtless invite you to share their food and water, but they will expect you to return their hospitality.*

119

The ¡Kung Bushmen's Environment

The ¡Kung live in the Kalahari Desert of southwestern Africa, a harsh, semidesert environment. Their territory belongs to several African nations, chiefly Botswana and Namibia. The Kalahari Desert is a vast basin of sand, occupying almost a third of the African subcontinent. Much of the Kalahari is too dry to sustain human habitation, but in the more northerly parts, around places like Dobe and Nyae Nyae, where the ¡Kung live, there is enough rain to support drought-resistant plants, grasses, scattered trees, and the animals that feed upon them. There are many kinds of antelope, like eland, kudu, and gemsbok; there are warthogs, hares, and tortoises and also giraffe. (There are predators too, like lions and hyena, but the ¡Kung don't hunt these for food.) The rainy season leaves temporary pools of surface water and greens up the landscape so plants bear fruits, nuts, berries, and seeds. But rains are localized and unpredictable; while some areas receive abundant rainfall, others nearby may suffer drought. The whole region experiences drought approximately two years out of every five, with severe drought one year in four. There are dry riverbeds in the Kalahari, but they are rarely filled by runoff, perhaps only once in a decade. The ¡Kung are sustained during the dry season by a small number of permanent water holes, where underground water comes to the surface.

The Kalahari is "big sky country," flat and monotonous, with endless vistas of brush out to the horizon. Outsiders easily lose their way in the markerless landscape. To this austere landscape is joined a harsh climate. During the hot, dry season of September and October, temperatures reach 115° F in the shade, 126° F in the sun, and the temperature of the sand reaches 140° F. The Kalahari winter of May to August is cold and dry, with nighttime temperatures often below freezing (Marshall, pp. 62–71; Lee, 1979, pp. 87–88).

Who Are the ¡Kung Bushmen?

There are actually several distinct peoples in adjacent parts of Namibia and Botswana who are all considered ¡Kung, though they have different names for themselves. For example, the ¡Kung who live around Nyae Nyae, Namibia, call themselves *Ju /wasi* ("the real people"). All the ¡Kung peoples share a distinctive physical appearance and a common family of languages. The ¡Kung are quite small in stature (the men under 5 feet 3 inches, the women considerably under 5 feet) and they have light brown or "yellow" skin, small, heart-shaped faces with wide-apart eyes, eyefolds, and flat-bridged noses. Physically they are very different from the black Bantu-speaking people of Africa, who are tall and dark-skinned.

All the ¡Kung peoples speak one of three related "click languages," which will probably seem quite unusual to you. Click languages include a dozen or so click sounds, made by clicking the tongue against the teeth, the roof of the mouth, the cheek, and so on, as if you were going "tsk tsk" or signaling to a horse. The clicks usually function as consonants in forming words. The ¡Kung themselves have no written language so only anthropologists have attempted to write down these click sounds and they have developed a system of denoting the different clicks with symbols like these: ¡, /, //. The ¡ in ¡Kung is a click sound.

In southern Africa, the ¡Kung are also linked to other peoples who speak languages unlike their own and who are also somewhat different from them in stature and skin color. These are the Nama-speaking peoples of the Kalahari region and the so-called Cape Bushmen of South Africa. All these peoples (and there are at least 10 distinct groups in all) have been called Bushmen in southern Africa. The name seems to be derived from a Dutch term, *bossiesman,* which means "bandit," and it is an insulting term the early white settlers used to refer contemptuously to the native peoples they found in South Africa who hunted and gathered and who resisted when settlers took their land. Later, the Bushmen were called the *San,* a name used by Nama-speakers, and still later, in Botswana, they have been called *Basarwa,* which means "those without cattle." We have chosen to call the ¡Kung "Bushmen" in this chapter (despite the racist and sexist overtones of the name), because the ¡Kung are now calling themselves Bushmen, emphasizing their ties to hunting and gathering peoples all over southern Africa (Gordon, pp. 4–8; Kelso, p. 51; Wood, personal communication).

Why Study the ¡Kung Bushmen?

Now is the time to ask yourself. "Am I reacting to the ¡Kung in an ethnocentric way?" Are you saying to yourself, "I have nothing to learn from these 'savages' who can't even read and write and go around in animal skins with bows and arrows?" Studying the ¡Kung Bushmen is a good lesson in the advantages of **cultural relativism.** If you can set aside your prejudgment of the ¡Kung as "deprived" or "primitive," you will find out how well their society works to help them survive and prosper in the Kalahari Desert. We think you will find that the ¡Kung have much to teach you: about human history, about living without war or inequality, and about living with nature without destroying it.

The Evolution of Human Societies

Using research by anthropologists, archeologists, and historians, sociologists have concluded that in all of human history there have been just four basic kinds of societies. The first human societies were **hunter-gatherer bands,** like the ¡Kung Bushmen. Humans, and their prehuman ancestors before them, lived like this for hundreds of thousands and perhaps millions of years. They lived in small nomadic bands, following game and harvesting wild foods. It was only about 10,000 years ago that humans learned to raise their own food. They settled down, often along rivers, and made gardens and raised tame animals. These people lived in **horticultural villages.** At about this same time, other peoples began to live as **pastoralists,** herding animals and often moving about with their herds. Approximately 6,000 years ago what we think of as "civilization" began with the invention of agriculture. Agriculture applied new technologies (the plow) and new methods (fertilizing and rotating crops) so people could farm the same fields generation after generation. Farming raised more food and made it possible for some people to live on food others grew. They became artisans, priests, monks and nuns, kings and queens, professional soldiers, sailors, cathedral builders, artists, scientists and inventors, and all the other inhabitants of cities in **agricultural states.** Finally, the most recent type of society to develop (in the last 250 years) is that of **industrial nations,** in which farming has become so productive that most people can devote their lives to other work, producing goods in factories, building large cities, inventing new technologies, waging war, and so forth. All four types of societies still exist today, but there are fewer and fewer hunter-gatherer and horticultural societies.[1]

The Importance of Hunter-Gatherers

Since the first humans were foragers, sociologists and anthropologists have long regarded hunter-gatherer bands as the cradles of human nature and culture. The first families must have been formed in hunter-gatherer bands, the first specialized roles and the first religions. It is easy to speculate (but difficult to prove) that early conditions of foraging bands fundamentally shaped human nature. Those who study hunter-gatherer societies have often asked whether widespread human characteristics—like competitiveness, or aggression—are a heritage from those first societies.

It is difficult to learn much about societies that existed 50,000 or 100,000 years ago, when all the world's peoples were hunter-gatherers. Archeologists dig up fossilized human and animal bones and the remains of hearths and sometimes huts, weapons, garbage heaps, and fossilized pollen, but these remains can tell us little about how people interacted in prehistoric times. To learn about humanity's ancient past, anthropologists and sociologists have turned to hunter-gatherer societies that still exist today. They have hoped that the study of the ¡Kung will open a window on the common ancestors of all humans—the ancient hunter-gatherer peoples.

Hunter-Gatherers and Human Nature

When you study the ¡Kung you must put away stereotyped images of "cavemen" fighting each other in a brutal competition for survival. The ¡Kung are a peaceful people and in this they are quite typical of hunter-gatherers. They avoid conflict and competition and share what they have so that everyone can survive. They have no formal leaders, no privileged class or deprived lower class. They don't hate or fight their neighbors. Though they live in a harsh environment, their lives are not brutal or debased. They value generosity and graciousness, joking and kidding around, and they find plenty of time for relaxation, playing music and singing, dressing up, and holding ceremonial dances, like parties that go on all night. If this is what our earliest ancestors were like, then we cannot blame our own greed and violence on our evolutionary heritage.

Living with Nature

The ¡Kung exemplify a kind of society we may well call the most successful human way of life of all times. The hunter-gatherer life sustained humanity for millions of years. Variations of foraging cultures allowed people to live in many different environments, gentle or harsh: by the shore, in forests, open grasslands, deserts, rain forests, and arctic tundra. Wherever they live, hunter-gatherers live

---

[1]Sociologists owe this commonly used classification scheme to Gerhard and Jean Lenski. See Lenski, Nolan, and Lenski, pp. 78–89.

close to nature: Their food comes directly from nature, and everything they use—houses, tools, clothing, containers, jewelry, and weapons—is made by hand from natural materials. Hunter-gatherers use nature, but they don't use it up. They live in such a way that they don't kill off the animals they depend upon; they don't use up the water or pollute the land. They can go on living on the same land for thousands and thousands of years without harming it. Sociologists call this **sustainability.** In the last 10,000 years, since people learned to cultivate seeds and plants and domesticate animals, human impact on the environment has constantly increased. Industrial society now pollutes the air and water and land. It pumps carbon dioxide into the atmosphere, creating a "greenhouse effect," and it alters ecosystems so many animal species become endangered or extinct. Many people are now asking: Is our industrial way of life sustainable? Perhaps we can learn from the ¡Kung Bushmen about creating an environmentally sustainable society.

HISTORY OF THE BUSHMEN

We know very little about the history of the Bushmen for all the thousands of years before their contact with Europeans in the seventeenth century. There are some artifacts unearthed by archeologists and there are reports by early white settlers about meetings with Bushmen on their arrival in southern Africa, but evidence is very thin. The modern history of the Bushmen, recorded first by white settlers, then by colonial governments, and now by African governments, began in the seventeenth century. It is a tragic story of genocide and displacement.

Settlers and the Bushmen

In the seventeenth century, an estimated 200,000 Bushmen lived all over southern Africa—in the desert, in the mountains, on grasslands, and along the coasts. When the Dutch settled the Cape of Good Hope region at the southern tip of Africa in the 1650s, an indigenous (native) group of Bushmen, called the Khoi, were living there, fishing, hunting, gathering, and herding cattle and goats. Seizing their good land, the Dutch slaughtered the Khoi and drove them northward.

Other groups of Bushmen lived in more remote areas, in small bands and without domesticated animals. The Dutch were especially contemptuous of them and considered them "wild" people, little better than animals. In the eighteenth century, white settlers moved north and almost completely exterminated the Bushmen, killing the men and enslaving the women and children. Some Bushmen fought back, raiding settlers' farms and stealing cattle, and in remote areas they were able to hold off the whites for years. By the end of the nineteenth century, the Bushmen had been virtually wiped out in all of the country of South Africa. Further north, however, in the harsh lands of the Kalahari Desert, where no whites wished to settle, Bushmen continued to live as hunter-gatherers.

In the late nineteenth century, the Kalahari Desert Bushmen came into contact with another group of settlers: Bantu-speaking blacks from southeastern Africa. Relationships between the Bushmen and the Bantu peoples were not always harmonious. Both sides tell stories of armed conflict, cattle theft, and disputes over women, and the Bantu considered the Bushmen an inferior people. However, these forms of conflict have never become as extreme as the European genocide against the Bushmen, and in the twentieth century, trade and intermarriage between Bushmen and Bantu have peacefully developed. As a result of intermarriage, some Bushmen who live along the eastern edge of the Kalahari have come to resemble their Bantu neighbors physically. Two different Bantu cattle-herding peoples, the Tswana and the Herero, settled the margins of the Kalahari. ¡Kung men worked for the Tswana as trackers and porters, and later as cattle herders, receiving tobacco and cow's milk in exchange for seasonal or temporary work. Many ¡Kung, especially in Botswana, became attached to Herero farms, as unpaid dependents (Lee, 1979, pp. 32–33, 77–84; Lee, 1984, pp. 17–18; Lee, 1978, pp. 94–96; Silberbauer, p. 181).

The Fate of Hunter-Gatherers

As recently as 100 years ago, there were dozens of foraging peoples still living in isolation in the most remote corners of the globe—in the deserts of Africa and Australia, the rain forests of the Amazon, Africa, and New Guinea, and the arctic wastes of Canada. Today, the ¡Kung are one of the last surviving foraging groups (along with some Eskimos and some Australian aborigines). Modern societies have not been kind to indigenous foraging peoples. Industrial societies have penetrated every corner of the earth, exploring, searching for precious metals or oil, for trees to log or land to clear for farming and ranching. Everywhere, they have dismissed indigenous hunter-gatherer peoples as subhuman savages. Settlers and explorers have not hesitated to kill indigenous peoples or take away their land, their means of survival. Western diseases spread through indigenous populations in devastating epidemics, and the bewildered survivors were converted by missionaries and enticed or forced into working for the outsiders. Under the assault of modern societies, indigenous cultures all over the world have disappeared. Surviving hunter-gatherers have been forced into the least desirable environments on earth. Even as you read this book, the last of the ¡Kung may be abandoning the foraging life. Your children will grow up in a world in which hunters and gatherers are a lost part of history, not real peoples linking us to the human past.

Today, most ¡Kung work on ranches and farms in Botswana and Namibia. They are the poorest, most despised people in those countries, often earning no wages at all for their work. The ¡Kung have no government of their own, but they live, nevertheless, in a world of modern nations, and government action shapes their lives. For example, when a fence was erected along the border between Botswana and Namibia, customary ¡Kung patterns of gathering and hunting were disrupted. After 1970, in Namibia, the ¡Kung were caught between sides in the war of liberation from South African rule, and recruited by the South African forces as trackers and soldiers. Both Botswana and Namibia have also directly intervened in ¡Kung affairs, taking some ¡Kung lands away and designating special areas where they have encouraged Bushmen to live. In Botswana, the government put thousands of acres of ¡Kung land into a game reserve where the ¡Kung are permitted to live only by hunting and gathering, using traditional weapons. In

Namibia, the government made a special "Bushmanland" reserve for the ¡Kung. There the government has dug wells and built schools, encouraging the ¡Kung to settle in one place and live partly as herders and partly as hunter-gatherers (Lee, 1979, pp. 424-431; 1984, pp. 147–150).

Anthropologists and the ¡Kung Bushmen

The ¡Kung are not only one of the last remaining foraging peoples, they have been studied with exceptional thoroughness. From the early 1950s, through the present, anthropologists, linguists, archeologists, musicologists, and ecologists have almost continuously lived with and observed one or another group of ¡Kung. These social scientists made a very detailed record of ¡Kung life in books and films, which we will draw on in this account.

The first major studies of the ¡Kung were done by Lorna and Laurence Marshall in the 1950s. The Marshalls made many trips to the Kalahari, accompanied by their daughter Elizabeth Marshall Thomas, who wrote a famous book about the Bushmen, *The Harmless People,* and their son, John Marshall, who filmed ¡Kung daily life. In the 1970s, anthropologist Richard B. Lee and his team studied several groups of ¡Kung, as reported in his books, *The ¡Kung San* and *The Dobe ¡Kung.* Today, a new generation of anthropologists has joined those studying the ¡Kung, including John Yellen, Susan Kent, Pat Draper, James Denbow, Edwin Wilmsen, Robert Hitchcock, Robert Gordon, Megan Biesele, and Claire Ritchie. Their primary focus has been on how ¡Kung culture is now changing as the ¡Kung Bushmen settle in villages and adopt cattle herding.

Some present-day anthropologists (like Robert Gordon and Edwin Wilmsen) (Gordon, pp. 1–12, 64–129, Wilmsen, pp. 10–12, 15–32) have questioned the portrait of the ¡Kung Bushmen painted by earlier anthropologists. These scholars, they suggest, were too eager to discover in the ¡Kung an isolated living survival of Stone Age times. They caution that for a long time—perhaps as long as 2000 years—Bantu and Khoi herders lived near Bushmen, and well-used routes for trade in iron, glass beads, and shells passed through Bushman territory. Bushmen, they contend, have long herded animals and traded goods when they could.

This chapter first describes the ¡Kung who live as hunter-gatherers. You must keep in mind that relatively few ¡Kung still follow this way of life today—only a few thousand, at most. Even in the 1950s and 1960s, when there were many more people living the traditional foraging life, the ¡Kung were not fossils of the past. Prehistoric hunter-gatherers lived in a world of hunter-gatherers. Then, the whole world was wilderness; there were no towns, no stores, no roads, no lands cleared for farming. Small bands of people traveled about following game and harvesting wild plants, and meeting another band was a rare and important event. Nowadays, humans are so numerous they are crowding out other species, and the remaining wilderness shrinks year by year. It is difficult to picture a time when the total human population was small and its survival insecure. We can use our knowledge of present-day hunter-gatherers to help us picture the past, but we must remember that the ancient world of foragers is gone. Today, hunter-gatherer peoples are surrounded by more modern societies and often exploited by them.

¡KUNG CULTURE: A DESIGN FOR LIVING

You can do a brief "thought experiment" to help you understand ¡Kung culture. Imagine yourself and your friends suddenly transported to the Kalahari Desert and abandoned there. Will you survive? Unlike the animals of the Kalahari, you will not know instinctively how to find water or food or shelter, how to avoid poisonous snakes and lions, or how to organize your group life. You will lack special physical adaptations to desert life. Your evolved human capacity to create culture will have to see you through.

The ¡Kung, like all human societies, have learned how to secure the necessities of life. They divide up their tasks efficiently. They have learned to keep order, resolve conflicts, and protect the group from outside threats. Their beliefs about the meaning of life sustain them. Even reproduction is not just left to nature; the ¡Kung make sure they have enough children, but not too many, and they teach their children how to live in their society and their difficult environment.

Sociology textbooks often adopt anthropologist Clyde Kluckhohn's definition of **culture** as "a design for living." Every human group must solve the basic problems of adapting to their environment: groups do so through **culture** and **social structure,** and if they are successful, the group survives. But there are many possible "designs for living."[2]

Foraging: A Successful Cultural Adaptation

Even in their harsh environment the ¡Kung have found a way to live that is environmentally sustainable, psychologically rewarding, and physically healthy. Four elements of ¡Kung culture make possible a more than adequate living in the Kalahari Desert. These are: the ¡Kung's comprehensive **knowledge** of their environment and its food sources; the custom of **nomadism,** or movement from one temporary encampment to another; customs of childbearing and childrearing that result in **population limitation;** and **values** that stress sharing, modesty, and cooperation.

Knowledge

Foremost in importance is the ¡Kung's detailed knowledge of their environment, itself a form of control over nature. Knowledge of plants, water sources, and animal habits enables the ¡Kung to use the desert as a larder, neither cultivating nor storing food, but rather turning systematically from one resource to another, each in its season. To some degree, knowledge is gender-based, since women gather plants and men hunt animals, but both women and men have some basic store of knowledge about animal tracks and plant properties.

¡Kung hunters are superb trackers. Not only can they identify animals from their tracks in the sand and their droppings, they are able to deduce detailed information from tracks. They can single out the tracks of a single animal (perhaps the

---

[2]See, for example, the chapters on culture in *Sociology* by Gelles and Levine, which begin with discussion of Kluckhohn's 1949 book, *Mirror for Man* (New York: McGraw-Hill, 1949) (Gelles and Levine, p. 84).

one injured by an arrow) from those of a herd, tell if it is male or female, old or young, whether it is injured and how badly. Examining the freshness of tracks, ¡Kung men can deduce how long ago an animal passed, whether it was feeding, how fast it was going, whether it passed during the morning or afternoon (Did it seek the shade to the east or west of bushes and trees?) or at night. Both men and women can read human footprints in the sand, identifying the tracks of every individual.

Intimate knowledge of resources makes the foraging life possible. The ¡Kung know and name hundreds of plants, insects, animals, and birds. Tiny ¡Kung arrows derive their lethal power from a poison coating made from the larvae and parasites of three different kinds of beetles.[3] In the dry season, when plants wither to near invisibility, ¡Kung women unerringly locate underground water-storing roots from the evidence of a few tiny leaves hidden in the dry grass. They know exactly when each plant resource will be ready to harvest, under various weather conditions. And they know how much water each permanent and temporary water hole can be expected to provide, so they are never caught short.

Nomadism

The ¡Kung adapt themselves to the desert by living in small **nomadic bands.** The ¡Kung have no permanent place of residence, but they cannot be said to wander either. They move about the desert in a planned, rational fashion, making temporary camps to exploit local resources of water and food, then move on when these become scarce. In the dry season, they retreat to permanent water holes. In this way, the ¡Kung neither wear out nor pollute the desert; they distribute their impact over a wide area.

But nomadism means traveling light. When the ¡Kung move, they carry on their backs all their possessions, plus their young children. In fact, all of a person's belongings can fit into a leather bag the size of an overnight carrier that weighs no more than 12 to 15 pounds. Possessions include a woman's *kaross* (her leather all-purpose garment and blanket), her digging stick, items of personal adornment like beads and headbands, ostrich eggshell water holders, and, nowadays, an iron pot. A man carries his hunting kit—arrows, bow and quiver, and his fire-making kit; other possessions include musical instruments, toys, pipes, ceremonial rattles, tortoise shell bowls, nets, and leather bags. All ¡Kung possessions (except the pot) are handmade and can readily be made anew. Houses are built at each camp out of branches and grasses, and abandoned when the camp is moved. The ¡Kung possess little, but until they become involved in the modern cash economy, they desire no more, and feel no deprivation.

Population Control

Ultimately, the desert can support the ¡Kung because they keep their population proportionate to its resources. In the 1970s, in the central Kalahari, population density was no more than one person per each 4 to 6 square miles! (Silberbauer, p. 184). Significantly, it is a low birth rate, rather than an usually high death rate that keeps

---

[3]The poison acts on the central nervous system, through the bloodstream, so animals killed by the poison can safely be eaten.

A ¡Kung hunter takes careful aim with his bow and arrow. His flimsy-looking arrow has a poison-coated tip and it is made to wound, not kill. Later, when the poison has done its work, weakening the quarry, the hunter will return and make his kill up close with a spear.

the ¡Kung population small. ¡Kung women reach puberty late, and generally don't have their first child until their late teens. Thereafter, children are widely spaced, without modern means of birth control, with an interval of approximately four years between babies. How this spacing is achieved has fascinated anthropologists. Richard B. Lee concludes that the nomadic foraging life and population control are closely linked. ¡Kung women nurse their children for as long as four years, and during that time they carry them everywhere, on daily foraging trips as well as on longer migrations, and they carry them in such a fashion that the child can nurse at will. Nursing is known to inhibit ovulation, but in most societies it is an ineffective means of birth control. Lee argues that ¡Kung babies nurse so frequently that ovulation is more effectively inhibited. ¡Kung women who settle on Bantu cattle ranches or farms carry their babies less and also give birth at more frequent intervals.

The ¡Kung understand the importance of spacing their children: It is very difficult for a mother to carry two children at once and, also, since young children live so entirely on their mother's milk, the ¡Kung believe that if a mother had two babies nursing, her milk would be insufficient and both would probably die. **Infanticide** (the killing of newborn infants) is infrequently practiced, but seen as a possible tragic necessity should a new sibling come too soon after the birth of a baby or in the rare case of twins. Infant and child mortality is high by modern western standards, but not compared to most poor agricultural societies. Close to 20 percent of ¡Kung children die before their first birthday, and only half of those born live long enough to marry (Shostak, p. 182).

The Value of Sharing

Critical to iKung survival is the emphasis they place on sharing. The worst one can say of a person is that he or she is "far-hearted" or stingy. Generosity, graciousness, and modesty are highly valued. Indeed, it would be fair to say that sharing is a subject of constant discussion among the iKung, with the question, "Who will give me food?" always on people's minds.

From the **functionalist perspective,** iKung sharing makes sense; it helps the society to survive. You could say that sharing is the iKung "social security system." They cannot store food for future use and they cannot buy food with money or any other goods, so when food is scarce, life is threatened. A man could be the iKung's best hunter, but if he is injured or falls ill, there is no unemployment insurance or welfare, no savings account or pension plan. He must rely on the people in his family and band to feed him. Everyone needs to help others, so they can be helped in turn. A person who shares gets something else of value in return: prestige or social advantage. A hunter who shares shows he is fit to be a husband, or qualified to be a hunting partner (Roue, p. 24).

Sharing is not only a prime value in iKung culture, it is a constant practice integral to their way of life. Sharing takes place on many levels. The plant foods women gather are cooked and shared with their immediate families. Big game is shared on a wider basis. The hunter to whom the meat belongs cuts it into large chunks and distributes these among his immediate relatives: his wife, in-laws, parents, and siblings. These recipients give some of their share to those who eat at their fire, but they also cut much of the meat into smaller pieces and make presents of these to their relatives, who pass it on in turn to theirs. In the end, everyone in a camp shares the meat, not in a wholesale distribution, but as a personal gift from some connection, and the meat is quickly consumed. The idea of a person hoarding meat is horrifying to the iKung: it seems savage and uncivilized. "Lions might do that; people could not," they explain. Lorna Marshall noted that in one large dry-season encampment, the meat of a single eland (a large antelope) was ultimately distributed to 63 individuals (Marshall, p. 302).

But the iKung struggle with sharing; it doesn't always come easily and sometimes hunger or possessiveness wins out over generosity. People grumble if someone keeps a particularly desirable ornament or tool, instead of passing it on as a gift. Disputes often arise over the sharing of food. iKung customs facilitate sharing by blurring the ownership of meat. Meat belongs not to the man who brings it down, but to the owner of the arrow which first penetrates the quarry. And a hunter will usually carry arrows borrowed or received as gifts from many other individuals in addition to his own. Even a poor hunter may thus come to be the owner of meat, and people will not be put in the position of constantly receiving gifts of meat from the same superior hunter.

Sharing takes place on a wider basis too: between bands as well as within them. Kalahari resources are unevenly distributed, since localized drought may temporarily render one area barren while another is productive. At times like these, whole bands of individual families visit relatives in more fertile or better-watered areas. At another time, when conditions are different, they will reciprocate as hosts. Sharing evens out inequalities among the iKung, between youthful and aging families, between talented and inept hunters, women and men, and people in different areas. Sharing constantly reinstates equality, ensuring that differences in individual ability or luck will not accumulate into institutionalized economic or status stratification.

An Integrated Culture

Knowledge, nomadism, low population growth, and sharing are critical elements of ¡Kung culture. Each supports the other, and all allow the ¡Kung to prosper in their harsh environment. We can say that ¡Kung Bushman society has a high degree of **cultural integration:** The different elements of the culture are consistent and fit together. For example, knowledge about resources, and norms and values concerning sharing make possible the nomadic way of life. Nomadism, in turn, holds down population growth, so the community does not outgrow its resources, or have too many babies to carry. Small, homogeneous, simple societies like the ¡Kung often have a high level of cultural integration.

Internal consistency like this is satisfying: People agree about most things; they share the same values and a single way of life. But integrated cultures are also fragile. Disruption of one of their elements may seriously damage or destroy the whole. For example, when the ¡Kung settle temporarily at Bantu cattle posts, women may have children so closely spaced as to prevent a return to the foraging life. Acquisition of cattle, goats, or chickens makes nomadism difficult too, but water and plant resources may be too scarce to permit settling in one place. Under pressures like these, ¡Kung society is now disintegrating.

How Hard Is the Foraging Life?

Until recently, life in hunter-gatherer societies was believed to be harsh and difficult, with constant labor the only shield against starvation, and population kept from outrunning resources only by famine, disease, and infanticide. In the last few decades, studies of the ¡Kung Bushmen and other foraging societies have resulted in a much rosier view of foraging societies and, by implication, of early human history. One of the most significant new insights is that foragers don't work very hard. In fact, they spend fewer hours working, and enjoy more hours of leisure, than people in agricultural and modern industrial societies. In a typical band observed by Lee, women went out gathering on an average of 9 out of 28 days. Counting all foraging, toolmaking and fixing, and housework, women put in an average workweek of 40 hours. ¡Kung men spent more days in hunting, an average of 12 out of every 28 days, and counting all hunting, gathering, toolmaking and fixing, and housework, their average workweek was 44½ hours. Even at this low level of work, the ¡Kung are generally adequately nourished, and they have infant mortality rates and adult life expectancies somewhat better than those of most agricultural societies.[4]

---

[4]Richard B. Lee collected these data in 1964. See Lee, 1979, pp. 254–280. Lee notes that work in child care was not included in the calculations, but if it had been, the work totals for women would have been considerably higher, since they do 60 to 80 percent of all care of young children.

Work and Affluence

The ¡Kung Bushmen work little, but from our modern western point of view, they are poor and deprived. It is important to understand that ¡Kung living traditionally don't feel deprived. They don't crave permanent houses, running water, refrigerators, Jeeps, or diapers. They accept occasional hunger, secure in the knowledge that there will be food soon enough. In effect, the ¡Kung have made a trade-off—living at a low level of material affluence, they needn't work much, and can enjoy a great deal of leisure. And, in reality, since they live in a sparse environment, greater work would not necessarily produce greater abundance over the long run; it might instead disturb the ecological balance. For example, more intensive hunting might temporarily provide abundant meat, but it might also threaten the welfare of the wild herds and, therefore, ultimately the survival of the ¡Kung.

Leisure

The ¡Kung Bushmen devote their leisure to nurturing group life, cultivating relationships among individuals, and elaborating their culture. Perhaps it was the abundant leisure of foragers that allowed our ancestors to create human culture, incrementally freeing humanity from the bonds of instinct and biological necessity.

Those who study the ¡Kung all note that they are great talkers. They spend an enormous amount of time sitting around their campfires and talking, joking, arguing, exchanging news, telling stories, repeating the events of a hunt, planning tomorrow's hunting or gathering. There is a constant buzz of conversation in a

Surrounded by miles of open land, this band of ¡Kung, adults and children, men and women, cluster close together, talking, telling stories, joking and arguing in typical Bushman fashion.

¡Kung camp, and uproarious laughter breaks out often. Women and girls sit close together at the campfire, their shoulders and knees touching, as do the men and boys. Members of a ¡Kung band truly seem to enjoy each others' company.

Playing Games. Unlike the children of farming and herding societies, ¡Kung children do not have to work. This is, in its way, a sign of affluence: You could say that the ¡Kung enjoy such abundance that they don't need the labor of their children (or of old people) to support the band. Since children don't go to school either, they are free to play all day long, until, in their teen years, girls and boys begin to accompany their elders in gathering and hunting. Adults also like to play games when they are at leisure in camp or in the evenings.

The games the ¡Kung play reveal much about their culture. There are no games in which people keep score or care greatly about winning or losing. Games are all played in groups, and in many, the players are bound together in rhythmic chorus and close physical contact. Typical is the ball game played by girls who stand in a line, singing and clapping. Each girl takes the ball in turn at the right point in the music, dances with it, then tosses it to the next in line (Marshall, pp. 313, 322, 332–336).

A Musical Culture. Music is not only a part of ¡Kung games, but a constant accompaniment to camp life. The ¡Kung have a rich musical culture in which everyone participates in some way. Their homemade instruments make subtle, vibrant sounds, and their compositions are always complex. The traditional *guashi* is a stringed instrument made from a hollowed-out log strung with animal sinew or hair. There is also a traditional one-string violin, and the more recently introduced drums (adapted from their Bantu neighbors) and the thumb piano, a handheld instrument made of wood and strips of tin. Women as well as men play the *guashi* and thumb piano. Talented men even produce music by plucking their upended bows. People carry instruments with them on trips, and traveling or in camp, they often sit listening to a musician, sometimes softly improvising a sung harmony interwoven with the intricate rhythm (Biesele, pp. 165–166; Thomas, pp. 223–225; Shostak, pp, 14, 310; Marshall, pp. 363–375).

Music is a means of individual self-expression for the ¡Kung. People who are troubled or sad or bothered by some trying incident may sit alone and compose "mood music"—songs with titles, but without words, that touchingly express emotions, often wistful or ironic. One song Elizabeth Marshall Thomas heard, called "Bitter Melons," expressed the musician's feelings when he returned to a remembered field of melons, but found them too bitter to eat. Another song expressed the composer's guilt and sorrow about an incident when his brother-in-law, lost in the bush near camp, had shouted to the band, and no one had bothered to answer him (Thomas, pp. 122–123). Some songs are mocking, and they are sung under cover of darkness, with words that reproach an individual for misbehavior.

There are also sacred songs, like the eland song, the gemsbok song, the giraffe song, and the sun song, which are part of the religious and ceremonial life of the group. These songs are sung at sacred trance dances, and some are also sung at important ceremonies, like the eland song sung by women at the ceremony for an adolescent's first menstruation.

Sacred Dances. Group ceremonies, called trance dances, are a regular feature of ¡Kung life, held on an average every ten days, with dances more frequent during dry season, when the nearness of several bands at a water hole makes social life more intense and exciting. Dances involve everyone in the band or bands, and last entire nights, with the women seated in a line or circle, shoulder to shoulder, singing the sacred songs and clapping complex rhythmic accompaniments. The men, their steps emphasized by the shaking of cocoon rattles tied around their legs, dance themselves into a trance in which they can converse with the spirits and heal the sick. Children excitedly dance and clap along, and then, as the night wears on, fall asleep in their mothers' laps.

Trance dances may begin spontaneously, as fun, often initiated by children, or they may be arranged in response to serious illness or misfortune. Trance medicine, *n/um,* is a kind of power, "owned" by the people who have learned how to achieve a trance state and use it to cure others. About half the adult men and a third of the women have achieved trance at some time. A smaller number are accomplished healers, the greatest of whom may travel from camp to camp when needed.

In trance, healers are able to draw illness out of the bodies of the sick and throw it away. The ¡Kung believe sickness (and misfortune and death) are caused by tiny invisible arrows shot into the sick person by the spirits of the dead. These spirits are not malevolent, but lonely, and wish the living to be with them. The spirits are especially likely to take away a person who is ill-treated by others. In trance, healers lay their hands on the afflicted persons and draw the arrows into their own bodies. Then, at a moment of crisis, healers violently shudder and shriek, hurling the arrows away again. It is believed that, in deep trance, healers' spirits can leave their bodies to meet and talk with the spirits of the dead, to find out why they want to take a sick person and try to persuade them to reconsider.

Though they may begin as social events, dances become serious ceremony when people enter trance, for it can be a frightening and exhausting experience. *N/um* is thought to be a substance in the dancer, which the music, the smoke and fire, and the strenuous dancing of the ceremony heat up. When *n/um* comes to a boil, it bursts into the brain and the dancer enters trance. The dancer trembles, sweats, and chokes for breath. The world spins and the dancer sees visions and can walk on coals without being burned. To learn how to enter and control trance, a person needs an experienced teacher, usually a relative of the same sex, who dances with the apprentice, massages tired limbs and offers reassuring restraint if the new dancer becomes wildly disoriented. Though not everyone chooses to become a healer, and some people's *n/um* is unusually strong, practically everyone who wants to achieve trance can do so; healing is not reserved for a privileged few (Biesele, pp. 167–168; Shostak, pp. 291–299; Lee, 1984, pp. 109–113).

Megan Biesele emphasizes that the dancers' *n/um* cannot be activated without the support of singers (or drummers for the women's drum dance). Singing actually protects the dancers as their spirits leave their bodies. The trance dance is thus "a concerted effort by the entire community to banish misfortune," and a central unifying force in ¡Kung life. As Emile Durkheim pointed out a century ago in *The Elementary Forms of the Religious Life,* dances like these are important shared experiences. Joining together in a sacred and risky ceremony intensifies group feeling, strengthening the bonds of group solidarity. While the ¡Kung may think of their dances as serving a practical-spiritual purpose—curing the sick—dances also fulfill a **latent function,** a secondary purpose of which the ¡Kung themselves are unaware, that of drawing the group closer together (Durkheim, 1965, p. 432).

As a student of sociology, you will recognize that trance dances are both religious and medical. There are no ¡Kung hospitals or doctors, though the role of "healer" is one of the few specialized roles in ¡Kung society. There are no ¡Kung priests or churches: Everyone participates in sacred dances and many people learn to enter trance. But sacred dances are nevertheless part of religious life, as Durkheim recognized. Through the dances the ¡Kung enter the realm of the sacred and communicate with spirits. They seek other worldly help for their misfortunes and affirm their beliefs.

Inventing Culture. In studying ¡Kung trance dances, we have a rare opportunity to see that culture is not simply learned and passed on, but is also constantly created and re-created, by real individuals. Traditionally, the gemsbok song was sung at trance dances, but within living memory, a new song, the giraffe song, was composed, by a woman, old Be, to whom the song came complete as a revelation from God. She taught it to her husband, who taught it to others, and this song became so popular that it largely replaced the gemsbok song. Also, while traditionally only men danced and entered trance, quite recently a women's trance dance, the drum dance, was invented, and it has swept ¡Kung society, with women in band after band learning from each other how to enter trance (Biesele, p. 162; Shostak, p. 297; Lee, 1984, pp. 113–115).

Gift Giving and Visiting. A great deal of the ¡Kung's abundant leisure is devoted to cultivating relationships—in talk and games, music making, and ceremony—that reinforce group solidarity. Leisure activities also link individuals in ties of friendship and reciprocal obligation. People all over the northern ¡Kung area are connected in face-to-face acquaintance through visiting. In rainy season, individuals, couples, and small family groups break off from their bands to visit relatives, especially people they like (Marshall, pp. 180–181; Lee, 1979, p. 72).

Visits are often occasions for gift giving, though gifts are also bestowed within the band, and exchanged by spouses. Gift giving is a constant preoccupation and a subject of talk second in prominence only to food. Interaction about gifts expresses feelings and carries weight in relationships. People talk about whom they plan to give gifts to; sometimes they complain about gifts they have received, or about people who take too long to reciprocate gifts. A person may ask someone for the gift of a particular object, as a way of inviting a closer relationship, or to cause discomfort because of jealousy or anger. It would be very rude to refuse a gift, and one must reciprocate, but not too soon, for owing a return gift links people together in friendship and is really the whole point of the exercise.

The objects given as gifts are really of secondary importance to the relationships created and sustained. Anyone can make any of the objects in daily use, or readily borrow them, and people tend to keep the gifts they receive for just a short while, before passing them on as gifts to someone else. People give objects in common use: ostrich shell bead headbands and necklaces, musical instruments, wooden bowls, arrows, pipes, dance rattles, or valued materials like eland fat (Marshall, pp. 303–305, 309–310).

SOCIAL STRUCTURE AND GROUP LIFE

One important lesson you can learn from studying the íKung Bushmen is that people create social structure themselves, through interaction. When you live in a large, complex society, statuses and roles and institutions often seem like "givens." You are confronted with politicians or bosses, teachers or nurses, schools or courts, and you may feel you have had nothing to do with creating them. In íKung society, it is clear that statuses and roles emerge as the result of repeated interaction between individuals. With the íKung, we can see the building of social structure very clearly, because íKung society is limited to the family and the band. The íKung are distinctive (though typical of hunting and gathering societies) in that they have an extremely limited selection of statuses, roles, groups, and institutions. There are no chiefs or officials, no police officers, priests, managers, employees, teachers, doctors, servants, or generals, or any of a long list of specialized statuses and roles that may be found in your society. There are no committees, gangs, classes, clans, teams, parliaments, or clubs. Nor are there churches, courts, prisons, hospitals, schools, armies, governments, markets, or businesses. Because there is no central authority in íKung society, íKung Bushmen have a lot of individual freedom. They are not in the habit of taking orders from anyone, and if a person doesn't like what others are doing, their most usual response is to pick up and leave.

íKung society is a social system based on kinship: The band, the family, and kin statuses comprise all social structure and must serve all needs. It is most helpful to think of íKung society not as socially impoverished by its lack of varied social structure, but as focused with extraordinary intensity on family relationships. Since social structure is created and maintained through interaction, it is easy to understand that the íKung are constantly involved in forming and elaborating family relations.

The Family: Putting Flexibility First

The small **nuclear family** (the reproductive unit of parents and children) is the basic unit of íKung society. íKung families are "modular" and flexible. Nuclear family modules may link together to form larger **extended families,** and extended families may also break up into their constituent nuclear units. A series of nuclear and extended families link together to form a band, but bands are not necessarily permanent arrangements: some families may leave and others join, and sometimes a band will break up entirely. The modular structure of íKung families and bands may readily be seen as a form of **cultural adaptation,** permitting flexible adjustment of group size to available resources.

Creating Nuclear Families

While a couple and their children form a long-lasting, firmly bonded group in ¡Kung society, nuclear families never live independently. (However, they may temporarily go off visiting on their own.) Nuclear families are small. In the 1950s, 1960s, and 1970s, anthropologists found that the average ¡Kung woman gave birth to only four to five children altogether, and the average family comprised only two to three living children. Marriage creates nuclear families, and also links them in larger extended families and in an even broader kinship network.

When a couple marries, the ¡Kung expect the husband to move in with his new wife's family. Typically, they explain this custom in terms of food. The boy must feed his wife's parents, who are getting old, and he must feed his bride, they say, and prove he is capable and responsible (Marshall, p. 169). Members of the same band are not forbidden to marry, but such marriages are unusual. Consequently, marriages usually involve some reshuffling of band membership. This is especially so since the new husband may bring others with him to his wife's band. He remains responsible for his parents and dependents, and they may come with him. ¡Kung men are allowed to have more than one wife **(polygyny),** though this practice is rare, and in such a case, a man will bring his first wife, their children, and perhaps her relatives with him (in addition to his own), when he joins his new wife's family.

There is no set duration for this **bride service** with the wife's family (people say it should last long enough for three children to be born), but afterward a man has the right to return to his own people, taking his wife and dependents. He may or may not do this, depending on how well he gets along with his wife's band and what kinds of resources are available to each band. The couple and their dependents may in fact move back and forth between his relatives and hers (Marshall, p. 170). One way of understanding this is to say that ¡Kung society is **ambilocal:** people live with either the husband's or the wife's relatives. It is also **bilateral:** they reckon kinship on both their mother's and their father's sides.

The Band: Linking Families

There is no rigid pattern for band formation. Band members are always related to each other in some fashion (through ties of blood or marriage), but the actual linkages vary. The band grows like a chain, as in-marrying spouses bring their parents, siblings, and spouses, who in turn bring theirs. But band members are not mandated by kinship ties to remain together. People choose to stay in a band because they get along well living and working together. If they don't get along, families are free to leave the band, affiliating themselves with relatives in some other band. This is a real option, frequently exercised. Often families break off from their band to visit others—to exchange gifts, or news, or arrange a marriage, or attend a ceremony. Because bands are flexible, people can adjust the size of their group to environmental conditions and resources. Most people, Lorna Marshall found, have relatives who are parents, offspring, or siblings in five to thirteen other bands (Marshall, pp. 180–181, 195, 200). But everyone belongs to a family and a band; there are no unattached people in ¡Kung society.

Dabe's Story: The Visitors

Dabe saw the straggling line first. A dozen people approached slowly through the bush. Dabe broke into a smile as he recognized his mother's favorite brother /Gao at the head of the line. /Gao had once lived for two years with Dabe's band and had taught Dabe to track and hunt. Dabe rushed to meet his uncle and shouted to attract his attention. /Gao embraced Dabe and croaked out a sad and weary tale. /Gao's band's water hole had run dry and they had walked north for six days, searching the area for Dabe's band. /Gao's infant daughter had died three days ago when her mother's milk dried up. As /Gao spoke, Dabe's mother Karu rushed forward and embraced her brother.

Then /Gao's wife limped up, and her mother and brother and his family, and his wife's widowed sister and her sons. Karu brought water that had been stored in ostrich eggshells; soon the travelers had their first deep drink of good water in days. An hour later, Dabe's father Kwi and several other men of the band appeared, returning from a hunt. Kwi greeted his relatives warmly and invited them to make their camp next to his. Later, he gave them a share of the eland he had killed, but his heart was full of anxiety. There was not enough water here for even two small bands. How would they all survive?

The next day it was decided: /Gao and his band would stay with Dabe and Karu and Kwi. They were too worn to go further. But the other people in Dabe's band decided to go to stay with their relatives at Nyae Nyae, where there was a permanent water hole and the rains usually began first.

Kinship: Elaborating Connections

¡Kung kinship is rudimentary in some ways, extraordinarily complex in others. The ¡Kung are not much interested in keeping track of relatives more than two generations back in time, or beyond second cousins. But they have developed several interesting devices for creating extra kinship bonds, weaving additional threads into the net of family that unites all the ¡Kung Bushmen.

The K'ausi and the N'ore

An important part of ¡Kung kinship has to do with the relationship of bands to their territories. Every band is attached to a territory—a water hole and the land and resources surrounding it, called a *n'ore*. It would be impossible for a band to exist without a *n'ore* (and since the number of water holes is limited, this serves to limit the number of bands). Each band is identified with a group of related older people, who have lived in the band a long time—usually siblings or cousins, who are considered to be the "owners" or *k'ausi* of the *n'ore*. Visitors traveling through a territory would ask the *k'ausi* for permission to gather plant foods and use the water hole.

The *k'ausi* are not formal leaders. They "own" the resources, but can't give them away or sell them; neither can they decide who joins the band, or tell people what to do. They may not necessarily be the informal leaders of the band either; they may be too old or lacking in the personal qualities needed for leadership. Leadership is then likely to be exercised by someone else who has a strong personality (but is not arrogant or selfish) and who has qualities of wisdom and judgment (Lee, 1979, pp. 61–67; 1984, p. 88).

Generations and the Joking Relationship

Another kinship principle profoundly shapes life in ¡Kung society: the principle of alternating generations (Lee, 1984, pp. 63–66). ¡Kung kinship terms pair up alternating generations. You, your grandparents, and your grandchildren share a special kin relationship; so do your parents and your children. Special reciprocal kin terms are used by the alternating pairs.

Just to make all this more complicated, there is another principle related to alternating generations: the joking relationship. All of a ¡Kung person's kin are either people they joke with or people they avoid. The "joking relationship" is relaxed, affectionate, and familiar; the "avoidance relationship" is respectful and formal. Generally speaking, you joke with relatives in your generation, your grandparents' generation and your grandchildren's generation, and you avoid relatives in your parents' and your children's generations. An important rule is that you may never marry someone in the avoidance relationship.

Xama's Story: The Joking Relationship

At the end of the long dry season, when everyone was waiting impatiently for the rains to begin, five bands gathered at the large permanent water hole at Nyae Nyae. They had to—it was practically the only water left—but it was also a wonderful distraction from worries about the rain. Xama thought this was the best time of the year. She saw her married older brother, and her best friend who had gone to live with her husband's band. Almost every night there was a trance dance at one camp or another. Xama was 16 and knew she was ready now to get married.

At the water hole, Xama met her mother's uncle / 'Ase, who had long ago left Xama's band to do his bride service in his wife's band. "Come walk with me," he laughed, "I am so old that I need help from my grandchildren." Xama laughed also. In his mid-thirties, / 'Ase was muscular and smooth-faced. He stood half a head taller than Xama; he was known as "Tall / 'Ase." "Here is someone who makes me feel small," / 'Ase said, as a hazel-eyed young man walked into view. As tall as / 'Ase, Tu was in his early twenties and, in Xama's eyes, very handsome.

"This is Tu," / 'Ase introduced the young man, "he is your cousin's cousin." This made Tu a marriageable partner for Xama, and after a few comments, / 'Ase left the couple alone. In a few days Xama had decided that the future would offer few better opportunities than the tall young man with the hazel eyes. But there were problems. Xama's aunt confronted her and said, "You must not joke with Tu; people are talking. Tu is the brother of your uncle's second wife. You cannot marry him; he is of your parents' generation."

Xama was stunned and frightened, but Tu reassured her. "I am your cousin's cousin; that's what's most important, People will see that." Tu's father and brother argued openly with Xama's mother. "Tu and Xama," they said, "could marry." No one could agree and Tu and Xama were miserable. Tu's father said he would take them to his cousin's band. They wouldn't see any problem with the marriage. The young couple waited anxiously for the rains to come and make travel possible.

Fictive Kin: Making Kinship Really Complicated

Here is the tricky part: the ¡Kung Bushmen take the whole kinship structure—relationships by blood and marriage, alternating generations, joking and avoidance relationships—and apply it to fictive (imaginary) kin. The system is based on names. People who have your name address your kin as theirs—they call your wife, "wife," your father "father," and so forth. And you can do the same: Anyone with your mother's name you can address as "mother," anyone with your son's name you may call "son," and so on. Anyone with your sibling's name or your grandparent's name stands in a joking relationship to you. Those with your father's name or your child's, you treat with avoidance. Also, and very important, you may not marry anyone who shares the name of a relative you are forbidden to marry (your sibling, or parent, or child, or sibling's child).

Fictive kinship extends the benefits of kinship to everyone who bears a ¡Kung name. With it, no one among the whole people need be a stranger or an outsider. In the very few cases in which people have no blood relatives, they live in a band with fictive kin. It also makes kinship a complex intellectual challenge, since there are very few ¡Kung names (only about 35 first names for each sex, and no last names) (Lee, 1984, pp. 68–71).

Why do the ¡Kung bother to maintain such an elaborate kinship system? You may find the **functionalist perspective** very helpful in understanding ¡Kung kinship. **Functionalists** always ask: How does this practice (or norm, or institution) help society function smoothly? Talcott Parsons, a famous American sociologist, was always concerned to determine whether a particular cultural feature helps a society to survive (then it is "functional") or whether it harms the society (then it is "dysfunctional"). It is clear that in a society like the ¡Kung Bushmen, which lacks specialized roles, the elaborate kinship system is functional because it finds places for all people. It helps the society function smoothly by ensuring that any two members of ¡Kung society will always know where they stand in relation to each other, and what roles they should play. Depending on their actual kinship, their ages, and their names, individuals will quickly establish kinship status and determine whether they have a joking or an avoidance relationship.

Roles: Focusing on Gender

In addition to kinship and age, the other fundamental basis of ¡Kung status and role is gender. More than anything else, who you are and what you do in life is determined by your gender. Male and female are the basic "specialties" in ¡Kung society; there are no other specialized occupations. One way of putting this is to say that the ¡Kung, like other hunting and gathering societies, have only the most basic **division of labor,** for there are only two jobs, two economic roles. And since these roles are gender roles, they are part of family life. In effect, there is no economy separate from the family and the band.

Is There a "Breadwinner" Role?

¡Kung women and men both "commute" to work (Fisher, p. 103). The work roles of men and women are different, but there is no sense in which women do "housework" and men "go to work."

Niuhka's Story: The Gatherers

Niuhka is hungry, but happy. Her brother found a field of tsin beans while hunting and she is off to harvest them. Tsin beans have been scarce, so many women are eager to come along. Even Niuhka's mother, who is less active than she once was, wants to come. Gathering tsin beans is work, but it's also a social occasion, a break in routine. Twikwe, Niuhka's best friend plays a tune on her thumb piano as they walk along, and the women join in, singing a rhythmic chorus. Even though Niuhka is burdened with her heavy toddler, whom she carries in her leather kaross, her step is light and her face is smiling.

Everyone seems lifted by the prospect of the beans. Even Dasina, whose running fight with her husband has made her sullen for weeks, is smiling and singing. Suddenly, as the women enter the bean field, a duiker, a tiny antelope, breaks from its hiding place and dashes away. The women take up the chase with enthusiastic shouts. Although the duiker can race faster than any ¡Kung, it is young and confused and runs in circles. Njuhka and Twikwe pelt it with stones, knocking it over, but the duiker recovers and bounds off. All the women are disappointed. On other harvesting trips they have run down small game and feasted on the meat.

Soon the women turn to the work of harvesting beans and by afternoon have collected a huge pile, which they roll in their karosses. With her kaross tied around her waist, each woman will carry 15 to 30 pounds of beans, the babies perched on top. Weary and joking, the women return home, knowing they can rest in camp for three or four days without further gathering.

Women's Work

The food women collect constitutes about 75 percent of the ¡Kung diet. Gathering is not random; the women have a plan and a clear objective. They know where fruits are ripe or roots and tubers may be found. When the band moves camp, women carry all their belongings and their young children. Lee estimates that each year the average ¡Kung woman carries her child 1,500 miles. Women also gather wood, tend fires, and cook vegetable foods. They build shelters and repair them and keep the family's living area clear of ash and grasses. They make household objects like ostrich eggshell water holders, tortoise shell bowls, and personal ornaments. Women don't use bows and arrows or spears to hunt, but they do kill snakes and tortoises and birds and, occasionally, even small animals (Marshall, pp. 92, 97, 102; Lee, 1979, pp. 310–312).

Men's Work

Hunting is the focus of male activity and talk. Men hunt small game with spears, clubs, or snares, and they hunt big game with bow and poisoned arrow. Their bows are lightweight. The poison-tipped arrows wound but don't kill. Men must track their wounded prey so that when the poison has done its work, they can kill the animal up close with a spear. Men hunt on an irregular basis, sometimes alone, but by preference in groups of two to four. They may stay around camp for weeks at a time, then hunt for several days in a row, but averaged out, they hunt around two or three days week.

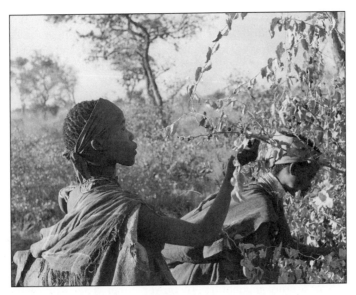

These young women have walked out from camp for the day, to a place where they know grewia berries are ripe. Behind them stretches the Kalahari Desert: rolling grasslands, punctuated with clusters of trees and bushes.

/Toma's Story: The Hunters

/Toma and Nieisi were very tired. They had followed kudu tracks all day without sighting the animals. "Let's go back to camp," sighed /Toma; "I'm tired, my back hurts. Nieisi will rub my back." "Your wife will rub her belly in hunger if we return without meat," Nieisi protested. "Let's go on just a little longer." /Toma and Nieisi were lucky. They suddenly came upon the kudu in the slanting light of late afternoon, grazing as they settled for the night. Crawling to a clump of bushes only a few feet from the kudu, /Toma used his bow. The poisoned arrow hit a young male kudu in the flank and it fled. By morning, the poison would weaken and then paralyze the 300-pound animal. /Toma and Nieisi hurried back to the camp. They would need help to carry the meat.

The next morning they returned to the hunt with four more men from their band. They soon found the wounded kudu, but it was closely watched by a pair of lions. Nieisi tried to chase the lions: "Go lions, this is our meat, not yours!" he commanded, tossing a clod of earth in the big cats' direction. The lions would not move and growled alarmingly as Nieisi tossed another clod.

/Toma raised his bow, but only in frustration. The lions would devour the foolish hunters long before the weak iKung poison could do its work. /Toma turned toward camp and shouted at Nieisi: "Now we can all rub our bellies!" "There are other kudu to hunt," Nieisi called out, but /Toma kept walking toward camp.

Game is used for many purposes besides food; almost nothing is wasted. Men make animal hides into clothing and bags; bone and horn are used for tools, sinews for bowstrings and nets. Men craft all their hunting gear—bows, arrows, quivers, spears, clubs, and implements for trapping. They collect the beetle larvae from which arrow poison is distilled and carefully prepare and spread the poison. Men also butcher and cook meat, especially the meat of large animals. They light fires, by twirling sticks, or in recent decades, by use of a flint and tinder. At a ¡Kung campground, both men and women are engaged in domestic tasks. Men know how to gather and sometimes do so—when they return empty-handed from a hunt, or when they go with women on overnight gathering trips (Lee, 1979, pp. 216–226; Marshall, pp. 124, 132–137).

SOCIAL INEQUALITY

Inequality in ¡Kung Bushman society is notable mostly for its absence. There is very little inequality of any kind. As we have seen, there are no economic or **class** inequalities: Sharing and gift giving ensure that food and material objects are distributed equally in families and bands. Visiting evens out resources between bands and *n'ore*. There are not inequalities of **power** either. The ¡Kung have no chiefs and the position of the **k'ausi** is mostly ceremonial. Informal leaders do develop in bands, but they don't have the power to give orders or make people do things against their wills. They lead by example and by their interpersonal skills. The only kind of inequality discernable in ¡Kung society is **status** inequality. Some people enjoy more prestige and respect than others, perhaps because of their skill as hunters or musicians or healers, or perhaps because of their pleasant personalities. But their prestige doesn't result in increased wealth or power. Admired individuals don't eat better or have more possessions than others; they aren't given special titles or privileges. They may be sought out in marriages or as band members. But take note: These status inequalities are personal, not social; they result from individuals' personal traits, not from their membership in social groups, like classes or races. The only status inequality in ¡Kung society that is social in nature is inequality between men and women. Gender inequality does exist, but it is minimal.

Gender Inequality

Women and men are not perfectly equal in ¡Kung society, but they come pretty close. Women work longer hours than men, in gathering, child care, and household work, but their enormous contribution to subsistence is recognized, and the food they gather is considered theirs. Men don't scorn women's work, and they do sometimes go gathering. Women have a great deal of autonomy and power. They are not expected to obey men; they don't wait on men, and they don't eat inferior food or less than men. Women are seldom physically assaulted or coerced by men, and in fact, women hit men about as frequently as they are struck by them. Women have a voice in group discussions and a say in making arrangements. There are no formal statuses or laws that give power to men (Marshall, p. 177).

In marriage too, women are not disadvantaged. Mothers and fathers share authority over children, and divorces are as likely to be initiated by women as by men. Because of bride service, young women don't end up as powerless newcomers in their husbands' families. And finally, though there is polygyny (multiple wives) and not polyandry (multiple husbands), its rarity seems to be the result of women's firm opposition.

Gender and Personality

In societies where men and women are very unequal, they are often socialized to develop personality traits that reinforce their inequality. In such societies, boys are taught to be aggressive and domineering and girls to be passive and dependent. Personality differences between ¡Kung men and women are minimal. The ¡Kung find conflict and violence abhorrent (as we shall soon see) and they disapprove of men who are aggressive, boastful, or dominating. It is no compliment to say that a man is a fighter, and in ¡Kung culture boys are never urged or taught to fight. Men who are easygoing and skillful and who help ease tensions in the group are preferred. Self-assertion, demandingness, and boldness are also discouraged in women, but perhaps slightly more so than in men. Women are expected to be gentle, modest, and gracious, and to comply with the wishes of others (Marshall, p. 176).

Gender Segregation

In many societies, women's lower status is reflected in their extensive segregation from men and from public life in general. Among the ¡Kung, women and men are segregated in some of their roles, but overall, the degree of segregation is not great. Most of the time, women and men work separately, each going into the bush with friends and relatives of their own gender. But this separation is not rigid. Parties of men and women do go gathering together, especially in major expeditions to the mongongo groves, or the tsin bean fields, and these are usually rather festive occasions. Women are sometimes part of the party that returns to track down and carry home big game fatally wounded in a hunt. Within the camp, men and women sit on opposite sides of the fire, but beyond this, there is a great deal of mixing of men and women, and boys and girls. Children of both sexes play together, and spouses are commonly real companions, sitting and talking by their fire and even arranging "getaways" to visit relatives or go gathering together in the bush.

The "Masters of Meat"

Anthropologists disagree about just how equal ¡Kung men and women are. Lorna Marshall argued that ¡Kung men did enjoy an advantage over women, an advantage in influence and prestige, which stemmed from the glamour of hunting. As she explained it, "There is no splendid excitement in returning home with vegetables." People crave meat and they call men the "masters of meat" and "the owners of hunting" (Marshall, p. 178). News of success in a hunt, particularly of big game, spreads rapidly even beyond the camp. Visitors arrive and everyone feasts and parties. Hunting confers not only prestige, however, but also concrete influence. Women distribute their plant food within their own families, but men distribute the enticing meat widely, and their gifts are a kind of investment, which gathers in honor and obligations, and grows into influence (Fisher, p. 215).

But more recently, Susan Kent has replied, "Only foreign anthropologists consider hunting as somehow better than collecting [gathering], or as an activity in which everyone should want to participate" (Kent, 1995, p. 520).

DEVIANCE AND SOCIAL CONTROL

Do you think that there is more deviance in your society or in ¡Kung Bushman society? If you think about this you will see that it is puzzling. The ¡Kung have no laws, or police or courts, no authority figures to make rules or mete out punishments. There are no **formal sanctions**—positive or negative—to make people conform: no diplomas to work for, no scholarships for merit, no promotions, no jobs to win or lose, no jail sentences, parole, or court martials. The ¡Kung rely entirely on the **informal sanctions** of small group life. Negative sanctions include the mocking song heard in the darkness, gossip and ridicule, teasing and avoidance. The ¡Kung fear having others laugh at them. Positive sanctions include group approval, loving attention, and companionship. Inclusion in group life is emotionally so essential that these informal sanctions are highly effective.

While there certainly is deviance in ¡Kung society, there are no **deviant roles** or **deviant careers.** There are no gang members, or burglars, no confidence men, no punk rockers, no cross-dressers who inhabit subcultures condemned as deviant by the rest of their society. Most of the time, members of ¡Kung society accept group norms and act and talk and think in ways that are expected of them. But they sometimes commit deviant acts, like failing to share food, or fighting, or boasting, or engaging in adultery, or even killing another person.

Deviance and Social Interaction

In the small ¡Kung bands, many norms concern how people are expected to interact with each other, and much of ¡Kung deviance involves disapproved modes of interaction. Sociologists distinguish four types of interaction, found in all societies: **social exchange, cooperation, competition,** and **conflict.** In every society, people value some of these forms of interaction and they disapprove of others. For the ¡Kung, exchange and cooperation are desired, competition and conflict feared and avoided.

Social Exchange and Cooperation

Many sociologists see exchange as a universally important interaction process, and the ¡Kung would agree. They tend to see the world in terms of exchanges (you give me a gift and then I'll give you one; you give me meat when you are successful hunting, and then I return the favor; you extend hospitality to my family or band when we are in your territory, and later we will do the same for you). In exchange, each person gives something in order to get something else—gifts, assistance, love, food, attention, companionship, and so forth. Like people in other societies, the ¡Kung are careful to reciprocate appropriately. Their society, like others, has many norms which sociologists call **norms of reciprocity.** These norms tell people what to exchange, how, with whom, and when. The ¡Kung worry about whether this relative or that deserves a shoulder of the antelope, or whether it would be better to give the hindquarter as well, and they think carefully about the timing of gifts as well as their nature—to reciprocate too quickly, or to wait too long could both be insulting.

People usually can find some way to reciprocate. Those who are too old or handicapped to hunt or gather can stay in camp with the children, or shell nuts or make music. People who fail to reciprocate are teased, reproached, or avoided. Some people work harder than others at reciprocal gift giving, spending many hours making ostrich shell beads and jewelry, for example. They are rewarded with an extensive network of social connections from whom they can expect gifts, perhaps help in matchmaking, or a place they will be welcome to visit.

For the ¡Kung, exchange often takes the form of cooperation, when people pitch in and pool their resources to achieve a common goal. We see this in the dry-season sharing of permanent water holes, in the help ¡Kung give each other in carrying home large kills, or heavy mongongo nuts. Most games illustrate and teach cooperation, as the whole group works together to keep the ball aloft, or the rhythm going. In one popular game, girls make a circle, each girl crooking one leg around her neighbor's, then hop in unison. When one falls, the circle collapses and the game is over.

Competition

Like cooperation, competition requires agreed-upon social rules, but competition is repugnant to the ¡Kung, and they work constantly to squelch competitive tendencies in individuals and suppress arrogance in those more talented or successful. Acting competitive is a form of deviance for the ¡Kung.

¡Kung norms call for extreme modesty in presenting one's accomplishments. A man whose arrow badly wounds an antelope will return to his hearth silent and dejected. Asked about the hunt, he will doubtfully admit that he just might have grazed his quarry. Then the camp will celebrate, for they know this means the hunter has scored a certain hit and there will probably be meat tomorrow. As one Xai/Xai man, /Gaugo, explained to Richard Lee, when the carrying party finds the kill, they will loudly disparage the meat:

> You mean you have dragged us all the way out here to make us cart home your pile of bones? Oh, if I had known it was this thin, I wouldn't have come. (Lee, 1984, p. 49)

The ¡Kung call this "insulting the meat." Anyone who shows open pride is relentlessly teased, and the object of their pride disparaged. Tomazho, a famous healer, explained:

> When a young man kills much meat, he comes to think of himself as a chief or a big man, and he thinks of the rest of us as his servants or inferiors. We can't accept this. We refuse one who boasts, for someday his pride will make him kill somebody. So we always speak of his meat as worthless. In this way we cool his heart and make him gentle. (Lee, 1984, pp. 48–50)

Conflict

Conflict occurs when normative consensus breaks down, but actually, in most cases, the events of a conflict follow an accepted script, escalating through stages recognizable to all. In conflict, people try to meet their goals by destroying an opponent. The ¡Kung are horrified, and very much frightened by conflict, especially violent conflict, and make every effort to prevent disagreements from escalating into physical fighting. Much as they oppose conflict, the ¡Kung are only moderately successful in preventing it. In the worst case, arguments progress to insults and then into wrestling and hitting, followed by a general melee in which many people may be wounded or killed (Lee, 1984, pp. 93–95; 1979, pp. 396–399).

Kushe's Story: The Fight

It seems like it has gone on all day. As Kushe sits shelling mongongo nuts, she carries on an endless shrill monologue, complaining about her husband. "He is so stingy; too stingy," goes the refrain. "He doesn't give me presents. He doesn't bring home enough meat." The whole band ignores her, and her husband's parents, who are visiting, tactfully disappear into the bush. By the time Ukwane and his brother-in-law return from hunting, the tension is so high you can practically see it. Ukwane begins to butcher the kudu and hands the first share to his mother. Kushe jumps between them, furious: "You're not going to give me any, are you?" she demands. Taken aback, Ukwane tries to deflect her with kidding: "No, of course not; I never give you anything." Kushe is beside herself. "That's right," she screams, "you don't; no food and no babies," as she hits and claws at him. Amazed by the suddenness of this emotional storm, Ukwane grabs Kushe and literally throws her out of his way. Kushe runs back and assaults him again. Ukwane's mother and Kushe's mother are now pushing and shouting at each other. Momentarily shocked, the rest of the group finds its feet and leaps into action, separating and holding the combatants. Everyone is talking and shouting and milling about.

Tempers have cooled by the following morning, but Ukwane wants no part of Kushe or her family. "They are like warthogs, not people!" Ukwane's mother spits out. "They all look like warthogs," grunts his father. Ukwane rises, declaring, "I want to go to hunt kudu, not to live among beasts!" Having said this in a voice loud enough to carry across the camp, Ukwane leads his parents off on the long trek to his brother's camp near the Herero village.

Managing Conflict. How do the ¡Kung ensure that most conflicts do not escalate to the point of violence? After all, they cannot call the police or campus security. While there are no separate political or legal institutions, the ¡Kung do have norms and procedures for handling conflict—within the band and the family.

One way the ¡Kung manage conflict is by providing plentiful opportunity for harmless venting of complaints. The ¡Kung are an exceptionally verbal people, and feelings like grief, envy, resentment, anger, or alarm are readily expressed in conversation. A great deal of the constant interchange in ¡Kung groups takes the form of semiserious argument, called "a talk," in which real discontents are jokingly aired. In such sessions, people complain about others' laziness or stinginess, about people who don't distribute meat properly, or don't reciprocate gifts generously. (Though complaints like these are common, the underlying problem in uncontrolled, fatal fights is usually adultery, or anger over a previous homicide.) "Talks" are potentially dangerous, but most of the time, the danger is defused by laughter.

A "Fight." If "talking" fails, then people lose their good nature and begin an angry argument. When they begin to make sexual insults (*za*) against each other, then you know that anger will mount and actual physical violence is likely. Women are as likely as men to be involved in hand-to-hand violence, with men or with other women. In most cases, once people separate the combatants, they are usually able to use joking to calm everyone down.

Conflict Control. Separation in fact is one of the most effective means of limiting conflict available to the iKung. It is relatively easy for one party or the other in a dispute to pick up and leave the group temporarily, and people often do so. Conflict avoidance and flexible group composition are closely intertwined, with conflict-induced separations keeping groups small, and flexible group composition making conflict avoidance possible.

The most extreme form of conflict management practiced by the iKung (and the one that comes closest to the exercise of political authority) is group execution. It is a last resort to even the score when people hold a grudge for a previous murder, or to put an end to fighting caused by a single, dangerously violent individual. Richard B. Lee has recorded several such cases, in one of which a whole community joined in shooting and stabbing a probably psychotic killer (Lee, 1984, p. 96; 1979, pp. 393–395).

Since the Tswana and the Herero have settled in the Kalahari, the iKung have been glad to make use of their legal institutions to manage conflict. As early as 1948, the Tswana appointed a iKung-speaking Tswana, Isak Utigile, as "headman" (really a kind of justice of the peace, or magistrate) of the iKung, and his "court" became very popular among the iKung as a place for mediation of disputes by a trusted authority (Lee, 1979, p. 396; 1984, pp. 96–97). Nowadays, as the iKung settle down in villages, people are less able to avoid conflict by leaving the group, so they are turning more and more frequently to Herero or Tswana headmen or to government officials to mediate disputes. Susan Kent describes a Bushman village in Botswana where villagers turned repeatedly to the game scout (the nearest government official) in cases of conflict (Kent, pp. 703–712).

SOCIALIZATION

One reason why there is relatively little deviance in iKung society is that socialization is quite successful. iKung Bushmen learn to play new roles all through life, as they move from childhood, through adulthood, to old age. These age-specific roles are in fact the major roles in iKung society since, besides the basic gender division, there are no other specialized roles. Like the rest of life, socialization takes place in the family and the band, and people are socialized by their friends and relatives. There is no formal socialization, since there are no schools or other formal institutions. However, there are formal ceremonies that mark important life transitions.

In the past, when the iKung Bushmen lived by traditional hunting and gathering, children could rely on their adult roles being just like their parents'. Adults had valuable knowledge and skills to transmit to children, and old people's long experience with the conditions of bush life made them respected advisers. Life was filled with difficulties, but had a reliable consistency from generation to generation. No ¡Kung children needed to worry about what they would be when they grew up; but they didn't have very many choices either. Everyone had to accommodate his or her talents to the small number of gender and kinship roles that existed.

Today, the situation is changing, and as the ¡Kung leave the hunting and gathering life, the experience of elders becomes less relevant to young people, and adolescents are faced with life choices never imagined by their parents. We will first examine socialization through the life cycle of the ¡Kung in traditional hunter-gatherer bands, and then describe how the ¡Kung are responding to current conditions.

Childhood Socialization

The ¡Kung begin their lives with an immensely secure early childhood. Babies sleep beside their mothers at night and are carried all day in slings that permit constant skin-to-skin contact. They have free access to the breast, and nurse on demand, several times an hour. The ¡Kung believe babies need no training or discipline. Young children are carried and nursed up to the age of 3 or even 4, but once out of infancy, they spend more time out of their mothers' arms—in affectionate play with their fathers, held by the various aunts and uncles, grandparents, and cousins who surround them in the band, and often carried, like dolls, by the older siblings.

But then, when children are 3 or 4 years old, they are suddenly required to stop breast-feeding, relinquish the role of an infant, and adopt the much more independent role of a child. ¡Kung mothers bear children with an average birth interval of four years. Ideally, a new pregnancy occurs because the still-nursing toddler is self-weaning to solid food. Much of the time, however, the toddler is still emotionally wedded to nursing, and with the new pregnancy, mother and child enter a stressful period of angry conflict. The child feels rage and rejection, sometimes still unresolved by the time of the new birth. But the weaning crisis gradually abates as the 4-year-old tires of hanging around mother and infant and is drawn off into the more exciting life of the children's play group (Shostak, pp. 57–58).

There is no worry about whether children will succeed in learning new roles; no debate over proper methods of childrearing; no controversy about the contents of school curriculum. The ¡Kung assume that in the normal course of their lives, children will learn what they need to know and become prepared for adult life.

Children Socialize Each Other

Children from about ages 7 to 12 spend almost all their time in each others' company, playing in mixed-age and often mixed-sex groups. They play in the cleared central "plaza" of the camp or, even more often, in a nearby "children's village," out of sight, but not out of hearing of the adults. Children play traditional games, give their smaller siblings rides on an old kaross, or on their backs, and endlessly "play house." Girls build rough shelters and pair off with boys or with each other as "mommies and daddies." Children gather berries or roots in the nearby bush, snare small birds or collect caterpillars, or pretend to kill and butcher an animal. Girls and boys hold their own "pretend" trance dances. Away from disapproving parents, children also experiment with sex, imitating parents glimpsed in the dark, looking and touching, but not initiating actual intercourse (Lee, 1979, p. 236; Shostak, p. 83; Marshall, pp. 318–319). A great deal of children's play is obviously **anticipatory socialization,** in which they learn by observing and imitating the roles they will play as adults.

Gai's Story: Learning to Be a Man

"We are masters of the meat," shouts 9-year-old Gai, as he leads two younger boys in a mock hunt through the tall grass. Gai and //Oma use their toy bows to shoot at the grasshoppers they disturb as they run. Suddenly a shout from the youngest boy, Gwe, reveals a 3-foot-long grass snake. The three boys chase the snake, shooting at it, tossing rocks, and finally killing it with a branch used as a club. "We must cook our meat!" exclaims Gai, as they build a fire and roast the unfortunate snake.

Gai enjoys his new role as "hunter" and distributes meat to the younger boys. Four girls, including Karu, an 8-year-old who often plays "house" with Gai, look on hungrily, but no food comes their way. Finally Karu shouts, "Where is my food? I am your wife; you have to give me some!"

Gai's pals are beside themselves with laughter. Karu, nearly a head shorter than Gai, chases him around the clearing. What starts as a game soon becomes a tug of war, as Karu grabs the charred snake and Gai pulls back on the other end. The snake splits and the pair are dumped on the ground. Karu and Gai scream at each other until Karu's older sister arrives and shouts at both of them, "You're acting like a bunch of babies! Grown-ups share their food, especially husbands and wives!"

Actually, children learn a great deal from each other. Older children are patient with younger ones who try to join their games, and instruct them in the proper way to play. Older children act as peacemakers and mediators in the frequent minor conflicts of the informal play group. They often intervene when one child teases another, grabs someone's melon or toy, or when disagreements turn to physical fighting. They punish aggression—generally with ridicule—and give comfort to the victims. Also, they sometimes make fun of children who don't participate in games, or who play badly (Eibl-Eibesfeldt, p. 135). As children grow up, they gradually move from freely expressing aggression to controlling aggression in others, then to an adulthood in which suppressing their own aggressive, competitive impulses will be expected.

Adults Socialize Children

Children spend a great deal of time with adults of all ages, and learn from them by imitation and informal instruction. They learn to control their tempers and avoid offending others. When young children fight, mothers' most common response is to separate or distract them. Mothers may scold and compel the return of a grabbed object. Though threats of beatings are common, actual physical punishment is rare (Eibl-Eibesfeldt, pp. 132–133, 135).

Children also learn the many norms of daily life. They learn to receive food in outstretched hands, not to grab, to wait until asked to share food; to take a modest serving from a passed bowl, and to eat with restraint, not revealing eagerness. They are scolded for greed or stealing. Girls and boys also learn the norms of sexual modesty. They learn that adults do not hug or kiss each other in public. Girls learn to sit modestly, so their genitals are not visible. Both girls and boys learn that it is dangerous to sit where a person of the opposite sex has sat. The ¡Kung believe that if a man sits in a place touched by a woman's genitals, his ability to hunt will be impaired, and if a woman sits in a man's place, she will get an infection (Marshall, pp. 244, 249, 293–294, 311).

In adolescence, children begin to go gathering or hunting with adults, in order to learn these vital skills. Girls begin to gather in earnest as soon as they marry, which among some ¡Kung groups used to be as young as 10 or 12. (It is now closer to 16 for most ¡Kung.) But even then, the young wife gathers in the company of her mother, or perhaps her aunt or sisters. The transition to adult responsibilities is gradual. At about the age of 12, boys' fathers give them their first small bows and arrows and quivers, and they begin to hunt birds and rabbits. This is a time when they may also accompany an older man, perhaps a grandfather, in setting snares and tending a trapline. Finally comes the big step of going with their fathers, uncles, and older brothers on a hunt (Shostak, pp. 83–84).

Rites of Passage to Adulthood

In traditional ¡Kung society, major events mark the passage to adulthood: for boys, the first kill of a large animal, and *choma*, initiation into manhood; and for girls, first menstruation and marriage. All four of these events are marked by public ceremonies; they are the **rites of passage** that mark and celebrate a person's change in status before the whole community.

The First Buck Ceremony

A boy becomes a fully adult hunter when he kills his first big antelope with a poisoned arrow. This milestone event traditionally was achieved between the ages of 15 and 18, but nowadays, as young men spend more time working on Bantu cattle posts, it may occur much later. Killing the first big animal is the result of hard work on hunting, and this is recognized with two important ceremonies—for the first male and first female animals killed.

These ceremonies are male business, performed while the women are out of camp. The young man is given small cuts and tattoos on his chest, back, and arms; these mark him as a hunter in the eyes of the world. Further cuts are rituals to strengthen his vision, stamina, aim, and determination. Then the men gather to cook and eat some of the young hunter's meat. The ritual ends with the dramatic tale of a hunt (Lee, 1979, pp. 236–240). After killing his first buck, a young man is considered eligible for marriage.

Choma

Sometime between the ages of 15 and 20, boys participate in *choma,* a sacred six-week-long initiation rite. *Choma* is an elaborate rite, in which sacred male knowledge is passed on to a new generation. It is usually held every few years during the winter dry season when several bands gather at a permanent water hole, bringing together a large enough group of boys. *Choma* is a challenging experience of hunger, cold, and thirst. The boys sing the men's songs and dance to exhaustion. Like the first buck ceremony, *choma* is performed away from women (Lee, 1979, p. 365; Shostak, p. 239).

Marriage

Marriage is an important life transition for both men and women. First marriages are usually arranged by parents or other close relatives (who will also arrange subsequent marriages if the spouses are still young). Arranging a marriage involves a lot of visiting, discussions, and gift giving, and it may actually be difficult to find a suitable mate within the restrictions of actual and fictive kinship. The marriage ceremony itself is an almost casual, hearthside occasion, attended mostly by children. Marriage and first menstruation are two important life transitions for girls that are marked by formal ceremony. It will probably seem quite strange to you that of the two events, a traditional ¡Kung girl would be likely to experience marriage first. Neither event signals an abrupt transition to adulthood, and marriage especially should be thought of more as a process—beginning with marriage negotiations and ending with the birth of a child—than as a sudden change of status.

But learning to play the role of a wife is a very difficult, and often long transition for a ¡Kung girl. Girls typically resist marriage. They are usually preadolescent, and they are in no hurry to grow up. The disparity in ages and sexual maturity of the bride and groom is a source of real difficulties. The groom is sexually mature, but he is expected to marry a child and wait, often as long as five years, before he has sex with her. During that time he must sleep by her side, live with and help her family, and probably put up with her rejection, fear, and anger. Young men find this situation very frustrating, but they usually accept it, because marriageable girls are scarce. Polygyny, though uncommon, unbalances sex ratios, and young men know that if they reject a marriage, they may have to wait for another potential bride to grow up. Newly married girls are often frightened. Frequently an adult woman, usually a close relative, sleeps next to the bride on her wedding night, and longer, to reassure her, but nevertheless, a girl's introduction to adult sex is likely to be traumatic. Sexual relations may be postponed for years, but will be unavoidable as soon as she begins menstruation (at about 16) (Shostak, pp. 129–130, 148, 150).

Khoana's Story: The Bride

When she wakes up, Kai doesn't see her daughter in her usual place, sleeping next to her fire. Could it be, she wonders happily, that Khoana has relented and agreed to sleep beside her new husband in their hut? But Khoana isn't in the hut and Kai's pleasure turns to panic. That girl has surely run away again! Hours later, they find her sleeping beneath a mongongo tree, hidden by sand dunes. "Are you crazy, girl," shouts Kai, "a lion could have eaten you!" Khoana bursts into tears and begins ripping the bracelets off her arms. "I won't go back to him. I'm afraid. I'm still a child; I'm not old enough yet for marriage."

¡Kung society tolerates a girl's free expression of her objection to marriage. She may rage and storm and may even threaten or attempt suicide. Basically, if she insists, a girl can force an end to her marriage, either by driving her husband away with unpleasantness or by enrolling family members on her side. Divorce is very common in the early years of marriage, before children are born, and it is usually initiated by the wife. It is common for a girl to enter several such "trial marriages" before finally having children and settling down to a stable marriage (Shostak, pp. 130–131, 148).

First Menstruation

The onset of menstruation is celebrated in a more public, ceremonial manner than is marriage. The girl, elaborately ornamented, stays in a special hut, while the women of the band dance and sing in a sometimes suggestive fashion. Men must not see the girl, but they watch the dancing women from a distance, making bawdy comments. The rite marks sexual maturity, but not full adulthood. Girls are unlikely to conceive a baby for about two years after menstruation begins, and in this period, their relatives still help them with gathering, cooking, and other household tasks, while they continue to play with their friends (Shostak, p. 149).

After her first menstruation, a ¡Kung girl usually begins to settle down, with her original or a new husband. She may come to love her husband and enjoy a period of romance before the first child is born. The married couple grow into an easy, relatively equal relationship, in which they go about together, exchange opinions, and make decisions jointly. Fear of her husband usually eases into acceptance and even enjoyment of sex. Also, the girl may come to enjoy the status of married woman, the presents given her by her husband and his family, and the meat he brings to her fire (Shostak, p. 150).

With the birth of a first child, a woman becomes fully adult. She and her husband are now referred to as the parents of their children ("/Toma's father" or "Nisa's mother") rather than by their childhood names, and they settle down to their major life roles in rearing children and provisioning their household. The ¡Kung love and enjoy children and wish to have many, though not too closely spaced.

New Roles in Maturity

Growing into mature adulthood and then old age, ¡Kung adults must adjust to new roles. Both men and women in maturity find opportunities to express their talents, as hunters, storytellers, artisans, musicians, healers, and informal leaders. A few men will be able to enjoy the advantages of polygynous marriage. But because of relatively high death rates, almost every adult has experienced the death of at least one child, and many the death of a spouse. Family roles change as the result of deaths.

The ¡Kung are adequately nourished, in good physical condition, and suffer little from stress or diet-related diseases. But lacking modern antibiotics and other medicines, infectious and parasitic diseases like influenza, pneumonia, gastroenteritis, tuberculosis, and malaria take a high toll of children and adults. Close-knit nuclear and extended households are repeatedly disrupted by death. The ¡Kung support each other in deeply felt mourning. People travel to attend funerals;

women publicly cry and wail, and men sometimes also cry. Family members struggle to understand the death of a child or sibling, asking why God would take a person so prematurely. But after a relatively short time, relatives and friends encourage the bereaved to stop mourning.

Death often causes the reorganization of families. After the death of the head of an extended family, the group may split up, with some of its constituent nuclear families leaving the band. There are many more widows than widowers, and they almost always marry again. Some remarriages also take place after divorce, which is relatively infrequent among adults, but readily accomplished by mutual consent, or as the result of one spouse leaving the other. No formal grounds for divorce are necessary, and there is no property to divide. Children remain with their mothers, except for teenage boys who may choose to stay with their fathers, or visit with both parents.

Polygyny

Adulthood is also the time when some ¡Kung men (approximately 5 percent at any time) are able to achieve their fantasy of having more than one wife. Polygyny has real advantages: a new sexual partner, more children, another person to gather food, and the forging of a whole new set of relationships with in-laws in another band, another *n'ore*. A second marriage may increase a man's status or political influence (Shostak, p. 169). But there are serious disadvantages too. A man must be a very good hunter to attempt polygyny, and he may even then regret his disruptive second marriage. The first wife will probably object, feel jealous and rejected; the two wives may fight so bitterly that the second one leaves. Polygynous marriages have the greatest chance of success when the second wife is the widowed sister, or the unmarried younger sister of the first (Shostak, pp. 170–171).

The Roles of the Old

Few of the ¡Kung live to old age: Barely 20 percent of those born reach age 60, but those who do will, on the average, live another ten years. The old are relatively free of high blood pressure, heart disease, and deafness and many are still vigorous. Old widows (over 40 percent of the women over 60) may marry again, or live with children or grandchildren. Old people are treated with respect and often have an influential voice in the group. The older they are, the more likely they are to be the *k'ausi* of their band. Old people are consulted because their experience is valuable. They know how people are related, who married whom, and who is comparatively older or younger. They have seen so many seasons go by that they know where to find food under unusual conditions. They know the recent history of the people and the region and the folktales, songs, and legends. As long as the group continues to live the traditional hunting and gathering life, old people play an important role in the band.

Healthy old people continue to forage, but on a reduced scale. Old women may gather closer to home, old men may set snares and gather along with their wives. But most old people contribute little food; they are supported by sharing with their relatives. Old age may be a time of intense religious exploration, especially for

women, who often wait until their children are grown before learning trance dancing and healing. For some people, spiritual powers strengthen with age; they
achieve great control over their ability to enter trance and become valued healers
and teach apprentices how to enter trance and cure.

For some people, old age is a satisfying time. If they are surrounded by children willing to provide for them, and grandchildren to be loved and cared for, they
may enjoy inclusion in the life of the band: sharing the feasts and dances, telling
and hearing the stories, sharing gossip, debating the merits of marriages. But for
those who outlive their children and spouses (one-fifth of all women, but relatively
few men) and become a burden on those with less affection for them, old age may
be far less pleasant (Shostak, pp. 324–325).

SOCIAL CHANGE AND THE FUTURE

Three Families

*Tiikay grew up and lives today on a white-owned farm. His father had been "blackbirded"
(abducted) from a hunting and gathering iKung band by white settlers and forced to work
herding cattle. Now Tiikay knows no other life. He lives with his wife and children and
other relatives in the little iKung encampment attached to the farm. Tiikay and his family
live in a hut they built of scrap tin. They wear western clothes and a locked trunk holds their
wealth: beads and extra clothing and blankets. They eat cornmeal given to them by the
farmer and cooked in a bucket over the fire, supplemented by vegetables from their garden.
They receive no wages, but the farmer also gives them milk and occasionally a cow or goat as
a Christmas present. Tiikay has managed to build up his own herd of two cows and a bull
which the farmer allows him to graze. Tiikay's problems start there. He would like to leave
the farm and live independently as a herder, but he owns no land. His wages are so low that
it is impossible for him to save up any money to buy land. If he leaves the farm he will have
to sell or eat his cattle, for there will be nowhere to graze them. Tiikay feels he is stuck.*

*Niai was raised on a Herero cattle ranch, and after marriage she and her husband Bo
worked for three years on another ranch. Then, however, bigger ranches began buying up
the land and they could get no more work. Niai and Bo moved to Chumkwe (in Namibia)
where the government was settling Bushmen, giving them food rations and land for gardens. Bo hated it there and he began drinking and getting into fights with other men. Niai
left Bo and now supports their four children on government food relief, the charity of relatives, and occasional prostitution. Niai's situation is serious: she has gonorrhea and AIDS
is inexorably making its way toward her remote region. Bo speaks despairingly, in a tone-
less, flat voice, of his inability to find work, and says that when he is not drunk he thinks
more and more of suicide.*

*/Gau was raised in the bush, but after working for two years in a South African gold mine,
he settled with his wife Niuhka at Chumkwe to be near the health clinic and the school for
their two children. But /Gau and Niuhka would like to leave Chumkwe. A lively trade in
home-brewed liquor has sprung up around the store, which sells sugar to women who make
the brew and sell it by the glass. Behind the store, people drink all day and party and dance
to radio music. They quarrel and fights break out. /Gau and Niuhka feel their children are
becoming disrespectful and they fear the effects of the liquor trade on their growing boys.
They have decided, together with Niuhka's parents, her sister and her sister's husband, and*

his older brother and his family, to return to living in the bush in Ni uhka's family n'ore, now in Bushmanland. Ni uhka and her mother have been able to sell enough handicrafts to the foundation to buy tools and seeds, and /Gau's brother has three cows and a bull. They plan to live in a village in the bush where the government has sunk a well. They will supplement cattle herding with hunting and gathering, skills still familiar to family members. They hope they can make a go of it.

These three families represent the three possible futures before the !Kung Bushmen. Which future lies ahead for most of the !Kung is unclear, but we can say with assurance that they will not be able to live as traditional foragers, isolated from outside influence. Expanding ranches, roads, planes, schools, stores, missionaries, and wars bring the outside to them and they must respond to changes not of their making.

The Forces of Change

!Kung life has changed in a classic pattern, repeated all over the world now for four centuries. Starting in the nineteenth century, new peoples came to the Kalahari Desert (the Tswana, the Herero, and the Europeans) and they introduced new technologies, new goods, and new ways of living. At first, the pace of change was slow, and !Kung culture was able to adapt and absorb the new elements.

First, the !Kung enthusiastically adopted the use of iron arrowheads and cooking pots, and the smoking of tobacco. They hammered arrowheads out of wire cut from the new fences (and later from extra wires cattle herders learned to leave next to their fences to protect them), but they could only get pots and tobacco by trade or in exchange for work. Young men became accustomed to working on Tswana and Herero cattle posts, as herders, hunters, or trackers, for a period of a few years before marriage or early in marriage. They earned little or no money, but were able to give their relatives gifts of milk and meat.

Some !Kung stayed permanently as farmhands among the Herero or Tswana. The children played together and learned each others' languages, and !Kung women married and had affairs with Herero and Tswana men. But !Kung men didn't marry black women, because the women's status was higher than theirs, though there were occasional affairs.

After 1950, !Kung men extended the pattern of early paid labor by traveling to the South African gold mines on months- or years-long work contracts. With their wages, they bought donkeys and saddles, and brought home blankets and clothes to give as gifts. They also brought gonorrhea, familiarity with money, and a taste for store-bought goods, radio music, and liquor.

Change in the Post-Colonial Era

In the nineteenth and early twentieth centuries, change came slowly to the Bushmen. Throughout the 1950s, most !Kung continued to live as hunters and gatherers. But starting in the 1960s, change became rapid, as Bushmen were evicted from their traditional lands and forced into towns or onto reservations. Today, only a small minority still live as nomadic foragers.

Ranchers Move In. Rapid change began for the Bushmen when Tswana and Herero entrepreneurs started large-scale cattle ranching in the Kalahari. By the end of the 1960s, 460 ¡Kung Bushmen at Dobe were sharing their nine water holes with 350 Herero and Tswana who owned 4,500 head of cattle and 1,800 goats (Shostak, p. 347). Around the margins of the Kalahari, water holes became contaminated by animal droppings and new diseases spread. Grazing cattle stripped bare the area around the water holes and encroached farther and farther into ¡Kung foraging territory, frightening away the game and trampling plant foods (Shostak, pp. 215–217; Silberbauer, pp. 181–184).

In Botswana, wealthy Tswana cattle ranchers moved onto traditional Bushman lands in the 1980s. The government gave them ranches of up to 25,000 acres, free of charge. Today in Botswana, along the northern edge of the Kalahari, there are an estimated 12,300 Bushmen, making up 43 percent of the population, but comprising only 2 percent of landowners. Here ranches average 17,300 acres and most are absentee owned and run by managers. The president of Botswana, Quett Masire, owns seven of these ranches and his two brothers each own two. Bushmen working on the ranches average $12.50 a month in wages (Kelso, pp. 51–53).

Botswana is an unusual country because of its mineral wealth; gem-quality diamonds are mined there and there is oil as well. Botswana's GNP has grown 13 percent a year since independence, an unusually rapid rate of growth for a developing country, but the Bushmen have not benefitted from the strong economy. Income is very unequally distributed in Botswana: The poorest half of the population receives only one-sixth of total earnings and the richest 20 percent receives two-thirds of all income. The government is eager to develop diamond and oil reserves, since over 60 percent of government revenues come from these sources. More than half the land occupied by Bushmen is now being explored by mineral companies. In 1998 the Botswana government began forcing the local Khwe Bushmen off their land because diamond deposits had just been discovered there (Kelso, pp. 51–53; Africa News Service).

The Governments Take Action. Looking back over the past 40 years, we can see that government action has had an even bigger impact on the Bushmen than have the ranchers. In 1960, Namibia was Southwest Africa, a territory ruled by white South Africa. During the 1960s, the government took over the lands where the ¡Kung Bushmen lived and created a park called Bushmanland. Most of it was a gamepark; another large portion the government gave to Herero cattle-ranchers, and another area was used to settle a group of Bushmen from Angola. The ¡Kung Bushmen were allotted a portion of the park which was called Eastern Bushmanland. This area was about 2,470 square miles, or approximately 10 percent of the former ¡Kung territory (Butler, pp. 20–23; McNeil, Nov. 13, 1997, p. A3).

The government also began urging Bushmen to move to Chumkwe, the administrative center for Bushmanland. In Chumkwe the government provided a school and a clinic, and there was a bar, a general store, and a gas station. In the 1970s and 80s, Bushmen also settled at other, smaller villages where the government sank boreholes (deep wells) to reach underground aquifers. Now there are 37 villages in Eastern Bushmanland, where 1,200 to 1,300 ¡Kung live, gardening, herding cattle, and selling crafts. ¡Kung Bushmen in Bushmanland are allowed to hunt and gather, but they may use only traditional weapons and kill only their traditional prey (McNeil, p. A3, Wood, personal communication).

In Namibia the long war for independence from South Africa, fought by the Southwest African People's Organization (SWAPO), had a violent effect on the Bushmen. Fighting raged through ¡Kung territory and many ¡Kung were hired by the South African government as soldiers and trackers. After two decades of fighting, the war ended in 1990 with the withdrawal of South African forces, and former ¡Kung soldiers, who had been paid as much as $200 a month, were left stranded. Many had never learned the traditional ¡Kung way of life, and they were fearful of the new Namibian society against which they had fought (Keller, p. A4; Lee, 1984, pp. 147–149).

In both Namibia and Botswana new black governments have been highly sensitive to problems of racial segregation, recalling *apartheid,* the South African system of legally mandated segregation. Both governments have decided that they can best pursue both their national interests and the good of the Bushmen by promoting integration of the Bushmen into the dominant Bantu society. So they oppose segregating Bushmen; but what this means in reality is that they want the Bushmen to leave the hunting and gathering life for settled cattle herding; to live in villages, like the Bantu, and go to school.

In Botswana, many Bushmen still live in and around the Central Kalahari Game Reserve, facing constant pressure from the government to move to resettlement camps, where the government provides schools, clinics, fields, seed and fertilizer, and then, when the rains fail, welfare, in the form of cornmeal or other flour. Of 39,000 Bushmen in Botswana, only 3,000 continue to live in the traditional way, and 5,000 live in resettlement camps. The others work on ranches, live in independent settlements within the reserve, or squat (live illegally) on lands that once were theirs but are now part of private ranches. Bushmen living in independent settlements struggle constantly to defend their lands against forced removal by the government or invasion by cattle straying from nearby overgrazed ranches (Kelso, pp. 51–53).

Foreign Nongovernmental Organizations Step In. In both Namibia and Botswana, anthropologists have played important roles in founding and funding organizations to help the Bushmen defend themselves against invasion by ranchers and relocation by the government. When anthropologist John Marshall visited Chumkwe in 1970, he was shocked at the squalor, disorder, and dependency he found there. He organized the Bushman Development Foundation, which fought against government efforts to make all of Bushmanland into a nature preserve, forcing all the ¡Kung to live at Chumkwe. The Bushman Development Foundation has encouraged Bushmen to live in independent villages around Nyae Nyae in Eastern Bushmanland, helping them with cattle, gardens and wells, and the legal registration of land and water rights. In Botswana anthropologists founded the

Kalahari People's Fund, which plays a similar role there (Shostak, pp. 347–348; Lee, 1984, pp. 142–144; Marshall and Ritchie, pp. vi., vii, 5–13; 153–157; Butler, pp. 20–24).

In 1993 the Namibian Ministry of Environment and Tourism established a plan called LIFE (Living in a Finite Environment) to help seven Namibian communities, including Nyae Nyae. This plan involves several foreign agencies. $14.6 million is provided by the U.S. Agency for International Development, and the World Wildlife Fund is implementing the plan to create "conservancies," areas where people and wildlife coexist, with the people managing the wildlife. The Bushmen will share fees paid by big gamehunters and they will earn money as trackers. In Botswana similar plans are funded mostly by the Scandinavian countries, especially Norway (Butler, pp. 24–25; Kelso, p. 53).

Consequences of the Settled Life

Life is very different for the ¡Kung Bushman today. More modern people have pushed them off their lands; governments have tried to settle them on reservations; and foreign aid organizations now play a big role in their lives. Now that you know what has happened to the Bushmen in the modern world, you can readily understand the recent histories of other indigenous peoples, because similar events have

As the Bushmen's land and water are taken for cattle ranches, diamond mines, and resorts, the resources for their traditional gathering and hunting economy vanish. In this staged photograph of "progress," young Bushmen in discarded western clothing share a schoolbook. Forcible settlement and cheap consumer goods speed the destruction of the traditional Bushman cultures.

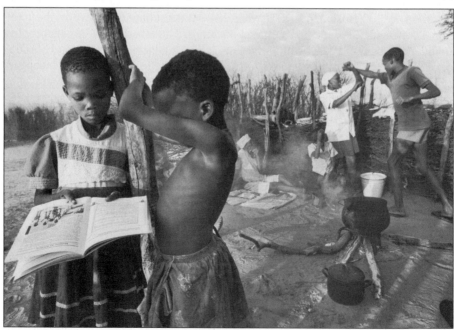

taken place all over the world—in Australia and New Guinea, in the Amazon, in the frozen north of Canada, in Mexico and Guatemala, in the Himalayas and elsewhere.

Can we draw up a balance sheet of gains and losses? Has contact with the modern world helped the ¡Kung or harmed them? The settled life is less demanding physically, and access to rudimentary health clinics is sometimes available. As a result, ¡Kung lifespans have lengthened. Settled in villages, the ¡Kung come into contact with a wider world, learning from Bantu-speaking neighbors and sending their children to school. But as the ¡Kung have been drawn into modern society, they have suffered some dramatic losses.

Sharing and cooperation among the members of each band have given way to a focus on individual families, who must act selfishly, for their own good only. Inequality has grown, and women and old people have become more isolated and less respected.

The ¡Kung themselves recognize that as they make the switch to settled herding, they are both securing their independence and irretrievably changing their society. Richard Lee points out the important contrasts between foraging and herding and farming as ways of life. Foraging is based on sharing, and the ¡Kung created a whole social structure erected on the immediate distribution of food and widespread gift giving. But farmers must save: They cannot kill the cow to feed relatives, or eat up their harvest at once, so traditional ¡Kung norms and kinship patterns are unsuited for settled life. Those ¡Kung who wish to succeed as farmers must be willing to offend their relatives and cut themselves off from kinship webs so carefully cultivated in the foraging life (Lee, 1984, pp. 137–138).

Settling down usually proves to be an irrevocable choice. Once settled in a village, the ¡Kung are tied down by schooling and babies, and find it very difficult to leave again. As we have seen, living a sedentary life, women have babies in more rapid succession, making a return to foraging impossible. And if the ¡Kung are to defend their land and herds, it is very important for their children to go to school. Illiterate, they are at a tremendous disadvantage dealing with the government and the law.

A New Relationship to the Land

Like other hunter-gatherers around the world, the ¡Kung Bushmen lived in intimate association with the land, but they didn't think of themselves as owning it. They didn't think of land as something that could be owned, and they disapproved of individual ownership anyhow. But living as villagers in Botswana and Namibia, the ¡Kung must own their land, individually or collectively, in order to keep it. Also, their new way of life encourages a new attitude to the land. In the past, the ¡Kung lived in harmony with their environment. Their numbers were small and their population grew slowly, if at all, and they did not exhaust the water or the animal and plant life of the Kalahari. Now, hunting with guns and horses, the Bushmen can hunt down all the animals around their villages. Modern society makes people think differently; it makes resources seem infinite. If there are no more antelope, or if there are more ¡Kung, you can raise goats, and if the goats are not enough, you can work for money and buy meat. Meat seems an endless, not a limited resource; only the individual's power to get it may be limited.

Today, the inhabitants of the Kalahari Desert are using its fragile environment in new, more destructive ways. Herding itself is not inherently damaging to the desert. Just as wild animals graze the Kalahari, so too can herds of goats and cattle. But the human and animal population of the Kalahari is increasing rapidly, placing unsustainable demands on the land and water. Commercial ranches cluster around the permanent water holes and the new boreholes and large numbers of cattle strip away all plant life. Africans call this process **desertification,** since the denuded land becomes a real desert, in which trees and grasses do not grow back and the wind erodes the soil. When rain falls, the ground doesn't hold it, and the water table gradually drops. Ranchers must then move on to less desirable, drier land, which is all the sooner exhausted. As a growing human population tries to graze more and more cattle, the process of desertification accelerates. Population growth, displacement, and desertification feed each other in a destructive cycle.

New Patterns of Work

Increasingly, the ¡Kung Bushmen find they must work for others, for wages, or make things for sale. They are no longer able to live independently, self-sufficient in the Kalahari Desert. They have become dependent on farmers and ranchers for employment, or even on tourists who buy their crafts or pay to look at them pretending to hunt (McNeil, Nov. 13, 1997, Daley). They are dependent too on foreign relief agencies, which help Bushmen settle on the land and defend their interests. Also, many Bushmen have become dependent on government welfare—mostly handouts of flour—when they move into towns. In many cases, even Bushmen who try to live independently, as herders at the new villages, still need government food rations in order to survive. While they may have more possessions, better houses, animals to ride instead of walking, these Bushmen have lost something valuable: their independence. They have become a very small part of a global economy, dressing up as hunter-gatherers for European and American tourists, raising cattle and mining gold for export, hoping to buy goods, like flashlights, iron pots, sneakers, or radios that have been imported from other countries.

Changing Roles and Relationships

Anthropologist John Yellen's detailed study of the Dobe ¡Kung has convinced him that accumulation of possessions changes relationships among the ¡Kung. Once craft sales made it possible for the ¡Kung at Dobe to make money and buy possessions, they began hoarding, rather than sharing with others through gift-giving. Ashamed of not sharing, they sought privacy, building their huts farther apart and facing their doors away from each other. Living in larger, more substantial huts, the ¡Kung began to spend more time indoors, cooking at indoor hearths instead of outdoors in the shared central space, and storing their possessions indoors, sometimes in locked trunks, rather than outdoors, hung casually in trees and on fences. People spent less time together as a band, and more time separately in individual families (Yellen, pp. 96–105).

It follows too, that once people cease to share everything, inequality immediately grows, for some are more successful than others. In Namibia new differences in wealth have been particularly extreme, as certain individuals who allied them-

selves with the South African government during the war with SWAPO received
large rewards (one woman worked making tourists films, a man became a cabinet
minister in the regional white-dominated government, and others were well-paid as
soldiers in the South African army). People who were able to establish claims to
land and acquire cattle prospered, while their less lucky or less entrepreneurial relatives ended up landless and dependent (Lee, 1984, p. 148; Wilmsen, pp. 247–257).

The sedentary life and the accumulation of possessions have also affected
¡Kung patterns of conflict resolution. Yellen found that heavy possessions tied
down the Dobe ¡Kung. When serious conflicts developed between individuals,
they could no longer resolve them in the usual way by traveling to join relatives
elsewhere. As a result, the Dobe ¡Kung turned to Bantu chiefs for arbitration. They
became more and more involved with the Bantus, more dependent on individual
Bantus, and more likely to intermarry (Yellen, pp. 96–105).

Gender Inequalities. Inequalities between men and women have also grown
among the ¡Kung living in villages and towns, leaving women in a more dependent, subordinate position. In their old hunting and gathering days, all life for the
¡Kung was family life, but modern society draws a line between "public" and "private" life. In most cases, ¡Kung men are more able than women to get paid work,
so their work takes them out more into the public realm. They learn more about
dealing with other ethnic groups, with ranchers and farmers and the government.
Men control the money they bring home and the possessions they buy with it.
Women become more tied to the home by housework, carrying water and wood,
repairing houses and cooking food. The work they do is devalued because it is unpaid; it no longer appears to be work. Tied down by babies, no longer the main
providers of food, women become more dependent on men (Draper, 1975, p. 85;
Draper and Cashdan, 1988, p. 361).

Government programs and programs developed by western aid agencies often
reinforce gender inequalities. They make jobs available to men, but not to women,
or they give cows or agricultural tools to men alone. Furthermore, when ¡Kung
groups live near Bantu-speaking people or work for them, they adopt their customs and beliefs along with their technology. Bantu-speaking societies are
strongly male-dominated. Men own the cattle and the fields, male and female roles
are sharply differentiated, and men control political decision making. Women lack
legal rights and sons are preferred to daughters. These patterns influence nearby
¡Kung societies (Kent, 1995, pp. 528–534).

In sedentary villages, old people too lose some of the respect they once enjoyed. Old people find village life easier than the old nomadic existence, but their
traditional knowledge becomes superfluous. They know nothing of cows, wells,
and arithmetic. Once the *k'ausi* of *n'ores,* they have no authority with government
land boards.

A Damaged Sense of Self

For the ¡Kung, as for other isolated indigenous peoples around the world,
contact with modern society often damages individuals' self-esteem. If tourists,
dressed in gaily colored sports clothes, pay to look at you, almost naked, as if you

were an animal in a zoo, you begin to feel less than fully human. You begin to feel inferior. The tourists seem fabulously rich; they spend more on craft items in a day than the ¡Kung earn in a month or even a year. Compared to them, the ¡Kung feel poor. Even the neighboring Bantu-speaking peoples are richer than the Bushmen; they have cows and permanent houses with dried mud walls and tin roofs. Many ¡Kung admire the Bantu-speakers, respect their chiefs, and wish to adopt their system of farming and herding, their norms for relationships between men and women. But the ¡Kung are seen as inferior by their Bantu-speaking neighbors. When you want to be like people who reject you, that is psychologically wounding.

Sociology offers some powerful concepts to help you understand the psychological state of the ¡Kung Bushmen. One is the concept of **marginality,** associated with two famous American sociologists, Louis Wirth and Robert E. Park. The "marginal man," said Park, "lives in two worlds in both of which he is more or less a stranger" (Park, p. 356; Wirth, p. 73). Marginality is an important American concept because it describes so well the situation of many immigrants, who find they are changed by the American experience. They no longer fit into the society they came from, while at the same time, they are not fully accepted in the dominant American society. The Bushmen experience marginality when the hunting and gathering life no longer seems sufficient to them, but they are still rejected by Bantus and whites in modern Namibia and Botswana.

Anomie. The most famous sociological concept that can help you understand the Bushmen is Emile Durkheim's concept of **anomie.** Anomie means literally a state of normlessness, a social condition in which shared norms no longer effectively regulate individual desires. Durkheim saw anomie occurring in times of rapid social change, when old norms fail to apply to new conditions, and people are no longer sure what they can expect in life (Durkheim, 1951 pp. 248–250). Anomie is a condition of society, not a psychological state, but it is regularly associated with certain individual symptoms like depression, feelings of meaninglessness and aimlessness. When societies suffer from anomie, Durkheim said, rates of suicide rise, and we notice nowadays that rates of alcohol and drug abuse rise too. The concept of anomie can help us understand many ¡Kung groups, especially those around the larger towns like Chumkwe, who seem to have lost their social moorings. Caught between the values of a lost culture, and those of another, not yet their own, some town-dwelling ¡Kung have lapsed into unemployment, dependency, drunkenness, and violence.

The Future: Adaptation and Anomie

Looking toward the future we have to ask: Will the Bushmen remain stranded between the hunting and gathering life to which they cannot return and the larger societies of Botswana and Namibia (which have so far rejected them)? Susan Kent reports on one group of Bushmen, the Kutse Basarwa (who are not ¡Kung) who have settled in villages and taken up herding, without abandoning sharing or gender equality (Kent, 1995). This group has been able (so far) to integrate a new livelihood into their old culture. Most iKung have moved further away from their traditions, but some have succeeded in adapting elements of their old culture to new circumstances. For example, in many villages, the iKung use donkeys to travel to the mongongo nut groves and bring back sacks of this traditional wild food, still an important part of the iKung diet. Some iKung men maintain their tracking and hunting skills, now using rifles on horseback as paid huntsmen of the Herero and Tswana. The trance dance and the drum dance have endured and even grown in importance in villages where Tswana and Herero neighbors attend the popular dances along with the iKung and even send for iKung healers in time of illness (Shostak, p. 219). Intermarrying iKung and Bantu have invented the new status of *swara*—brothers-in-law by intermarriage—who are elaborately jovial and cordial with each other, avoiding potential anger at the "theft" of a sister, and disguising the real inequality in a situation where Bantus marry iKung women, but iKung men never marry Bantu women (Lee, 1984, p. 127).

It may be that for Bushmen the most favorable outcome will be to blend gradually into Bantu society. The children of iKung/Bantu marriages think of themselves as Bantu. As they attend school and become educated, increasingly they think of themselves as Botswanan or Namibian, not Bantu or iKung. At the same time, there are terrible losses—to dependency and drunkenness, violence and disease—among those groups of Bushman who have failed to find a new place for themselves in society.

Thinking Sociologically

1. Explain what the authors mean when they say that the iKung "live close to nature."
2. Can you use the functionalist perspective to explain why the iKung Bushmen emphasize sharing, why they are nomadic, and why they have small families?
3. What are the most important social groups in iKung society?
4. Compare the status and roles of women in iKung society and in Japanese society. Is the status of women in your society more similar to that of iKung women or that of Japanese women?
5. Which of the four types of social interaction (social exchange, cooperation, competition, and conflict) predominate in iKung society? How about in your own society?
6. What effects has the spread of large-scale commercial farming had in Mexico and in the Kalahari Desert?
7. When iKung bands settle down in villages, how do their roles and relationships and sense of self change?
8. Use the Internet to find out about another indigenous people threatened by social change and compare their situation to that of the iKung.

For Further Reading

LEE, RICHARD, *The iKung San.* Cambridge: Cambridge University Press, 1979.
LEE, RICHARD B., *The Dobe iKung.* New York: Holt, 1984.
SHOSTAK, MARJORIE, *Nisa.* Cambridge, MA: Harvard University Press, 1981.
THOMAS, ELIZABETH MARSHALL, *The Harmless People.* New York: Knopf, 1959.

Bibliography

Africa South of the Sahara, 1995, Europa Publications, Ltd., 24th edition.

AFRICAN NEWS SERVICE, "Botswana's Hidden Agenda in Kalahari Bushmen Eviction," Mar. 27, 1998, Doc ID GG19980330020000139.

BIESELE, MEGAN, "Religion and Folklore," in Phillip V. Tobias, ed., *The Bushmen: San Hunters and Herders of Southern Africa.* Cape Town: Human & Rousseau, 1978, pp. 162, 165–168.

BUTLER, VICTORIA, "Bushmen at a Crossroads," *International Wildlife,* Vol. 27, no. 4 (July–August, 1997), pp. 20–27.

DALEY, SUZANNE, "Endangered Bushmen Find Refuge in a Game Park," *The New York Times,* Jan. 18, 1996, p. A4.

DRAPER, PAT, "Kung Women: Contrasts in Sexual Egalitarianism in Foraging and Sedentary Contexts," in Reyna Reiter, ed., *Towards an Anthropology of Women.* New York: Monthly Review Press, 1975.

DRAPER, PAT, AND E. CASHDAN, "Technological Change and Child Behavior among the ¡Kung," *Ethnology,* Vol. 27 (1988), pp. 339–365.

DRAPER, PAT, AND M. KRANICHFELD, "Coming In From the Bush: Settled Life by the ¡Kung and Their Accommodation to Bantu Neighbors," *Human Ecology,* Vol. 18 (1990), pp. 363–384.

DURKHEIM, EMILE, *Suicide.* New York: The Free Press, 1951.

———, *The Elementary Forms of the Religious Life.* New York: Free Press, 1915, 1965.

EIBL-EIBESFELDT, IRENAUS, "Early Socialization in the ¡Xo Bushmen," in Phillip V. Tobias, ed., *The Bushmen: San Hunters and Herders of Southern Africa.* Cape Town: Human & Rousseau, 1978, pp. 132–135.

FISHER, HELEN E., *The Anatomy of Love.* New York: W. W. Norton, 1992.

GELLES, RICHARD J., AND ANN LEVINE, *Sociology, An Introduction,* 6th ed. New York: McGraw-Hill, 1999.

GORDON, ROBERT J., *The Bushman Myth: The Making of a Namibian Underclass.* Boulder, CO: Westview Press, 1992.

HITCHCOCK, ROBERT, "Decentralization and Development among the Ju/wasi in Namibia," *Cultural Survival Quarterly,* Vol. 12, No. 3 (1988), pp. 31–33.

KELLER, BILL, "Misfits of Peace: Is This the End of the Bushmen?" *The New York Times,* May 10, 1993, p. A4.

KELSO, CASEY, "The Landless Bushmen," *Africa Report,* Vol. 38, no. 2 (March–April 1993), pp. 51–53.

KENT, SUSAN, "And Justice for All: The Development of Political Centralization among Newly Sedentary Foragers," *American Anthropologist,* Vol. 91, no. 3 (Sept. 1989), pp. 703–712.

———, "Does Sendentarization Promote Gender Inequality: A Case Study from the Kalahari," *Journal of the Royal Anthropological Institute,* Vol. 1, no. 3 (Sept. 1995), pp. 513–537.

LEE, RICHARD B., "Ecology of a Contemporary San People," in Phillip V. Tobias, ed., *The Bushmen: San Hunters and Herders of Southern Africa.* Cape Town: Human & Rousseau, 1978, pp. 94–96.

———, *The ¡Kung San.* Cambridge: Cambridge University Press, 1979.

———, *The Dobe ¡Kung.* New York: Holt, 1984.

LEE, RICHARD B., AND IRVEN DEVORE, eds., *Kalahari Hunter-Gatherers.* Cambridge, MA: Harvard University Press, 1976.

LENSKI, GERHARD, PATRICK NOLAN, AND JEAN LENSKI, *Human Societies: An Introduction to Macrosociology,* 6th ed. New York: McGraw-Hill, 1991.

MARSHALL, JOHN, AND CLAIRE RITCHIE, *Where Are the Ju/wasi of Nyae Nyae?* Cape Town: University of Cape Town African Studies Program, 1984.

MARSHALL, LORNA, *The ¡Kung of Nyae Nyae.* Cambridge, MA: Harvard University Press, 1976.

MCNEIL, DONALD G., JR., "In Bushmanland, Hunters' Tradition Turns to Dust," *The New York Times,* Nov. 13, 1997, p. A3.

———, "Aids Stalking Africa's Struggling Economies," *The New York Times,* Nov. 15, 1998, pp. 1, 20.

PARK, ROBERT E., *Race and Culture.* New York: The Free Press, 1950.

ROUE, MARIE, "An Economy of Sharing: There Is No Place for Selfish Individualism in Nomadic Hunter-Gatherer Societies," *UNESCO Courier* (January 1998), pp. 23–25.

SHOSTAK, MARJORIE, *Nisa.* Cambridge, MA: Harvard University Press, 1981.

SILBERBAUER, GEORGE B., "The Future of the Bushmen," in Phillip V. Tobias, ed., *The Bushmen: San Hunters and Herders of Southern Africa.* Cape Town: Human & Rousseau, 1978, p. 181.

THOMAS, ELIZABETH MARSHALL, *The Harmless People.* New York: Knopf, 1959.

TOBIAS, PHILLIP V., ed., *The Bushmen: San Hunters and Herders of Southern Africa.* Cape Town: Human & Rousseau, 1978.

WILMSEN, EDWIN N., *Land Filled with Flies: A Political Economy of the Kalahari.* Chicago: University of Chicago Press, 1989.

WIRTH, LOUIS, *The Ghetto.* Chicago: University of Chicago Press, 1928, 1956.

WOOD, ERIC, personal communication, 1995.

YELLEN, JOHN E., "The Transformation of the Kalahari ¡Kung," *Scientific American* (Apr. 1990), pp. 96–105.

EGYPT

 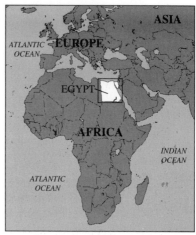

You can reach Cairo, Egypt's capital in a short flight from anywhere in the Middle East or the Mediterranean. Athens, Rome, Damascus, and Jerusalem are only hours (or minutes) away. You will set down in one of the oldest human civilizations. Thirty centuries before Christ there were cities, scholars, and kings in Egypt.

LOCATION: Egypt rests in Africa's northeast corner bordered by Israel and the Red Sea on the east, the Sudan on the south, Libya to the west, and the Mediterranean Sea to the north.

AREA: 384,000 square miles or 1,113,600 square kilometers. Egypt is as large as Texas and New Mexico combined or about the size of Ontario.

LAND: Egypt is mostly desert. Population is concentrated in the Nile Valley and on the Delta—one of the world's most densely settled areas.

CLIMATE: Hot and dry. The coast gets 8 inches of rain per year, while south of Cairo there is almost none. Egypt is hot from May to October (up to 107° F) and cooler from November to April (55 to 70° F).

POPULATION: In 2000 there were 68 million people; 36 percent were under the age of 15. By 2025 population is projected to reach 98 million.

INCOME: An average of U.S. $1,065 GDP per person in 1995. 21 percent of Egyptians live in absolute poverty.

EDUCATION: 39 percent of Egyptian women are literate, as are 64 percent of Egyptian men.

RELIGION: 91 percent of Egyptians are Sunni Muslims; at least 5 percent are Coptic Christians.

MINORITIES: Coptic Christians and Saidis—people from the southern part of Egypt.

CHAPTER 4

Egypt: Faith, Gender, and Class

INTRODUCTION

It would be a good idea to start this chapter by thinking about what you already know about Egypt. When you think of Egypt, do pyramids, palm trees, and mummies come to mind? Do you think of veiled women and Muslims kneeling in prayer? Does your mind turn to violence in the Middle East and militant Islamic fundamentalists? For many people, Egypt is a faraway place with an exotic past and a frightening present. Why should you learn more about it?

One good reason to study Egypt is that it is an Islamic society and today everyone needs to know something about Islam. Islam is one of the world's great religions, practiced by more than 900 million people worldwide. Followers of Islam are known as Muslims. The three nations with the largest Muslim populations are Indonesia, Pakistan, and Bangladesh, but there are millions of Muslims in other parts of the world too, including Egypt, Morocco, Algeria, and Nigeria in Africa; Saudi Arabia, Iran, Iraq, Jordan, and Syria in the Middle East (Lippman, 1990, pp. ix, x).

Another reason to learn more about Egypt is that it is an important third world nation, one of many former European colonies struggling with poverty, economic development, and rapid population growth. Like other societies in Africa, Asia, and Latin America, Egypt is also struggling to define its attitude toward the West in the post–Cold War world. Because of its sensitive geographic location—in the Arab oil-producing region, near Israel, in Africa, and not far from Europe, conflict in Egypt makes the news and reverberates around the world.

A final reason to study Egypt is that if you come from a western nation, you will find Egypt very different from your own society. You will learn a lot from contrasting the two. Three aspects of Egyptian society are absolutely central: faith, gender, and class. In Egypt the Islamic faith imbues all aspects of life: People understand the values they cherish and the norms they follow in religious terms. They debate government and law and politics in the light of their religion.

Class contrasts are unavoidable in Egypt. There are sophisticated young men and women who live in luxury apartments in Cairo's modern high-rise apartment towers, who would not be out of place in New York, Paris, or London. Their clothing comes from Milan and Paris, their luxury cars from Germany, their electronics from Japan, and their income from high-level jobs in Egypt's banking and legal establishments. Not far from the apartments of such wealthy Egyptians, poor people fill the narrow alleys of Cairo's oldest quarters. Many are recent migrants from villages in southern Egypt, where electricity, doctors, and clean water have yet to make an appearance.

The aspect of Egyptian society that may make the greatest impression on you is the contrasting roles played by men and women. Egyptian men and women have different religious obligations, different family responsibilities, and different legal rights. In public and private, Egyptian men and women usually carry on their lives separately from each other. Let us introduce you to three Egyptians who illustrate these important aspects of their society.

Three Egyptians: Their Stories

Saad is tired. At 14 he rises very early each morning to study for his high school classes. His father is a small shopkeeper, but Saad badly wants to be a professional with a good salary and a house in a fashionable part of the city. He interrupts his studies only for a cup of tea, a roll, and morning prayers. As busy as he might be, Saad, like his father Ibrahim, prays five times a day. Ibrahim has a "raisin" on his forehead: a small dark bruise raised by touching his forehead to the ground thousands of times in a long lifetime of prayer. Although the future that Saad dreams of may be very different from his father's, Saad cannot imagine a life outside Islam. It is as much a part of him as his family, his friends, and his hopes. Every morning Saad spends the long walk to school listening to the Quran (the holy book of Islam) recited on his Walkman.

Fatima, 27, lives in the village of Bani Hasan in Upper, or southern, Egypt. Her husband Hussain is away in Saudi Arabia, working in construction. The money he sends home has paid for an extra room built onto the house, and an extra acre of land. Fatima and her children live with Hussain's parents, his two brothers, and his older brother's wife and three children. Fatima has never left her village; it is hard for her to imagine Hussain in a big city like Riyadh. Fatima stayed in school through fourth grade, so she can help her children a little with their homework and she can read the Quran. She worries about her husband, so far away, but life goes on much as usual, since she spends most of her time in the company of her mother-in-law and her sister-in-law. The three women work in the kitchen together and in the fields. At quiet moments in the late afternoon, they relax together chatting in the courtyard while the children play.

Anwar is a 31-year-old manager. Young, ambitious, self-confident, he hopes to rise in Egypt's business circles. He is a graduate of Cairo's American University and he holds a graduate degree in business from Michigan State. Employed by a large construction company, Anwar is already expanding his range of contacts. Not the least of these is Asya, his fiancé whose relatives hold important posts in business and government. Anwar is fluent in English and French and travels frequently to Europe and America. He met Asya, then a student in Paris, while consulting with a large French civil engineering company. In Cairo, Anwar lives with his parents and younger sisters in the affluent Garden City neighborhood. Cosmopolitan as he is, Anwar is devoted to his family, especially to his mother. He is concerned about his sister Mina, who wants to study literature in the United States. America is a fine place for a business degree, but is it any place for a carefully protected young woman? Anwar is a Muslim, but not a very active one. Though he rarely goes to the mosque, he is careful not to offend his more religious co-workers.

To understand why Islam is fundamental to Egyptian culture, how class inequalities have come to divide Egyptian society so deeply, and why the position of women is the subject of such passionate debate in contemporary Egypt, you need information about Egypt's long and fascinating history.

EGYPT'S HISTORY

Because of its geographic location, Egypt has been a crossroads of cultures ever since the beginning of human civilization. In the past, Egyptians invented new technologies, arts, and sciences and many of these spread to other societies. But Egypt's location also made it vulnerable to invasion. Although it was one of the world's first nations, Egypt suffered conquest after conquest by other societies that successively imposed their cultures and social structures. Egypt embraced some of the invading societies and absorbed their cultures, but resisted others. In its long history Egypt has changed its language and religion three times. After the ancient pharaonic period (c. 3100 B.C.–671 B.C.), Egypt was conquered and became part of the Greek and Roman empires (333 B.C.–A.D. 641). Next came the Arab-Islamic conquest of Egypt, and the long period of Islamic civilization (641–1798) which followed. In recent centuries, Egypt was conquered once again, this time by Europeans, and subjected to European colonialism (1798–1952). Then, in the mid-twentieth century, Egypt entered its present era of postcolonial independence (1952–present). Throughout its history, Egypt has been an intellectual and cultural center. The great library at Alexandria brought together all the knowledge of the ancient world. Later, Cairo became an important focus for Islamic scholarship. And in the nineteenth and twentieth centuries, Cairo was the literary and cultural leader of the Arab world, a magnet for novelists, filmmakers, journalists, and political activists, who argued and inspired each other in the literary coffee houses and shaped cultural life in the whole Arab world.

The Pharaonic Period

One of the world's first great civilizations developed in Egypt. Egyptians began farming as early as 9,000 years ago, and by 4,000 years ago they had built towns, and wealthy people lived in elaborate houses, adorned with gold and glass ornaments, musical instruments, pottery, and cloth. Merchants traveled and traded with other societies in Africa and the Middle East. By 3000 B.C. the reign of the pharaohs began, which lasted nearly 3,000 years. Pharaonic Egypt created some of the first government bureaucracies, complete with record keepers and tax collectors. The power of the pharaohs and the energy and knowledge they commanded is still visible today in their surviving monuments: the pyramids, temples, deserted cities, and tombs of the Egyptian desert.

Greek and Roman Empires

Pharaonic Egypt lasted until 332 B.C., when Alexander the Great conquered Egypt—one step in a stunning series of victories over all of Greece and then over the armies of Asia and Africa. Alexander was the young ruler of Macedonia, a small, poor country in the Balkans, but he put together a historic empire. After Alexander's death, one of his generals, Ptolemy, took over rule of Egypt. Ptolemy and his successors drew Egypt into the Greek world. Greek replaced Coptic, the ancient language of Egypt. Egyptian decorative arts began to follow Greek artistic ideas and depictions of Egyptian gods began to resemble Greek gods. Ptolemy and his successors built a new capital city, Alexandria, on the shore of the Mediterranean, facing toward Europe.

Greek conquest brought great changes to the lives of Egyptian men and especially Egyptian women. Women had been respected in pharaonic Egypt. There were important female deities and priestesses, and women and men were equal before the law. Women could own property and sue for divorce and they could socialize freely in public with men (Ahmed, pp. 31–33). All this changed with the Greek conquest. In Greek civilization, free women (as opposed to slaves) were **secluded** (that is, they were kept separate from men and out of public view). They could not be seen by any men except close relatives. Men engaged in public life—in the marketplace, the gymnasium, and the political assembly—while women stayed home in special rooms at the back of the house. Greek women were expected to be silent and submissive, and most important, to provide male heirs for a society that was focused on the male line. Women could not own property and anything they inherited was held in trust for them by male relatives (Ahmed, pp. 28–31).

The Roman Conquest and Christianity

Not long after Alexander's conquests, the city of Rome came to dominate much of Mediterranean Europe. Then, in the first century B.C., Rome defeated the Ptolemies and added Egypt to the expanding Roman Empire, which now ringed the Mediterranean Sea. International trade led to a burst of economic and intellectual productivity in Egypt. Egypt grew the wheat for Rome's bread, and Alexandria became the intellectual center of the entire Roman world.

In the years after Christ's birth, Christianity came to Alexandria and found a receptive audience. For several centuries, Christianity spread throughout Egypt, gradually replacing the worship of the ancient gods of the Nile. Christian ideas about women were similar to Greek ideas. Early Christian women were frequently covered from head to toe in voluminous gowns and veils and they were strictly segregated in order to protect men from temptation (Ahmed, pp. 35–36).

But while Christianity blossomed in Egypt, the Roman Empire declined. The empire had grown so large, stretching from the Atlantic Ocean to the Red Sea, that Rome could not effectively rule it. In the fourth century A.D., Rome divided itself into an Eastern and a Western Empire. The Eastern Empire, which included Egypt, was to be ruled from the ancient city of Byzantium (today Istanbul, in Turkey). Byzantium proved to be a less friendly ruler than Rome. The Byzantine rulers objected to the way Egyptians practiced Christianity and persecuted Coptic (Egyptian) Christians. By the seventh century, Egyptians regarded the Byzantines less as brothers in Christ and more as hated tyrants.

The Arab/Islamic Conquest

When the seventh century began, Egypt was a Christian country; its language was Greek and it identified with the cultural traditions of Greece, Rome, and Jerusalem. All this was to change forever with the explosive growth of a new religion: Islam. Islam originated in the Arabian city of Mecca (now in Saudi Arabia), at that time a crossroads of trade between India and the Byzantine Empire. In the seventh century, Muhammad, a 42-year-old merchant, had a revelation from God and announced a new faith—Islam—that built upon Arab culture, Christianity, and Judaism. By 632 Muhammad's followers dominated Arabia. In 639 the militant followers of the new faith swept across the borders of the Byzantine Empire and rapidly conquered Egypt, Syria, and Palestine. In the decades that followed, they swept beyond Egypt, west through North Africa, and on to Spain and east to the borders of China.

Although the Arabs came as conquerors, they were not entirely unwelcome in Egypt. The bitterness that Egyptians felt toward the Byzantines led them to stand aside as the Arabs crushed the Byzantine forces. The Arabs, for their part, demanded much less than had the Byzantines: Only obedience and taxes were required. Although the Arabs devoutly wished for converts to their new faith, they did not forcibly convert Egyptians—whether Christians or Jews or worshipers of the ancient gods.

Islam gradually transformed Egyptian society. Arabic became the common language of Egypt, replacing Coptic, the language of ancient Egypt, and the Greek of the Greco-Roman period. Cairo, a new Islamic city, replaced Alexandria in importance and became a world center of Islamic learning. By the fourteenth century, most Egyptians had embraced Islam, and Islamic beliefs and practices became a fundamental part of Egyptian culture. (However, a minority remained Christians. About 6 percent of Egyptians today are Copts, Coptic Christians.) Arab literature, music, and the arts were absorbed into Egyptian culture.

Islam didn't much change the status of women in Egypt. It shared Christian gender norms and attitudes toward women. Islam did give Egyptian women limited rights to sue for divorce and a limited right to inherit, but it also introduced into Egypt the Arab practice of **polygyny** (which allowed men to marry more than one wife) (Ahmed, p. 33).

European Colonialism

For many centuries after the foundation of Islam, the Islamic world was a center of trade, knowledge, and wealth. At the same time Europe declined into its "Dark Ages," a period when government disintegrated, knowledge was lost, and trade withered. But by the fourteenth and fifteenth centuries, Europe began to develop and expand, gradually pushing aside the Islamic world. Europeans forced Arab rulers out of Spain in 1492. They took over trade with India in the sixteenth century, and in 1798, a French army, led by Napoleon, conquered Egypt itself. The French were soon expelled by the British and Turks, with whom they were at war, but European political and economic domination of Egypt continued. England, in particular, believed it had a major interest in Egypt; it wanted Egyptian customers for its products and it wanted to control the Suez Canal, the most direct route to India, Great Britain's largest colony.

Some Egyptians prospered during this colonial period of European domination. An elite of landowners, government officials, and professionals, who cooperated with the Europeans, came under the influence of European culture and ideas.

They adopted French (rather than Arabic) as their everyday language and sent their sons to schools where they were taught in French and read European books. They ate European food, drank wine, and read European literature. Many thought and wrote about how a society could be at once modern and Islamic. Egypt's elite also absorbed European ideas about democracy, the right of nations to self-rule, and the need for equality between women and men. During the colonial period, some affluent Egyptian women publicly removed their veils and participated in the political struggle for independence. However, for most Egyptians life became much harder during the colonial period. Many peasants lost their land, weavers, tailors and other skilled workers could not compete against machine-made European goods, and the growing ranks of industrial workers labored long hours for very low wages. Poor Egyptians had little contact with European culture: They spoke Arabic and took consolation in Islam. Both the economic and the cultural distance between rich and poor widened.

The European powers made increasingly restrictive demands on the Egyptian government, and in 1882 a revolt against these restrictions by the Egyptian army led to the occupation of Egypt by the British. From 1882 through 1954, the object of modern Egyptian politics was the end of the British occupation. Although a popular revolt in 1919 led the British to proclaim Egypt independent in 1921, the British army remained in occupation and the newly created king and parliament were dominated by the British ambassador. In 1952, following a humiliating defeat of the Egyptian army by the forces of Israel, the newly independent Jewish state, a group of junior officers deposed King Farouk and took control of the government. In 1954 these officers, led by Gamal Abdul Nasser, expelled the British army and created real independence for Egypt for the first time in 100 years.

An Independent Egypt

It is ironic that western ideas played so large a role in Egypt's revolt against European domination. Nasser, Egypt's greatest twentieth-century figure, transformed Egypt's government and economy and greatly improved the lives of the poorest Egyptians. While he respected Islam, Nasser looked to the West, to the United States, the Soviet Union, and Europe for political values and institutional models. Nasser moved his country in the direction of a **secular** (that is, not religious) authority: a system of business law separate from Islamic family law, a school system separate from religious education, and western-style parliamentary government separate from religious authority. Nasser established a public school system that was open to all but the poorest Egyptians, and open to women as well as men. He chose to build a **socialist** economy, in which most enterprises were government-owned and the government was the society's largest employer.

Nasser also challenged Egypt's deep economic inequalities, particularly in the countryside. His first target was the great landowning families who owned more than a third of Egypt's land. Nasser seized the land belonging to the royal family and required the other rich families to sell more than half their land. He redistributed this land to hundreds of thousands of poor peasant families. Many poor families received no land, and even those who did acquired only very small plots, but all felt grateful to Nasser; they felt released from oppressive landlords and they hoped to be given more land in the future (Hooglund, pp. 122–123; Mitchell, T., pp. 22–23).

Taha's Story: The Peasant

Taha was a young man in his teens when Gamal Abdul Nasser deposed the king, but it is still a glowing day in his memory. Not only was the honor of the country restored, but the cruelty of the greedy landlords and their agents came to an end. As a young boy, Taha would rise to find a sickle before his family's home, a signal that a day's badly paid work was demanded by the landlord. Refusal to work was met with threats and beatings. Young Taha could feel the contempt of the landlords who drove out from Cairo in their luxurious automobiles. When Nasser made these fat Cairenes sell their land, they left Egypt. This made a good deal of sense to Taha; he thought of these rich people as foreigners. Nasser's revolt enabled Taha to buy three acres of fertile Delta soil. He married and raised three sons and a daughter in a freedom and prosperity he could never have imagined before Nasser: enough to eat, a radio, a television, and school for his children. At Nasser's death, Taha traveled to Cairo for the first time. Carrying a green palm frond, symbol of eternal life, Taha and hundreds of thousands of peasants followed Egypt's president to his grave. Gamal Abdul Nasser has been dead more than 20 years, but for Taha, there is no one like him.

Egypt's peasants benefited in a limited way from Nasser's land reform. But Nasser's attack against the great landowners transformed the rural middle class. They bought much of the land the elite was forced to sell and turned themselves into prosperous commercial farmers (Vatikiotis, pp. 396–399).

Politics in Independent Egypt

Nasser won wide support from Egyptians because he helped many people become more prosperous and he succeeded in evicting the British. At the same time, however, he severely restricted democracy. The army crushed strikes and suppressed militant Islamic groups and jailed their leaders.

In 1956 the British, French, and Israeli armies once again invaded Egypt. Britain and France wanted to reassert their control over the region, and Israel wanted to end Nasser's support of the Palestinians who attacked Israel. Although Egypt's armies were defeated in the fighting with Israel, Nasser persuaded the United States and the Soviet Union to force the invaders to withdraw. Nasser emerged as the hero, not only of Egypt, but of the Arab world as a whole. Strengthened by political and economic support from the Soviet Union, Nasser led Egypt into a period of prosperity and international leadership. Other Arab countries recognized Nasser as the leader of "pan-Arabism," a movement for political unity among Arab nations. "Nonaligned" countries—those like India and Yugoslavia, that sought to avoid becoming a part of either the Soviet bloc or the U.S.-led western block—also looked to Nasser for leadership.

But much of Egypt's progress was brought to a halt by the 1967 war with Israel. Israel defeated Egypt's armed forces so completely that it humiliated both the Egyptian leadership and ordinary Egyptians. Many Egyptian soldiers were killed or injured and Egypt's economy was shattered by the closing of the Suez Canal, the capture of the country's developing oil fields in the Sinai Peninsula, and the wave of refugees that poured out of war-torn areas.

In the remaining years of his life, Nasser struggled to undo the damage of the war, but it remained for his successor, Anwar Sadat, to bring about the withdrawal of Israel's army from Egypt. In 1973 Egyptian forces crossed the canal and forced the Israeli army back into the Sinai Desert. Although Israel's forces later recrossed the canal, isolating the Egyptian army, and moved into Egypt's heartland, the initial defeats of the 1973 war forced Israel to negotiate a withdrawal from the Nile Valley.

Egypt Today

After the exciting intellectual ferment of the 1920s, 30s, and 40s, and after the triumph of independence and the heady early Nasser years, Egyptians have found their country's progress disappointing and frustrating. Egypt never recovered its leadership of the Arab world after the 1967 defeat and the 1979 Camp David treaty with Israel. Both Anwar Sadat and Hosni Mubarak, his successor, sought peace with Israel and alliance with the United States. They were rewarded with huge sums of U.S. foreign aid, but earned the contempt of many Arab nations.

Social tensions within Egypt increased as Egypt's economy failed to keep pace with the growing size and expectations of its population. In 1947 there were 19 million Egyptians; by 2000 there were 68 million. In the 1950s, millions of Egyptians moved from the countryside to the city and found work and housing in an expanding economy. By the 1990s, there was neither work nor housing for poor Egyptians who continued to flock to Cairo, Alexandria, and other cities. In recent decades, more than 2 million Egyptians have been forced to find work outside the country, mostly in the oil-rich nations of the Middle East and the Persian Gulf.

Anwar Sadat attempted to restore Egypt's economic health by fostering private investment in Egypt and encouraging private enterprise. In doing so, he reversed Nasser's long-standing policy of favoring state enterprises—such as the government oil companies—at the expense of privately owned businesses. Sadat's policy failed to bring substantial benefits to most Egyptians and many people came to believe that this policy of *infitah* (or "opening the door") created benefits only for a few rich business owners. Despite his foreign policy successes, Sadat faced growing hostility in the streets. In October 1981, during a celebration of the 1973 war against Israel, Anwar Sadat was assassinated by members of an elite military unit.

Sadat's successor, Hosni Mubarak, was an air force general, unknown to most Egyptians. He stepped to the helm of a country increasingly torn by economic inequality and political conflict. For many Egyptians, it seems that Egypt has tried both western alternatives—socialism under Nasser and capitalism under Sadat—and both have failed. As Egyptians search for another alternative, the *Islamist movement* (or Islamic fundamentalist movement) has grown in size and influence. *Islamists* demand an Islamic state—a society government by religious leaders, according to the laws of Islam. Sociologists call such a state a **theocracy.** Islamic theocracies can be found today in Iran, Saudi Arabia, Afganistan, and Pakistan. Mubarak, fighting against the Islamists, has resorted increasingly to police repression, eliminating free speech and political choice, and infuriating the many Egyptians who wish their society to be a western-style democracy. Egypt today is increasingly squeezed between an antidemocratic Islamist movement and an undemocratic government.

EGYPTIAN CULTURE

Many Egyptians today believe their society must choose between a culture based on Islam and a secular culture imported from the modern West. Western culture is probably familiar to you, but Islamic culture is likely a subject you know little about. We can make good use of sociological concepts in exploring the character of Islamic culture.

Egyptians find it difficult to understand that for most people in Europe and America, religion is often irrelevant to daily life, engaging people only on certain occasions and in special places. In Europe and America, people accept the idea that some aspects of life are ruled by government and law and others by religion. They are used to disagreements between religion and science. Sociologists call western societies **secular societies.** It is commonly said that Islam is a culture, a way of life, as well as a religion. In Egypt even people who are not devout Muslims (and even those who are Christians) live in a world filled with Islamic values and norms. Phrases such as *insha' Allah* (God willing) and *alhamdu lillah* (thanks be to God) fill everyday conversation. Egyptians use these expressions easily and sincerely. We might say that even though Egypt has not gone so far as to become a theocracy, nevertheless, it is a **sacred society,** a society in which religious ideas and values are applied to every aspect of life.

Islamic Beliefs, Norms, and Values

Any Muslim will tell you that it is easy to get to know Islam; you need to begin with the five pillars of faith: declaring belief in God, prayer, charity, fasting during the holy month of Ramadan, and pilgrimage. Each of these fundamentals reveals important Islamic beliefs and each has major implications for the conduct of everyday life.

Declaring Belief

Five times a day, in the largest cities and the smallest villages, the voice of *muezzin* (the prayer caller) cries out from the *minaret* (the highest tower) of the *mosque* (the Islamic house of worship). Nowadays the voice is likely to be recorded and broadcast over a public address system.

> God is great (Allahu Akbar), God is great, God is great. I witness that there is no god but Allah. I witness that there is no God but Allah. I witness that Muhammad is his messenger. I witness that Muhammad is his messenger. Come to prayer, come to prayer. Come to prosperity, come to prosperity. God is great. God is great. There is no God but Allah. (Esposito, 1991*a*, p. 89)

The call is echoed by Muslims indoors and out, who all join in affirming their belief. They thus daily and repeatedly declare their faith: their faith in Allah, the God of Islam, and their belief in one single god ("there is no god but Allah"). You may take **monotheism** (the belief that there is only one god) for granted, but in the history of the world's religions, monotheism is relatively unusual. Most of the world's religions recognize many gods, major and minor. For example, when you read about Japan in Chapter 1, you learned that all the major religions of Asia—Buddhism,

Hinduism, Taoism, and Shinto—honor multiple gods. Islam, Christianity, and Judaism all believe in a single god, and he is the same god, the god of Moses and Abraham. Islam recognizes Jesus as one of the four prophets—Moses, David, Jesus, and Muhammad—but Jesus is not believed to be the son of God.

All that is necessary to become a Muslim is to make the affirmation of faith: "There is no god but God (Allah), and Muhammad is the messenger of God" in the presence of other believers. But professing faith in God commits you to accepting the word of God, as transmitted through his messenger Muhammad and recorded literally in the *Quran,* the holy book. The word *Islam* actually means "submission" in Arabic, meaning submission to the will of God. "Muslim" means one who submits (Lippman, 1990, p. 1).

Values and Norms. Muslims believe in a Judgment Day on which each person will be sent by God either to paradise or to hell. Islam tells people that God is stern, and on Judgment Day terrible agonies await the sinner, while paradise is filled with delights. Pious Muslims fear the wrath of God if they do not live by Islamic values and norms. For example, Islam values honesty, modesty and chastity, charity toward the less fortunate, and religious faith. To be virtuous and win paradise, the good man or woman must strive to submit to God, to make life a spiritual exercise so that in every situation he or she struggles to act virtuously, not for worldly benefit, but to honor God. It is important to follow detailed norms, but they must be obeyed in the spirit of faith.

The good Muslim does not drink alcohol, or profit from lending money, or gamble, gossip, or seek revenge. The good Muslim does not have sex outside marriage, gives to charity, helps orphans, and of course carries out the prescribed religious obligations of prayer, charity, fasting, and pilgrimage. Many of these norms are described in the Quran, which is so important that many Egyptian men and boys try to memorize it in its entirety. In Egypt the Quran is chanted continually on the radio, and in the traditional schools that boys attend. Over one-third of the millions of cassette tapes sold in Egypt yearly are Quran readings, and the most popular readers are treated with the acclaim of rock stars. A recent public performance by a Quranic star attracted 600,000 people (Jehl, March 6, 1996, p. A4). Other Islamic norms are recorded in the *hadith,* the collection of Muhammad's words as interpreted by religious scholars. *Sharia* is the name of the code of law based on Islam, the only law in Islamic theocracies. In Egypt *Sharia* law holds for cases involving family and marriage, but the rest of civil and business law is secular (Rodenbeck, p. 105; Campo, p. 105; Lippman, 1990, pp. 30–32).

Prayer and the Social Construction of Time

Prayer is the second of the five pillars of faith. Muslims are required to pray five times a day: at sunrise, noon, midafternoon, sunset, and night, in response to the call to prayer. Daily prayers may be recited alone or in company, in a mosque or at one's place of work. In rural areas, men may keep clear a small spot in their fields for daily prayer. In busy cities, traffic may be blocked by rows of men kneeling for the noon prayer. Some people, who are not religious, or not Muslims, do

On a busy Cairo street, traffic comes to a halt for noonday prayers. Public space in Egyptian cities is "male" space and all those praying in the street are men. Since they face toward Mecca, they easily arrange themselves in neat rows. Not all Egyptians, not even all Muslims, pray regularly. Behind those at prayer you can see other people on errands and at work.

not pray, but those who do are completely unself-conscious about it. Everyone takes for granted the brief interruptions in life's activity that punctuate the day.

Many norms prescribe the proper way to pray. People take off their shoes before entering a mosque and they ritually wash themselves before prayer, washing their faces, hands, and feet at a fountain, or perhaps just sprinkling a few drops of water if that is all that is possible. All believers face in the direction of Mecca (the city, today in Saudi Arabia, where Muhammad first heard the word of God) when they pray, so if there are many praying together, you will see them lined up in orderly rows. In daily prayer people recite standard texts; they don't make individual appeals to God. Recitation is accompanied by sequences of bows and prostrations, when people kneel, then lower their foreheads to the ground. Women generally pray separately from men, since the postures of prayer might prove immodest. In the street or the field, people avoid touching the dirty ground by praying on a small rug or even a piece of cardboard (Bassiouni, pp. 30–31). There is tension in Islam between the "official" religion of the mosque and the holy texts and the folk religion practiced by villagers and the urban poor. They often visit shrines and make personal appeals to popular saints. These practices are condemned by Muslim clergy.

Prayer Structures Time. How is time ordinarily divided in your society? Do you think in terms of the week and the weekend? The hours of classes? The time the coffee cart comes around in the office, lunchtime, and the end of the workday? In Muslim countries like Egypt, the hours of prayer divide the day, marking the passage of time as clearly as the clock. Businesses open after the morning prayer and the best bargains may be found before the call to noon prayer (Rodenbeck, p. 105).

In Egypt Friday is the day of special religious observance. The week hurries toward Friday, when schools and government offices are closed. Women who work in private businesses, as typists or engineers, struggle to finish work early so they can go home and clean their houses by Friday afternoon, when the eye of God will be upon them. In towns and villages, the Friday market is the largest, since people flock into town for Friday prayers. People gather in the markets to shop for sugar, tea, or cassette tapes (Fakhouri, pp. 51–52; Campo, pp. 126–127).

On Fridays, Islamic tradition requires that Muslim men pray together in the mosque. Women may attend too, but it is not required. The prayer leader or *imam* leads Friday prayers and also delivers a sermon. He is not a priest, but rather an ordinary worshiper, normally someone with extra religious training. In a city, the *imam* is probably a person who has done a great deal of special study, but in a village he would likely be an artisan who has studied for a few years at a village religious school (Lippman, 1990, p. 14).

Finally, in Egypt religious holidays punctuate the year. The most important of these is *Ramadan,* which lasts for a whole month. Because the Islamic calendar is a lunar calendar, Ramadan begins on a different date in each year and it is not associated with a particular season. Observance of Ramadan is so demanding that people must structure their year around it.

Ramadan and the Value of Unity

Observance of Ramadan is another of the pillars of Islam. Ramadan is the Arabic name of the month in which God began to reveal the Quran to Muhammad and the month when Muhammad's small army won its first battle, at Badr in 624. During Ramadan all Muslim adults must fast from dawn until dark (neither eating nor drinking anything) unless they are pregnant, nursing, traveling, or ill, and refrain from smoking and sex. Fasting teaches self-restraint and also compassion for the poor and hungry. You can imagine how these obligations disrupt normal life during Ramadan. Especially when the fast occurs during hot weather, life slows to a crawl, with people working shorter hours and resting indoors as much as possible away from the desiccating sun. Families rise before dawn to eat the leftovers from the previous night's dinner and to take their last long drinks of water before the sun rises. Then, after dark, everyone celebrates, with a feast called the *iftar* ("breakfast"). Even the poorest Egyptians, who rarely see meat on their tables, will scrimp and save to eat meat during Ramadan.

Like daily prayers, Ramadan vividly demonstrates the cultural and religious unity of Muslims. The rigors of fasting are shared and people feel linked in common endeavor with their community, their nation, and the worldwide community of Islam. In cities and towns all over the country, people who have fasted will sit before tables piled high with food and drink, waiting for the broadcast cannon shot with which Radio Cairo announces sunset prayers and the end of the fast. Radio and television, which often act as instruments of secularization, work in this case to reinforce the culture of a sacred society (Esposito, 1991*a*, pp. 91–92).

Charity and the Value of Equality

Charity (or *zakat*) is a major Islamic value and it is one of the five pillars of Islam. All Muslims are obliged, as an act of worship of God, to support Muslims in need and the Islamic faith. Some Muslims interpret *zakat* as requiring them to give a fixed percentage of their income and wealth to charity every year; or to leave money to charity in their wills. Others donate money to help build mosques. During Ramadan, charity-givers spend hundreds of dollars a day provisioning free *iftar* meals on the streets for the poor, feeding as many as 2,000 people a day. Egyptians also give money to the homeless on the streets or outside mosques (Bassiouni, pp. 30–31; Lippman, 1990, p. 19; Campo, pp. 122–124; Jehl, January 23, 1998).

Consideration for the needy is part of Islam's traditional emphasis on equality. In the mosque, all are equal; there are no preferred pews for the rich or influential—all kneel together. Anyone can lead prayers and give the sermon; there is no church hierarchy, no official priests or sacraments, no recognized saints, no monks or nuns. Islam also requires that the rich respect the poor, even though they may be ragged and hungry. Kindness and compassion are the essence of what Egyptians refer to as *saddaqa*. The Quran warns, "A kind word with forgiveness is better than charity followed by insult" (Bassiouni, p. 30). Much of the moral energy and appeal of "fundamentalist" Islam comes from a sense that the rich and powerful have long since ceased to care about the needs of ordinary Muslims. Even when help does come from government agencies, it often comes with a kind of contempt that is especially resented because it violates the sacred norms of Islam. In the absence of government services Islamist groups have organized clinics, built housing, and provided loans for the poor, and this dedication to charity earns them the respect of other Muslims and attracts many followers (Campo, pp. 130–137; Lippman, 1990, pp. 78–90; Hedges, Oct. 4, 1993, p. A8).

Pilgrimage: A Culmination of Faith

The final pillar of faith and the last major obligation of all Muslims is to make the pilgrimage or *hajj* to Mecca at least once in their lifetime. Both personally and socially the pilgrimage sums up the meaning of Islamic faith. To make the journey to Mecca is certainly an affirmation of faith. In the past, when pilgrims journeyed overland, it was a grueling trip. Today, airplanes ease the journey, but it is still challenging, especially in summer. Also, for many Egyptians, the *hajj* represents an enormous expense, the fruit of many years' savings, and perhaps a person's single trip ever away from his or her village. As prayer and holy days structure the Islamic day and year, planning and making the pilgrimage are key events in a lifetime. In many villages you will see "pilgrimage murals," depicting the airplane and Mecca and the crowds, painted on the outside walls of their houses by those who have made the *hajj*.

Finally, the pilgrimage expresses with special emphasis the Islamic values of community and equality. The pilgrimage is a yearly event, taking place only on specified days. During that short time, hundreds of thousands, even millions of pilgrims pour into Mecca from all over the world. In the huge crowds which walk through the required rites of the pilgrimage—trekking to the Sacred Mosque and back and forth to other holy places—you will see people of many races, speaking dozens of languages, visibly united by their Islamic faith. Symbolically, they all put on the special clothing of the pilgrimage, white wraps for the men and loose white dresses, without facial veils, for the women, reminding them that in Islam differences of race and class are surmounted (Lippman, 1990, pp. 22–27).

The Value of Community in Egyptian Culture

Egyptians treat their society as a collection of families and villages. Egyptians' attitude toward each other is generally trusting, not fearful or suspicious. Even modern Cairo, despite its rapid growth and millions of residents, remains a place of intensely personal contacts (Abu-Lughod, L., p. 71). While city neighborhoods may include migrants from all over Egypt, residents emphasize their closeness, even to strangers, by addressing each other by kin terms. A younger woman calls an older, unrelated man "uncle." Women the same age call each other "sister." Egypt is a "touch" society (but only in same-gender interaction). Men greet their friends and relatives by kissing first on one cheek, then the other. Men may hold hands as they walk and women walk down the streets together arm in arm. Egyptians of the same gender are comfortable standing quite close to each other when they talk, and they smile a lot and look intensely into each other's eyes. Egyptians don't hesitate to intervene with neighbors or even strangers if there is a problem. An argument on the street between a vendor and a customer or between two young men brings all the merchants out of their stores and gathers a crowd of passersby. Those nearby willingly jump in and take sides or calm down the antagonists. In a way, the propensity of Egyptians to get involved permits them to dramatize disagreements. Antagonists shout, pound on tables, make threatening gestures, and wave their arms. People rely on others, even strangers, to stop their conflict before it escalates too far (Wilson, pp. 108–109).

In every situation, Egyptians would rather be with others than alone. It is easy for them to establish a sense of community within a crowd of strangers. Sociologist Andrea Rugh describes how affluent Egyptians pitch their umbrellas close to one another on the beach, rather than seeking privacy. Expensive movie theaters and cheap buses fill up in the same way: People sit next to others already seated, rather than spreading out. Visiting is a major leisure-time activity in Egypt. Friends and relatives spend a great deal of time just sitting around and talking and visits last for hours. Even in illness, Egyptians prefer company. A man who has a headache, or a fever, will be surrounded by a stream of friends and relatives who bring him soda, food, aspirin, and advice. Hospitals are crowded with relatives and friends visiting patients. Egyptians also will make considerable sacrifices to live out their lives in the company of their families. Andrea Rugh describes a young city woman who refused a good job as a live-in companion to a wealthy widow. Despite the fact that her family was so poor they could hardly feed her, she regarded this well-paid job with horror, because she would have to sleep in a room alone, apart from her family (Rugh, 1984, p. 36–38). A sly joke about the unsophisticated Saidis of southern Egypt reveals not only how Egyptians from the big cities of Cairo and Alexandria feel about Saidis, but also the comfort that all Egyptians take in the presence of their countrymen:

An Alexandrian, a Cairene, and a Saidi are stranded in the desert with no transportation and no water. Suddenly a genie appears and offers each of them one wish. The young man from Alexandria wishes that he was back on that city's beautiful beach—and in a flash he is gone. The Cairene wishes to be returned to the Hussein Mosque in Cairo—and in an instant he too vanishes. The genie then approaches the Saidi and asks, "what is your wish?" "I'm so lonely," cries the Saidi, "can't you bring my friends back?" (Rodenbeck, p. 100)

In the countryside, people live in a village, not spread out in farmsteads in the fields. Houses are tightly clustered, along narrow alleys, filled with children, water buffalo, and the bustle of everyday life. A village teacher asks children to find what's missing in a chalked outline of a peasant home, and their immediate reply is "the neighbors" (Fakhouri, pp. 17–21). According to a familiar Arabic saying, "the most important thing about a house is its neighbors" (Fluehr-Lobban, p. 58).

The Importance of Personal Ties

In Egypt, when people have problems they must solve, they rely on personal contacts. To find an apartment, a job, or a spouse, people turn first to their relatives, then to neighbors and friends. Friendship in Egypt is an active, intense relationship that takes a lot of time and energy. Friends constantly do favors for each other. In fact, you don't really have to even ask for a favor. If you express a wish— "I just feel like getting out of the city today"—a friend will feel obliged to help make it happen for you. A friendship implies a commitment, even if you have long been out of touch. Andrea Rugh describes a middle-aged, middle-class Egyptian woman in difficult economic circumstances who is sure that the president's wife will help her. After all, they went to college together, 30 years before (Wilson, p. 149; Rugh, 1984, p. 40)! A network of favors given and received: a car borrowed, the children watched, money lent, binds individuals tightly together.

But at the same time, Egyptians are reluctant to commit themselves to large, impersonal organizations like big businesses, labor unions, activist groups, or political parties. In Cairo's poorest squatter settlements, people struggle bravely and inventively to survive. They use all their informal, personal connections to tap into municipal electric lines, to connect with the right bureaucrat to enroll their children in school, but unlike their counterparts in Latin America and South Asia, they rarely engage in organized collective action. Protest campaigns against factory pollution are rare, and rallies, marches, or riots are even rarer. (Bayat, pp. 2–5; Hopkins and Mehanna, pp. 2–3).

In a similar preference for the personal and informal over the formal and institutional, Egyptians may make great efforts to turn large groups into close-knit units. Men who own businesses, for example, will organize their enterprises around family connections even when this limits their expansion or economic flexibility. Egyptian businessmen like to think of themselves as "fathers" to their employees and often expect their employees to behave like children might: running employers' little personal errands and seeking their boss's advice on personal matters (Rugh, 1984, p. 43).

The Value of Generosity in Egyptian Culture

Linked to Egyptians' broad sense of community is the value they place on generosity and hospitality. Anthropologist Carolyn Fluehr-Lobban traces Egyptian generosity to the influence of Arab culture, now absorbed into Islam. She describes the ancient nomadic desert life of the Arabs, when everyone might someday be a traveler, dependent on strangers for shelter, life-saving water, and food. Today, Fluehr-Lobban says, "generosity . . . is a core value in Arab society the importance of which has not diminished over the centuries or been fundamentally transformed by urban life and empire, by class division and social stratification." A generous person is a moral person, and everyone looks for generosity in friends, marriage partners, and politicians (p. 46). Thus, in Egypt today, shopkeepers offer their customers tea and a pleasant chat, motorists stop to offer help to a driver with a flat tire, bureaucrats offer coffee when you visit their office, and relatives and friends visit each other often, sitting down to tables piled with food and drink, as high as family finances afford. Visitors are urged to stay longer, eat more, and have another cup of tea.

Fluehr-Lobban also explains that in Egypt "sharing is so deeply engrained that to notice its expression is an oddity." It would be very impolite to refuse the offered cup of tea, and impolite as well to thank your host for it. Generosity is **normative:** It is expected and you don't have to thank people for their generosity. People in Egypt don't say thank-you to the store clerk or the taxi driver or the waiter. On the other hand, if someone is generous to you, it would be polite to reciprocate at some later time. You should invite your host to your home, and you may bring fruit or candy to the family of the person who fixed your flat tire (p. 46).

Egyptians prize a quality of lightheartedness they call *dem-khefeef.* Those who have it ease the burdens everyone bears by gently laughing and joking, making light of their troubles, and poking fun at their own feelings. Egyptians love to tell jokes and they treasure their comic movie actors who bring the whole country together in laughing acknowledgment of their absurd problems (Fernea, 1970, p. 279).

The Value of Honor

Egyptians will tell you that their family's honor is utterly precious to them. Individuals are judged by the reputations of their familities and when Egyptians think about their own personal honor, they are thinking about how their actions will reflect upon their families. Carolyn Fluehr-Lobban defines honor as "the pride and dignity that a family possesses due to its longstanding good reputation in the community for producing upright men and women who behave themselves well, marry well, raise proper children, and above all adhere to the principles and practices of the religion of Islam" (p. 52). In everyday life, people try to avoid shameful behavior so they won't dishonor themselves and their families. Even future generations of their family would have to live with the dishonor. Use of foul language is shameful, so is losing one's temper, or gossiping in a way that harms others; failing to help a relative or neighbor when one could really do so is shameful, as is failing in one's obligation to support family members (Fluehr-Lobban, p. 53).

It is difficult to discuss honor without describing Egyptian gender roles, because maintaining honor places different obligations on men and women and much shameful behavior is sexual in nature. Requirements for propriety are more demanding of women than men and much smaller infractions of sexual norms endanger a woman's honor and bring shame on her family.

Honor and Women's Roles

A woman's honor is based on chastity and modesty. Women shouldn't start conversations with strange men, or smile at them, or make direct eye contact with them. Such behavior seems flirtatious and endangers a woman's reputation. A wife, alone in the house, or with other women only, would not open the door to her husband's friend, nor would he wish to enter because it might appear improper (Wilson, p. 91). Egyptian women never think of wearing shorts or short skirts or sleeveless blouses, or even bathing suits at the beach. Marriage is considered the most important event in a woman's life and an honorable young woman "saves herself" for marriage, avoiding interaction with young men that might spoil her reputation. Virginity is a special treasure, which a girl and her family carefully preserve and guard until marriage. Lost virginity is a disaster for a young woman, for whom marriage will likely become impossible, and for her shamed family. Consider this incident: A 10-year-old daughter of an affluent family crashed her bicycle into a wall and tore her hymen. Her family rushed her to the doctor, who wrote an affidavit describing the injury. This document preserved the girl's marriageability.

Egyptians' beliefs about sexuality underlie the importance they place on chastity and modesty. Egyptians look on sexual desire as something natural to men and women. They assume that men's desire for sex is easily aroused by the sight or company of non-kin women, and they believe that men cannot be expected to control themselves once aroused. That means women are a dangerous temptation to men. Egyptians use a special word, *fitna,* meaning sexual disorder and chaos, to highlight the danger of sexual desire (Shalkamy, p. 5). This way of thinking dates far back in Egyptian history, to the Greek and early Christian eras. If women are dangerously tempting to men, then they should act in such a way as to avoid attracting male desire and men should protect their female relatives from unrelated men. In Egypt people think that women require *hudud,* "boundaries" in Arabic, like the walls of a house which form a protected space. In Arabic both a house without secure outside walls, and a woman without a *hijab,* a covering veil, are described as *awra,* or naked (Mernissi, pp. 6–8).

Modest Dress. Women should dress modestly, in a way that conceals their sexual attractiveness. The Quran, in a passage often cited as the source of modesty norms for women, required the wives of the prophets to cover themselves:

> And say to the believing women that they should lower their gaze and guard their modesty; that they should not display their beauty and charms except what (normally) appears of them; that they should draw their veils over their bosoms and display their beauty only to their husbands. (Quoted in Esposito, 1991*a*, p. 99)

This passage in the Quran is rather vague and there are a number of different ways for women to dress modestly in Egypt today. Poor village women wear traditional dress when they go out in public: long, loose cotton robes, often black, but sometimes flowered, with a shawl thrown over their heads. Recent migrants to cities often wear such dress too. In cities more stylish women may adopt western dress, wearing skirts and jackets or dresses with waists, but with long skirts, long sleeves, and high necks. Suit jackets with turtlenecks are very acceptable. Alternatively, women may adopt the new "Islamic dress," a loose-fitting gown with no waist, a high neck and long sleeves, topped by some sort of *hijab* (usually translated as "veil," but actually a scarf or hood that fully covers the hair and neck). Women in poor urban neighborhoods may wear any of these styles. On the street in Cairo, about half the women who pass by are wearing the hijab. Indoors, they remove the hijab and often put on a cooler, less enveloping dress. In the big western-style hotels and the fanciest restaurants you can still see women dressed in the latest western fashions, but their clothes are increasingly conservative.

Purity. There is a traditional custom in Egypt, practiced today by both Muslim and Christian Egyptians, which is linked to norms about virginity and chastity. Its proponents call the custom **female circumcision,** but Egyptian feminists who have campaigned against it call the custom **female genital cutting.** In female circumcision, the clitoris is wholly or partially removed. It is an ancient North African custom that has nothing to do with Islam.[1] The mutilation, usually performed on pre-adolescent girls is painful and risky, since it may result in hemorrhage, infections, incontinence, or later difficulty in childbirth. At least 85 percent

---

[1]Unicef (the United Nations Children's Fund) estimates that 130 million women, most of them in Africa, have undergone genital cutting. Seven nations account for 75 percent of the cases of female genital cutting in Africa: Egypt, Ethiopia, Kenya, Nigeria, Somalia, and Sudan. The mutilation is banned in eight countries: Burkina Faso, the Central African Republic, Djibouti, Egypt, Ghana, Guinea, Senegal, and Togo (Crossette, Jan. 18, 1999, p. A10).

of Egyptian women have been circumcised and most plan to have their daughters circumcised as well. Folk beliefs hold that an uncircumcised girl will be dangerously masculine and will be wild and chase after men. Most women believe that it will be harder for their daughters to find husbands if they are uncircumcised. Egyptian feminists and human rights groups have been fighting female genital cutting since the 1970s, when the famous writer Nawal al-Saadawi (who was also a medical doctor and the Minister of Public Health) was first imprisoned for her opposition to it. Egypt's highest court ruled female genital cutting illegal in 1997. Some Islamic authorities argue that since the practice is not mentioned in the Quran, it is not required. Other, more conservative religious leaders argue that since the Quran does not forbid female circumcision it should be allowed (Fakhouri, pp. 86–87; Atiya, pp. 11–13; Crossette, December 29, 1997, p. A3; WIN News, Summer, 1997, pp. 31–32; "Jail Term in Egypt for Mutilation Death," *The New York Times,* December 16, 1997, p. A3; "Egypt to Appeal Ruling on Genital Cutting," *The New York Times,* July 12, 1997, p. 3).

Female genital cutting is often the place where westerners draw the line on **cultural relativism;** where their tolerance for cultural diversity runs out and **ethnocentrism** begins. It is a good place to start thinking carefully about ethnocentrism. Is it ethnocentric to condemn female genital cutting? Can you condemn it without being ethnocentric? Must sociologists accept uncritically every aspect of each culture? Women's organizations in Africa make it very clear that they welcome your support for their efforts to end the practice, but western criticism that depicts their societies as backward or barbaric is unwelcome and makes their struggle harder. (See Fernea, 1998, pp. 269–272.)

Seclusion. Separate social spaces for women and men also protect women from the attentions of men and protect men from sexual impulses. Traditionally, a woman's male relatives protected her by supporting her, so she had no need to go out into the world to make her way. A husband's wish to keep his wife hidden at home showed how much he loved and valued her. If a woman had to venture out in public, it was proper for her male relatives to accompany her.

Today, even though few women are completely secluded at home, Egyptian women will tell you that they appreciate the protection their male relatives give them. By protecting women, men guard their families' reputations: Sexual indiscretions imply that the men of the family are too weak or careless to protect their women. In the conservative countryside, a young woman who meets alone with an admirer, or a married woman seen with a man not her husband, still commits a terrible violation of Egyptian **mores.** She would be suspected of forbidden sexual activity. Her husband or brothers or father might well lock her inside the house, or even beat her. If the family agrees that adultery has taken place, custom allows her husband to kill her, to "wash away the shame with blood" and restore the family's honor. Such murders, considered "crimes of honor," are punished with prison terms of only one to three years, rather than the usual death penalty (Fluehr-Lobban, p. 55; Daniszewski, p. A09).

You can see that a woman who dresses modestly and limits her public interaction is seen as honorable and brings honor to her family. Nowadays, many Egyptian women work outside their homes and attend school and college, but even so, men and women tend to gather separately. We call this **gender segregation.** After dinner at a family party, men and women gravitate into separate rooms. The public realm clearly belongs to men. Even in the daytime, there are more men than women in the streets, and men gather in mosques and cafés. After dark almost everyone outside is male. Men stroll with friends, sit in restaurants, and go to the movies. In the day-time, women walk outside together, linked arm in arm. They may go with their children to the movies, and they gather in each other's homes. In poor neighbor-hoods, women move freely through the alleyways near their houses, fetching water or food from the market, or calling children in for meals, but not venturing far afield.

When women must travel to and from work or school, this creates problems, because there are no clear norms specifying how men should treat unrelated women, particularly strangers, in public places. There is a traditional assumption that any woman away from the protection and seclusion of her family, especially at night, is sexually available, a prostitute. Even when it is clear that respectable women are on their way to work, they are often harassed (MacLeod, p. 63).

Sex. After all this discussion of sex and danger, it is important to stress that Muslim culture in Egypt is not opposed to sexual pleasure. Sex itself is not seen as sinful, and celibacy is not admired. (Islam has no celibate clergy, no monks or nuns.) When men get together they talk about sex and make sexual jokes and puns. So do women, when they talk together. Coptic Christians in Egypt think of Mus-lim culture as sensual and sexual (Forsythe, p. 71). For Muslims, it is sexual pleas-ure outside marriage that is condemned, not sex itself. Thus, religious authorities have no objection to marital sex that is not for the purpose of procreation. When modern birth control technology was first introduced into Egypt, the religious au-thorities considered it and decided they had no objection—as long as it was used by married couples only. Today, the Egyptian government officially promotes the use of birth control. We must acknowledge, however, that when Egyptians accept sexual pleasure in marriage, they are thinking mostly of men. After all, female genital cutting certainly inhibits women's pleasure. Women's sexuality seems a very strong and dangerous force and it makes Egyptians uneasy.

Honor and Men's Roles

Gender roles in Egypt are seen as **complementary,** not unequal; men and women have differing obligations and rights and both must live up to expectations for families to survive and society to function properly. While Egyptian men cer-tainly enjoy wider freedoms than women, they too must constantly protect their honor and the honor of their families and clans. Men have many role obligations. To avoid shame, they must protect their female relatives—their mothers, sisters, wives and daughters—accompanying them in public and watching to make sure that no man compromises their reputations. The obligation to protect women ex-tends to supporting them. A husband must feed, clothe, and shelter his wife and children, and any other female relative dependent on him. If his wife works, a married man would still pay for food, clothing, and housing out of his own earnings and his wife would decide what to do with her wages, usually spending the money on school fees and supplies, household equipment, and extras for the children (Hoodfar, pp. 5–7). A man who could not find work to support his wife would feel shamed. He would feel shamed if his wife paid the bill in a restaurant, or drove while he was in the car. Like young women, young men are expected to make marriage their goal; to behave properly so other families won't reject them. Drinking, chasing after women, swearing, getting into trouble with the police all dishonor the man and his family. Young men are expected to marry as soon as they can afford it and to be chaste in the meantime.

A man's obligations go beyond avoiding shame. Every man must also defend his family against disrespect and insult. A man whose neighbor shouts insults at him in a drunken quarrel would be dishonored. So too would a man whose wife, gossip suggests, flirts with others. If one man steals crops from another man's field, it is an insult to the victim and his whole clan. Even an accidental death might still be seen as an assault on the honor of the victim's family.

In the traditional setting of a rural village, with strong family and clan ties, all these slights to honor must be erased; a man cannot ignore an insult or injury, even though Islam condemns revenge. If he does not respond to insult, a man will be seen as weak and unmanly. His family too will be obliged to back him or revenge him, and they may be drawn into disastrous and criminal violence. You might say that this is one reason why drinking alcohol and gossiping are both so much condemned in Islamic culture: They pave the way to conflict, insult, and destructive revenge.

Ibrahim and Ismail's Story: The Quarrel

Ibrahim and Ismail had quarreled for years over a piece of land that Ismail had inherited, but no one in El Mina thought this would lead to bloodshed. Both men were hot-tempered, but not foolish. Neither of them wanted to provoke a feud that might leave their sons and nephews dead. On a hot July day though the men parted after unusually bitter words. Driving off in his truck, shouting at Ismail, Ibrahim accidentally struck his rival's 11-year-old niece. The girl lapsed into a deep coma and died. Tension soared as everyone feared that Ismail and his brothers would strike at Ibrahim's family.

When the girl died, Ibrahim and his brothers left El Mina for their mother's village. There, his grandfather urged Ibrahim to find a way to end the dispute. Everyone talked about a feud 30 years earlier that had taken many lives.

Three days later, Ismail was approached by a man respected for his role in ending disputes. He asked Ismail's family to accept a traditional court which would set conditions for a peaceful resolution. Ismail and his kin agreed and all concerned met at the home of a man who was on good terms with both families. After long discussion, all agreed that while the girl's death had been an accident, her family should receive some compensation. They also agreed to resolve the dishonorable squabble that indirectly caused the accident. Ibrahim's family agreed to pay the substantial sum of 500 dollars to the girl's family and to give up their claims to the disputed land. In return Ismail's family agreed not to seek blood vengeance. Tension gradually eased and Ibrahim was relieved that he and his family could go about their lives without fear of sudden and deadly assault.

Given the importance of defending family honor, it is fortunate that Egyptian tradition provides peaceful ways of resolving affronts to honor. Tradition gives a victim's family only three days for violent revenge, and it permits the wrongdoer and his relatives to protect themselves by fleeing to their mother's kin. The institution of the traditional court allows older, often more powerful relatives to mediate a settlement (Fakhouri, pp. 109–114; Ghosh, pp. 69–70, 135–137). It is a testament to the effectiveness of these customs that while norms call for men to defend their honor, the murder rate in Egypt is in fact very low (only 0.5 per 100,000 persons per year, as compared to 9.1 per 100,000 in the United States). (See Table 1.2, p. 26.)

Honor and Role Conflict

In Egypt now, men's and women's roles are changing. More and more Egyptians are leaving the countryside for the cities, and more young people are attending high school and university. Urbanization and education offer new freedoms and pose new challenges for both men and women.

Changing Male Roles. In the city, men find themselves less burdened by the demands of clan loyalty and traditional notions of honor. On the other hand, they must confront a shortage of city jobs. Unemployment threatens not only family survival, but also male honor. A man without a job cannot marry and young Egyptian men are reluctantly postponing mariage until they can find jobs and save enough money. In 1960 only 36 percent of Egyptian men aged 25–29 were single; but by 1990 the figure was 47 percent (U.S. Census, International Data Base). An unemployed man, whose wife or daughters work, may feel deeply humiliated and anxious. Unemployment is a particular threat for "over-educated" men whose high school or college degrees qualify them to do office work. They may feel entitled to government jobs but find no jobs at all. Egyptian psychologists and human rights activists note a rise in violence against women, which they say is fueled by male frustration and anger (Daniszewski, p. A09). Many men, suffering new status anxieties, turn to another role which confirms their masculinity and importance: the role of the observant Muslim. In Islamic societies, religion has an atmosphere of masculinity; the mosque is a male place and the history of Islam as a militant, fighting religion adds to its masculine tone. Attending mosque, praying, making the pilgrimage, demanding strict compliance with the laws of Islam are all activities which make a man more manly. Islamic fundamentalist groups, which stress the primacy of men and call for the withdrawal of women from the workplace and public life, also attract many men.

Changing Female Roles. Women have also experienced changes in roles and new anxieties. Starting in Nasser's time, women gained new freedoms: to attend high school and university and then work in thousands of new jobs as schoolteachers and secretaries, doctors, lawyers, and engineers. Today approximately 30 percent of Egyptian women work for wages outside their homes—in offices, factories, stores, and on farms. The government supports working women by giving maternity leave to those who are government employees and by making free

TABLE 4.1. Women's Economic and Political Roles, 1990–1996:
Egyptian women are less likely to work as managers than Mexican women,
but are more likely to do so than Japanese women.

	Percent of All Managers Who Are Women*	Percent of All Technical and Professional Workers Who Are Women*	Percent of All Members of the National Legislature Who Are Women**
Egypt	16%	29%	2%
Germany	26	43	26
Japan	9	42	8
Mexico	20	44	14
USA	43	53	21

Source: *Human Development Database, United Nations, 1997
  **Statistics Division of the United Nations Secretariat, http://www.un.org/Depts/unsd/gender

birth control available at government clinics. Nasser also encouraged women's political participation and women now serve in the parliament (the National Assembly) as well as in neighborhood and village councils (Ibrahim, B., pp. 294–295). (See Table 1.3, p. 40.) Finally, as more families move to the cities and more men leave Egypt as migrant workers, more women find themselves, at least temporarily, the heads of their families. It is mostly younger women who work; their mothers' generation was much less likely to venture away from home. That means working women can often rely on their mothers-in-law or other female relatives for help with child care. Nevertheless, working outside the home is fraught with conflicts and complications.

First of all, "housewife" is a highly respected, honorable role in Egypt. Especially among poor Egyptians, a woman who is a good housekeeper, who can always stretch the budget to feed the family, arrange good marriages for her children, and solve their medical problems, is admired by all her neighbors and relatives. People recognize her wisdom and hard work and go to her for advice. The idea of a woman being "just a housewife" is foreign to Egyptian culture. Many poor women who must work outside their homes—in factories, as servants, as peddlers, or market women—would prefer not to. The role of housewife is much more rewarding than their menial, heavy, and poorly paid work. Educated, middle-class women are in a different situation. Many are clerical workers and secretaries, and their work is not particularly challenging or well-paid (they file papers and run copy machines and keep simple accounts). Government offices are very much overstaffed and everyone spends a lot of time drinking tea and chatting. Nevertheless, women employees greatly enjoy office life, with its bustle of visitors and links to a larger world. Many young, educated, middle-class women work before marriage and sometimes after it as well.

Role Conflicts. However desirable or undesirable it is, working creates many **role conflicts** for women, situations in which the expectations of one of their roles are incompatible with those of another. These role conflicts occur because Egyptian

women are torn between two opposing trends. The first is a trend toward more freedom and equality for women, as they move out of their houses into a greater role in
public life through education and jobs. The second trend is the religious revival,
spearheaded by the Islamist movement, sweeping Egypt and other Muslim countries. Being a good Muslim woman (or man) is now an important concern for many
Egyptians and the Islamist movements highlight the issue with their demands to return to traditional "family values," traditional women's roles, and a sexually reseg-
regated public order. Every Egyptian woman must find some way of dealing with
the role conflicts that result (MacLeod, pp. 107–115; Fernea, 1998, pp. 240–288).

Role Conflicts and Modest Dress. Think about your society for a moment.
Does the way people dress have symbolic meaning? Do people use their clothes to
tell the world who they are and what they believe? A business suit or jeans, loose
pants or fitted ones, expensive watches, nose rings, briefcases and backpacks all
convey social messages. The same thing is true in Egypt. A small minority of
Egyptian women have chosen to solve their role conflicts by giving up their new
freedoms, embracing Islam in a kind of born-again movement, and returning to the
traditional role of a Muslim woman—staying at home as a wife and mother and
avoiding public life. Many of these very religious women symbolize their religious
committment by adopting full "Islamic dress,"—typically a long, full, unfitted
gown in a solid light color, topped by a hijab—a full scarf pulled forward to conceal the hair and tied or pinned under the chin to cover the neck. A few women,
but very few, even wear a face veil, concealing all but their eyes. For these women
veiling has religious meaning.

Many more women adopt a modified version of full Islamic dress, usually
wearing the hijab over modest, conservative clothes—a long skirt, with a blazer or
tunic, or a full dress, often in soft colors or flower prints. For some of these
women adopting the hijab has political meaning; it makes a political statement
about Egyptian or Muslim identity. Their dress is a visible rejection of western
influence—of the lure of western fashion and western-style advertising and marketing. Many such women also reject western feminism, which they see as fo-
menting unnecessary hostility between women and men. But they look to the
Quran for a genuinely Islamic legitimation of changing women's roles, attending
Quranic study groups which reinterpret the Quran, stressing passages which address men and women as spiritual equals (El-Gawhary, pp. 26–27; Fernea,
pp. 241–245). But most of the women who now wear the hijab do so for practical
reasons, to solve their role conflicts by finding a compromise, a way to be both a
working woman and an honorable Muslim woman. Islamic dress solves problems
for upwardly mobile working women. It declares that a woman respects Islamic
values, even though she leaves her home. It declares that a woman is a bureaucrat
or an engineer or other professional, not a sex object. It reassures her father or
husband or fiance. Islamic dress also reduces sexual harassment in public places.
Men who annoy a woman wearing western dress break only a poorly defined secular norm, but men who harass a woman in Islamic dress profane Islam; they violate one of the sacred **mores.** Several sociologists have even argued that women in
Islamic dress find it easier to interact with men, since their dress defines the situation as nonsexual, as this university student explained:

Thuraya Al-Ghindi (right), chief music censor for the Egyptian government, works with two assistants. They are listening to a tape of the Cranberries to make sure it includes no sexually suggestive lyrics, before it is approved for sale in Egypt. All CDs, cassettes, and videotapes are censored. Mrs. Al-Ghindi wears a businesslike western outfit, while her two assistants wear the *hijab* over modern "Islamic dress"—full gowns with long sleeves and high necks.

Before I wore the veil, I always worried what people might think when they saw me speak to a man in the cafeteria or outside the class. I even wondered what the man himself thought of me. Since I wore the veil, I don't worry anymore. No one is going to accuse me of immorality. (Quoted in Mule and Barthel, p. 330. See also Ahmed, p. 224; Fernea, p. 244.)

Zaynab's Story: A Good Wife

Zaynab met her future husband, Kamal, an engineer, at the government office where she still works. Zaynab's father Mamduh, a mechanic for Egyptair, the national airline, was delighted. He had begun to despair that Zaynab, already 24, would ever marry, but now she would—and an engineer at that. What a catch for an uneducated man's daughter! Mamduh hoped Zaynab would leave her job and stay home where a wife and mother should be. When Mamduh was a boy in a tiny village in Upper Egypt, no woman left her home. But after the birth of her children, Zaynab returned to her office. "It's my life," she said, "my friends are there. Besides, no family can live on one income; Kamal, the children, and I would starve!"

Mamduh was not entirely surprised. Zaynab had turned down a previous offer of marriage from a young man who had demanded that she leave her work. But Zaynab astonished her entire family in 1997 by announcing that from then on she would wear "Islamic dress," the hijab over a loose dress. Zaynab, her parents, and her husband were not especially religious.

Kamal thought it was ridiculous that the wife of an educated man should "cover herself," but Zaynab persisted. "Men do not respect a woman on Cairo's streets," she argued, "only a 'covered woman' will be left alone. Besides, even women at the university are 'covered'." (MacLeod, pp. 110–124; Ahmed, pp. 222–225; Mule and Barthel, pp. 328–331)

Islamic Law and Women's Rights Today. Some Egyptian feminists have reacted very negatively to the adoption of "Islamic dress," even in its less extreme forms. Most of these women are older and identify strongly with western culture and western ideas about the rights of the individual. Many of them came to maturity just as middle and upper class Egyptian women were embracing college education, careers, and western clothing styles. For them the choice of Islamic dress represents a step backwards. They identify traditional Islam with obstacles to equal rights for women. But for many younger women what is important is that *Sharia* does guarantee women important rights, even if they are not the same rights men enjoy. Young women find the Islamic norms embodied in *Sharia* an important protection against the difficulties of life in a poor and male-dominated society. *Sharia,* for example, provides that a woman retains the right to the property she owns at the time of marriage. She also has sole ownership of any new property she acquires in the course of her marriage; her wages or her inheritance are hers, not her husband's (Hoodfar, pp. 5–7, 12–14). It was well into the nineteenth century before even a few European societies gave women such rights. People don't always fully comply with Islamic law, but a claim made under it is not easily denied. In Egypt *Sharia* is taken far more seriously than western principles of human or women's rights.

SOCIAL STRUCTURE AND GROUP LIFE

All over Egypt, people strive to live in ways that express their values. They try to be good Muslims, honorable men and women, loyal members of their families. But everywhere, they are constrained by the social structures of their communities: by the availability of housing, the types of work they can get, the very physical layout of their surroundings, and the level of supervision of women and girls it permits. In both agricultural villages and in city neighborhoods, marriage, family, and community are the center of Egyptians' lives, but they take different forms. Also, in all settings, people center their lives around gender-segregated groups of friends, relatives, and neighbors, but these too vary in different social contexts.

Social Structure in the Countryside

Today, half of all Egyptians live in rural areas. Roads, buses, radio and television, schools, and health clinics link villages to modern cities, and villagers themselves move to the city or abroad to find work, but villages remain a distinctive social environment. Think for a moment of the geography of Egypt: Life hugs the Nile. Green fields line its banks, interspersed with villages; but not far from the river, the barren sand begins. As a result, the countryside is crowded. People use as much of the good, irrigated land as possible for growing crops; so families never build houses in the midst of their farmland. They all live in houses clustered together in villages, along narrow, winding lanes. Men head out of the village each morning to work in their fields, which may be scattered in different locations. Poor families may have just a couple of rooms, built around a courtyard; rich families occupy a walled compound, with offices, storerooms, kitchen, and living quarters. In Egypt's heat, where rain may not fall for years at a time, much of daily life takes place out of doors in the courtyards where women prepare food and bake in outdoor ovens, on the rooftops, in the streets, and in the village center, where the mosque, the market, the coffeehouse, and the school are located (Fakhouri, pp. 119–123; Early, pp. 41–48; Rugh, 1984, pp. 1–4).

Egyptian peasants or *fellahin,* as they are called in Arabic, must cooperate with each other in order to prosper. Without rain, agriculture is entirely dependent on irrigation from the Nile's water. A village's land may be miles from the river and channels must be dug and maintained to sustain the flow of water to each field. *Fellahin* must work together to keep the irrigation system working and share the water. No single farmer and no single family could do it alone.

The Extended Family

The basic rural cooperative group is the **extended family,** an economic unit of production and consumption. Such a family might include an older married couple, their two adult sons and their wives and children, and perhaps, if one of those children is old enough, a grandson and his wife and children. The constituent **nuclear families** may all live in one building or in separate houses. Either way, they operate as a single household. Extended family members carry out household tasks, work in the fields, and take care of the very young and the very old. When a father with married sons dies, the extended household formed by his sons' families dissolves. Each son then creates his own extended family including his sons, their wives, and children (Fakhouri, pp. 55–63).

The Clan

In villages related extended families are linked together in **clans,** theoretically descended from a long-ago common male ancestor. The men of a clan, especially the elders, usually form a tight-knit social group. They are brothers, cousins, brothers-in-law, neighbors, and lifelong friends, who have played and gone to school together as children. They have spent their lives helping each other in the fields, sitting together in the coffeehouse, attending the same weddings and funerals. In practical terms, clans are political alliances of men. Village politics often consists of the maneuverings of rival clans (Fakhouri, pp. 56–57).

Family and clan membership are the most important source of identity in the village, far more important than an individual's wealth and possessions. *Fellahin* actually reject wealth as a genuine source of prestige. Prestige is instead a product of the collective prominence of one's clan and personal qualities such as generosity and courage. A man who openly sought recognition based on his wealth—his land or his television or other possessions—would be dismissed with such traditional retorts as "What makes you better than I am? We're from the same family." Clans actually try to moderate the economic inequalities among their members. Wealthy members of a clan are encouraged to pay for religious festivals and to distribute food to the poor in accordance with Islam and local custom (Fakhouri, p. 74).

Marriage

Villages are conservative places and marriage is a very important matter to rural extended families. Everyone is expected to marry and in most cases the choice of a spouse is a family decision. Since a newly married couple becomes part of the husband's family, the bride and her relatives must be acceptable to the groom's whole family, and especially to his mother, who is often the one who actually searches for and selects the bride. The bride's family, if they are wise, must concern themselves not only with the groom, but with the whole extended family with whom their daughter will live. Consequently, village marriages are a matter of careful negotiation between families. The wishes of the prospective bride and groom are secondary to the interests of their families, and may not even be consulted at all. Young women are especially powerless in this process. Even though Islamic law requires that they consent to their marriages, in practice they often are not asked. In the past, girls were given in marriage so young (as early as the age of 12 and sometimes before puberty) that they were not yet ready to form an attraction to any man. (Of course, this was the point of early marriage; it preserved the virginity and chastity of girls by ensuring they were already wed when their sexual interest awakened.) Nowadays, 58 percent of all Egyptian women aged 20–24 are married, while only 17 percent of the men that age are married because of the difficulty of finding good jobs (Fluehr-Lobban, p. 65; United Nations, *Demographic Yearbook, 1995,* p. 549). (See Figure 2.1, p. 80.)

Egyptians do not date before marriage, not even in the city, but young city residents may have more say in choosing a spouse than villagers do. Their parents may suggest and cajole: "Why not marry your cousin Muhammad?" "I wish you would marry a girl from the village." However, young people's ability to choose for themselves is limited by their difficulty in getting to know those of the opposite sex. A middle-class Egyptian man might see a young woman at a wedding or a festival or she might be a customer in the store where he works. Perhaps their eyes will meet; perhaps she will shyly smile. Attraction can be communicated just as clearly through glances as through open flirtation. Then the young man and his father will ask around: How old is she? What family is she from? Does she have a good reputation? Is she educated? Is she pleasant and easy to get along with? If the answers are positive, the young man's father would contact the young woman's parents and proceed in arranging the marriage (Wilson, pp. 127–132).

The Marriage Contract. Arranging a marriage is a complex process, culminating in the signing of a marriage contract. This is a detailed document that includes an agreement about what the groom and his family will give to the couple's new household—carpeting, furniture, kitchen equipment—and what sum of money they will give the bride. This money becomes the bride's own property. The bride may require that the contract include a promise by her husband never to take any additional wives, or to permit her to work. While **polygyny** (the practice of a

**TABLE 4.2. Percent Married, Divorced, or Widowed at Selected Ages
for Latest Available Year, 1986–1995:**
Egyptians Marry Early and Rarely Divorce

	Percent Married 15–19	Percent Married 20–24	Divorced or Separated 40–45	Widowed 45–49
Females				
Egypt	14%	58%	3%	16%
Mexico	15	51	5	7
USA	3	27	21	4
Germany	2	23	10	4
Japan	1	14	5	3
Males				
Egypt	9	17	1	1
Mexico	5	37	2	1
USA	1	17	16	1
Germany	0*	10	8	1
Japan	0*	10	1	3

*Indicates less than 0.5%
Source: International Data Base, United States Census, http://www.census.gov/ipc/www/idbsprd.html

man marrying more than one wife) is legal in Egypt, as in most Islamic societies, it is actually quite rare. Definitive data are hard to find, but experts estimate that throughout the Middle East only 3 to 4 percent of women are wives in polygynous marriages (Omran and Roudi, p. 31). Few men can afford polygyny and few would attempt it against their wive's objections, so it is most common when a first marriage has produced no children.

The six months or a year between the signing of the marriage contract and the wedding is the closest Egyptians come to dating. Then the young man may visit his fiancée's house and get to know his future wife—in the company of her relatives—or the young couple may actually be permitted to go out together.

Weddings are joyous events in Egypt. They are one of the few occasions when young men and women can socialize together, perhaps even flirt with each other or see each other dance, albeit under the careful observation of their parents and relatives. Traditionally, weddings lasted for as long as a week of music, dancing, and feasting, culminating in a public procession of the groom and his friends and family to the house of the bride, where they picked up the bride and her entourage and accompanied her to the groom's house, to the music of a hired band. Today, in cities, weddings are one-evening events often held in big downtown hotels (Fluehr-Lobban, pp. 70–71; Fakhouri, pp. 63–70).

Divorce. Divorce is permitted in Egypt, but divorce rates are rather low. For every hundred marriages in Egypt in 1994, there were only 17 divorces. (Compare this to the United States, where there were 50 divorces for every hundred marriages.)

In Egypt only 3 percent of all women aged 40–45 are divorced, while in the United States the corresponding figure is 21 percent (*UN Demographic Yearbook,* 1995, pp. 542, 561). According to Islamic law, an Egyptian man may divorce his wife easily, just by stating three times "I divorce thee." It is not that easy in reality; he must file legal papers and relatives often try to arrange a reconciliation. Legally, women are permitted to divorce their husbands, but only on certain grounds like maltreatment or impotence. However, a woman's family may pressure her to stay with her husband because if she is divorced they will be responsible for supporting her. Also, in cases of divorce, the woman may keep her daughters until they are 10 years old and her sons until they are 8, but after that the father may legally take over their custody. These problems of course discourage women from trying to divorce. Another interesting Egyptian custom has helped to hold down divorce rates. The sum of money the groom customarily gives the bride at marriage has grown to be very large, and it is usually divided into two parts: the "prompt" and the "deferred." The "deferred" part must be paid only at the time of a divorce, so it is kind of an insurance policy against divorce (Fluehr-Lobban, pp. 64, 69, 116–117, 124–130; Wilson, pp. 132–134). (See Table 4.2.)

The Patriarchal Family

One important part of Egyptian marriage norms will probably puzzle you, until you understand more about Egyptian families. Both rural and urban Egyptians agree that the ideal marriage partner for a man is a paternal first cousin—a daughter of his father's brother. A more distant cousin on his father's side would also be preferable to a nonrelative. Marrying someone who is not kin is called "stranger marriage" (Fluehr-Lobban, pp. 65–67). The ideal cousin marriage is not often attainable in practice; only one marriage in five is actually between first cousins (Fakhouri, pp. 63–64).

Cousin marriage is preferred in Egypt because families are **patriarchal.** A patriarchy is a male-dominated social order, in which men enjoy more power, and greater rights, privileges, and prestige than women. In rural Egypt both men and women think that the family should be patriarchal. First of all, inheritance is **patrilineal,** that is, the family name and most of the land are inherited through the male line. People think of themselves as part of their father's family, not their mother's family. When the children of brothers marry, wealth and property can be kept within the extended family. Since the families know and trust each other, it is also easier to negotiate the marriage, and the bride's family can have confidence she will be well-treated by her in-laws, who are her own kin.

In fact, if two brothers marry their children to each other, the young bride may be able to remain in the same household as her mother. This is because rural marriages are **patrilocal,** that is, on marriage a bride moves to her husband's home and joins the household there, which includes his parents, his brothers, and their wives and children. As a result, except in cases of cousin marriage, women must leave their parental home, but relationships between fathers and sons and brothers are enduring; these relatives live and work together for their whole lives. The relationship between a father and son is very important in Egyptian culture: it is the ideal model for male interaction. A younger man respects and obeys an older man, particularly an older male relative (Fakhouri, pp. 61–63). Think about it: This means that if you are a young Egyptian man in a rural village, you will live with and obey your father until he dies.

Women are not without influence and respect in the patriarchal family, but their position is subordinate and their influence indirect. Traditionally, a married woman's allies are her sons, her father, and sometimes, her brothers. Sons and mothers are close in Egyptian society and adult sons, of course, continue to live in their mother's household. They are expected to take their mother's part in quarrels and to support and protect her (Early, p. 67). A mother of many adult sons is an influential person in an Egyptian village. Conversely, a married woman who has no sons has little influence in her household (Fakhouri, pp. 27–28, 61–63). Women are respected not only for their sons, but for their labor and knowledge. Men know that the family's prosperity depends as much upon the mother's household labor, management skills, and help in the fields as it does upon the men's work. Women often market a family's surplus produce or prepare cheeses to sell in the market. These cash sales are frequently a crucial part of the family's income and strengthen the woman's place in her husband's family. By virtue of her contact with the marketplace, her children's schools, and health clinics, a rural woman may also be more sophisticated than her husband, and the family may rely upon her knowledge. But there are strict limits to her assertion of influence. She may confront her husband in private, argue with him, or refuse him, but she will never do so in public.

Village Women and Group Life

Men dominate the public life of the village: You may see them in the coffeehouse, the mosque, and the marketplace, but women enjoy their own separate, more private group life. One of the greatest sources of satisfaction that countrywomen have is the community of women who share an extended household. These women share **primary** ties, bonds that are close, personal, and intimate (Sadat, pp. 181–190). Sisters-in-law and the unmarried daughters of their household work together to prepare food, store crops, make clothing, and do the housekeeping. Village festivals, weddings, and funerals bring together large groups of women. After a funeral, a bereaved woman's home fills with her female relatives and neighbors. Day after day they bring cooked dishes and sit together crying and wailing and praising and telling stories about the deceased individual. Women visit each other on ordinary days too, and sit chatting over coffee and snacks, surrounded by their children. They exchange news of the village, analyze other people's problems and personalities, and give each other advice. The importance of the community of women in Egyptian life is marked by the many jokes men tell about the power of gossiping women.

Social Structure in the City

Egyptians have been city dwellers for thousands of years, so urban life is very much a part of Egyptian culture. In the past century, Egypt's urban population has expanded rapidly. Migrants from the countryside have poured into Cairo, Alexandria, and other cities, so that today nearly half of all Egyptians live in urban areas. Cairo is an exceptionally crowded city; it packs in almost 100,000 people per square mile.

TABLE 4.3. Urban Concentration, 1994–1995:
One in every six Egyptians lives in Cairo, the country's largest city,
but only one in every 25 Germans lives in Berlin, the largest city in Germany.

	Largest City in the Country	Population of Largest City	Percent of the Urban Population Living in the Largest City	Percent of the Total Population Living in the Largest City
Egypt	Cairo	9,665,000	36%	16%
Germany	Berlin	*3,472,000	5	4
Japan	Tokyo	25,013,000	26	20
Mexico	Mexico City	15,643,000	23	18
USA	New York	16,329,000	8	6

Source: Human Development Database, United Nations, 1997
   *Statistics Division of the United Nations Secretariat, http://www.un.org/Depts/unsd/demog

(See Table 4.3.) Some poor Egyptians live in squatter settlements and others in the densely settled and colorful old downtown districts like Bulaq which are well-known in Egyptian literature and folklore. The people of these neighborhoods are known as the *ibn al balad* or *baladi*. The term literally means "sons of the place." Many *baladi* families are only recently arrived in the city from the countryside, but others have lived in Bulaq or similar neighborhoods for generations. These urbanites resemble rural *fellahin* in their dress and their observance of tradition, but they contrast strongly with rural Egyptians in their cultural sophistication, their ability to do business, and their willingness to assert themselves publicly (Early, pp. 59–61).

In crowded poor neighborhoods old four- and five-story apartment buildings face each other across unpaved, rutted alleys, many no more than six feet wide. Lines of laundry hang criss-cross overhead, and in front of shops racks of merchandise encroach on the street. Coffeehouses place benches and tables out in front of the café. Peddlers sell clothing, sweets, vegetables, and prepared foods like beans in various sauces. Storefront workshops produce furniture, shoes, jewelry, and even industrial machinery, spilling some of their operations out into the alleys. Cars can pass through these crowded streets only with great difficulty; goats, sheep, and buffalos stand in muddy corners chewing grain, and donkey carts clog the intersections. In Cairo, neighborhoods like Bulaq exist in a world of their own; government agencies do not venture inside. There is no mail delivery, no police patrol, no fire station. There are no public schools (Weaver, April 12, 1993, p. 85).

The Family in Poor Neighborhoods

In Cairo, as in Egypt's villages, people want to have close ties with their extended families, to live with them in the same buildings or at least in the same neighborhood. But the housing shortage makes this difficult. As adult children marry, they may be unable to find apartments near their parents, and so the extended family may be scattered, married siblings living in different neighborhoods, perhaps far from their parents. Family members may find it hard to get together regularly. In this situation, people have to make choices about which ex-

A large traditional market in Cairo supplies basic goods. The vendor in the foreground is wearing a traditional *gallibiyya* (a loose gown). Behind him a peddler sells bread. In a central market like this, visited by people from many neighborhoods, buyers, sellers, and passersby are mostly men. Women are more likely to be found closer to home in smaller neighborhood markets.

tended family members they remain close to. Sometimes two siblings will manage to buy apartments in the same building, so that they can share child care and home appliances and spend time together (MacLeod, p. 37). Interestingly, it is often sisters who make such arrangements, making female relatives the center of extended family life in a way that is impossible in villages.

As in the village, single young adults never live independently. They remain in their parents' home until they marry. The only exception is young men who migrate to other countries to find work. They disrupt traditional family patterns, both by leaving and by postponing marriage.

When the children of poor city families succeed in moving up in the world, they don't leave behind their family loyalties, and often don't leave their neighborhoods. Though they may seek western-style education and western consumer goods, middle-class Egyptians continue to put family first, socializing by preference with relatives, and seeking out traditional cross-cousin marriages. They take seriously their obligations to relatives: to be generous, to support the helpless, and to reciprocate favors.

Urban Reciprocity Networks and Social Groups

Patterns of reciprocity in *baladi* neighborhoods often revolve around the domestic roles of women. Women help each other by watching each other's sick children, plugging in a long extension cord for a neighbor without electricity, marketing for one another, exchanging small gifts, and raising each other's morale as the grind of daily life takes its toll. Women who work can extend their networks further: co-workers trade information about the best doctors, good tutors for their children, or the right bureaucrat to see for a visa. **Reciprocity networks** also extend beyond the urban neighborhood, to relatives in the villages of residents' birth, and to wealthier, more educated relatives in richer neighborhoods who may be called upon for help. People with good networks have a better chance of succeeding in life (Early, pp. 9–11, 75–80; Rugh, 1984, pp. 89–101).

While poor urban women spend less time with relatives than their village sisters, they still have a rich group life with other women. Women form loan cooperatives to raise money for weddings and the purchase of sewing machines, televisions, and other expensive items. Sewing cooperatives, with one skilled woman teaching others how to sew, so they can do piecework in their homes, are often linked to informal schools in which illiterate women and their daughters learn to read and write and do arithmetic. Women with leadership abilities become an important neighborhood force in such quasi-political organizations. If they understand how government bureaucracies work—how to get a passport or a job, or how to get a place for a son or daughter in school—they become informal local power brokers, advocating for their neighbors and linking them to government officials.

In the city, the clan is no longer the center of men's social life. Instead, men look to social groups called *shilla*. These are small groups bound by friendship or family ties—friends from the village or from school, a group of brothers and their friends, and some of their friends' brothers. Often the members of a *shilla* have a regular table in the coffeehouse or a regular weekly get-together, and they are also mutual-aid networks. A group member who has prospered and moved high in the government bureaucracy will expect to help his friends and relatives. Islamic fundamental organizations have successfully adapted the structures of male group life. They call themselves a group of brothers, or a community of men, and offer men an active group life in religious study groups, political meetings, and community improvement associations, and the resources of the organization and its well-placed members. Fundamentalist "brotherhood" networks interweave, linking legal political and religious groups with illegal paramilitary and terrorist organizations.

Urban Male and Female Roles

Urban families, like their rural counterparts, are patriarchal, but the economic realities of city life have altered gender roles and given city women more independence and greater influence in the choice of their husbands. In rural Egypt, land is the foundation of life, and men control the land. Groups of men are tied together by common interests, cemented by kinship, and work together to cultivate, irrigate, and harvest the land. This unity of work and family gives men tremendous power. While peasant women often work in the fields, they have little opportunity to become economically independent. In the city, *baladi* men are not as united as rural men, nor do they have a monopoly on earning money. Women work in offices and factories; they sell produce or cooked foods in the streets, or even own and manage coffeehouses. They have much more opportunity to spend time away from their male relatives and the supervision of their families. As a result *baladi* women are more nearly equal to their spouses than are their country sisters. The *bint al balad* (daughter of the place) is a positive stereotype of the urban woman as a strong character, boldly confronting the world to help her husband and family, asserting her personality and sex appeal. Songs, novels, plays, and films have portrayed the *bint al balad* for at least a century (Early, pp. 44–45; Sholkamy, p. 203).

Huda's Story: A City Girl

On Huda's 15th birthday she met her brother's friend Ali in the street as her brother walked her to work. Her 20-year-old brother amused her and guarded her reputation as they walked through the neighborhood. Huda decided that Ali was the most handsome young man in Cairo. She was delighted when her brother revealed that Ali returned her interest. Unfortunately, there was no easy way for the two to meet. They were not relatives and their mothers disliked one another. Worst of all, in her father's eyes, would be the fact that Ali was a Saidi, from a part of Egypt that had the reputation of breeding fools and hotheads. Huda's father was from the Delta and considered the people of the Delta sophisticated and clever, not clods like the Saidis.

But Huda was not without resources. Some days later she and her friend Idil were walking home from work. They linked arms and chatted as they walked. Remarkably they encountered Ali and Huda's brother Ahmed. Ali and Ahmed strolled a few paces ahead of Huda and Idil. To any casual observer Ahmed and Ali ignored Huda and Idil, each couple taken up by their own conversations. But someone listening to what they said would see an interesting pattern. "I can't wait to see the Nights," said Huda to Idil, referring to a popular TV soap opera. Ali then commented to Ahmed, "I watch the Nights whenever I can." In this way Huda and Ali exchanged the first of many conversations. Huda's aunt Fatima watched the four from her balcony and was not fooled for a minute. Fatima considered telling Huda's mother, her older sister, but she recalled that she too had once been young and in love with a handsome Saidi.

SOCIAL INEQUALITY IN EGYPT

Egyptians have a lot in common with each other: their long shared history as a nation, the culture of Islam, a single language, similar family and community structures, a centralized government and school system. But at the same time, Egyptians are deeply divided by social inequalities. We have seen that because of gender inequality Egyptian men and women inhabit quite separate social worlds. Class inequality divides Egyptians as radically as does gender inequality.

Class Inequality

Sociologists use the term **class inequality** in discussing several related matters. They use it to talk about inequalities in the distribution of economic resources like income and wealth and to ask how broadly or narrowly these resources are spread through the society. They also use it to discuss **social classes,** groups of people whose economic resources and lifestyles are similar, and which may form real, self-identified social groups. Finally, sociologists use the term *class inequality* in discussing **social mobility,** the extent to which people in different social classes have a chance to move up or down in the social stratification system.

The class stratification system in Egypt is quite distinctive. It bears the imprint of Egypt's history as a socialist society, when the government took control of land and capital and strove to distribute resources more equally. It also shows the effects of Egypt's recent "opening" to capitalism and global business. Today, most Egyptians are quite poor. Egypt's yearly Gross National Product averages only U.S. $1,065 per person. Almost half of all Egyptians have incomes below their society's official poverty line, and the poorest 20 percent of all Egyptians have an average per person income equivalent in purchasing power to $1,653 in the United States (Schmidt, p. 10). At the very top of the stratification hierarchy there is a very small class of very wealthy Egyptians—probably no more than 1 percent of the population. A good way to understand Egyptian class inequality is to say that the top and the bottom of the Egyptian hierarchy are very far apart, but most people cluster near the bottom. As a result, if you examine distribution of income by quintiles (see Figure 2.2, p. 92), you will find that Egypt has a relatively equal distribution of incomes—much more equal than Mexico, for example. In 1991, the most recent year for which income distribution data is available, the richest 20 percent of all Egyptians received 4.7 times as much total income as the poorest 20 percent. (The poorest 20 percent of Egyptians received 8.7 percent of all income and the richest 20 percent received 41.1 percent.) Data on earnings by occupation reveal a similar level of inequality: Skilled workers earn 6 times as much as unskilled workers, and supervisory and professional employees earn 12 times more than laborers (World Bank Development Report, pp. 222–223; U.S. Department of Labor, p. 1).

Economic Resources and Social Class

For any society, knowing about income and wealth distribution gives us only half the picture of class inequality. We also want to know who these people are: Who are the Egyptians in the top income fifth? Who are the poorest Egyptians? Where do they live and what is the source of their earnings? The legacy of Egypt's socialist economy is quite clear. Even today, when it is official government policy to encourage private enterprise, few Egyptians own or work for privately owned companies. Agriculture and government employment are the main sources of income. A very large number of Egyptians can get no regular employment at all; they make their way as best they can in the **informal sector** or else migrate abroad to find work.

Only one-third of Egyptian workers are employed in the private sector—in industry or manufacturing, retail sales, or services. One-third of all workers are government employees, working either in the government bureaucracy, the army, in the civil service (as postal clerks, teachers, bus drivers, mail carriers, etc.), or in government-owned companies like the Helwan Steelworks, the state-owned oil industry, or the Suez Canal Company. State-owned factories produce 70 percent of Egypt's industrial output—everything from steel to clothing (Hedges, July 17,

1994, p. A6; *The Economist* p. 4). As a result, ownership of businesses, the "means of production" in Karl Marx's sense, isn't the most important source of income or class position in Egyptian society. Much more important is a person's **power,** or access to government-controlled resources. In Egypt, unequal access to government power results in unequal rewards. People who can get jobs as government employees (as skilled factory workers, clerical workers, or professionals) enjoy an enviable job security, even though their pay is usually low. They are likely to treat their jobs as economic resources—a way to get medical insurance, or a way to find jobs, or contracts or connections, for relatives and friends. They may supplement their wages by accepting bribes for ordinary services or by skimming government funds that come through their hands. They don't hesitate to skip work when their family needs them and they may even leave work early every day to go to a better-paid, but less secure second job.

Even for those who are not government employees, access to government resources is critical to prosperity. Owners of private businesses operate in an economy which is largely government-owned. Banks are government-owned, as is transportation, and many industrial supplies must be purchased from government factories. Import and export licenses must be granted by the government and paperwork must find its way through the vast government bureaucracy. Business owners can't use their property profitability without government permission.

The same is true in agriculture. Ninety-five percent of Egyptian farms are tiny—below 5 acres. Many of these landowners have the government to thank for their holdings, having received them in the post-1952 land redistribution. But new landowners didn't receive outright ownership of their land. They were required to join farm cooperatives which decide what crops should be grown, supply seeds and fertilizer, storage, transportation, and marketing. Farmers are given credit by government banks and sell their crops to the government at prices the government sets. Egyptians look upon their government officials very differently than do the Japanese. In their eyes the bureaucracy certainly is not a rational, dispassionate agency committed to the public good. Ministries and bureaucrats operate in their own self-interest and they are open to influence and bribery. To get ahead, Egyptians need good connections, through family or *shilla* networks.

Social Classes in Rural Egypt

Twenty-five million Egyptians are dependent on agriculture for their livelihood and most of them are very poor. In the 10 years between 1981 and 1991, the number of poor rural families doubled. Many are landless agricultural workers, dependent for survival on employment on neighboring farms, seasonally or by the day. They are the lowest rung of the rural stratification system. About 1 million Egyptians (occupying 62 percent of all farms) are sharecroppers, farming land for which they must pay rent in the form of a percentage of their crop. A smaller number of tenant farmers pay their rent in cash. The rest of the farmers own their own land, but almost all of them (95 percent) have very small farms—under 5 acres (Kurian, 1992, p. 568). They are better off than the landless, but are still poor and, as we have seen, dependent on the support and goodwill of the government. (See Table 2.2, p. 96.)

Since such an overwhelming percentage of rural Egyptians are poor, it is easy to miss the rural elite. As a result of the land redistributions, there are relatively few large farms. Only 5 percent of farms are larger than 5 acres—but these farmers own 49 percent of the land! Egyptian soil is so fertile that 5–20 acres is a good size for a commercial farm and the owner will be quite prosperous. Such farmers usually live locally and farm their land with hired labor. They are part of a rural upper class, together with village professionals like the town lawyer and doctor and perhaps a successful storekeeper. They live in comfortable houses, with gardens and shaded courtyards, and employ servants. Villagers look up to them and they are able to send their children to university in the city.

But while these landowners are the elite of village society, in national terms they are not part of the upper class. This distinction belongs only to the largest landowners—one-tenth of 1 percent of farmers who own more than 50 acres of land. These farmers don't live locally; they let their land out to tenant farmers, hire a manager, and live in the city. Many of them are actually foreign corporations from Saudi Arabia, Europe, or the United States that buy Egyptian land and employ landless laborers to produce crops like cotton and sugar for export.

Social Classes in Urban Egypt

Class differences are highly visible in Egyptian cities too, and city residents are aware of the hierarchy of classes and where they stand in it (MacLeod, p. 34). In Cairo people of different classes live in distinctively different neighborhoods. The poorest live on the dusty fringes of the city in squatter settlements. Those who are luckier or slightly better off live in old crowded downtown slums like Bulaq or in the concrete high-rise towers of government-built "satellite cities" on the outskirts of town. More prosperous people live in spacious neighborhoods with solid apartment houses and paved streets. The wealthy elite are found in downtown luxury apartment towers or in gracious, tree-lined enclaves of private homes. Different social classes spend their leisure in different places too: the poor in the coffeehouses and on the rooftops of their quarter; the middle class in their homes and in the downtown coffeehouses, restaurants, and movie theaters; the rich in country clubs and modern western hotels. Only the rich own cars; everyone else must ride the slow, sputtering buses, jammed with people, or else walk. People of different classes dress differently too. Lower-class men are likely to wear the traditional *gallibiyya,* a long, loose cotton shirt, and lower-class women wear a loose black cotton overgown with a black head scarf when they are out in public. Middle-class Egyptian men generally wear western-style clothing and middle-class women wear some form of modern "modest dress," often home-sewn. The upper classes are easily identified by their fashionable clothes, imported from Europe (MacLeod, p. 34).

The Lower Class. Overall, at least 35 percent of Egyptian families fall below the very low official poverty line, and the percentage has almost doubled since 1990. The impoverished population in Egypt's cities has been growing rapidly; urban poverty increased more than 50 percent between 1981 and 1991. Early in the 1990s more than half the households in Cairo and adjoining Giza (with an av-

In Cairo's poorest squatter settlements carrying water is one of the daily tasks of women and children. Goats help keep the district clean by scavenging garbage, while cheese made from their milk provides essential nutrients in a monotonous diet of beans and grains.

erage of 4.6 members) had household incomes below $1,100 per year. Six million Cairo residents are now living in squatter communities. There are more than 100 such illegal settlements, self-built quarters of shacks and tents, on the desert outskirts of the city, without electricity, piped water, schools, or health clinics. Sewage runs in open ditches in the street. There is no safe drinking water and health problems are rampant. Some of these squatter settlements are built in the city's cemeteries, where poor people have moved into the stone tombs in which rich Egyptians inter family members' remains (*The Economist,* p. 10; Bayat, pp. 1,5; Rodenbeck, p. 84; Abu-Lughod, J., p. 218). (See Table 2.1, p. 96.)

Most of the poorest Egyptians find work only in the **informal sector** which employs an estimated 26 percent of all Egyptian workers. Informal sector is often a polite way of saying that people scrounge for work. They work off-the-books, often as temporary laborers, or they work as unlicensed street vendors, outside the regular markets, outside the tax system, sometimes selling "pirate" goods—illegal copies of cassette tapes or foreign designer clothes. More than 200,000 street vendors flood Cairo's downtown. Thousands of people work the garbage dumps of big cities, picking through the trash for recyclable materials to sell. Others buy and sell old clothes from door to door, shine shoes, hawk newspapers on the street. Organized groups illegally control the streets of a quarter, where they park and protect cars for a fee. Some informal sector workers are educated, recent graduates unable to find work, or government workers who need second jobs. They make use of their literacy and bureaucratic know-how, by writing letters for illiterate Egyptians or taking sidewalk passport photos. Hundreds work as "facilitators," freelance guides to the bureaucracy, who for a fee will help people find their way through the bewildering corridors of Mugamma, Cairo's huge government building (Rodenbeck, p. 80; Hedges, June 7, 1994, p. A4; Bayat, p. 4).

The Middle Class. When thinking about Egyptian social class, you must remember the sociological concept of **relative poverty.** Many Egyptians consider themselves middle class, even though their incomes are barely above poverty line, because their family has two rooms to live in rather than one, or owns a radio. In the same situation, you would consider yourself desperately poor. About half of all Egyptians (and about three-quarters of urban Egyptians) identify with the middle class, but actually their circumstances vary greatly. Saad Edin Ibrahim divides the Cairo middle class into three **strata** (or layers); the lower middle stratum (including 26.5 percent of Cairenes), the middle stratum (36.1 percent), and the upper middle stratum (15.3 percent) (cited in MacLeod, pp. 34–35). The lower middle class includes manual workers who, in many other societies, would consider themselves "working class."

Egypt's industrial workforce is small, only about 10 percent of the whole labor force, mostly in government-owned enterprises. Relatively skilled industrial workers, who are literate and secure in their jobs, tend to think of themselves as middle class, dress like middle-class people, and have middle-class aspirations for their children. They see themselves as socially equal to other government employees, like clerks or lower civil service workers, whose wages are indeed similar. In fact, their wives and daughters very well may be clerical workers. The bottom of the lower middle class lives barely above the poverty line and they live in the same neighborhoods as the poor.

Those who are better off may have a larger apartment, with perhaps as many as four rooms, a TV, refrigerator, and maybe a few other appliances. In cases in which the husband has a skilled job in a private company the family will be better off, since pay is much higher in private companies than in the public sector, though jobs are less secure. Many lower-middle-class families would be poor were it not for income earned by the wife, who works in a regular job in the formal economy (MacLeod, p. 36). Women are rapidly entering the labor force today, with almost 50 percent of women aged 20 to 39 in paid work (U.S. Department of Labor, p. 6). Twelve percent of industrial workers are women (Hooglund, p. 130).

The middle stratum of the middle class has a more secure hold on its class position. They are university educated and many are young professionals or senior clerical workers in the government bureaucracy. They are self-employed workers in the skilled trades, like plumbers and electricians, or they are shopkeepers or small merchants. Many live in the *baladi* neighborhoods where their businesses are located, but they are actually quite prosperous (Barakat, pp. 89–90; Rodenbeck, p. 82). Middle-middle-class people live in much better apartments, usually of three or four rooms, and they have more elaborate home furnishings and appliances. They expect their children to go to a university.

The upper middle class shades off into the upper class. These people are much more secure than the rest of the middle class. They are established professionals, government bureaucrats, army officers, the prosperous owners of private businesses. Upper-middle-class Egyptians live in air-conditioned modern apartment houses, or in large apartments in old-fashioned middle-class districts. Their homes may be lavishly furnished with inherited antiques or modern European furniture. They can afford servants and even perhaps to send their children to a university abroad.

The Upper Class. The Egyptian upper class is very small, but it is growing. Ibrahim estimates the upper class in Cairo, the national center of business and government, as not more than 1 percent of the population. According to Hooglund, in 1990, only 2,000 families in all of Egypt had incomes above $14,000 per year, so you can imagine how small the upper class is (Ibrahim, cited in MacLeod, p. 35; Hooglund, p. 114). The upper class includes the elites of the government bureaucracy and the top managers of government-owned industries. It includes the most successful owners of private capital—entrepreneurs, big wholesale merchants who engage in international trade, and the owners of big construction firms favored by government contracts. The most successful professionals who work for the public and private elites are members of this class too. The occupations of upper class individuals and the sources of their wealth are varied, but they are linked together by business ties, social relationships, and kinship. Upper-class people are dependent on each other to maintain their wealth. After all, exporters need government licenses and permissions; lawyers need clients, and bureaucrats, no matter how powerful, earn relatively low wages; they use their official positions and their contacts in the private sector in order to earn upper-class incomes, often through private commissions. For example, in recent years President Mubarak's sons have become very wealthy acting as business agents in the airline industry. They earned commissions from foreign airplane manufacturers when they negotiated contracts to supply planes to Egypt's government-owned airline.

Old and New Wealth. In Egypt today there is an old upper class and a new upper class. The old upper class was formed in colonial era Egypt, though many of its members were able to preserve their wealth and connections in socialist Egypt. This elite formed a small, self-conscious group in Cairo and Alexandria. They lived amid family antiques in a few exclusive, guarded villa neighborhoods, spoke French, and supported Egyptian literature and theater. Their children attended exclusive private schools together and they socialized together at English-style country clubs. This elite still prospers in Egypt, but since it always sought to live privately and conceal its wealth, the old elite is overshadowed today by the newly rich.

Egypt's new millionaires have made their money since Sadat's *infitah*, the opening to global capitalism. Some are the sons of old elite families, but others are enterprising operators, some of really modest background, who parlayed their positions in the bureaucracy, or their gift for speculation, into tremendous wealth. Some of the newly rich have made their money in industrial production—steel, appliances, aircraft, but others have profited from currency speculation, or from skimming business loans from international banks. Ex-officials and their sons grew rich from bribes paid by western multinational corporations eager to break into Egypt's markets for arms, aircraft, communications systems, etc. Others made their fortunes investing in the oil-rich Gulf States and have brought back both their new wealth and Islamist styles of dress, architecture, and piety. As new money flows into Egypt, a whole secondary layer of business people has grown wealthy selling consumer goods to the newly rich. They are architects and developers, interior decorators, advertising consultants, dealers in cars, jacuzzis, and cell phones. Entertainers, lawyers, and doctors who serve the rich have also prospered (*The Economist*, p. 6; Raafat, January 6, 1996).

The newly rich have not hesitated to show off their wealth, making the contrast between rich and poor more obvious to everyone. A huge new apartment tower in the suburb of Giza boasts "villas" of 17,000 square feet each, selling for up to $15 million. A new golf course, constructed in the desert on the road to Suez, has carefully watered and manicured green fairways and 300 villas, advertised as "a lifestyle for the privileged few." It sits right next to a bleak, rundown group of concrete public housing blocks, surrounded by eroded sand and blowing trash, home to 20,000 (Ibrahim, Y., August 17, 1995, p. A4; Ajami, pp. 235–237).

Ahmad's Story: The Developer

Ahmad Moustafa looked out over the Nile from the balcony of his Zemalek apartment. At 54 he wished his country had done as well as he had in these turbulent times. He marvelled at his own capacity to find a way to profit in every circumstance. A Mercedes, a luxury apartment in Cairo's most fashionable quarter, hand-tailored suits made in Italy, a glamorous wife, and a son to follow in his footsteps—not bad!

When the monarchy ended in 1952 and the estates of large landowners were broken up, Ahmad's father took the family to live quietly at one of their country properties. But Ahmad went to university, did his army service, and finished his degree in engineering. A classmate helped him get a job in the Ministry of Construction and then he married the daughter of his commanding officer.

In the 1980s, Ahmad saw the opportunities in luxury construction. He went into partnership with his old classmate and they pooled their resources. His father-in-law helped him get a bank loan and with 10 million pounds in hand they were able to buy an old colonial mansion in Garden City from the squabbling heirs who had just inherited it. The house cleared away, they planned 16 apartments, sold for 2,400,000 pounds each, and a well-timed "gift" to a crucial colleague in the ministry and others at the city council made it possible to build two extra floors, another four apartments. In the end, accounting for construction costs and bribes, net profits amounted to 24,000,000 pounds. Ahmad never looked back: three more apartment complexes, a golf course, and now the condo development in the resort at Sharm el Sheikh. Ahmad's son manages land acquisition and is soon to marry the daughter of one of the top bureaucrats of a major bank. They may well fly all the guests to Sharm for the wedding.

Social Mobility in Egypt

For ordinary Egyptians today opportunities for upward mobility are shrinking. Population growth outpaces job growth and young people face high rates of unemployment. This situation is particularly upsetting to Egyptians because their expectations were formed during several decades of rapid economic growth after the 1952 revolution, when living standards rose and opportunities for upward mobility expanded rapidly.

Closed and Open Systems. Sociologists make a theoretical distinction between two kinds of societies: **closed stratification systems** and **open stratification systems.** In closed systems, people must remain in the social class into which they were born and no amount of talent or effort can have any effect. In contrast, in open systems, parents are unable to pass any advantage on to their children. All children have an equal chance to prosper or fail, based only on their ability and hard work. In real life, no stratification system is completely closed or completely open, but it is useful to think about the two theoretical extremes in order to understand the situation in Egypt today. Before Nasser and the revolution of 1952, Egypt's stratification system was based primarily on inherited land and wealth. It was very difficult for people who didn't have these to acquire any. After 1952, Egypt changed from a rather closed system to a more open one, and opportunities for social mobility increased.

The Revolution and Social Mobility. Nasser created vastly more opportunities for Egyptians in two ways. First, he expelled the existing upper class, by ending colonialism and nationalizing almost all Egyptian businesses. European managers, Greek, Christian, and Jewish merchants, and even wealthy Muslim business owners fled the country. Their departure deprived Egypt of their skills, but created many new openings for those loyal to the revolution (Kurian, 1992, p. 550). A new class of Egyptian managers grew. Second, Nasser quickly moved to create a modern economy under state ownership. Economic expansion laid the foundation for a new middle class, and Nasser deliberately poured the nation's resources into training Egyptians for modern industrial jobs. He opened schools and universities and made education available to ordinary Egyptians. He created a modern health care system as well. Suddenly teachers, doctors, nurses, engineers, architects, accountants, managers, and industrial workers were required in great numbers. To encourage young people to go to school, Nasser promised each college graduate a job in the bureaucracy or in government-owned industry. In Nasser's time, the sons of postal workers became doctors, and the sons of peasants became skilled workers (MacLeod, pp. 31–34; Fakhouri, pp. 40–45; Vatikiotis, pp. 390–396, 457–458). (See Table 4.4, p. 210.)

Shrinking Opportunities Today. Today Egyptians find it hard to keep their standard of living from slipping and they fear their children will fall into a lower social class than their own. Every year 400,000 to 500,000 people enter the labor force for the first time and half of them cannot find jobs (Hedges, July 17, 1994, p. A6). The official unemployment rate stands at 10 percent, and that isn't counting the 3 million workers (one-quarter of the total labor force) who cannot find regular jobs, but work in the informal sector (U.S. Department of Labor, pp. 1, 4). It is two decades now since the government found it could no longer promise a job to every university graduate. However, Egyptians still look to education as the

TABLE 4.4. Increases in Secondary Education of Females and Males:
Egypt and Mexico have rapidly expanded their secondary school enrollment since 1970.

	Percent of Females 12–17 Enrolled in Secondary Education		Percent of Males 12–17 Enrolled in Secondary Education	
	1970	1996	1970	1996
Egypt	19%	70%	38%	80%
Germany	Data Not Available	101*	Data Not Available	103*
Japan	86	107*	87	105*
Mexico	18	59	27	58
United States	84	98	83	97

*Figures larger than 100 percent indicate that portions of the population older than 12–17 are enrolled in secondary school.
Source: http://unescostat.unesco.org//Yearbook/Indicator

route out of poverty, and even quite modest jobs as clerks or semiskilled workers require a high school degree. Many educated young people find their expectations disappointed though. Nearly one-quarter of those unemployed in Cairo today hold university degrees (Rodenbeck, p, 82). Young men without jobs cannot marry, and until they marry they cannot leave their parents' homes. Intensified competition and unsatisfied aspirations fuel social unrest.

Migration. The most common response to shrinking opportunities is migration. About 2 1/2 million Egyptian men—out of a labor force of 22 million—work outside Egypt today, mostly in the Persian Gulf states: Saudi Arabia, Kuwait, Jordan, and Libya. (Some Egyptians have even tried to work as illegal migrants in Israel!) Men don't take their families abroad with them and women never become migrant workers. Migrant work pays well: that is its great attraction. Those working abroad send home an average of $1,600 apiece yearly. Don't think of migrant labor as something done only by the poor and unskilled. Men of every class work abroad, especially the insecure children of the rural and urban middle classes—the sons of small landowners, shopkeepers, and government bureaucrats. They often work as engineers, teachers, and doctors. Egyptian universities graduate a great many students with degrees in education—more than 17,000 per year—but 80 percent of them go abroad to teach (Kurian, 1992, p. 569). (See Table 4.5.) Plunging oil prices in the late 1990s have hurt the economies of the Gulf states and restricted opportunities there for Egyptians. Egyptians are reminded of their vulnerability in the world economy.

Idris' Story: The Teacher

Idris had always thought of himself as a man with a bright future. His parents had been born in the countryside, but in the flush times of the early sixties they came to Cairo. Idris was a bright child and did well in school, and his parents believed his intelligence and hard work would bring success. But this was not to be. By the time Idris left teachers' college in the early 1980s, there were no jobs for teachers in Egypt. For two miserable years he searched desperately for any job, but only found work tutoring neighborhood children to pass their exams.

TABLE 4.5. Money Sent Home:
Egyptians and Mexicans working abroad contribute billions to the Egyptian
and Mexican economies.

	Value of Money Sent Home by Those Working Abroad in U.S. Dollars		Money Sent Home as a Percent of the Gross Domestic Product
	1992	1995	1995
Egypt	$5,430,000,000	$5,070,000,000	11%
Mexico	$2,070,000,000	$3,710,000,000	2

Sources: United Nations Human Development Database, 1997
    The State in a Changing World, Oxford University Press, 1997

Idris was rescued by the offer of a job as a teacher's assistant in a private school in Kuwait. A college friend was teaching there and had some small influence. Idris was delighted, even though working in Kuwait meant leaving his family. He arrived in Kuwait penniless; the bribe he paid for his exit visa took the last of his cash.

But then Idris hated Kuwait. Even though he was an educated man, an Arab, and a Muslim, he was treated with contempt. And he thought Kuwait was a wasteland—no culture, no night life, no nothing. Idris lived with other Egyptians, rarely going out and sending most of his money home to his family. They needed it too. His father's wages as a factory worker failed to keep pace with rising prices.

On one of his infrequent visits home, Idris married Aisha, whom he had known since childhood, and in the middle of the Kuwaiti school year he became the father of twins. He couldn't even return home for their birth; it was either a hospital room for Aisha or an airline ticket for him. What, thought Idris, had become of his life? What hope could there be for the future? Even in eight or ten years, when his name finally came up on the waiting list for a teaching job in Egypt, the salary would never be enough to support his wife and family and also help his parents.

Compared to the tremendous class and gender inequalities in Egyptian society, other status inequalities seem minor. There are racial and religious inequalities in Egypt, but they are of lesser importance.

Racial Inequality in Egypt

Egypt is a racially mixed society. Its people come from Africa, the Middle East, Central Asia, and Europe, but they have been mixing and intermarrying for thousands of years. As a result, Egyptians vary in their skin colors and facial features. There is no doubt that light skin is a source of prestige. Before the 1952 revolution, many families in the landowning elite were aristocrats descended from Egypt's earlier rulers (including Greeks, Turks, and Macedonians). They were conscious of their lighter skin and sought similar spouses for their children (Hooglund, p. 119). Today light skin is still associated with elite status, with wealth and power. Movie stars and women in advertisements tend to have light skin. On the other hand, skin color is only one of many sources of prestige in

Egypt, including gender, education, occupation, family background, and city origins. Furthermore, while Egyptians are aware of skin color, they are not race-conscious. That is, they do not classify people by race: "she is black," or "he is white." They might note that among a family of siblings, some have lighter skin and others darker skin, but they would not feel a need to decide if the family was "white" or "black." Another way of putting this is to say that race is not a **master status** in Egypt. Skin tone does not determine a person's access to jobs, education, or choice of spouse in any major way.

Religious Inequality

The majority of Egyptians are Muslims. Coptic Christians are a religious **minority group** in Egypt. Copts make up somewhere between 5 percent and 20 percent of the population. The true total is a matter is dispute, since the government does not enumerate Copts. Some people say the government is afraid to know how large the Coptic minority has grown. Sociologically speaking, Copts are a minority not just in numbers, but in terms of their lack of power. Arabic-speaking Muslims are the social **majority** in Egypt, and were so even when their numbers were small, because they controlled the military, the government, and the laws. At many points in Egyptian history, the Muslim majority permitted Copts to maintain their own communities and religious institutions, as long as they accepted their subordination to Muslim authority. At other times, Coptic institutions and property were attacked by the Muslim majority, despite their official protection under Islamic law. The situation was similar for the much smaller Jewish minority in Egypt (Nisan, pp. 115–121; Ibrahim, Y., Mar. 15, 1993, pp. A1, A8).

The Life of a Religious Minority

Egypt's Coptic community has traditionally been divided between those living in Cairo and Alexandria and those living in rural areas in Upper Egypt. Before the twentieth century, urban Copts often served as clerks and administrators for Egypt's Muslim rulers. Boutros Boutros-Ghali, former secretary general of the United Nations, is descended from a prominent Coptic family with a long tradition of government service. When Copts were forced out of government positions by the British colonial administration, they turned to the professions and many became doctors and pharmacists (Nisan, pp. 122–127). Affluent, urban Copts have little informal social contact with their Muslim neighbors, except to some extent when they attend a university. But the situation is far different for poor Copts in the countryside and the cities.

Poor Coptic Christians and Muslims are often neighbors and they come into close social contact as part of the same neighborhood social networks. Coptic and Muslim women shop for one another, watch each other's children, and lend each other money. Christian and Muslim neighbors attend each other's weddings and funerals and participate in the more social aspects of each other's religious celebrations. For example, it would not be unusual for Christian men to attend their town's annual festival at the Muslim shrine, nor would it be strange for a Muslim woman to go to Easter services with her Christian neighbor (Early, p. 73).

In some ways, Copts can be considered a highly **assimilated** minority, one which has taken on the culture of the dominant group. Copts cannot easily be distinguished from their Muslim neighbors. Centuries ago, Copts adopted Arabic as their daily language; the ancient Coptic language is rarely used. Copts wear the same clothing as other Egyptians and eat the same foods too. In daily life, only a visible cross or a Christian name (such as Butros) distinguishes Copt from Muslim (Hooglund, pp. 141–142).

Increasing Discrimination

Today, however, as economic conditions worsen in Egypt, and competition for scarce jobs and housing increases, Copts are experiencing more prejudice and discrimination. Militant Islamic groups have pressured the government to define Egypt as an Islamic state, ruled by Islamic laws. These groups frighten Copts and make them feel like outsiders in their own country. Terrorist fundamentalists have attacked and killed Copts and vandalized and burned churches. As many as 150 to 200 Copts have been killed and the government for several years stationed police guards outside churches. Coptic children are now shunned by their public school classmates, and women with the traditional tattooed cross are taunted and attacked in public. Copts say that despite its official opposition to terrorism, the government encourages attacks on them. Construction of new churches has not been allowed for 30 years and Copts have been barred from positions in the government, the army, the police force, and universities. In their efforts to appear pro-Islam, government officials sometimes make statements that reflect deep hostility toward the Coptic minority (Nisan, pp. 127–133, Ibrahim, Y., Mar. 15, 1993, pp. A1, A8; Ajami, pp. 206–209; Jehl, March 15, 1997, p. A3).

SOCIAL CHANGE AND THE FUTURE

Egypt today is in an unstable situation. The society is plagued by serious economic and social problems and life for most Egyptians has noticeably worsened over the past 25 years. Politically, Egypt is torn by conflict over whether the nation should be an Islamic state, ruled by *Sharia,* a secular democracy, or the mostly secular military dictatorship it is now. Increasing poverty and growing economic inequality exacerbate political tensions.

Economic Growth and Increasing Poverty

Egypt's economy today is in a very contradictory state: Gas tanks are full, but dinner plates are empty. Rich Egyptians now buy so many Mercedes-Benz cars that the company started an assembly plant in Egypt to serve local demand. At the same time, most Egyptians can afford to eat meat only a handful of times a year. The economy looks good: Under pressure from the International Monetary Fund, and with the help of United States foreign aid and debt relief, Egypt has begun to develop a private economy. Economic growth reached 5 percent in 1998, with inflation at an admirably low 4 percent and almost no budget deficit. New suburbs and Mediterranean villas have been built and there are new privately owned businesses. Some businesses that were government-owned have been privatized too. There are now privately owned steel companies, appliance manufacturers, telecommunications companies, aircraft manufacturers, and lots of construction businesses (*The Economist,* pp. 1–5).

The downside is that most of the new big businesses are owned by the sons of the old upper class who are well-connected to the governing elite. Outside of that upper crust, most new businesses are tiny; they are the shoestring operations, the local grocery and candy stores, the market stalls that serve a growing population. And job growth has not kept pace with population growth. There is a growing split between older, middle-class Egyptians who have jobs, houses, and schools for their children, and younger Egyptians, even middle-class people, who can't find jobs, can't marry, and can't afford housing. Poverty continues to intensify and the percentage of Egyptians who are poor is still growing (*The Economist,* pp. 1–5).

Even though Egypt is privatizing, the economy is still strangled by its traditional bureaucracy. It is a burden to both rich and poor. Nasser began to overstaff the bureaucracy decades ago in order to provide jobs for all educated Egyptians. Now bureaucrats start work at nine and leave at two and spend much of the time in between on tea breaks and conversation. They are poorly paid, so many use their positions merely as opportunities to collect bribes or help relatives advance their fortunes. Registering new property—a house or business you have bought—still requires 77 different bureaucratic procedures in 31 different offices! (Vatikiotis, pp. 406–411, *The Economist,* p. 4).

> *Egyptians find this joke very funny; it rings true to them: "U.S. President Clinton visits Cairo and insists on jogging through the streets. He meets a poor man who pours out his heart and tells him about his sick wife and his son who can't afford to marry. Clinton is very moved and when he gets back to Washington he calls President Mubarak and tells him, 'I've sent you $5,000. Please give it to Ibrahim Sayed of Bulak for me.' Mubarak calls in an aide. 'Here's $2,500 from Bill Clinton. Find Ibrahim Sayed in Bulak and give it to him.' The aide calls his assistant. 'Go to Bulak and find Ibrahim Sayed and give him this $1,000 from President Clinton.' The assistant calls his assistant. 'This $500 is from Bill Clinton. Find Ibrahim Sayed and give it to him.' The assistant calls his secretary. 'I want you to find Ibrahim Sayed and tell him Bill Clinton sends his regards.' "*

Corruption of those at the top is particularly resented. Egyptians complain about the "Gang of Sons," the children of a number of important officials in the government, including the sons of President Mubarak, who are believed to collect bribes and use their fathers' positions for business advantage (Weaver, 1995, p. 56). Many Egyptians believe that corruption has grown so great that it is preventing growth, while government officials are too corrupt to really want to change things.

Privatizing the Land

The Mubarak government's efforts to modernize and privatize the economy have had a big impact on rural Egyptians. Mubarak has substantially weakened the land reform laws instituted by Nasser and allowed foreign businesses to buy up huge tracts of fertile land (Mitchell, T., pp. 22–23). In 1997 Egypt's government ended the freeze on land rents and changed the law so landlords are now allowed to revoke leases. The changes in law came at the urging of the World Bank and the International Monetary Fund to move Egyptian agriculture toward mechanized cultivation of commercial crops like cotton and rice, for export, and away from **subsistence agriculture** (in which families grow food for their own consumption). The new law, No. 96, affects 6 million peasants, nearly 10 percent of the population, most of whom cannot afford the new market rents and risk dispossession. Some landowners hired armed guards to force tenants off their land, and some peasants were killed resisting. The potential for unrest and violence is so great that by 1998 the government decided to slow the pace of change, requiring landlords to go to court case by case to evict tenants (Jehl, December 27, 1997; Hirst, October 1, 1997, p. A16; Engel, January 4, 1998).

The Food Gap and Inequality

Today, Egypt suffers from a **food gap:** Despite rising agricultural production, the country must import food to feed its people. Money that might be spent on schools, housing, and health care is used for foreign wheat. Egypt's food gap is puzzling, because production of grain has kept up with and even exceeded population growth. The explanation lies in the use to which the grain is put. Increasingly, wheat and corn grown in Egypt are used as animal feeds to raise cattle for beef sold to those affluent Egyptians who can afford a diet rich in meat. Then the government must import wheat for subsidized sale to the poor. Half of all wheat is now imported. Also, foreign companies grow thousands of acres of cotton and sugar for export. Obviously, this also reduces domestic food production in Egypt (Metz, p. 358; Mitchell, T., p. 21). (See Table 4.6.)

Population Problems

Because Egypt's economy has grown little, it has proved difficult for the society to absorb its growing population—neither job growth nor housing construction have kept pace. In 1947 there were 19 million Egyptians, by 1976 there were nearly 37 million, and by 2000 there were 68 million. Although Egypt's population is not

TABLE 4.6 Dependence on Food Imports:
Despite substantial agricultural production, Mexico and Egypt import
very large amounts of basic grains to feed their populations.

	Egypt		Mexico	
	1970	1995	1970	1995
Tons of Grain Imports (Mostly Wheat)	1,260,000	7,934,000	845,000	6,791,000
Percent of Daily Calories from Grain Imports	13.6%	34.1%	5.3%	19.5%

Source: Food Balance Sheets for 1970 and 1995, Food and Agriculture Organization, On Line FAOSTAT DATABASE, Http://apps.fao.org/lim500/nphwrap.pl?FoodBalanceSheet&Domain = FoodBalanceSheet expected to increase as rapidly in the future, substantial growth is still expected. By some estimates, Egypt will have nearly 105 million people by 2025 (Omran and Roudi, p. 4).

The Demographic Transition

Egypt, like many other developing countries is in the midst of very important changes in population patterns. **Demographers** (the scientists who study population) call these changes a **demographic transition.** Before 1950, Egypt had a high birthrate, but there was a high death rate too. Many babies failed to survive to adulthood and consequently population growth was slow. Then, after 1950, there was a big change. Death rates fell rapidly: In 1950 24 people out of every 1,000 Egyptians died every year; by 1990 only 8 out of every 1,000 died yearly. This striking drop in death rates started when the Nasser government embarked on a huge campaign to make free or low-cost health care available to all Egyptians. Between 1952 and 1976 government expenditure on public health increased 500 percent. At the same time, however, birthrates stayed high, so in consequence, population soared. Recently Egypt has entered another stage in the **demographic** transition: Birthrates are falling, while death rates remain low. As a result, the rate at which its population is growing has slowed. In 1950 the birthrate in Egypt was 48 births yearly for every 1,000 Egyptians, but by 1990 the birthrate had fallen to 33 per 1,000 yearly. Birthrates continue to fall, but so far the rates are still high enough to keep population expanding (Hooglund, pp. 124, 148–152; Omran and Rondi, p. 4). (See Figure 4.1.)

Urbanization and Population Growth

Better health care brought down death rates. What changes made birthrates fall? One critical change has been the migration of people from the countryside to the cities and their involvement in an urban economy. In 1950 only one Egyptian in three lived in an urban area, but by 1990 half of all Egyptians lived in cities. In 1992 rural women had an average of five children each, but urban women had only three. In the cities, women in the paid labor force are likely to have fewer children. Also, city families see that educated children earn more than those who are barely literate. If a family thinks it likely that they will be able to send their children to school, then it pays to have fewer children so they will be able to afford to educate them. Conversely, a very poor family that knows education is out of the question will find it more rational to have many children, all of whom can work and bring in some income to help the family.

It is puzzling though, that despite urbanization, Egypt's birthrate has declined more slowly than demographers expected. There are a variety of reasons for this, but one is apparently the influence of surrounding countries which are eager to increase, rather than reduce, their populations. Libya, Iraq, Kuwait, and other oil-rich states with relatively small populations have tried to encourage people to have large families. Youssef Courbage argues that the enormous numbers of young Egyptian men working in these countries have been very influenced by their values. At the same time that education and urbanization tend to reduce the number of children women desire, work abroad tends to reinforce male preferences for larger families (Courbage, pp. 19–22).

FIGURE 4.1. Comparing Birthrates and Death rates in Egypt and Japan, 1980–2000

In Egypt both birthrates and death rates (per 1,000) are falling, but birthrates still far exceed death rates and the population is rapidly growing. Egypt's population in 1980 was 42 million and is projected to reach 68 million by 2000.

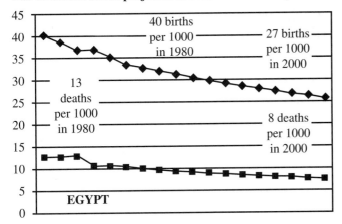

Japan's birthrates and death rates have converged and population growth has slowed. There were 117 million Japanese in 1980, 124 million in 1990, and only 2 million more—126 million—are projected by 2000.

Source: International Data Base, United States Census, http://www.census.gov/lpc/www/idsprd.html

Population Policy

Since 1966 Egypt's government has encouraged family planning and the use of contraceptives to limit population increase. The government has created a national network of family planning clinics, conducted an extensive media campaign in favor of small families, and made contraceptives widely available. These efforts have not been as successful as the government hoped: Egyptians tend to distrust anything that their government promotes. Nevertheless, it is clear that programs to reduce family size have met with some success. In 1992 almost half of all married Egyptian women reported that they used a modern contraceptive method such

TABLE 4.7. Population Momentum:
Births—and the total population—rise despite the fall in the number
of births per woman. The rising number of births reflects the growing
number of women in the childbearing years.

	Women in the Childbearing Years 15–49	Births	Average Number of Births to a Woman in Her Childbearing Years*	Population
Egypt				
1960	6,200,000	1,200,000	6.6	27,000,000
1980	9,800,000	1,700,000	5.5	43,000,000
2000	15,800,000	1,800,000	3.2	68,000,000
Mexico				
1960	13,900,000	1,800,000	6.7	56,000,000
1980	16,000,000	2,400,000	4.7	69,000,000
2000	20,800,000	2,500,000	3.5	85,000,000

* Total Fertility Rate
Source: International Data Base, United States Census, http://www.census.gov/ipc/www/idbsprd.html

as the diaphragm or the intrauterine device. The same survey also reported that 67 percent of married women wanted no more children (Omran and Roudi, p. 13). But despite these very real successes, the number of Egyptians continues to rise, due in part to the **momentum factor.** Each family is having fewer children, but there are so many more families that population growth continues at a rapid rate. (See Table 4.7.)

Environmental Damage: The Unintended Consequences of Economic Growth

In the 1950s, Gamal Abdul Nasser attempted to increase Egypt's productivity in two ways: by farming more land and by developing heavy industry. His approach to development was heavily influenced by American and European ideas about irrigation and industrialization. These policies had serious unintended consequences when applied to Egypt. Americans and Europeans now know that industrialization and irrigation projects can damage even hardy environments. In a fragile environment such as Egypt's, development produced as much damage in a decade as it did in a century or more in the United States.

Many of Egypt's environmental problems concern water and farmland. The Aswan Dam was the most important element in Nasser's plan to increase agricultural production. In the short run, the dam was a great success: It controlled the destructiveness of the Nile's annual flood, it permitted more effective allocation of irrigation water, and new land was brought under cultivation. A lake, Lake Nasser, formed behind the Aswan Dam. As time went on, however, the Aswan Dam produced more and more negative effects. The absence of the annual flood severely reduced agricultural productivity. In the past, the flood brought soil from central Africa to the banks of the Nile. This new soil gave the Nile Valley its remarkable fertility. The land is now less productive and more reliant on expensive fertilizers. The reduced flow of the Nile has also increased the salinity of the water at the northern edge of the Delta where the Nile meets the sea. Eventually, this could make the land too salty for farming. The absence of the annual flood has also facilitated the spread of parasitic diseases. As population increases in Egypt and north Africa, the Nile increasingly becomes an object of conflict. In Egypt illegal construction of housing along the Nile has removed one million acres of land from agricultural production. Countries like Ethiopia, further south in Africa, at the headwaters of the Nile need more water as their population grows, so tapping the waters of the Nile becomes a source of international dispute (Hooglund, pp. 100, 150; Hedges, Dec. 18, 1993, p. A5; Jehl, March 25, 1997, p. A4; Hirst, Oct. 1, 1997, p. A16).

Industrial Pollution

In the 1950s and the 1960s, influenced by ideas shared by virtually all economists at the time, Nasser worked to introduce heavy industry to Egypt. One of the centerpieces of this effort was the mammoth steelworks of the Helwan industrial complex. This project transformed the countryside and the lives of the people. Villages that existed on the fringes of the modern world gained electricity, paved roads, schools, radio and television, modern consumer products, and the wages that permitted people to buy them. But now, several decades later, these same villages are paying an environmental toll for industrial development: Water and air are polluted, the land has lost some of its fertility, and agricultural produce is contaminated by industrial wastes. Industrial pollution from petrochemical plants has begun to wear away Egypt's most famous tourist attraction, the pyramids. The survival of these ancient monuments is also threatened by an eight-lane highway and its fumes and pollution. Not only pyramids, but people are endangered by Egypt's burgeoning auto traffic. Cairo's air is dangerously polluted with lead (Ethelson, pp. 4–5; Hedges, Nov. 26, 1993; Dec. 10, 1994, p. 4; Jehl, April 4, 1997, p. A4).

The Islamic Alternative

If you were a young Egyptian, what would you think about the future? If you were rich, you would feel optimistic about free-market capitalism, but if you were poor you might conclude that socialism didn't work and capitalism doesn't help either. In this discouraging, confusing time, the Islamists proclaim, "Islam Is The Solution!" Disillusioned with western policies that don't seem to work, many Egyptians are attracted to an answer that comes out of their own Arab, Muslim traditions.

The Islamist or Islamic fundamentalist movement is a world movement. At the end of the twentieth century it is probably the most important such religious/political movement. The Islamists won their earliest victory in the 1979 revolution which overthrew the Shah of Iran and installed a strict Islamic republic. Fundamentalist movements in Egypt, as in Algeria and Malaysia, seek political power, in many cases through violence and revolution, in order to overthrow secular government and create a theocracy, a government of religious leaders, ruled by *Sharia,* Islamic law. (You should realize that other religious fundamentalisms—Hindu fundamentalism in India, Jewish fundamentalism in Israel, and Christian fundamentalism in the United States of America are also important political movements today.) Islamic rule promises an end to corruption, a more equal society, and a society that will prosper because it is god-fearing and moral. Islamic rule also promises to moderate the harsh inequalities of capitalism, by forbidding speculation and loan sharking, enforcing charity, and requiring the wealthy to invest their money productively, creating jobs for others and goods and services for the community. Many Muslims see in Islamic fundamentalism the hope of "something uniquely Islamic between capitalism and socialism that will marry private enterprise with social justice and a sense of family and community" (Smith, pp. 85–88).

In Egypt the Islamist movements have attracted a great deal of sympathy and support because they help poor and middle-class Egyptians, especially in poor areas where government institutions—schools, health clinics, police, etc.—are wholly lacking. In Cairo in 1992 there was a terrible earthquake in which hundreds of people were killed and thousands lost their homes. While the government stood by passively, the Islamists responded immediately with food, blankets, tents, and housing. Today the Islamists run health clinics, schools, day-care centers, and furniture factories to provide jobs to the unemployed. They sell meat at discount prices to the poor and give free books and tutoring to poor children. They help young professionals like doctors, dentists, and lawyers by giving them loans to set up clinics and offices and by underwriting health and life insurance policies. Islamic militants seem earnest and dedicated, and above all, honest, especially in contrast to Egypt's corrupt government (Weaver, 1993, p. 82, 1995, p. 61; Hasan, pp. 60–63).

Nabeel's Story: The Sympathizer

Ever since he was a small boy, Nabeel had loved cars, trucks, tanks, planes—things that moved. His parents despaired when he failed the high school entrance examination, but he thrived in the local technical and vocational school, learning to be a mechanic. On graduation, Nabeel looked for a job in Asyut, the city in Upper Egypt where he was raised, but there was little work to be found, only unskilled and poorly paid labor. Unhappy, but resigned to the need, Nabeel left to join one of his uncles in Cairo who promised to help him find work. Nabeel's uncle found a job for him repairing postal vans, but the pay was low and he had to make a large payment to the garage manager "for his help." After three years, Nabeel, now 22, owned only his clothes and a few books. His wages fed him, but let him save little. When his mother was ill, Nabeel sent most of his small savings to pay for doctors and medicines.

Cairo was not the bright promise it had once seemed. He was poor, had no future, and every day rich men and women drove past him in expensive cars and foreign clothes. Nabeel was shocked by the women in Cairo; they walked the street uncovered and immodest. Bared bosoms were displayed on every movie poster! It was all part of the influence of the afrangi—*the westernized Egyptians who thought and acted as foreigners, not Egyptians, and not Muslims.*

Later that year, Nabeel's mother came to visit him in Cairo and he took her to a free health clinic run by the Muslim Brotherhood. There were dedicated young doctors there who took their work seriously. The doctor really listened to Nabeel's mother and she was able to diagnose her breathing problems and get the asthma under control. Nabeel was overjoyed, but he was also furious at the government clinics that had made his mother wait and wait, then hadn't helped her. Nabeel listened to sermons by imams who sympathized with al Jihad. They called for an Islamic Egypt where the government would care about ordinary Egyptians and there would be jobs and decent wages for all. "Perhaps," thought Nabeel, "this is the path we need to follow."

Revolutionary Islam

The Islamist movement in Egypt dates back to the 1920s when the Muslim Brotherhood formed to oppose British colonial rule. After independence it went on to campaign for an Islamic state. Banned for an attempt on Nasser's life in 1954, the group was suppressed. Despite the ban the group still exists today, tolerated by the government as a moderate, nonterrorist alternative to newer, more militant groups. There are over 40 Islamist groups in all now, but they operate in alliances and under the leadership of the two most important groups—*Gama'a al-Islamiya* (The Islamic Group) and *al-Jihad.* These groups were suppressed by Nasser but encouraged by Sadat in order to foster opposition to the socialist movements he saw as his enemies. Foolish man—his assassination in 1981 was carried out by the military wing of al-Jihad (Weaver, 1993, p. 76).

Islamist groups in Egypt follow classic revolutionary strategies. Their revolutionary terrorist wings use violence against individuals in order to change their society. Attacks on tourists aim to bring on an economic crisis, since Egypt's economy is so dependent on tourism. Attacks on Copts and especially on intellectuals and religious figures who dispute fundamentalist theology assert the power of the Islamists to interpret and impose Islamic law. Most casualties have been in fighting between fundamentalists and the police. Fundamentalists hope that the more vicious the government repression of the movement, the more ordinary Egyptians will sympathize with them. So far, it hasn't worked; Egyptians are accustomed to stable, powerful central government and a civil political dialogue. The public was especially horrified by the 1994 stabbing of one of Egypt's most venerated novelists, Naguib Mafouz, a Nobel Prize winner, who has criticized both the militants and the Mubarak government. Then, the 1997 massacre of tourists visiting the temples at Luxor drove most Egyptians into support of the government they usually condemn and even split the Islamist movement.

The Islamists have been much more successful in their strategy of penetrating existing institutions. Gama'a has recruited on college campuses and elected "Islamic" slates to leadership of trade unions and professional associations. It has sent its members into the courts, the hospitals, and the bar, and probably the army too (Weaver, 1993, p. 80). Probably most important, Islamic activists are now strongly represented among Egypt's 850,000 poorly paid schoolteachers and they have, according to Mary Ann Weaver, "basically seized control of the educational system, assaulting secular thought, altering school texts and playing cassettes of radical sermons of popular sheikhs in class" (1995, p. 63). A whole generation of Egyptian children is growing up under the influence of the fundamentalists.

Defining Deviance

A great many Egyptians—probably a majority—are in sympathy with the fundamentalists' declared values; they agree that chastity, modesty, honesty, sobriety, and obedience to the will of Allah are of utmost importance. If free elections were permitted in Egypt, the legal Islamist parties would probably gain many seats in the legislature. But when it comes to actual norms and especially when it comes to sanctions for deviant behavior, many people find the militants go too far.

In the 1990s, in poor neighborhoods dominated by Gama'a, groups of young male militants armed with knives and guns went about enforcing *Sharia* (Islamic law), as their religious leaders, their *sheikhs* defined it. They burned video shops selling tapes they considered immoral—tapes which showed men and women touching, or which seemed insulting to Islam. They forced Coptic shopkeepers to remove images of the Virgin Mary and forced women and girls as young as six or seven to wear the hijab (Weaver, 1993, p. 61). The sheikhs who set policy for Gama'a are acting as what sociologist Howard S. Becker called **moral entrepreneurs,** people who create and enforce new norms in societies (Becker, H.S., 1963).

Dissent and Deviance

Islamic militants have not only tried to define behavioral norms, they have insisted on their authority to set norms for what may be said in writing in Egyptian society. During the 90s they mounted a powerful attack on Egypt's secular intellectuals, accusing certain writers of heresy and apostasy, crimes punishable by death under Sharia. It began in 1992 with the assassination of Farag Foda, a well-known author who wrote as a Muslim, but critized the fundamentalists and rebutted their claim to know the only true Islam. Then came the attack on the novelist Naguib Mafouz, and in the late 90s, the famous case of Nasr Hamed Abu Zeid, a professor of Arabic literature, whose work was a scholarly and erudite analysis of early Islamic texts. Abu Zeid was targeted as a secularist for daring to discuss the Quran as a text subject to interpretation. He was declared apostate and then Islamist lawyers went to court to dissolve his marriage on the ground that an apostate could not be married to a Muslim woman. Abu Zeid eventually fled Egypt. In these cases and others, the government has acted quickly in cases of assault, but permitted legal attacks like those on Abu Zeid. Further, the government has really tried to ingratiate itself with Islamist sympathizers, by giving more power to what it sees as "moderate" Islamic authorities. Thus the official sheikhs of Al-Azhar, the Islamic university, have been given the power to censor all books and films. Egyptian publishing has withered. In a country that used to be a literary center, only 375 books were published in 1997. And the government has suppressed dissent generally, for example, jailing a journalist and a professor who tried to help tenant farmers organize against Law 96 (Miller, pp B7, B9; Ajami, pp. 205–221; Weaver, 1995, pp. 57–58).

Then, starting in 1992, the Mubarak government struck back against Islamist violence. They cordoned off Islamist neighborhoods and invaded with thousands of troops. There were gun battles and thousands of militants were arrested, held illegally in jails and tortured. In 1994 Human Rights Watch estimated that over

20,000 Islamists were imprisoned. Every terrorist act has been followed by immediate arrests, summary convictions, and executions (Weaver, 1995, pp. 61–62; Ajami, pp. 202–203; Hasan, pp. 60–63). By the end of the 1990s, the government had killed or imprisoned so many Islamists that their movement really seemed to be in retreat—Gama'a and Al Jihad had stopped working openly and acts of terrorism seemed at a halt (*The Economist,* p. 15).

Egypt's Future

In the 1990s in Egypt, quite ordinary, acceptable behaviors like renting an Egyptian movie, buying groceries on a Friday afternoon, criticizing a government policy, or examining the history of Islam suddenly were redefined as serious deviance. It made many Egyptians uneasy. And a small, influential group of middle-class Egyptians were appalled. These were the more westernized intellectuals who hoped for increased personal freedom, broadened public debate, more guarantees of civil rights, and greater democracy in Egypt. Egyptians find themselves caught between conflicting definitions of deviance. Are the secular intellectuals wrong to want freedom of expression? Are the militants wrong to want people to follow Islamic law? Is the government wrong to meet terrorism with violence? The conflict is very frightening because it evokes the spectres of fundamentalism in two other societies: Algeria and Afganistan, where things are much worse than in Egypt. In Algeria conflict between the fundamentalists and the military-backed government has resulted in a bloody civil war, with 70,000 civilians killed thus far, mostly villagers massacred by one side or the other. In Afganistan an extremist Islamic group called the Taliban has taken power and imposed a particularly harsh version of *Sharia.* People are forced to attend public sessions in which the hands of thieves are amputated and those convicted of adultery are stoned to death. Music and movies are banned. Women must cover their entire bodies, including their faces, and religious police beat and arrest women seen in public with even an inch of wrist showing. Women are forbidden to work or attend school and cannot even leave their houses without a male escort (Miller, J., January 31, 1998, p. 89; Sciolino, October 13, 1996, p. 4E).

In every Islamic society today—from Egypt to Iran—there is worry about the Taliban and debate over the interpretation of Islamic law. There is conflict between those who would interpret *Sharia* very strictly and impose extreme penalties for deviance and those who want a more liberal Islam, with more rights and freedom for women and more openness to exchange of ideas.

What will happen in Egypt in the near future? Will the Islamists succeed in taking power? If so, how restrictively will they apply Islamic law? Between an entrenched dictatorship, defending its power by military force, and an armed fundamentalist movement, will there be any room for democracy and civil rights? Will either the government or the Islamists manage to solve Egypt's economic problems and improve life for the Egyptian majority? Whatever happens, it will have a big impact on the Arab world, the Muslim world, Africa, and Europe, both because of Egypt's strategic location and especially because Egypt has for so long been the intellectual leader of the Arab world.

Thinking Sociologically

1. Explain why sociologists consider Egypt a sacred society and Japan a secular society.
2. How do Islamic norms shape daily life in Egypt?
3. What are the norms for "modest dress" in your society?
4. How has modernization changed the roles Egyptian women play? Has it changed the roles of ¡Kung women in the same way?
5. Is it ethnocentric to condemn female genital cutting?
6. What role conflicts do women in your society experience? What strategies do women pursue to resolve them?
7. In what ways are rural Egyptian families patriarchal? Are ¡Kung families patriarchal? How about families in your society?
8. Discuss the importance of work in the informal sector and work abroad for Egyptians and Mexicans. Is there an informal sector in your society? Who works in it?
9. Is the social stratification system in Egypt becoming more open or more closed? How about the stratification system in your society?
10. Based on what you have read in this chapter, do you think the Islamic fundamentalist movement in Egypt will become stronger or weaker in the next few years?
11. In what ways has the experience of colonization shaped the cultures of Egypt and Mexico? How has it affected attitudes towards the West?

For Further Reading

AHMED, LILA, *Women and Gender in Islam.* New Haven, CT: Yale University Press, 1992.
ATIYA, NAYARA, *Khul-Khaal: Five Egyptian Women Tell Their Stories.* Syracuse, NY: Syracuse University Press, 1982.
FERNEA, ELIZABETH WARNOCK, *In Search of Islamic Feminism.* New York: Doubleday, 1998.
FERNEA, ELIZABETH WARNOCK, AND ROBERT A., *The Arab World, Forty Years of Change,* Anchor, 1997.
FLUEHR-LOBBAN, CAROLYN, *Islamic Society in Practice.* Gainesville: University Press of Florida, 1994.
LIPPMAN, THOMAS, *Understanding Islam: An Introduction to the Muslim World.* New York: Penguin, 1990.
MACLEOD, ARLENE, *Accommodating Protest: Working Women, The New Veiling and Change in Cairo.* New York: Columbia University Press, 1993.
RODENBECK, JOHN, ed., *Cairo.* Singapore: APA Publications, 1992.
RUGH, ANDREA, *Family in Contemporary Egypt.* Syracuse, NY: Syracuse University Press, 1984.
SPRINGBORG, ROBERT, *Mubarak's Egypt: Fragmentation of the Political Order.* Boulder, CO: Westview Press, 1989.
WILSON, SUSAN, *Culture Shock: Egypt.* Portland, Oregon: Graphic Arts Center Publishing Co., 1998.

Bibliography

ABU-LUGHOD, Janet L., *Changing Cities.* New York: HarperCollins, 1991.
ABU-LUGHOD, Lila, "Islam and Public Culture: The Politics of Egyptian Television Serials," *Middle East Report,* Vol. 23, no. 1 (Jan.–Feb. 1993), pp. 25–30.
AHMED, LILA, *Women and Gender in Islam.* New Haven, CT: Yale University Press, 1992.

AJAMI, FOUAD, *The Dream Palace of the Arabs: A Generation's Odyssey.* New York: Pantheon Books, 1998.

ALDRED, CYRIL, *The Egyptians,* revised and enlarged edition. London: Thames and Hudson, 1984.

ATIYA, NAYARA, *Khul-Khaal: Five Egyptian Women Tell Their Stories.* Syracuse, NY: Syracuse University Press, 1982.

BARAKAT, HALIM, *The Arab World: Society: Culture and State.* Berkeley: University of California Press, 1993.

BASSIOUNI, M. CHERIF, *An Introduction to Islam.* Chicago: Rand McNally, 1989.

BAYAT, ASEF, "Cairo's Poor: Dilemmas of Survival and Solidarity," *Middle East Research and Information Project,* June, 1997, http://www.merip,org.

BINDER, LEONARD, *In a Moment of Enthusiasm: Political Power and the Second Stratum in Egypt.* Chicago: University of Chicago Press, 1978.

CAMPO, JUAN EDUARDO, *The Other Side of Paradise: Explorations into the Religious Meanings of Domestic Space in Islam.* Columbia: University of South Carolina Press, 1991.

CLARKE, LYNDA, "Suicide," in John Esposito, ed., *The Oxford Encyclopedia of the Modern Islamic World,* Vol. 4. New York: Oxford University Press, 1995, pp. 133–135.

COURBAGE, YOUSSEF, "Demographic Change in the Arab World: The Impact of Migration, Education and Taxes in Egypt and Morocco," *Middle East Report,* Vol. 24, no. 5 (Sept.–Oct. 1994), pp. 19–22.

CROSSETTE, BARBARA, "Court Backs Egypt's Ban on Mutilation," *The New York Times,* Dec. 29, 1997, p. A3.

———, "Senegal Bans Genital Cutting of Girls," *The New York Times,* Jan. 18, 1999, p. A10.

DANISZEWSKI, JOHN, "Disabling Acid Attacks on Women are on the Rise in Egypt, *Los Angeles Times,* June 1, 1997, p. A09.

DEPARTMENT OF ECONOMIC AND SOCIAL INFORMATION AND POLICY ANALYSIS, STATISTICAL DIVISION, *Statistical Yearbook,* 38th ed. New York: United Nations, 1993.

EARLY, EVELYN, *Baladi Women of Cairo: Playing with an Egg and a Stone.* Boulder, CO: Lynne Rienner, 1993.

THE ECONOMIST, "A Survey of Egypt: New and Old," March 20, 1998, pp. 1–18.

EL-Gawhary, Karim, "An Interview with Heba Ra'uf Ezzat," *Middle East Report,* Vol. 24, no. 6 (Nov.–Dec. 1994), pp. 26–27.

EL-MESSIRI, SAWSAN, "Traditional Urban Women in Cairo," in Lois Beck and Nikki Keddie, eds., *Women in the Muslim World.* Cambridge, MA: Harvard University Press, 1978.

ELMUSA, SHARIF, "The Economy," in Helen Chapin Metz, ed., *Egypt: A Country Study,* 5th ed. Washington, DC: Federal Research Division, Library of Congress, 1991.

ESPOSITO, JOHN, *Islam: The Straight Path.* New York: Oxford University Press, 1991*a*.

———, *Islam and Politics.* Syracuse, NY: Syracuse University Press, 1991*b*.

———, *The Islamic Threat.* New York: Oxford University Press, 1992.

ETHELSON, SALLY, "Gender, Population, Environment," *Middle East Report,* Vol. 24, no. 5 (Sept.–Oct. 1994), pp. 2–5.

FAKHOURI, HANI, *Kafr El-Elow: An Egyptian Village in Transition.* New York: Holt, 1972.

FAY, MARY Ann, "Historical Setting," in Helen Chapin Metz, ed., *Egypt: A Country Study,* 5th ed. Washington, DC: Federal Research Division, Library of Congress, 1991.

FERNEA, ELIZABETH WARNOCK, *A View of the Nile.* Garden City, NY: Doubleday & Co., 1970.

———, *In Search of Islamic Feminism.* New York: Doubleday, 1998.

FERNEA, ELIZABETH WARNOCK, AND ROBERT A., *The Arab World: Forty Years of Change.* New York: Anchor, 1997.

FLUEHR-LOBBAN, CAROLYN, *Islamic Society in Practice.* Gainsville: University Press of Florida, 1994.

FORSYTHE, LOUISE, "Edwar-al-Kharat: Sexuality in Contemporary Egyptian Literature," *Polytext,* Vol. 10 (Spring, 1994), pp. 69–84.

FRIEDMAN, THOMAS, "Almost Egypt," *The New York Times,* Oct. 25, 1995, p. A21.

GHOSH, AMITAV, *In an Antique Land.* New York: Knopf, 1993.

HASAN, SANA, "My Lost Egypt," *The New York Times Magazine,* Oct. 25, 1995, pp. 60–63.

HEDGES, CHRIS, "As Egypt Votes on Mubarak, He Faces Rising Peril," *The New York Times,* Oct. 4, 1993, p. A8.

———, "Industrious Egypt Is Choking Its People to Death," *The New York Times,* Nov. 26, 1993, p. A4.

———, "Bananas Become Fruit of Egypt–Israel Friendship," *The New York Times,* Dec. 18, 1993, p. A5.

———, "In Bureaucrats' Castle, Everyone Else Is a Beggar," *The New York Times,* June 7, 1994, p. A4.

———, "Domestic Problems Hurt Rising Stature of Egypt," *The New York Times,* July 17, 1994, p. A6.

———, "Peasants See the Promised Land Snatched Away," *The New York Times,* Sept. 28, 1994, p. 4.

———, "An Airline Fears Cairo Will Kill It with Rules," *The New York Times,* Nov. 12, 1994, p. 11.

HIRST, DAVID, "Reaping Worry Along the Nile," *Newsday,* Oct. 1, 1997, p. A16.

HOODFAR, HOMA, "The Impact of Male Migration on Domestic Budgeting: Egyptian Women Striving for an Islamic Budgeting Pattern, *Journal of Comparative Family Studies,* Vol. 28, no. 2 (Summer, 1997), pp. 73–99.

HOOGLUND, ERIC, "The Society and Its Environment," in Helen Chapin Metz, ed., *Egypt: A Country Study,* 5th ed. Washington, DC: Federal Research Division, Library of Congress, 1991.

HOPKINS, NICHOLAS, AND SOHAIR MEHANNA, "Pollution, Popular Perception and Grassroots Environmental Activism," *Middle East Research and Information Project,* June, 1997, http://www.merip.org.

HUBELL, STEPHEN, "Cairo's People," in John Rodenbeck, ed., *Cairo.* Singapore: APA Publications, 1992.

IBRAHIM, BARBARA, "Cairo's Factory Women," in Elizabeth Fernea, ed., *Women and the Family in the Middle East: New Voices of Change.* Austin: University of Texas Press, 1985.

IBRAHIM, YOUSSEF, "With Islam in Vogue, Egypt Follows in Its Fashion," *The New York Times,* Feb. 3, 1993, p. A6.

———, "Muslims' Fury Falls on Egypt's Christians," *The New York Times,* Mar. 15, 1993, pp. A1, A8.

JEHL, DOUGLAS, "Above the City's Din, Always the Voice of Allah," *The New York Times,* Mar. 6, 1996, p. A4.

———, "Killings Erode Cairo's Claim to 'Control' Militants," *The New York Times,* Mar. 15, 1997, p. A3.

———, "Yes, This Is the Nile, but Don't Go Near the Water," *The New York Times,* Mar. 25, 1997, p. A4.

———, "Under the Cairo Sun, the Leaden Skies Can Kill," *The New York Times,* Apr. 4, 1997, p. A4.

———, "Egyptian Farmers Resist End of Freeze on Rents," *The New York Times,* Dec. 27, 1997, p. A6.

KURIAN, GEORGE, *The New Book of World Rankings,* 3d ed. New York: Facts on File, 1991.

———, ed., *Encyclopedia of the Third World,* Vol. 1. New York: Facts on File, 1992.

LIPPMAN, THOMAS, *Egypt after Nasser.* New York: Paragon House, 1989.

———, *Understanding Islam: An Introduction to the Muslim World.* New York: Penguin, 1990.

MACLEOD, ARLENE, *Accommodating Protest: Working Women, The New Veiling and Change in Cairo.* New York: Columbia University Press, 1993.

MERNISSI, FATIMA, *Islam and Democracy.* Reading, MA: Addison-Wesley, 1992.

METZ, HELEN CHAPIN, *Egypt: A Country Study,* 5th ed. Washington, DC: Federal Research Division, Library of Congress, 1991.

MILLER, JUDITH, "With Freedom, Cairo Intellectuals Find New Stress," *The New York Times,* Jan. 31, 1998, pp. B7, B9.

MILLER, NEIL, "Background Search," *The Advocate,* June 13, 1995, p. 29.

MITCHELL, TIMOTHY, "America's Egypt: Discourse of the Development Industry," *Middle East Report* (Mar.–Apr. 1991), pp. 18–34.

MULE, PAT, AND DIANE BARTHEL, "The Return to the Veil: Individual Autonomy versus Social Esteem," *Sociological Forum,* Vol. 7, no. 2 (1992), pp. 323–332.

THE NEW YORK TIMES, "Egypt to Appeal Ruling on Genital Cutting," July 12, 1997, p. 3.

———, "Jail Term in Egypt for Mutilation Death," Dec. 16, 1997, p. A3.

NISAN, MORDECHAI, *Minorities in the Middle East.* London: McFarland, 1991.

O'CONNOR, DAVID, *A Short History of Ancient Egypt.* Pittsburgh: Carnegie Museum of Natural History, 1990.

OMRAN, ABDEL R., AND FARZANNEH ROUDI, "The Middle East Population Puzzle," *Population Bulletin,* Vol. 48, no. 1 (July 1993), pp. 1–39.

ROBINSON, FRANCIS, *Atlas of the Islamic World.* New York: Facts on File, 1982.

RODENBECK, MAX, "Religion," in John Rodenbeck, ed., *Cairo.* Singapore: APA Publications, 1992.

RUGH, ANDREA, *Family in Contemporary Egypt.* Syracuse, NY: Syracuse University Press, 1984.

———, *Reveal and Conceal: Dress in Contemporary Egypt.* Syracuse, NY: Syracuse University Press, 1986.

SADAT, JEHAN, *A Woman of Egypt.* New York: Simon & Schuster, 1987.

SCHMIDT, WILLIAM E., "A Deluge of Foreign Assistance Fails to Revive Egypt's Stricken Economy," *The New York Times,* Oct. 10, 1993, p. 10.

SCIOLINO, ELAINE, "The Many Faces of Islamic Law," *The New York Times,* Oct. 13, 1996, p. E4.

SHOLKAMY, HANIA M., "A Trade Like Any Other: Female Singers and Dancers in Egypt," (book review), *Middle Eastern Studies,* Vol. 32, no. 3 (July 1996), pp. 197–214.

SMITH, PAMELA ANN, "Where Capitalism Is Shaped by Islam," *Utne Reader* (Mar.-Apr. 1994), pp. 85–88.

SPRINGBORG, ROBERT, *Mubarak's Egypt: Fragmentation of the Political Order.* Boulder, CO: Westview Press, 1989.

STOWASSER, BARBARA, "Women's Issues in Modern Islamic Thought," in Judith Tucker, ed., *Arab Women: Old Boundaries, New Frontiers.* Bloomington: Indiana University Press, 1993.

UNITED NATIONS, *1995 Demographic Yearbook,* New York: 1997.

UNITED STATES DEPARTMENT OF LABOR, BUREAU OF INTERNATIONAL LABOR AFFAIRS, *Foreign Labor Trends: Egypt, 1992.*

VATIKIOTIS, PETER J., *The History of Egypt,* 3d ed. Baltimore: Johns Hopkins University Press, 1991.

WATERBURY, JOHN, *The Egypt of Sadat and Nasser: The Political Economy of Two Regimes.* Princeton, NJ: Princeton University Press, 1983.

WEAVER, MARY ANNE, "The Trail of the Sheikh," *The New Yorker,* Apr. 12, 1993, pp. 71–88.

———, "The Novelist and the Sheikh," *The New Yorker,* Jan. 30, 1995, pp. 52–69.

WILSON, SUSAN, *Culture Shock: Egypt.* Portland, Oregon: Graphic Arts Center Publishing Co., 1998.

WIN NEWS, "Egypt: New Research Shows Many More Women Mutilated," Vol. 23, no. 3 (Summer, 1997), pp. 31–33.

WOLF, MARGERY, "Uterine Families and the Women's Community," in James Spradley and David McCurdy, eds. *Conformity and Conflict: Readings in Cultural Anthropology,* 8th ed. New York: HarperCollins, 1994.

WORLD BANK, *World Bank Development Report, The State in a Changing World,* New York: Oxford University Press, 1998.

GERMANY

Five hours east of Montreal and New York by air, less than an hour from London and Paris lies Berlin, the capital of a reunited Germany, one of the most prosperous countries on earth and the birthplace of Albert Einstein, Ludwig van Beethoven, and other figures who shaped western civilization.

LOCATION: In the center of Europe. France, Belgium, and the Netherlands border Germany to the west; Denmark and the North Sea to the north; Poland and the Czech Republic to the east; and Austria and Switzerland to the south.

AREA: 135,000 square miles or 391,500 square kilometers; the size of California or Japan.

LAND: Lowlands in the north, highlands in the center, and a mountainous region in the south bordering the Alps.

CLIMATE: Temperate, similar to the northeastern United States, Canada, or Japan.

POPULATION: 82 million in 1998, expected to decline to 76 million in 2025.

Germany's population is aging: 15 percent are 65 or over.

INCOME: Germany is a wealthy industrial nation. Germans earned an average of $20,070 in per person purchasing power in 1997.

EDUCATION: The average adult (25+) has completed almost 12 years of school.

RELIGION: 42 percent Protestant; 35 percent Catholic.

MINORITIES: Germany has a large immigrant population. There are 2.2 million Turkish immigrants and their children, 800,000 Yugoslavs, 600,000 Italians, 350,000 Greeks. Germany has a significant Muslim minority and there are 50,000 Jews.

CHAPTER 5

Germany: Social Institutions and Social Change in a Modern Western Society

INTRODUCTION

"Periods of bliss are history's blank pages." Does this quotation from George Wilhelm Friedrich Hegel, Germany's most famous nineteenth-century philosopher, make sense to you? Hegel means that people are most likely to find private happiness in uneventful times. Historians write books about history's interesting periods—times of war, revolution, and social transformation—but for most people, these are very painful periods to live through.

If Hegel is right, modern Germans surely have been the most unhappy people. In the past century, Germans have lived through many successive social transformations. Germany was agricultural and then rapidly became industrialized at the end of the nineteenth century. Germans experienced humiliating defeat and devastation in two world wars and they lived under the greatest variety of political systems: a monarchy, a republic, a fascist state, an authoritarian Soviet satellite state, and a democracy. After World War II, East Germans and West Germans experienced two different economic systems: socialism and capitalism. Finally, east Germans today are finding their lives transformed as their society is absorbed into a reunified Germany.

It will be helpful for you to learn about German society for several reasons. First of all, you will become acquainted with all the varieties of political and economic institutions that are found in modern western societies. For example, Germans practice their own national variety of capitalism. If you live in a capitalist society, you will see that German capitalism is different from your nation's capitalism. Also, by studying Germany you will learn how changing social institutions shape people's lives. Sociologists, because they deal with real-life societies, cannot conduct experiments in the same way that physicists or even biologists can. But in the past 45 years, Germany has been a kind of natural experiment in the consequences of adopting two different sets of political and economic institutions. You can see how different institutions in East and West Germany shaped contrasting values and norms and interpersonal relationships.

Finally, it is important to study German society because so many important sociologists were German. They used their experiences with dictatorship and democracy, with bureaucracy and social inequality, in creating some of sociology's most important concepts and theories. To really understand Karl Marx's theories or Max Weber's works, you need to know about German society.

Social Change Today: Reunification

One of the most fascinating things about Germany is that dramatic social change is going on today. Reunification is an experiment in deliberately remaking social institutions that is happening before our eyes. Germany was originally divided into two separate states in the wake of its defeat in World War II. The eastern part of Germany, occupied by the Soviet Union, became East Germany (the German Democratic Republic, or GDR), a Soviet satellite state with a socialist economy, an authoritarian government, and sealed borders—symbolized by the famous Berlin Wall. The western part of Germany, occupied by Britain, France, and the United States, became West Germany (the Federal Republic of Germany, the FRG, or the Federal Republic, as Germans called it); a close ally of its former enemies in their fight against communism. West Germany became a western-style parliamentary democracy and one of the world's richest, most powerful capitalist economies. It was twice the size of East Germany and had a population 4 times larger (62.6 million, versus 16.4 million in the GDR in 1990) (Heilig, Buttner, and Lutz, p. 4).

Until Gorbachev came to power in the Soviet Union and loosened the Soviet hold on eastern Europe, no society had ever before abandoned socialism and adopted capitalism. Now, since 1988, East Germany, like Poland, Hungary, the Czech Republic, and many other former Soviet-bloc nations, has been engaged in adopting some form of democratic political institutions and capitalist economic institutions. In East Germany, the transformation has taken the particular form of reunification with West Germany, or, in reality, absorption into West Germany. West German institutions have remained essentially unchanged, while the former GDR (East Germany) has changed its government and economy, values and norms, and social group life. Acknowledging that the process of unification is not yet really complete, Germans refer to "the western Länder" (the states that composed the former West Germany) and "the eastern Länder" (the states that were East Germany). Recently they have taken to calling the unified Germany "the Berlin Republic" to distinguish it from the FRG and the GDR.

Inge's Story: In The New Germany

Since the Wende *(literally, the "turning," as in "a turning of the road," the term Germans use for the fall of the East German regime and reunification), life in Leipzig (in the former GDR) has changed more than Inge Reuter ever imagined. New Year's Eve, for example, Inge and her husband went out to a restaurant—alone. In the old days there were no restaurants worth going to, and no one had any money anyhow. They spent all their New Year's eves (and most other weekend nights as well) gathered around someone's kitchen table, eating bread and cheese, and drinking beer, laughing and singing and enjoying the company of family and friends. That was all they had: friends and plenty of time to enjoy them. No one worked very hard, because working hard didn't get you more pay, and even if it did, there was nothing to buy.*

Now Inge finds herself a successful businesswoman, and nostalgic for the old days. When the western companies began to build all the new shopping malls outside Leipzig, she started a cleaning company. She is busy all the time, hiring and training employees, supervising, getting new contracts, and doing her accounts far into the night. There are no more kitchen-table parties. It's not just time either: The old crowd has split up. Some, like Inge, have prospered, but others are still unemployed. They are no longer all in the same boat, and tensions have sprung up among them. Everyone is out for themselves now; working hard to earn money and busy spending it. It seems like things have become more important than friendship.

Life has changed too in western Germany, though not as drastically as in the east. As Germany struggles to absorb the east, there are new economic burdens and people in the west have seen their standard of living decline.

Joachim's Story: In the New Germany

Joachim Hasselblad has just completed his technical training in advertising, at the age of 26. He is very disappointed that the company with which he apprenticed has not hired him and he has only been able to find contract work. If he can keep the contracts coming without pause (not very likely, he assumes), he can make as much as $40,000. Not bad for the first year out of training, you might say. Joachim bitterly denies it. "I'm going to lose 40–50 percent to taxes! That's to pay for rebuilding the east, and to pay for all those pensioners in the east who never paid in with real German money, but will collect anyhow. And all they do is complain—after all we've done for them! Oh, I know," says Joachim, "its not just the east. It's the pressure of global competition. Employers can't afford high wages and pensions and long vacations and all the other benefits anymore. They are moving factories east to Poland and Slovakia. But why should it be my generation that has to pay the price?"

Inge and Joachim come from two different societies: East Germany and West Germany, but they are both Germans, and as Germans they do still have much in common. Forty-five years of division into two societies did not erase all their common heritage. Their societies have a history that was shared up until 1946 and it has left preoccupations and scars common to both societies. Also division did not entirely alter the German culture common to both East and West. Let us begin by examining the two Germanys' common history and culture.

GERMAN HISTORY: CENTRAL THEMES

First of all, Germany's national history is briefer than that of Egypt or Japan. Germany didn't even exist as a separate nation until modern times. Nevertheless, Germany's history has been very eventful. It is studded with wars, treaties, monarchs, changes of borders, and successive governments and policies. We cannot begin to tell you the whole involved story in a sociology text. Instead we will describe a few key issues that Germans have repeatedly fought over. The first is: Should Germany have a single government with centralized power or should it be a collection of small states with most power held on the local level? Over the centuries Germans have fought about this and they have also fought about whether Germany should be an authoritarian nation, with unrestricted power in the hands of its rulers, or whether it should be a democracy, with a constitution, a bill of rights, and a parliamentary system to give its citizens political say and protection from rulers' power. Finally, Germans have struggled about what protection the government owes its citizens against the impersonal destructiveness of market forces in an industrial society. In this battle, a system of social welfare protections has been the alternative to government control of the economy.

Centralized Power versus Local Power

Germany was not fully united as a nation-state until 1871. Before that, Germany experienced many centuries when periods of national unification alternated with fragmentation into small kingdoms. In the first and second centuries B.C., Germanic tribes settled the area that is now modern Germany, battling the Romans, and after the collapse of the Roman Empire they spread over northern Italy, Britain, and France. In early medieval times (A.D. 800) Charlemagne unified these peoples in an empire known in Germany as the First *Reich* (or empire) and elsewhere as the Holy Roman Empire. After Charlemagne's death, his empire broke up into hundreds of small kingdoms. Through the centuries they sometimes formed local unions, then broke up again. In modern times, centralization gained. Prussia was first united after the Thirty Years' War ended in 1648. In 1815, after Napoleon's defeat, the Congress of Vienna established a German Confederation of 39 monarchies, headed by Austria under Prince Metternich as chancellor. After the Franco-Prussian War, in 1871, German states voluntarily joined Prussia in a Second Reich, a new imperial Germany, led by the Prussian King Wilhelm I and his prime minister, Otto von Bismarck. This time the Reich took the form of a federal union, with all the small monarchies represented in a Federal Council.

Imperial ambitions for military might and global political power led Germany into World War I, a war the nation expected to win within months. When, after four grueling years of trench warfare, Germany finally conceded defeat, it lost some territory and was forced to disarm, but it remained one state through the Weimar Republic and Hitler's Third Reich. Only after World War II did Germany once again suffer division—into two separate states. But as we shall see, West Germany, the FRG, mindful of the harm done by Germany's past imperial ambitions, established itself as a federation of states, carefully balancing centralized power with the rights of separate state governments.

Authoritarianism versus Democracy

Germany has a long tradition of authoritarian rule and a much newer commitment to democracy. Monarchs with absolute power ruled Germany at least from the time of Charlemagne, and the most successful joined absolutism with empire, a strong military, and especially in the modern period, an efficient bureaucracy, which the monarch tried to keep subordinate. But in the nineteenth century, absolutism came under attack in Germany, from liberals influenced first by the French Revolution and later by German socialism.

During the time of the German Confederation some aristocrats, influenced by liberal thought, joined with officials of the bureaucracy to press Metternich for reforms like a constitution, parliamentary government, guarantees of civil liberties, and market freedoms. The French Revolution of 1830 inspired further efforts, and liberals, allied with artisans and peasants actually seized power briefly in the German Revolution of 1848. They succeeded in establishing a constitutional monarchy in the form of a federation of states. But the alliance among middle-class liberals and artisans and peasants soon broke down, because the latter two groups wanted more radical reform. Then conservatives seized their chance to restore monarchical absolutism.

It was Bismarck who healed the split between liberals and monarchists by dividing power between the king and parliament in such a way as finally to favor the king. His strategy of attracting the support of liberals through a policy of militarism and imperialism was to prove surprisingly durable, from the 1870s, straight up to World War I, and then, of course, in Hitler's Germany as well. Germans were continually attracted to the idea of military strength used to conquer an empire under the leadership of a heroic, absolute ruler.

One interlude in German history built democratic institutions. Germany's military defeat in World War I was accompanied by workers' revolts all over the country which deposed monarchies and replaced them with revolutionary councils. In Berlin, the Social Democratic Party proclaimed a federal republic, instituted a parliament, drafted a constitution with universal suffrage, and elected a president. The new republic was the Weimar Republic, named in reference to the birthplace of Germany's beloved poet Goethe, who symbolized German humanism, in contrast to Prussian despotism and militarism. But despite its democratic values, the Weimar Republic left the door open to authoritarianism. Bowing to German tradition, the republic created a strong president, elected for seven years with extensive powers. When communists put down an antidemocratic coup, Social Democrats allied themselves with the military to suppress the communists. This opened the way to extremism on both right and left and prepared the way for Hitler's rise in the desperate times of the depression of 1929–1933.

Once in power, Hitler established an extreme authoritarian dictatorship, arresting liberal, socialist, and communist critics, and putting all independent institutions under Nazi control. The secret police, special courts, and concentration camps were used to crush all opposition. State governments were replaced by appointed governors, trade unions were abolished, and other political parties were disbanded. Hitler appointed himself *führer* of the Third Reich. Nazi propaganda glorified the authoritarian state, the heroic leader, and military power. Military might was used for conquest, adding *lebensraum* (living space) to the new German empire, and for a racist genocide against the Jews, at least 6 million of whom were slaughtered in the Nazi holocaust.

After the Nazi defeat, the federal Republic was founded as a democracy, consciously building on the legacy of Weimar democracy. East Germany, while formally adopting democratic institutions, actually became another authoritarian regime.

Welfare Capitalism versus Socialism

Germany experienced a late and rapid industrialization during the final quarter of the nineteenth century. Primarily agricultural in 1875, by 1900 Germany employed more people in industry and mining than in farming. It became the biggest industrial power in Europe. Germans flocked to industrial cities and towns and population grew by 50 percent. Germany specialized in heavy industry: coal mining, iron production, and manufacture of chemicals and electrical equipment. Laboring under the oppressive conditions of early capitalism, industrial workers were attracted to Germany's tradition of Marxist socialism.

Marx wrote the *Communist Manifesto* in time for the Revolution of 1848. Characteristically, for Germany, it fused a demand for popular democracy with the call for socialism. In authoritarian Germany, these two goals were joined: Working people wanted the right to form trade unions, the right to political representation, and the power to control industry themselves. When the 1848 revolution was crushed, more than a million German republicans left their country for the United States. Others remained to form many democratic and socialist opposition parties, including the forerunner of today's Social Democratic Party.

Fear of socialism motivated every German government of the late nineteenth and early twentieth centuries. Bismarck, always the clever politician, succeeded both in repressing socialism and in co-opting it: He outlawed all Social Democratic organizations and trade unions, while at the same time attracting Social Democratic support by instituting comprehensive social insurance to protect workers against the cost of illness, accident, old age, and disability.

Later governments were more obvious in their opposition to socialism. After Bismarck the German monarchy pursued militaristic nationalism and overseas colonies to distract the public from social reform. Even the Weimar government, though founded with the help of revolutionaries and Social Democrats, became so fearful of socialists and communists that its president Hindenburg appointed Hitler chancellor rather than seek Social Democratic support. After World War II, Germany faced the future with a strong socialist tradition, an equally enduring history of opposition to socialism, and a culture that, since Bismarck, had assumed social welfare to be the government's business.

East and West Germans are united by their common history. They all understand Germany's historic conflicts over centralism, authoritarianism, and socialism. Germans are also united by a common culture inherited from their shared past.

GERMAN CULTURE: CONTINUITY AND CHANGE

Because Germany was for so long divided into separate monarchies, there are still regional variations in customs and identity. The cultures of Prussia (in the north) and Bavaria (in the south) are distinct. Nevertheless, we can easily single out certain enduring values and norms in German culture. Germans have long been known for their love of order, their respect for authority, their seriousness, hard work, and social responsibility. These values still animate Germans today in both the former GDR and the FRG.

Order

Germans prefer order in all aspects of their lives. Norms require promptness, tidiness and cleanliness, careful conformity to the law, and a proper formality in relating to others. If you have a business appointment with a German executive you must get right down to business, because when your time is up, the manager will become impatient and soon send you on your way (Hall and Hall, pp. 35, 53, 83–84). Social small talk will not be appreciated. If you are late to a job interview, there is no way you can get the job, and if you are late to dinner, your hosts will be insulted and annoyed. Stores close at 6:30 on weekdays and at noon on Saturdays (and are closed all day Sunday) so people are expected to be very well organized to get their shopping done in time. You can't run over and borrow a cup of sugar or a snow shovel from your neighbors either, because it would be shameful to admit to running out of anything (Hall and Hall, p. 39).

Germans also carefully order the space around them. Spending the day at the beach, West German families pile up sand as high as 4 feet in a wall around their blankets, defining their own private territories (Gannon, p. 75). In a business, the offices of different departments are separated by closed doors and the department chief carefully closes the door of his private office. It would be very rude to pick up or move a chair in someone's home or office in order to make yourself more comfortable (Hall and Hall, pp. 40–41). In a German hotel, the maid arranges a foreigner's jumbled shoes in a neat row and lines up the toothbrushes.

Obedience

Germans have long seen it as their duty to obey the law and to submit to the authorities—government officials, bureaucrats, police officers, and judges who make and enforce the laws. Ordinary Germans believe it is their duty to correct anyone they see disobeying the law. They don't hesitate to reproach strangers. On buses, people deposit their fares in a box on the "honor system" and an unknowing stranger who fails to put in the money will be hissed by all the passengers on the bus. Neighborhoods have informal rules about when and where you can wash your car, or hang out the laundry, or put out the trash, and people will reproach a neighbor whose windows are unwashed or whose lawn grows too high (Hall and Hall, p. 47).

Germans cross only when the light is green and let their dogs off the leash only in specially marked areas. In East Germany factories had special workers' committees that acted like courts. They could fine their co-workers or make them apologize in cases of fights or petty theft or damage to factory property.

While many other cultures rely on informal understandings, Germans like to make all the rules explicit. It is typically German to make thousands of detailed laws and regulations which people carefully obey to the letter. In each German state detailed laws specify how schools should operate: from the marking system to the types of punishments permitted. Businesses must conform with endless and growing legal regulations: health and safety laws, laws regulating competition, and laws specifying the structure of corporate boards and their membership.

Ulrich and Helga's Story: The Marriage Contract

Ulrich and Helga, after living together for a year, have decided to marry. Tonight they are sitting over glasses of wine with their friend Otto, a lawyer, to draw up a prenuptial agreement. "We agree to share domestic tasks equally," the document reads. "We will take turns in cooking, cleaning, and dishwashing, laundry, grocery shopping, and bill paying. We each agree to contribute 10 percent of our salaries monthly toward a fund for buying a house, to retain 10 percent for private use, and to place the rest in a joint bank account. We agree that each of us shall have the right to go out alone with male or female friends, but we pledge ourselves to sexual fidelity. We agree that if we have a child, Helga will stay at home for six years and, during that time, Ulrich will support her and the child." Ulrich, Helga, and Otto see nothing unusual about this document. All their married friends have done something similar and they believe it is good to discuss all these matters explicitly and reach a formal agreement.

Seriousness

Germans take life seriously. They are very concerned with ideas and principles and they insist on things being done right. Many observers have characterized German culture as "intellectual." West German TV features many earnest discussion programs in which people sit at round tables and solemnly debate current issues. The TV audience sits before them at smaller tables, sipping drinks and listening attentively (Buruma, p. 23). Germans are idealistic. They want to find the right principles and follow them, no matter what.

In the nineteenth century, Germany was a breeding ground for trade unionism and socialism, developing a tradition of working-class organization and an analysis of class conflict expressed most influentially by Karl Marx. German dedication to improving the condition of working people influenced societies all over the world, and particularly in the United States, where many German immigrants became involved in the antislavery movement, and the trade union and socialist movements. As immigrants in American, they fought successfully for higher wages, shorter hours, limits on child labor, safer working conditions, and recognition of contracts with labor unions.

Dedication to principle has had some admirable results, but some ghastly ones too. German fascination with absolute principles facilitated Nazism. People were willing to accept a simple principle—"Aryan supremacy"—that explained everything in life and told them what to do, and they closed their eyes to its immoral consequences. But you mustn't forget that German conscientiousness also underlay resistance to Hitler by some German aristocrats, Catholics, and Communists.

Hermann's Story: The Police Officer

Hermann Schnabel is a 17-year veteran of the Hamburg police force, recently promoted to detective. He has been assigned to track down foreigners who have overstayed their visas and are now in Germany illegally. One day Hermann is called by an angry landlord to a shabby walk-up apartment building on the industrial outskirts of the city. "That woman up there never pays her rent on time, and she looks so foreign and her apartment smells funny; I want you to investigate," the landlord demands. Climbing up to the top floor, Hermann finds a terrified woman who falls weeping at his feet. "Please don't arrest me," she pleads, "it's not for me, but for my daughter. If you send us home my relatives will circumcise her. Do you know what that means? I can't let her be mutilated like that." Hermann does know what it means. He has heard this story before. And this is on top of yesterday's encounter with an Algerian journalist who wrote an exposé of a fundamentalist militia. If he is sent home, the militia will hunt him down and kill him. Mumbling with embarrassment, Hermann takes a 20-mark bill out of his wallet and gives it to the woman, then flees.

Trudging back to the station house, Hermann feels anguished and torn. "It's my assignment," says one side of his mind; "it's my duty." "I can't do this," says another side. "I can hear my history teacher telling us, 'Germans must never simply acquiesce in persecution again.' " "How can I send foreigners home to be killed or mutilated?" Back at the station house, Hermann drags himself into his captain's office. "I can't do this," he says. "I want to resign from the illegal alien detail. Please, can you transfer me to another duty?" "Well Hermann, I'm not surprised," says the captain. "You're the third officer in the last four months to ask for transfer off this duty. Maybe I'll ask for a transfer too."

Careful Work

Dedication to work is another aspect of German seriousness. Germans are renowned for their hard work and efficiency and their "insistence on precision." Germany has long excelled in industries that produce quality goods to exacting standards, like machine tools, cars, cameras, arms, and small appliances. Cars like Mercedes Benz are built to be driven for hours on the German *autobahnnen* (highways) at speed over 100 miles an hour. German businesses, even retail stores, don't employ casual workers or part-time workers. They want only employees who are thoroughly trained, usually in two- to three-year apprenticeships that teach every detail of the business and stress the importance of "precision, cleanliness, and order." Business managers are slow to reach decisions, because they require a great deal of very detailed technical information. Slide presentations, reams of data, long histories of background events, are all carefully attended to and digested (Lewis, p. 375; Hamilton, p. 58)

The Burden of History

Not only do Germans take their principles and their work seriously, they take their history very seriously too. They worry about Germany's past susceptibility to authoritarian government, to racist ideologies, and to demagogues like Hitler. Do you come from a society with an ugly past? Is there racial oppression or genocide in your country's history? If so, you will understand some of the painful dilemmas Germans face. Young Germans long to put the Nazi horror behind them; to be part of a "normal nation." "How long do we have to keep apologizing?" they ask. But if they try to close the books on Nazism, doesn't that show insensitivity to Hitler's victims? And can they be sure there is no discrimination against racial minorities or Jews in Germany today? What about those neo-Nazi groups; they are few in number but seem to glory in Nazi rhetoric and regalia.

Taking Responsibility. In the aftermath of World War II, Germans hastened to forget the horrors of Nazism. But in the late 1960s, a new generation of young West Germans insisted on confronting the public with the truth about Nazi crimes. Germans began a serious national self-examination of their guilt, a process of *Trauerarbeit,* as they call it (the work of mourning) that continues to this day (Buruma, p. 21). Schools made study of the Holocaust a required part of the curriculum.

Government policy reflects Germans' fear of repeating the past. The constitution grants draftees the right to refuse to fight on grounds of conscience (Buruma, pp. 24–25). Germany has also made it state policy to welcome refugees from political persecution, despite Germans' discomfort with foreigners. And Germany has maintained a careful tolerance of free speech, despite distaste for nonconformists. Many analysts see Germans as very torn in their response to today's neo-Nazis, their wish to squelch all stirrings of Nazism warring with their commitment to free speech.

Questioning Authority. Since World War II, Germans have worried about the dangers in their traditional respect for authority. In Hitler's time, people treated Nazi groups with respect, as they paraded and drilled in their smart uniforms. After World War II, many Germans said that they had been "just obeying orders" when they massacred civilians and sent Jews off to concentration camps. If that was the result of obedience, West Germans reasoned, they were going to have to educate their children to resist authority and make their own moral choices. Nowadays, German school exams ask questions like "Discuss the problem of how an individual is to behave in a state based on false norms" (Buruma, pp. 183–184).

Divergent Values in East and West

Though East and West Germany had much in common, during the 45 years of their separation their cultures diverged. After all, the two societies were completely isolated from each other, divided by an armed border. East Germans were not allowed to cross the border, and West Germans could do so only with difficulty. For several decades even phone calls across the border were blocked. In the West, German culture was shaped by consumer capitalism and in the East it was changed by socialism.

West German Consumerism

West Germany became one of the world's most affluent societies. Yearly per person income was $23,030 in 1992, putting the West Germans behind only Japan, Sweden, and the United States in international income comparisons. In West Germany smooth, carefully engineered highways were filled with Mercedes Benzes, BMWs, Audis, and Porsches, zooming along at 100 miles per hour. Modern high-speed trains connected cities filled with upscale shopping districts and malls, sleek apartment towers, and new housing estates. Landmark buildings destroyed in World War II were perfectly rebuilt or restored. Few neighborhoods in West Ger-

How fitting that the Mercedes-Benz logo stands over this scene of German affluence. Economic success has been at the core of western German identity for many years, but Germans are uneasy now, as their economy encounters more global competition. Germany's history of racial genocide has also reemerged to haunt today's prosperity. Many of Germany's most respected firms have recently been tied to the use of Nazi-organized slave labor.

man cities were old or crumbling, dirty or neglected. You could not help but notice that this was a rich society. (See Table 5.1.)

The Value of Possessions. In West Germany, people were busy making money and spending it. They had many labor-saving devices but were always in a hurry. Meetings with friends were carefully scheduled on busy calendars. In many regions, the simplest single-family house cost $300,000 and people spent heavily on luxury furnishings: leather couches, oriental rugs, and original paintings. De-

TABLE 5.1 Measures of Affluence:
Americans, Germans, and Japanese have far more extensive connections to global communications, entertainment, and information than Egyptians and Mexicans do.

	Mobile Cellular Telephone Subscribers (per 100 people)	Televisions (per 100 people)	Internet Users (per 10,000 persons)	Personal Computers (per 100 people)
Egypt	0.01	9	0.15	*
Germany	3	55	141	14
Japan	3	62	43	12
Mexico	1	19	4	2
USA	9	78	671	30

* Data Not Available
Source: Human Development Database, 1987, United Nations

signer clothes and upscale cars and trendy sports equipment were the means to declare one's status and express an individual identity (Rademaekers, pp. 9–10). West Germans invested a great deal of money and time in their homes and they enjoyed their possessions in privacy.

The Value of Leisure. In recent decades, West Germans moved away from the traditional German dedication to work. They devoted themselves less to duty and more to pleasure. West Germans achieved the highest wages, the shortest work week, and the most holidays of any industrialized nation. They worked an average of 37 hours per week, compared to 41 in the United States, and over 60 in Japan. Plus, they got six weeks of paid vacation, with an extra month's pay at vacation time, a Christmas bonus, and noncash benefits equal in value to 80 percent of their take-home pay (Glouchevitch, pp. 112–113). On their long vacations, West Germans were dedicated travelers, filling the beaches of the Greek islands, Miami, and Cuba during the winter months and seeking the latest tropical resorts on remote Asian islands. Travel agents did a booming business in tour packages.

The Value of Individualism. West Germany was an **individualistic** society: People saw themselves as individuals, autonomous actors, free to join groups or remain separate. They valued their privacy and their right to speak as individuals. Businesses and politicians addressed citizens through advertising and the mass media, but people were expected to make individual decisions and act on the basis of their own needs and judgments. In West Germany it was not unusual or deviant behavior to belong to no group beyond the family, friendship circles, and a rather formal work group membership. Few West Germans did volunteer work with the elderly or any other needy group.

John Ardagh vividly described West Germans' sense of their separateness as individuals and their distance from the rest of society. For example, at a West German health club an elderly person needing help or a mother who needed someone to watch her child for a moment would not turn to other club members. If asked, their response would be "That's not my business—the officials (staff) are paid for that." The West German welfare state provided generous support for people who were disabled, addicted, or ex-prisoners. This is perhaps fortunate, since individual West Germans tried to avoid such people and felt no obligation to help them. No one described West German individualism more clearly than an old East Berlin couple, interviewed by *The New York Times* after reunification: "In the old East Germany people were closer. . . . We helped each other," they said, "In the west, people say this is my space, it is separate from you, and do not disturb my space" (Ardagh, pp. 526, 527–528; Cohen, p. D3).

East German Socialism

In the East consumer goods were drab and sometimes in short supply. Housing was cheaply built and often in disrepair. People had to take their vacation in East Germany or in nearby Soviet-bloc nations. Life moved slowly; people spent hours waiting in line in stores and for buses, but everyone seemed to have lots of time; time to go visiting, take coffee breaks, chat with a neighbor, or cheer up people at the old-age home (Darnton, pp. 297–309).

When Peter Marcuse visited the two Germanys in 1989, just before the Wall came down, he saw "the society of the elbows" and "the society of the coffee breaks." In West Germany he thought that people were always elbowing each other out of the way in their hurry to get to the cashier or on the plane. In East Germany he was amazed to find that all work at his office stopped every day at 10 A.M. sharp. The secretaries cleared off a table, laid a cloth and dishes, and put up the kettle, and everyone in the office came in and had coffee and cake and chatted together. No one answered the phones and appointments waited (Marcuse, p. 43). East German customs reflected distinctive values, different from those in the West.

The Value of Labor. Socialist theory holds that workers are the most important part of any economy, because their labor produces the goods on which wealth is based. Capitalists are really parasites who feed on workers, because they take their profits out of what workers produce. In East Germany there were no capitalists—no businesspeople, no entrepreneurs. To make a profit, or charge interest was seen as profoundly immoral. Socialist East Germany taught respect for labor. Each elementary school class was paired with a factory unit where they visited and helped out and got to know individual workers. Classes planted gardens and learned to use machinery. The East German government tried to give heroic workers as much publicity as entrepreneurs like Donald Trump received in the United States. The only problem was that people were aware that workers in East Germany didn't live as well as workers in capitalist West Germany.

Because they valued labor so highly, East Germans believed that people's jobs should be productive and satisfying, not mindless or debasing the way labor so often was in capitalist societies. This ideal came from the writing of Karl Marx. But East Germans frequently complained about their society for its failure to provide satisfying work. Shortages of supplies, or mixups in deliveries often shut down production, and because materials were of poor quality the goods produced were often shoddy. Everyone was employed, but there really wasn't enough work for everyone, so many people were working way below their capacities. These problems bothered people, because they really believed in the value of work.

The Value of Equality. Egalitarianism was a very strong value in East Germany. If ordinary working people are the real source of wealth, then it makes sense for everyone to be paid what workers are paid; no one deserves any more. East German society was strongly committed to providing necessities for all. Everyone had a job; there was no unemployment. Housing was very cheap, though its quality was poor. There was no homelessness. Basic foods like bread and cheese and beer were cheap. Health care was free, education was free, old people received pensions, and preschool day care was available to all. But luxuries were distrusted. The only car for sale was the sputtering, smelly Trabant; clothing was all cheap and styleless. **Conspicuous consumption,** acquiring possessions as signs of wealth and status, was condemned. In fact, a key event in undermining the East German regime after the fall of the Soviet Union was a series of revelations about the privileges of the ruling Communist Party elite. When East Germans learned that the party chief's wife traveled to Paris every month to get her hair cut, and that the party leadership lived in luxury homes in guarded compounds and drove Mercedes Benz cars, they were furious.

The Value of Collectivism. An important part of socialist culture in East Germany was belief in the virtues of group participation and distrust of individualism. People were expected to involve themselves in **collectives** (organized groups): to join youth organizations, women's organizations, the Communist Party; to attend meetings at their office or factory. Individualism was suppressed. If you avoided joining group life, and insisted on setting yourself apart, that was seen as "antisocial" and it was actually a legal offense.

East German **collectivism** was at one and the same time resented and absorbed. The coffee break Peter Marcuse observed was a benign aspect of East German collectivism. People did really become very involved with their co-workers socially and emotionally. They depended on friends and workmates for mutual aid, much more so than in the West. Friends helped each other find scarce goods and cope with bureaucracy. Typical friendship groups of perhaps two dozen people often linked individuals with very varied occupations, from doctors to auto mechanics, who all had contacts or skills to share with the group. But oddly enough, these warm, close-knit groups which exemplified the value of collectivism were in their own way a form of retreat from the demands of official socialism. East Germans called it "niche society" (*Nischengesellschaft*) and it was seen as a passive protest against the regime. Friendship groups were a substitute for official party organizations like the youth and women's groups that the government insisted people join. These groups were disliked and they disappeared immediately after reunification.

SOCIAL INSTITUTIONS OF THE TWO GERMANYS

In some ways the two Germanys were very similar: both were modern industrial societies with specialized social institutions. If you were a ¡Kung Bushman visiting Germany, you would probably notice little difference between the East and the West; the contrast with your own small-scale hunting and gathering society would be overwhelming. In both Germanys large-scale formal organizations—businesses, collective farms, parliaments, political parties, trade unions, management boards, planning boards, universities, armies, government ministries, and so forth—were critical to the functioning of society.

Bureaucracy

Max Weber, the most famous German sociologist of the early twentieth century, saw **bureaucracy** as the defining feature of modern industrial societies. As a person living in a modern society, you certainly have a feeling for what bureaucracy is. Weber saw **rationalization** as the essence of bureaucracy: formal rules and procedures for attaining specific goals are substituted for traditional or spontaneous forms of social relations.

In addition to formal rules, Weber saw some other special features in bureaucracies: People perform specialized jobs, and they are ranked in a hierarchy, so they take orders from superiors. Employees can make a career of work in a bureaucracy, climbing the levels of the hierarchy. Bureaucracies are also impersonal. They treat people as cases, not individuals, and they place great emphasis on careful record keeping. Weber argued that though it has definite drawbacks, bureaucracy is the most effective way to organize large numbers of people to serve practical, well-defined goals. He expected that whatever its political and economic system, any modern society would require bureaucracy (Gerth and Mills, pp. 196–216). Like Weber, we can certainly see bureaucracy well-illustrated in Germany. It is clear that German culture, with its stress on obeying authority and following the rules, is quite supportive of bureaucratic organizations. German bureaucrats take their jobs seriously and people trust them not be capricious or corrupt.

Katerina's Story: The Proper Bureaucrat

Katerina Wolf is a certified social worker in the office of Immigration Services in Berlin. Her department handles the cases of Ausseidler (ethnic German "resettlers") from lands that were once German, but were taken by the Soviet Union after Germany's defeat in World War II. Germany has a policy of accepting as a citizen anyone who is of German ancestry. Since the fall of the Soviet Union, three-quarters of a million Soviet Germans have applied.

Today, Stefan Z., an ethnic German who comes from East Prussia, has come to consult about his case. Katerina is looking down, studying his file while he sits down. When she looks up, she is stunned. He is the most handsome young man she has ever seen. Despite his accent, he has a beautiful voice and a winning smile; she can hardly focus on what he is saying. When she finally concentrates she understands two things: He is asking her out to coffee and he is asking her to speed up the process of getting state aid for an apartment. "But you're not even close to the top of the list," she exclaims in surprise; "there are many people before you." "Please, it's not for me," he begs, "my parents—they are old, sick—we have only a tiny room; it's not well-heated—they suffered for many years." "Just look at their papers," he pleads, unfolding a worn packet of letters from dissidents in the Soviet Union, Lutheran ministers, and even a TV personality. Folded between the pages is a 100-mark note. Katerina gasps. Forcing herself to respond, she shoves the papers toward Stefan and in a voice choked with anger she says, "You cannot do this—others are in need also. You are a German now; you must follow the rules—everyone does. This is not the East; not Russia!" Astonished at his rebuff, Stefan rises in awkward silence and moves toward the door. Katerina's eyes follow him; then she stares dumbly at the door until her supervisor approaches with a questioning look.

The Capitalist Economy in West Germany

In 1945 Germany lay in ruins after its surrender. The people were starving, the cities were smoldering rubbish heaps, about half the factories were destroyed, and roads and railroads were torn up by the bombing. Inflation made the German currency worthless, so people who had food or anything else of value refused to sell it. Germans call this time *die Stunde Null,* zero hour, the lowest point, which had to be a new beginning. But in capitalist West Germany, once rebuilding began, production grew with astonishing rapidity. They called it "the German economic miracle." People once again had enough food and clothing and shoes. Millions of houses were built and cities were reconstructed. By the 1950s, West Germany had achieved full employment and it exported more goods than any other country except the United States (Turner, pp. 59–62). By the 1980s, West Germany had become one of the world's richest countries, in the same league with the United States and Japan. You can learn about the basic features of capitalism—private property, competition for profits, and market forces—by studying West Germany.

Private Ownership

In Germany businesses are almost all privately owned and they compete in their efforts to make profits. This makes the economy very dynamic. You may be surprised to learn that Karl Marx was one of the first to recognize the productivity of capitalism. In his 1848 *Communist Manifesto* Marx wrote: "The bourgeoisie (that is, the class of capitalists) during its rule of scarce one hundred years, has created more massive and more colossal productive forces than have all preceding generations together" (Marx, pp. 13–14).

Many German businesses are corporations. They have no single owner; rather, shareholders have the right to vote on company decisions and the company is legally headed by boards of directors and run by managers appointed by the boards. German manufacturing companies are famous all over the world and some of their names may be familiar to you. Cars are produced by Daimler-Benz, BMW, Volkswagen, and Porsche. There are major chemical companies like Bayer, and electrical manufacturing companies like Siemens. Big banks like Deutsche Bank are also privately owned.

West Germany also has an unusually large number of middle-sized businesses (called the *Mittelstand*) which often are owned and managed by single individuals or families. These companies account for half of all west German production, employ two-thirds of all workers, and produce two-thirds of all exports. Many produce precision parts, like machine tools, parts for cars, and laser cutters. Farms are also privately owned. Most are very small (averaging about 35 acres) and they are owned by the families that work them. Less than 1 percent of the farms are larger than 120 acres (Glouchevitch, pp. 57, 63; Nyrop, pp. 182–184).

The Profit Motive and Competition

Like other capitalists, the owners and managers of west German firms are in business to make money. They try their best to maximize the profits of their enterprises in order to increase their own wealth and prestige. In search of profits, they try to produce and sell more, to produce more cheaply, to develop new products that customers will want to buy, and to find new customers for their products. In an economy based on the **profit motive,** businesses find themselves in **competition** with each other, for customers, and for the best workers and suppliers.

For example, in the 1960s, Volkswagen did fabulously well selling budget-model VW "Beetles" to buyers all over Europe and America. But as buyers became more affluent they abandoned the Beetle for more luxurious cars, made by other German and non-German manufacturers. VW profits fell and the company might even have gone out of business had it not designed several new, fancier cars and vans. Today buyers seem to want their cars to be big and powerful and luxurious and German companies are successful in international competition because they can meet this demand.

German firms also compete for capable workers, and workers compete for the best jobs. The most profitable companies are able to provide very fine apprenticeship programs that lead to well-paid jobs and opportunities for promotion. Many German high school students choose apprenticeship rather than university, and the programs run by big companies are considered very desirable. Students must compete for admission and companies have their pick of students with the best grades and recommendations, and the best presentation at interviews.

Market Forces

Capitalist economies are sometimes called **free-market systems** because, in theory at least, the interaction of supply and demand determines how much is produced, and by whom, and at what price it is sold. Adam Smith, the first theoretician of capitalist economies said that the market acts like an "invisible hand," directing workers to this firm, or capital investments to that firm. Smith was amazed at how smoothly the market worked, weeding out the inefficient and the overpriced, encouraging innovation, and giving the buyers what they demanded.

German-Style Capitalism

West Germany built one of the world's most successful capitalist economies, but it built in characteristically German style. German capitalism is different from Japanese capitalism and different from American capitalism. The particular nature of German capitalism is consistent with German culture and values.

When West Germany was established in 1949, the British and American forces wanted it to become like Adam Smith's ideal capitalist society: an economy of many small producers, all competing feverishly, and all subject to the operation of market forces, without government interference. Today this ideal is often called **laissez-faire capitalism.** But as soon as the West Germans began running their own government they set about controlling and limiting the operation of free-market forces. For laissez-faire competition they substituted government regulation, **oligopoly,** and labor-management cooperation. Germans call their economy a "social market economy."

Valuing order and social responsibility, Germans find the workings of free-market forces unacceptably cruel and disorderly. In unregulated competition, some companies become so successful that they drive out all others, becoming monopolies and destroying competition itself. Also, unregulated market economies often exhibit strong **business cycles,** periods of boom when profits rise, businesses grow, and more workers are hired, followed by terrible depressions when companies go bankrupt and many workers are unemployed. Workers may be forced to accept very low wages and bad working conditions, just to have a job. Even business owners in Germany want the government to step in to control free-market competition. For example, the head of the 100,000-member German Retail Trade Association recently explained why business owners are pleased with government restriction of business hours: "Germans need rules and regulations, and want a well-ordered, harmonious society, not the law of the jungle" (Whitney, Jan. 16, 1995, p. A6).

Government Regulation

Germans agree that it is right for the government to set the rules for business and use its power to make sure the economy works well. Complex laws regulate business practices, the use and disposal of toxic materials, the kinds of advertisements permitted, work conditions in factories and offices, how businesses should bargain with unions, and how corporate management should be structured. While Germans sometimes complain about the difficulty of complying with so many regulations, they think that their society is better off because of the role government plays in the economy.

The German government also uses its resources to steer the economy. The government makes plans for economic development (sometimes in coordination with industrial associations) and it gets business to do what it wants by using incentives. Tax breaks spur capital investment and are used to target investment in vital industries. Subsidies and tariffs protect small farmers against competition from large commercial farms (Nyrop, pp. 218–220). The most important way the German government intervenes in the economy is by providing benefits to workers to guarantee their security (see p. 262, "The Welfare State").

Oligopoly

West Germany allowed a good deal of **oligopoly** (situations in which a few very large firms dominate an industry), again for the purpose of making its capitalist economy more orderly and controlled. The firms in oligopolies can get together to control market forces instead of being at their mercy.

Today, Germany's biggest businesses and banks have **interlocking directorates.** They hold shares of each other's stock and bank representatives and directors of large companies sit on each other's supervisory boards. Through these connections they are able to cooperate with each other instead of competing. German companies also form industrial associations, in which the biggest companies lead others in planning investment and research for a whole industry.

Labor-Management Cooperation

German capitalism is distinctive in the emphasis it places on workers' security. In Germany, businesses must be profitable, but maintaining "the social peace" by recognizing the rights of labor is an equally important value. This is apparent in the organization of firms and in management goals.

Approximately one-third of German workers are union members and almost all of their unions belong to a powerful central federation, the German Trade Union Federation (DBG). Employers and unions run big businesses together in a unique system known as **codetermination.** By law, all big companies have two boards of directors, a management board and a supervisory board. Union representatives must make up half the members on the supervisory boards. The idea that workers should have a say in running the businesses where they are employed goes all the way back to nineteenth-century Marxism. German workers first demanded it in the revolution of 1848, and workers' councils were enacted into law for the first time in 1920 (Glouchevitch, pp. 134–142; Nyrop, pp. 232, 234). You can see that Marx's ideas had a big influence on West German society as well as on East German society.

Working together, unions and management have become allies in Germany. They join together to advocate increased capital investment by companies, which produces growth and more jobs, and they oppose investors' efforts to pay out company income in profits (Glouchevitch, pp. 106–107, 114). They advocate investment in industries that require skilled, well-paid workers and they avoid creating unskilled, low-wage jobs.

The Socialist Economy in East Germany

Socialism existed as an ideal before any society actually adopted a socialist economy. It was meant to be a new form of modern industrial society that would correct the defects and abuses of industrial capitalism. Now that you know something about capitalism, the logic of socialism will be easier to understand.

In the nineteenth century, Karl Marx was the social thinker most influential in describing and criticizing capitalism and calling for a socialist alternative. Marx was German, but he fled Germany and lived in France and finally England. The capitalism he saw in Europe was a harsh system. Factory workers toiled long hours in unsafe conditions for very low pay. Even young children were employed in factories. Every decade or so there was a financial crisis and a huge economic depression, and millions of workers found themselves without any means of support. The market economy, Marx said, far from being a miraculous system that automatically works for the public good, as Adam Smith claimed, is actually an irrational, ruinous system, in which successful business owners (**capitalists**) get richer and richer by **exploiting** their workers (that is, paying them less than the value of the products of their work). Marx also condemned the **irrationality** of capitalism, which he said produces what is profitable, not what the public needs. Marx expected that once workers knew about socialism, they would revolt against the capitalist system, seize control of their governments, and create worker-states, where working people would run the economy to benefit the public. Marx considered collective ownership, planning, and cooperation the essence of socialism.

The first socialist economy was created in the Soviet Union after the 1917 Bolshevik Revolution. Following World War II, variations of Soviet-style socialism were established in all the Soviet-bloc countries of eastern Europe: East Germany, Poland, Czechoslovakia, Hungary, Yugoslavia, Bulgaria, Romania, and Albania, and in other socialist countries like Cuba and Mozambique. In Asia, China adopted its own socialist system after Mao Zedong's revolutionary forces triumphed in 1949.

Collective Ownership

East Germany's postwar administration established socialism while the country was still occupied by the Soviet army. The first step was **collectivization,** when privately owned farms and businesses were turned into public property. In East Germany, collectivization began with the estates of great landowners (who owned approximately half the farmland). About two-thirds of this land was distributed to small farmers and the rest was organized into large collective farms. The businesses of active Nazis were seized and also certain types of enterprises considered essential, like banks and power utilities. These became "peoples' plants" operated at first by the administration of the Soviet Zone and later by the GDR. Later, many more firms were harassed out of business by taxation and difficulties with government supplies or price controls. By 1952 over three-quarters of industrial workers were employed in state-owned enterprises. Small farmers were also pressured to join collectives (Turner, p. 109). Collectivization continued until, by 1985, 95 percent of agricultural land was farmed by collectives and 98 percent of the labor force was employed in collectivized enterprises, which earned 96 percent of total national income (Burant, pp. 121–122; Ardagh, p. 373).

A Planned Economy

The East German economy was a **planned economy.** Economic decisions were not left to market forces; rather, various planning boards set economic goals and decided what would be produced, and by whom, and how resources would be used and at what prices products would be sold. The government not only planned the economy, it also commanded: It told the various economic institutions and actors what to do. For this reason, some sociologists call socialist economies **command economies.** Ideally, a planned economy would extend political democracy to the economy, because important economic decisions would be made by the people or their representatives, not by the tiny class of capitalists. A planned economy would work for the public good by producing what people really need and deliberately distributing it equally, so everyone would have at least the minimum to live in health and dignity. Congresses of the ruling Communist Party (called the SED) passed successive two-year and then five-year economic plans that decided what the society should invest in, where resources should go, and what trade should be permitted (Turner, pp. 111, 112).

Corporation, Not Profit Seeking

Socialists in East Germany expected that once collective ownership and a planned economy were created, new relationships among people would develop too. Socialist society would be humane: Competition would be replaced by cooperation; individual greed by a spirit of comradeship. People would no longer try to make profits by selling things or by exploiting others; instead they would do work that benefited everyone.

In fact, over the 40 years of socialism in East Germany, people did stop thinking in terms of profit. They thought of providing basic goods for everyone, and the idea of persuading people that they needed more and more so that you could sell more and make more money became foreign to them. When Peter Marcuse visited East Germany in 1989–1990 he talked with a hotel manager about the new private bicycle store down the road. The manager was puzzled: "When everyone has a bike, they won't be able to sell any more," he explained. The capitalist idea of inventing racing bikes, then mountain bikes, then dual-use bikes, and convincing people they needed them was totally beyond him (Marcuse, pp. 263–264).

German-Style Socialism

East German socialism had a lot in common with the socialist systems of other eastern European Soviet satellite states. In large measure this was so because Soviet domination set limits to what institutional variation was allowed. The socialist economy in East Germany was distinctive in that it was heavily industrial, it was run by a huge bureaucracy which was not corrupt, and it was quite productive. Serious, skilled East German workers turned out relatively high-quality goods in great demand throughout the socialist world. The GDR economy was also quite effective in raising the living standards of the poorest East Germans and making all citizens more equal.

Productivity

The East German system never aspired to produce luxuries for anyone. Its goals were to achieve material comfort and security for everyone, equally shared, and to build an economy collectively and democratically run by the people. An idealistic East German socialist told John Ardagh that "this society may be far from perfect, but at least we have eliminated real poverty, and that's more than you have done in the West." In terms of output, East Germany's socialist economy made great progress in the early postwar years, rapidly restoring production to prewar levels. This was quite a feat, considering that the East received no aid from the United States and instead had to pay reparations to the Soviet Union. The U.S.S.R. dismantled and took away factories producing 40 percent of East Germany's industrial goods; this was twice the damage done by the war. Also, the Soviets took 25 percent of East Germany's output, without compensation (Ardagh, pp. 371, 373; Turner, pp. 110–111).

Between 1963 and 1973, GDR national income grew at an annual rate of 5 percent and East Germany became the strongest Soviet-bloc economy. Consumer goods like cars, refrigerators, washing machines, and TVs became widely available. Much more housing was built. According to the World Bank, in 1974, per capita income was higher in the GDR than in Britain. But this was the high point of East German production. Thereafter, the oil crisis of the 1970s made it difficult for the GDR to sustain capital investment and production of consumer goods at the same time. Growth and improvement in living standards slowed (Turner, p. 139; Ardagh, p. 372; Steele, p. 7).

Collective Ownership

In East Germany, people took the idea of collective ownership very seriously. But large numbers of people rejected it. Their problems with collective ownership revolved around a central issue: When enterprises are "collectively" owned, who really owns and controls them? The people who work in them? All the people? The government? In East Germany, "collective ownership" was really **state ownership** and control. In effect the state owned the means of production in the name of the people and it acted, so it said, in their interests. The East German government really tried to make people feel like members of collectives. In every workplace there were dozens of committees and hundreds of meetings about the "plan," and employees made thousands of suggestions; but in actuality, the "plan" was made at the top levels of the party and orders came down from the top through all the levels of the party, down to each factory department, and everyone knew it.

East Germans themselves had never demanded collective ownership; they never made a socialist revolution. Collectivization was imposed by the Soviet Union, and many people didn't want it. The most common form of opposition was flight to the West by small farmers, small businesspeople, and workers too. By 1961, when the Berlin Wall was built, 2.5 million East Germans (from a total of 19 million in 1948) had fled their country. Many people defied collective ownership in a smaller, less risky way—they worked privately in addition to their regular jobs, doing house building, babysitting, car repair, dressmaking, and so on. This hidden private economy was probably quite large (Ardagh, pp. 390–391). Some east Germans believe their experience demonstrates that socialism is a hopeless failure, impossible to achieve. Others believe a truly democratic socialism might be possible, but that the Soviet Union never permitted East Germany to try it.

Planning and Bureaucracy

East Germany's experience is very interesting, because it shows something about the strengths and weaknesses of bureaucracy. A huge state-planning bureaucracy developed in East Germany. There were factory committees, regional and state planning boards, *Kombinaten,* the huge combines of factories, with their production quotas, joint prices, and distribution outlets. German-style, bureaucrats took their jobs relatively seriously. They were not open to bribery and they didn't use their power to favor their relatives. They behaved like good bureaucrats, systematically and rationally advancing the goals of their organization.

Nevertheless, Marx would have been greatly disappointed in the East German government bureaucracy. Marx had predicted that under socialism the state would need to rule for the proletariat at first; but eventually, as collective institutions developed, the state would "wither away" and the people would run their economy and society directly. This ideal future state would be **communism.** Neither East Germany nor any other socialist society has even come close. In all socialist societies, collective ownership has meant increased centralization of power in the hands of a ruling party and a swollen government bureaucracy.

Max Weber always said that Marx was wrong on this score. He believed no industrial society—capitalist or socialist—could do without bureaucracy. While aware of the advantages of bureaucracy for rationally coordinating large organizations, Weber would not have been surprised to hear about its limitations.

Planning in East Germany turned out to be clumsy and inefficient. You could say that it was like having the Department of Motor Vehicles run the whole economy. Once a plan had been made, it was very difficult to change it, even if it didn't seem to be working. Information from the factory moved very slowly up the layers of party bureaucracy. For example, if a condom factory had been sent too little latex, it would take a long time for word to get back to the planning boards and a long time for them to respond. Perhaps a bathing suit factory had received too much latex, but they just hid it away to compensate for future shortages. Factories often came to a stop when some vital material was lacking, or else everything waited while the factory manager made an information arrangement trading some parts he had stockpiled for the missing material stockpiled in some other factory.

> A lion in a GDR zoo complains to the zookeeper that he's being discriminated against. "All I ever get to eat is bananas and every now and then an apple, but the lion in the next cage gets meat all the time."
>
> "But there's a good reason for that," says the warden. "The lion next to you is in a cage planned for a lion, but you're in a cage planned for a monkey." (Marcuse, p. 127)

Recently economists have argued that defects in planning are an intrinsic, fateful flaw of socialism. Robert Heilbroner contends that it is impossible, in principle, for a large modern economy to be run by central planning. No one could ever build a computer with sufficient capacity to keep track of all the supplies, products, prices, and exchanges. Blind as it is, market allocation of production avoids this colossal bookkeeping task.

It seems clear that while the East German government was committed to raising standards of living, reliance on centralized planning caused many unforeseen problems. For example, it took the East German government until the 1970s to decide that building housing had to be a priority, and then the plan poured resources into housing. Investment was diverted away from factories, which kept on producing with old, outdated machinery. As a result, the quality of East German products declined, and it became harder to export them to countries outside the Soviet bloc. Also, aging factories and power plants spewed more and more pollution into the air and water and land. But since the plan called for increasing production of housing and consumer goods, this problem was ignored. This is one of the saddest defects of socialism: It proved to be no better, and perhaps worse, than capitalism at controlling environmental pollution (DeBardeleben, pp. 144–164).

Because planning was so clumsy and imprecise, it could deal best with highly standardized goods. Newly built housing endlessly repeated the same modular concrete apartment blocks; clothing was offered in only a couple of basic designs; even cars came in only one model. State-owned stores were identified only by number: "Women's Clothing Store #32," "Butcher Shop #1658." Such standardization, combined with the poor quality of much consumer goods, made East Germany a kind of "gray society," lacking color and variety, in sharp contrast to the bright lights, vivid advertising, and glittering shopping districts found in the West.

Economic Inequality in East and West

Despite the differences in their economic systems, the societies of East and West Germany shared a common commitment to reducing economic inequality. Both societies were relatively successful in limiting inequalities of income, and the welfare state further equalized families' resources. West Germany showed a moderate degree of income inequality. In the mid-1980s, the poorest quintile of West Germans received 7.0 percent of total income, while the richest fifth received 40.3 percent or 5.8 times as much (World Bank, 1993).[1]

Data on East German income distribution show that income was more equally distributed in the East than the West. In 1980 the poorest fifth of East German households received 12.2 percent of total income, and the richest fifth received 29.8 percent, approximately 2.5 times as much (United Nations, p. 7). In the East, in the 1980s, the average factory manager was paid only about twice as much as the average factory worker. In West Germany in 1990, a pay for a managing director averaged about 4.5 times that of an average factory worker (Ardagh, pp. 174, 374).

Ethnic, Religious, and Racial Minorities

While Germany has relatively mild income inequalities, racial, ethnic, and religious inequalities are more significant. West Germany first welcomed immigrants in the 1950s and 60s, when rapid economic growth led to labor shortages. The Federal Republic negotiated agreements with poorer countries to supply temporary laborers. These *gastarbeiter* ("guest workers") first came from Italy, Spain, and Greece, and later from Turkey, Morocco, Tunisia, and Yugoslavia. They worked at unskilled jobs in mines and factories and construction. In the beginning, single men immigrated to Germany, intending to earn money and return home. In fact, during the 1960s and early 70s, 14 million immigrants came to Germany and 11 million returned to their native countries.

Germany stopped recruiting temporary workers in 1973, but allowed remaining foreign workers to bring their families to join them in Germany. More recently, new groups of immigrants have come to Germany, particularly ethnic Germans from Poland, Rumania, and the former Soviet Union. Some of these ethnic Germans are actually German Jews. More than 22,000 Jews have settled in Germany since 1990, bringing the total number of Jews to about 50,000 (Friedrichs, pp. 1745–1746; Cowell, Sept. 24, 1995, p. 3). By 1998 there were 7 million foreign residents in Germany (almost all in the western Länder) making up 8 percent of the population. Germany now has the largest immigrant population of any country in Europe. One in five babies born in Germany today is not ethnically German. There are religious minorities too: not only Jews, but Muslims from Turkey, Yugoslavia, and North Africa. Immigrants are clustered in western German industrial cities; in 1995 23 percent of the population of Stuttgart was foreign-born, as was 22 percent of the population of Munich and 29 percent of Frankfurt (Friedrichs, p. 1754).

---

[1]In comparison, the richest quintile of Japanese received only 4.3 times as much as the poorest quintile. In Mexico, the richest fifth received 13.5 times as much income as the poorest fifth. And in the United States, the richest fifth received just under 9 times as much income as the poorest. (See Table 1.3, p. 40.)

Boys who are ethnic Turks learn to worship at a mosque in eastern Germany. Immigrants are an important part of the new unified Germany. After World War II, when the country was desperately short of labor, Germany recruited workers in Italy, Turkey, and elsewhere. Germans hoped these "guest workers" would return "home," but today ethnic Turks and many other former immigrants constitute more than one German in every ten.

Many countries have ethnic minorities and minority religious groups. In many cases minorities face prejudice, perhaps racial discrimination, perhaps obstacles to practicing their religion. Often they are poorer than the dominant national group. But in Germany the meaning of such inequalities is different. Their existence stimulates guilt and shame because it recalls the racial policies of Nazi Germany. Overall, ethnic minority group members in Germany are poorer than other Germans. Their poverty rate is triple the national rate and their unemployment rate is almost double the national rate (Friedrichs, p. 1750). Perhaps more importantly, ethnic minorities find themselves unwelcome in Germany, the more so if they are darker-skinned and Muslim. German citizens will readily tell a visitor, "Germany is not an immigration country." It is the common view that having German blood makes you German, and long residence, or even birth in Germany, does not if you are of foreign stock (Turner, p. 163; Ardagh, p. 276; Schlaes, pp. 19–20, 36).

As unemployment has increased in Germany, outspoken prejudice against foreigners, particularly Turks, has increased also, especially in eastern Germany and especially among the less educated. In 1992 and 1993 there was a shocking series of violent assaults on Turkish families and on immigrants seeking asylum. Turkish workers tend to live in run-down inner-city neighborhoods, somewhat separated from other Germans. Germans don't invite Turks into their homes, although German children do learn to tolerate their foreign classmates.

In a society as much given to legal regulation as Germany, it is significant that there are no laws against racial discrimination, other than in pay. Ads for jobs or apartments often say "only Germans," or "only Europeans," and bars often prohibit entry to Turks. By law, a German worker has preference over a foreigner for a job (Ardagh, pp. 287, 288, 297). It was only in 1998 that Germans took on the task of changing their outdated citizenship law that defined citizenship as a matter of German "blood." (See pp. 288–289.)

Representative Democracy in West Germany

There is no characteristically "German" form of government. In the past century, Germans have lived under the most varied political orders—from the small, independent kingdoms of the early nineteenth century, to the great monarchy which Prussia dominated at the end of the nineteenth century, and then on to the Weimar parliamentary democracy which fell to Nazi dictatorship. When the governments of the two Germanys were created after World War II, there were precedents for almost any modern form of government. West Germany embraced **democratic** political institutions and East Germany was given an **authoritarian** government.

The West German government was created under the influence of the occupying forces of the United States and Britain, who were determined to establish a democracy—that is, a political system in which the citizens choose their leaders and participate in making government decisions and the government functions according to rules set down in a constitution, which also guarantees basic human rights. But West Germans themselves, horrified by Nazi carnage, reached back in their history to identify with a German democratic tradition. It was no accident that they chose for their flag the red, gold, and black bands first carried by the republican revolutionaries of 1848, which was also the flag of the Weimar Republic. West Germany, like all modern societies, is much too big to be a **direct democracy** in which all the citizens actually meet together and directly make the decisions which affect their lives. Instead, it is an **indirect democracy, a representative democracy** in which people express their preferences by voting for the candidates of competing political parties.

A Federation of States

The particular type of representative democracy adopted in West Germany is characteristically German. It reflects both Germany's tragic history and its present-day values. With typical German thoroughness and attention to detail, the West German political system was designed to make it difficult for a dictator like Hitler ever to seize power again. First of all, West Germany chose to avoid a centralized government like that of Nazi Germany. Instead, West Germany adopted a **federal system** (like that of the United States and Canada). It consisted of 10 states, to which 5 additional states were added when Germany was reunified. Many of the states were based on old German principalities, which had united in past German confederations. In this federal system, the rights of the states limit the power of the central government. In Germany the states control education, radio and TV, police, environmental regulation, cultural affairs, and local government and planning (Turner, p. 39; Ardagh, p. 86).

Every state elects its own parliament and its own prime minister and has an office, a kind of embassy, in the federal capital. All personal income taxes and corporate taxes are shared 50–50 between the states and the federal government, although federal law ensures that tax rates are the same in all states.

Parliamentary Government

West Germany also chose a parliamentary system of representative democracy, similar to the governments of other western European democracies. In a parliamentary system, the head of the government (in Germany, the chancellor) is elected by the upper house of parliament, not directly by the citizens. The vote takes place along party lines, so when a particular party or coalition of parties wins a majority of seats, its leader almost automatically becomes chancellor.

The upper house of the parliament (or *Bundestag*) is the nation's most powerful political institution. The lower house (the *Bundesrat*) is composed of delegates of the states. Representatives are elected to the *Bundestag* following an intricate system of **proportional representation** designed to frustrate the seating of small extremist parties, like the Nazi Party. Every German casts two votes for representatives: one for a district candidate, elected as an individual, and one for a party list of candidates. Half the seats go to district candidates and half to party list candidates, in proportion to their party's share of the vote. Any party that fails to win either three election districts or 5 percent of the party lists is denied representation (Dalton, pp. 281–285; Turner, pp. 40–41). In Germany today, power is carefully divided between the federal government and the states, between the upper and lower houses of parliament, and among the parties.

Political Parties

Finally, as specified in the constitution of the Federal Republic, the West German political system is fundamentally a **party system.** Political parties, distinguished by their differing political perspectives, compete for votes. In parliament they follow party discipline; that is, their members almost always vote as blocs. Political parties make the system orderly. When they vote for a party or its candidates, voters know what they are getting. The party system keeps the government responsible to voters; legislators know that if they do not act as they promised, voters can always turn to another party and vote them out of office (Dalton, pp. 249–250).

In West Germany after World War II there were two major parties, the Christian Democratic Union and the Social Democratic Party; and two lasting minor parties, the Christian Social Union (which usually acted in coalition with the CDU) and the Free Democratic Party (which allied itself with either of the two major parties). The CDU was the party of the moderate right, advocating anticommunism and a commitment to capitalist economies. The SDP, the oldest German party, was traditionally committed to socialism and democracy, but since World War II, it has been a moderate left party, clearly anticommunist and oriented to a market economy, but with a strong belief in the welfare state (Dalton, pp. 251–276; Nyrop, pp. 264–273).

West Germans are also free to create other political organizations to make their opinions heard and to compete for political power. **Interest groups** speak for people who share common needs and problems. They lobby the government for desired legislation and policies. In the Federal Republic the "big four" interest groups are business, labor, the churches, and farmers, represented by organizations like the Federation of German Industries, the German Federation of Trade Unions, the Catholic Church and the Evangelical Church in Germany (an association of Protestant churches), and the German Farmers Association (Dalton, pp. 210–227).

Starting in the 1960s, new groups of political organizations developed which often challenged the traditional interest groups. These new groups, known collectively as the New Politics movement include environmentalist organizations, the women's movement, and the peace movement. In 1980 people involved in these groups created a new party—the Green Party, which became an influential minor party and in 1998 became the minor partner in a coalition government with the SPD. The Greens express younger Germans' serious concerns about pollution, nuclear weapons and nuclear power, militarism, gender inequality, and alienating work (Dalton, pp. 227–228, 266–269).

Constitutional Rights

The 1949 Basic Law (or constitution) which established the political system in West Germany, also granted citizens certain basic rights: freedom of speech and assembly, freedom of the press, equality before the law, religious freedom, and freedom from discrimination based on race, sex, religious or political beliefs, and the right to relief from military service on grounds of conscientious objection. All these rights had been lost under the Nazi regime, so restoring them was a very important step toward democracy. But ironically, the Nazi experience led the new German government to qualify some of these rights in order to protect the democracy. Thus, it is constitutional to ban parties that advocate the overthrow of democracy and this provision has been used against both Nazi and Communist parties. Similarly, the right of free speech cannot be used to attack democracy or to advocate Nazism. For example, publication of Hitler's book *Mein Kampf* is still banned in Germany today (Nyrop, p. 247). In recent years, West Germans have debated conscientiously about how far the right of free speech should license neo-Nazis who parade and publish anti-Semitic literature and wear Nazi symbols, and how much repression is necessary in order to protect democracy.

Authoritarian Government in East Germany

You must understand that East Germans did not choose their form of government. East Germany's government was created during the Soviet occupation after World War II and sustained until 1989 when Soviet domination ended. The GDR was what was called a "Soviet satellite state"—a country kept in the orbit of the Soviet Union's power by that country's threat of military force. East Germany tried once to escape Soviet domination in the uprising of 1953, which the Soviet army brutally put down. Afterwards, East Germans put up with their Soviet-installed regime as best they could. They learned to put aside the traditional value of obedience in favor of "working the system" in order to get by. For example, if you ordered parts to fix your car in the proper way, you could wait years for them, but West German money earned illegally and spent on the black market could get you what you needed right away. To get a good professional or technical job, or to qualify for it, you had to pretend to be an enthusiastic supporter of the regime. East Germans were schooled in petty disobedience and in contempt for authority.

When they were first created, East Germany's political institutions paralleled those of West Germany. There were five federated states, upper and lower houses of parliament, and a minister-president elected by a majority of the upper house (or People's Chamber). The Constitution of 1949 resembled West Germany's Basic Law, and guaranteed fundamental rights like freedom of assembly and speech, freedom of the press, religious freedom, the right to strike, and the right to emigrate.

But as early as 1947, these institutions of representative democracy became an empty shell, within which a second set of centralized and authoritarian political institutions developed. Real power became highly centralized in one party, the Social Unity Party or SED, and within the Party, in the hands of the top SED leaders, the *Politburo*. Early on, the states ceased to have any separate powers, and they were replaced by administrative districts in 1952 (Turner, p. 101). Although basic civil rights were formally guaranteed, in actuality those rights were denied in a repressive **police state** that permitted no opposition to SED rule.

A Sham Democracy

Officially, the East German state was a parliamentary democracy with a total of five competing parties. In fact, four of the parties were really puppets of the SED, run by leaders acceptable to the ruling party and never permitted to challenge SED power. This was how it worked: East Germans did not get to choose between candidates or party slates when they voted. An organization called the National Front put together a single slate of candidates, representing all five parties and also the "mass organizations" like trade unions, farmers' cooperatives, women's and youth organizations. East Germans could vote only for or against this "unity slate," and the vote was always reported as overwhelmingly in favor of it.

In any case, the power of the People's Chamber was very limited. It met only about six times a year, for a day at a time and unanimously passed only about a dozen bills a year, all submitted to it on direction from the Central Committee of the SED. Even Jonathan Steele, a sympathetic observer, commented, "there is no chance of voters exerting any influence against SED policy" (Steele, p. 145). Western critics of Soviet-style socialism argued that the SED had no intention of allowing democracy, since they knew that if East Germans had a choice they would vote out the SED and get rid of the socialist regime. This is probably true: When East Germans were given a choice in 1989–1990 after the collapse of the Soviet Union and the fall of the Berlin Wall, they voted to join West Germany and adopt its political and economic systems.

The One-Party State

Real power in East Germany was exercised by the political institutions of the SED. At the top was the *Politburo,* the supreme party organization, composed of about 25 senior officials, ministers, and army officers, and headed by the general secretary. Below was the Central Committee, then the Party Congress, then the regional congresses, and at the bottom the local party organizations. In theory, the *Politburo* was elected by the Central Committee, which was elected by the Party Congress and so on, but in reality, the top levels were self-selecting and party members had no influence on their choice. **Centralism** was the official principle of government in the GDR. Decisions were to be made at the top, and lower-level organizations were expected to act on orders without question.

In East Germany, the leaders of the SED lived in a separate guarded suburb outside Berlin. They selected the individuals who would get special training at party schools to become party officials. The party membership lacked access to the means for making their voices heard. For example, when the Party Congress issued a new Five-Year Plan, it was sent out to every branch of the party and state for discussion. Union locals met to discuss how the Plan would affect their work and to make suggestions. But union members were all full-time workers who met after work. They had no researchers or libraries or statisticians, and they were given only two weeks to discuss a proposed plan (Steele, p. 135). You can see that it would be very difficult for them to challenge a plan or even document any well-founded doubts. Party officials had an enormous advantage over them in resources, time, and power.

Democratic Centralism

Despite its centralization of power, SED leaders claimed that the GDR was, in fact, a democracy. It was not a parliamentary democracy like West Germany, but rather a new socialist kind of democracy they called **"democratic centralism."** The SED's leaders believed that a single party could integrate within itself all the different social groups so democracy would take place in debate within the party, not in competition among parties. SED leaders prided themselves on the high degree of political involvement among East Germans. They said political participation made East Germany more democratic than the western democracies, where citizens took little part in ongoing politics, most not even bothering to vote in elections every couple of years.

In East Germany, the government urged people to belong to the SED and other political parties, join mass organizations, run for office and join committees, and attend meetings—and large numbers of people did so. Approximately one in six East Germans over 18 (or about 2.3 million people) were SED members, and they belonged to over 84,000 local organizations. Nearly 100 percent of adults were trade union members. Hundreds of thousands more people were members of state legislatures or legislative committees, National Front committees, production councils, and PTAs. Millions joined youth and women's organizations (Burant, pp. 182, 187, 201; Dalton, p. 43).

GDR leaders proudly emphasized that people from all different classes participated in the SED and could rise to positions of power. The SED monitored the class background and current status of party members and described its membership as 56 percent working class (Steele, p. 142). They argued that the SED was democratic because all different classes were represented in it. In the West, people believed their society was democratic because many different views were represented in parliament, even though almost all representatives were middle class or upper class. In the East, it was relatively easy to join the party hierarchy, and in fact it was a major channel of upward mobility. But to rise to leadership, you had to be ideologically loyal. Thus, people from many classes were represented, but only one viewpoint—that of the SED—was allowed.

Gunter's Story: Criticizing the West

Gunter, a 53-year-old east German factory worker lived all his life under "democratic centralism." Since reunification, he has been introduced to western-style democracy, and he is critical of it. "In the GDR, a man like me or my son could hope to have a place in the life of the nation. In today's Germany, no one has a minute for you unless you drive a big car! Is this democracy? A democracy of the Mercedes? Everyone is free to have their say as long as they have money! Even the Socialists are Doktoren! When was the last time you saw a man with callused hands in the Bundestag? Honecker [past general secretary of the SED] was a fool, but he knew that in a democracy, everyone has a part."

A Police State

The East German government demanded political mobilization and ideological loyalty from its citizens, but just to make sure there was no opposition, the government suppressed all dissent. A large secret police force, a network of informers, a guarded border, and an army prevented the expression of opposition to the SED or to socialism, and prevented the penetration of seditious ideas from outside East German borders. Any group larger than seven people needed official permission to meet (Ferree, p. 96).

Censorship. In East Germany, the newspapers, radio, and television were all state-owned and state-run. News reporting was considered part of the campaign to build socialism, so events with the GDR and outside that might cast the regime in a bad light were simply not reported. For example, when the worker movement Solidarity challenged the Communist Party in Poland in 1980, it was never mentioned in the GDR news media. Newspapers and radio gave lots of news about sports and the arts, but there was no reporting on crime or consumer shortages. Party congresses were reported in predictable boring detail, economic reports were always positive, and headlines like "Delegates Unanimously Praise Workers' Collectives" were so obviously canned that they defeated their own purposes. TV programs were similarly relentlessly upbeat. Since most East Germans could tune in to West German TV, they learned about censored news anyhow, and it fed their cynicism about the GDR (Ardagh, pp. 391–392).

Prohibition of Travel. One of the things that angered East Germans most about their repressive regime was the ban on travel to the West. To leave East Germany or its Soviet-bloc neighbors you needed special government permission, seldom granted. Married couples were never permitted to exit at the same time and individuals, like athletes or musicians, permitted to tour the West were carefully watched by spies. Only old people were allowed to visit relatives in West Germany.

In 1961 construction of the Berlin Wall completed the sealing of the border between East and West. The entire border was fenced and guarded by 50,000 GDR border police, who patrolled a mined no-man's-land and were trained to shoot anyone attempting to cross.

The Threat of Force. Ultimately, the SED kept its power in East Germany through the threat and use of force against its citizens. There were police, secret police, border guards, a regular military, and volunteer militia units. East Germany's military was not large, but it was conspicuous. People were also aware of the threat of the Soviet army, which had been brutally used to put down rebellions in East German in 1953 and in Hungary in 1956.

Most sinister was the *Stasi,* the secret police, which in the very repressive days of the 1950s and 1960s imprisoned and tortured dissidents without trial. By the 1980s the *Stasi* was simply in the business of spying on people, looking for dissent. The secret police force was huge: It had a regular staff of 85,000, as many as half a million paid informers—ordinary people who spied on their co-workers, neighbors, friends, or even spouses—and secret files on a third of all GDR citizens. Until the Wende, no one knew how big the *Stasi* was. People just had the feeling that it was important to watch what you said all the time. When the true size of the *Stasi* operations was revealed after 1989, people were horrified and furious.

The Welfare State

When you read about the political and economic institutions of East Germany and West Germany, you see how very different the two societies were. But in one very important respect, both Germanys were similar. They were both **welfare states,** and welfare institutions worked effectively and met with popular approval in both societies. In both East and West, the welfare state meant the same thing: It meant that the government accepted responsibility for its citizens' social welfare. Germans today will tell you that welfare benefits support "the social peace" and relieve class tensions. Though their taxes are high, they believe the benefits are worth it. In the West, the welfare state meant that the government pledged to guarantee citizens the right to certain benefits and services, like health care and housing, even if they couldn't afford to buy them on the free market. The East German welfare state was more extensive than the West's but it was based on a similar belief that the government has an obligation to provide for the well-being of its citizens. Both societies also took responsibility for making certain that all young people were able to get an education that prepared them for a job.

The institutions of the welfare state date back long before the division of Germany. The welfare state began in the 1880s, under the rule of Kaiser Wilhelm I and his prime minister, Otto von Bismarck, as a conservative response to the trade union and socialist movements of the time. They instituted three historic components of a universal welfare system: national health insurance, accident insurance, and old-age/disability insurance. Unemployment insurance was added in 1927.

During the twentieth century other European countries followed Germany's example, establishing similar welfare programs. In the United States, where the obligation of the state to ensure the social welfare of its citizens is not fully accepted, only two of the usual welfare programs—old-age pensions and unemployment insurance—have been enacted.

The West German Welfare State

West Germany added to this basic welfare package. The government gives all parents a yearly family allowance for each child, regardless of income or marital status. There is also a program of rent allowances for low-income families, to make sure they can afford market rents and prevent homelessness. Finally, there is a small "welfare" component: allowances for people who for some reason cannot work (Nyrop, pp. 97–98).

West Germany's social insurance and welfare programs are expensive. Approximately one-third of the country's GNP is spent on health and welfare. Social programs are paid for by high income taxes, payroll taxes, and mandatory employer contributions. Health insurance, for example, is paid for by required contributions from employees and employers equal to about 6 percent of salary (Nyrop, 94; Glouchevitch, p. 111). (See Table 5.2.)

The East German Welfare State

In East Germany, the welfare state went even further. As Jonathan Steele reported, in East Germany the state "takes responsibility for providing almost everything from stable consumer prices to a job for every school leaver. People expect the state's promises to be kept. They make higher claims on it than most people do in the West" (Steele, p. 13). Although the overall standard of living in the East was much lower than in the West, no East German was excluded from education or health care for lack of money. No one was homeless or jobless; no elderly people or single mothers were left without social and financial support.

TABLE 5.2. Access to Health Care:
Although Germans and Japanese go to the doctor more often than Americans,
their societies spend less per capita on health care.

	National Legislation Requiring Health Insurance for Entire Population	Percent of Population Uninsured at Some Point in a Year, 1990	Per Capita Spending on Health (U.S. $), 1991	Average Number of Doctor Visits per Year, 1990
Germany	Yes	1	$1287	12
Japan	Yes	1	$1035	13
United States	No	26	$2566	5

Source: World Bank, *World Development Report 1993: Investing in Health.* New York: Oxford University Press, 1993.

Children and teachers from an East Berlin day-care center are out for an afternoon walk. Cars were scarce in East Germany, but high-quality, inexpensive day care was easily obtained by working mothers.

East Germany provided the standard European universal welfare institutions: health insurance, accident and disability insurance, old-age pensions, unemployment insurance, and family allowances. Health care was readily available, without charge, from state-employed medical professionals, so patients neither laid out money in advance nor filed paperwork. The quality of health care was high and the atmosphere caring.

Family benefits were generous: Women received six months' maternity leave at full pay for their first child, and a full year at reduced pay for subsequent children. Years spent caring for children were credited in figuring pensions. Families received allowances for their children until they reached age 18. Newly married young couples were given free "starter loans," with repayment waived incrementally as children were born. Day care was inexpensive and readily available (Edwards, p. 46).

Many additional benefits were provided through the workplace and administered by the unions, including holidays in union hotels, factory hospitals and clinics, day-care centers, sports facilities, adult classes, libraries, discount shops, and housing (Steele, p. 131; Burant, p. 98).

Finally, an important element in the East German welfare state was management of wages and prices through the Plan, which made basic goods available to everyone at subsidized prices, at the cost of making luxuries scarce and expensive. Prices of basic foods like bread and milk and sausage, rents, gas and electric, and commuter fares were frozen. Even the prices of theater and concert tickets and restaurants were subsidized. Rents were especially low: about 4 to 5 percent of average family income. (To imagine what this means, figure that a family earning $500 a week would pay only $25 a week in rent.) Forty percent of government spending went to these subsidies (Burant, pp. 88–89).

Educational Institutions

Germany has a highly effective educational system that will be of real interest to students from other societies. Education is treated with great seriousness and thoroughness and students make a smooth transition to adult jobs. Only students who are admitted to academic high schools, get good grades, and pass rigorous entrance exams are permitted to attend university, but those who are admitted pay no tuition and are given allowances for living expenses so they needn't work while they are in school. Most people who don't go to college undertake apprenticeships, a German tradition and a respected alternative to university education. However, even those in technical and vocational education must show their grades to employers when they seek jobs, so everyone works hard in school.

Georg's Story: The Apprentice

At 18, Georg Messer is in his final year of apprenticeship with the famous Konigsdorfer Shoe Company in Hamburg, training to be an Industriekaufmann, *an office worker in an industrial firm. Georg felt lucky to get this apprenticeship; it was highly competitive. One thousand graduates applied for 25 places. Konigsdorfer chose young men and women who were socially skilled and presentable and whose records attested to their ability to work hard and carefully. Having served in 12 different departments at Konigsdorfer, Georg is finishing his apprenticeship in the Cost Accounting Department, working closely with his mentor and applying new computer models to develop prices for the spring shoe line. He uses his knowledge of international exchange rates, import-export tariffs, and the costs of materials and labor, learned in the one-day-a-week formal instruction* (Berufsschule), *which is part of his apprenticeship.*

We asked Georg if he is ever sorry he didn't go to Gymnasium *(academic high school) and on to university. "No, not at all. Why should I be," he answered. "I was really getting tired of school by the time I was 15. This apprenticeship has let me out in the real world, and the one-day-a-week formal school makes sense, because I use what I learn in* Berufsschule *here at the factory. Did I tell you I've been offered a job, in the Cost Accounting Department? I can begin as soon as I take my qualifying exams. My bosses seem certain I'll pass. You know I'll have a responsible job with a real adult salary and plenty of room for advancement by the time I'm 18."*

Public education is controlled by the states in Germany and there is some variation from state to state in curriculum and educational philosophy, but the basic system is the same throughout the country, and 95 percent of children attend public school. States try hard to assure all students an equal start in primary school. Primary schools are neighborhood schools and richer and poorer children often attend school together, because neighborhoods often have diverse populations. Teachers are paid by the state and salaries are standard, but school buildings and equipment are supplied by the locality and vary greatly in quality. There is no **tracking** (ability grouping) at the primary level: All the children are taught the same lessons in heterogeneous classes.

But at the end of the fourth grade (in some states sixth grade) German children face a crucial life transition. Based on their grades, their teachers' assessments, and their parents' wishes, they will transfer to one of three types of secondary schools. From here on, German schools are seriously tracked and the kind of secondary school one attends has lasting life consequences (Hamilton, pp. 73–74, 77–78).

Three High School Tracks. Students considered to have the strongest academic ability go to academic high school (or *Gymnasium*) which they attend until age 19. It is roughly equivalent to American high school plus one or two years of college. In 1990 31 percent of German students attended *Gymnasium.* Most of them were from middle-class families. Students whose grades are satisfactory, and who pass a rigorous entrance exam are admitted to university, and about 75 percent of those qualified go right on to further study ("A Profile of the German Education System," p. 21; Hamilton, p. 85; Ardagh, p. 249). (See Table 5.3.)

Twenty-eight percent of German students move from primary school to technical institutes (or *Realschule*). These are vocational schools which specialize in commercial or technical fields and also provide some academic education. Technical institutes go through tenth grade and when students graduate at 16 they go on either to apprenticeship or to a technical college (*Fachhochschule*) which trains for careers like nursing or accountancy. Those who don't go on to technical colleges get jobs as lab technicians, precision mechanics, secretaries, or personnel managers, and so forth (after completing apprenticeships in these jobs). *Realschule* educate a true cross section of the German population.

The largest and least academically qualified group of students (33 percent) attend vocational high school (*Hauptschule*) until age 15.[2] These schools prepare

TABLE 5.3. *Postsecondary Education:
More young adults attend college in the United States than in Germany or Japan.

	Students in Post-secondary Schools as a Percent of Those 20–24		Women in Post-secondary Schools per 100,000 Population	For Every Woman in College in 1980,
	1980	1993	1993	Today There Are
Egypt	16	17	1056	101
Germany	**	36	1813	**
Japan	31	30	1861	140
Mexico	**	27	1333	146
USA	56	81	5834	110

* Postsecondary education includes post high school vocational and technical schools as well as community colleges, colleges, and universities.
** Data Not Available
Sources: The State in a Changing World, World Bank, Oxford, New York, 1997 *Human Development Database 1997,* United Nations, New York, 1997

[2]Another 8 percent of German students attend comprehensive high schools, which are uncommon in Germany ("A Profile of the German Education System," p. 21).

students for apprenticeship or work in manual, clerical, and semiskilled service jobs. They become construction workers, auto mechanics, file clerks, and sales-people in retail stores. The *Hauptschule* is usually a neighborhood school, often in the same building as the primary school, and its prestige is low. Students at *Hauptschule* are usually from working-class families (Hamilton, pp. 80, 85).

Second Chances. In recent years, Germany has modified its tracking system to allow more second chances to students who start out doing poorly, but later decide they want a university education. It is now possible for technical school students to switch over to the academic high school after graduation, though they often lose a year or two in making the switch. In some states as few as 2 percent do so, but in others up to 16 percent make the move up. Also, there are now adult-education courses which prepare people for college entrance later in life (Hamilton pp. 78–79; "A Profile of the German Education System," p. 21.)

Apprenticeship. The most impressive characteristic of German education is that in every track education is taken very seriously by both teachers and students, and at every level education culminates in marketable skills that qualify students for good, full-time jobs immediately upon graduation. For most students this is accomplished through a system of apprenticeship. More than 60 percent of all Germans 16 to 18 years old are apprentices who typically train for three years, spending four days a week in the workplace and one day a week in vocational school. Apprenticeships are provided by German companies, which pay for the training (Gittler and Scheuer, pp. 18–19).

Young people in Germany apprentice as auto mechanics and personnel managers, postal workers, computer programmers, graphic designers, copywriters, plumbers, railway conductors, shoe sales workers—for white-collar and blue-collar jobs in over 350 occupations. You might even think that German apprenticeships overtrain young people. Even relatively unskilled jobs are treated with the greatest seriousness. For example, shoe sales workers serve a full apprenticeship and learn about sales, sizing, cash-register operation, the process of shoe manufacture, and bookkeeping. Ordinary workers are very competent as a result, which adds to their status, and they are also qualified to advance to the next step of promotion. Every shoe salesperson has the knowledge necessary to be manager. More than half of all apprentices go to work for the company that trained them, but others move into jobs with companies not offering apprenticeships or into related occupations that don't have apprenticeships (Hamilton, pp. 35, 143–144). In Germany, the school-to-work transition is a smooth one; not just for an educated elite, but for students at every level of the educational system.

DEVIANCE AND SOCIAL CONTROL

In East Germany, because of collectivism, centralization, and police power, the state had tremendous power over individuals. The government was able to monitor what individuals did and said and use sanctions to ensure that people conformed. The government responded most severely to deviance it considered a political challenge to the SED or to socialism. A great deal of behavior seen elsewhere as private was defined as political in the GDR. For example, listening to rock music was considered a political act. In the West, in contrast, an emphasis on individualism, compartmentalization, and civil liberties shielded individuals from state power, and left them freer of official social controls. Using state power against political deviance makes the German government uncomfortable.

Totalitarian Social Controls

East Germany was often characterized by western critics as a **totalitarian state,** that is, a society in which the government intrudes into all aspects of public and private life, so that the individual is nowhere sheltered from state power. In a totalitarian state the government imposes its ideology through control of the media and education. It controls the police, the economy, and the ruling party. Through these institutions, the state exercises supreme power over individuals. In a totalitarian state there is no "independent public space" free of government control (Philipsen, p. 79).

Collectivism, Centralization, and Social Sanctions

It is important to understand that all formal East German social groups were in some way government-controlled. Some, like the party, the unions, the youth groups, and the Women's Federation were more tightly controlled, and others, like the work collectives and social clubs were more independent, but in every group there were party members pushing the party line and *Stasi* agents noting what people said and did. People were induced to participate in official organizations by means of powerful positive and negative social sanctions controlled by the SED.

Centralization meant that anything you did in one group could have consequences in every aspect of your life. People could not expect to be promoted at work unless they took leadership roles in basic organizations like the Youth Federation or Women's Federation (Scharf, pp. 141–142). Those who joined the party, enthusiastically gave their time to other voluntary groups, and voiced their belief in socialist ideology were more likely to be admitted to university, given responsible jobs and promotions, good apartments, even perhaps permission to travel to the West. You could lose these desirable rewards too. If your child defected to the West, you might lose your responsible job and get work only as a janitor; if you joined a church, your child might be turned down for the university; if you opposed the party line at work, you might never get a better apartment.

Adult Organizations. Adults were expected to join many official organizations—unions, of course, professional associations, sports leagues, the Women's Federation, volunteer social service groups, and possibly the SED or another party. Adult workers were also expected to participate in collectives in their place of work and about half did so. Collectives were social groups: They kept scrapbooks with pictures of members' families, records of members' health, and minutes of meetings. They went on picnics and trips and did weekend volunteer work maintaining the factory's summer camp and staging plays, concerts, or educational events (Steele, p. 136). Though East Germans felt coerced by this system, they also found personal satisfaction in it. People felt the work collectives, clubs, and volunteer groups were humane; they belonged and others cared about them.

Petra's Story: The Party Member

Petra is a hospital radiologist in Potsdam. In the old days, before 1990, she was a union member, a member of the Democratic Women's Federation and the Society for German-Soviet Friendship. Further, as an SED member, she played a role in the party organization in her hospital. She had been a swimmer since primary school and retained her membership in the sports league. Petra was busy, managing her household and children in addition to attending meetings after work, but she enjoyed meeting people and valued the respect with which her friends and co-workers viewed her accomplishments. She felt like she was a participant in making her society run.

Dieter's Story: The Drop-Out

For Petra's younger brother Dieter, reunification came just in time. Dieter, a musician, had not joined the Association of Composers and Musicians, and he had stopped going to meetings of the Free German Youth. He pierced his nose and hung out in the bars downtown with other "punk" youth. Dieter had completed an apprenticeship as a primary school music teacher, but somehow the government never placed him in a job. Now Dieter has moved to Berlin and found a job in a private nursery school. It doesn't pay very much and Dieter can't afford his own apartment, so he is still sleeping on the couch in the apartment where the other members of his band live. Dieter says he can live with that.

Youth Organizations. Children and teenagers spent a great deal of their time in organizations controlled by the government. First of all, all children attended the same kind of government-controlled schools (there were no private schools). Ninety-nine percent of them joined the Young Pioneers, the official children's organization, and 75 percent went on to join the Free German Youth, the official youth group from which the SED recruited new members. Children spent a lot of time after school and on weekends in Pioneer activities like cleaning up public areas, collecting paper for recycling, or helping old people to shop, carry coal, or shovel snow. Thousands attended Pioneer camp each summer as well (Steele, p. 175).

Teenagers were attracted to youth clubs, which offered discos and hobby groups, and cheap vacations, all under the watchful eyes of party cadre. Once they finished school or apprenticeship, young people were pressed to join youth commissions or youth teams on their first job. Youth teams in the workplace had their own "plan" to fulfill (Edwards, pp. 124, 129, 130, 135, 141, 144). In its mobilization and indoctrination of children, the GDR resembled the Nazi state.

Women and Group Life. Throughout its 50-year history the government of the GDR worked to bring women into the labor force, both for ideological and for political reasons. In ideological terms, Marxism teaches that "socially useful work" is an essential human activity and that no one can fully develop as a person without it. Paid work was politically desirable too, as a means of integrating women into East German society, making them part of the collectives, unions, and volunteer groups that were the fundamental social units. As early as 1950, the GDR began working to counter the Nazi belief that women belonged at home. By the 1980s, 88 percent of women aged 15 to 60 were either employed or in school, the highest percentage in any country in the world (Edwards, pp. 50, 78, 82). And East German women typically remained in the workforce throughout their childbearing years, supported by low-cost day-care centers, shorter hours, and time off for childbirth. Early in its history, East Germany was short of labor, so it helped to have women work. But by the 1980s, the GDR had trouble finding enough jobs for all its people. Still, women were urged to work—in response to political, not market priorities.

The Elderly. East Germany also tried to prevent isolation of elderly people. Old people were encouraged to continue at work, or maintain contact with their old collectives and unions, and to join old people's clubs or other clubs. Factories and primary schools were "twinned" with old people's homes or clubs. They visited the elderly, did repairs for them, and ran trips and parties for them. Union committees also kept in touch with retired members. In turn, elderly people frequently visited schools or youth groups to give talks about the past, the Nazi era, and the building of socialism. A separate adult volunteer society ran old people's clubs, delivered meals on wheels, and provided home aides (Edwards, pp. 170–172, 193–196).

The Effectiveness of Social Controls

Social control in East Germany was focused on preventing political opposition to the SED and its style of socialism. The government was less concerned with deviance it defined as nonpolitical, except insofar as it saw all crime as political because it reflected poorly upon the merits of socialist society. Ordinary crime was handled in a style that was unmistakably both socialist and German. There was great emphasis on responding to deviance within worker- or neighborhood-based collectives. For example, factory managers were required to report to the policy any workers "who show serious signs of developing a work-shy outlook, who try to obtain a livelihood in an unworthy way, who break work discipline through constant abuse of alcohol or who show by their social behavior that they need extra instruction" (quoted in Steele, p. 158).

Some deviance was handled within the factory itself. Workers elected conflict commissions of 8 to 10 members which acted as courts for disciplining fellow workers in cases of quarrels, insults, petty theft, or damage to factory property. These panels were taken seriously and were quite effective. They might require convicted individuals to apologize to another person or to the collective, to repair or pay for damage, be publicly reprimanded, or pay a fine. The party newspaper published conflict commission cases weekly. Local disputes commissions played the same role in residential neighborhoods, adjudicating cases involving quarrels, noise, drunk driving, or even child abuse. Offenders convicted by the regular courts were expected to return to their old jobs after imprisonment and be looked after and helped to go straight by their fellow workers (Steele, pp. 139, 140, 157).

East Germany kept an unusually large uniformed police force, and they maintained files on all citizens, regardless of whether or not they committed any crimes. But except in cases of "political crimes," the police operated in typically German legalistic fashion, processing crimes and complaints strictly by the book (Ardagh, p. 316).

Defining Political Deviance. East German statistics cannot be relied on for accuracy, but it seems likely that there were in fact relatively low crime rates. Political deviance was another matter entirely. East Germany's leaders understood that many people did not support the regime; they were, in one way or another, **dissidents.** Open dissidence was treated harshly. Dissidents and their families were blocked from universities, jobs, and apartments. They were watched and followed by the secret police, so others avoided them. In extreme cases they were jailed, or even expelled from the country. Even people who were not explicitly "political" but simply tried to "drop out" of conventional life were defined as anti-socialist. Hippies, folk musicians, punk rockers, and unconventional artists were all viewed with suspicion. When rock music came to East Germany in the 1970s, the SED considered it harmful and threatening. Much rock was individualistic: It explored private, subjective feelings, and other rock was critical of government and society. As early as 1976 the SED decided that only carefully controlled rock music could be played in official discos by "disco moderators," who received special training in Marxism-Leninism and could be trusted. All other rock music performances were banned (Ramet, pp. 91–92).

But despite its tremendous power to sanction deviance, the East German government was caught in a dilemma. Leaders wanted both to suppress dissent and to give the appearance that there was no dissent, that East Germans enthusiastically supported the SED. In particular, SED leaders wanted to play down the amount of violence required to keep their regime in power. As much as possible, they wanted to avoid the open use of force. Above all, they wanted to avoid a recurrence of open revolt like the June 1953 rebellion, put down in such an ugly way by Soviet troops. On the other hand, they weren't willing to let dissidents leave East Germany, because they were afraid that millions of people would do so, revealing the pervasiveness of discontent.

The government hoped that by involving all citizens, from early childhood, in government-controlled organizations, they could build willing support for the regime. Government and people engaged in a sort of silent struggle, with the government trying to control all aspects of its citizens' lives and the people trying to create private space shielded from state power. By trying to control so much of people's lives, the government turned every aspect of life into an arena of political struggle. Many people who were otherwise apolitical found themselves defined as dissidents and in opposition to the government. Many people retreated from the public realm to country cottages and gardens and the kitchen-table society of friends and family. Informal friendship circles were particularly important to young people. Among friends they listened to music, talked politics, defined individual identities, and participated in a youth culture which was outside of government control (Lemke, pp. 68–71).

In the mid-1970s, the SED, under the leadership of Erich Honecker, decided that it would be better to allow people selected safety valves for their discontent, rather than increase the level of repression. The SED selected two seemingly harmless outlets: television and the church. They decriminalized the watching of western TV, figuring that since so many of West Germany's serious-minded TV programs were devoted to social problems like poverty and drug abuse, watching western TV would decrease the attractiveness of the West. The SED also permitted the Protestant Church, harassed since the 1950s, to increase its level of activity. The church became the only institution independent of the state and it took on an enormously important role in opposing the East German regime (Ardagh, p. 384).

The Church and Dissent

East Germany is a traditionally Lutheran part of Germany and the Catholic Church is rather small and inactive there, so Honecker sought his rapprochement with the Lutheran Church, promising some degree of church independence in exchange for a pledge that the church would stay out of politics. Honecker hoped the church would attract discontented people and direct their energies into religion, not political opposition. As a result, the church came to offer "the only organized public alternative to the official value-system, and thus attracted many people not otherwise very religious" (Ardagh, p. 385). All kinds of deviants—homosexuals, punks, rebellious youth, rock musicians, peace activists, and would-be emigrants—were attracted to the church (Goeckel, pp. 211, 216–217).

The church hierarchy, pastors, and congregations constantly argued over the role of the church: How far should it go along with the state? How much should the church allow its premises to be used for dissent? This very discussion, which called into question the legitimacy of the government, was profoundly seditious, even when church authorities decided in the end to suppress political activity. The very existence of the church as an institution outside the hierarchies of the SED made the state nervous. Even in the 1980s, when the SED permitted the building of new churches, permitted religious programs on state radio, and permitted departments of theology to train ministers, the state still discriminated against church members and especially pastors. Their children were usually excluded from higher education. They were officially put in a special category, the *Sonderlinge*—literally "the peculiar"—with a very small admissions quota and active Christians were not permitted to become schoolteachers or government officials (Ardagh, p. 387; Darnton, p. 226).

In the late 1980s, as the domination of the SED weakened, the churches, somewhat reluctantly, became the natural focus of dissident activity. In many cities peace groups, environmentalist groups, and human rights groups began meeting in churches and they pressured church officials to allow and protect greater freedom of speech within the church. Concerts and church services arranged by these groups drew more and more people and became weekly events that spilled over into candlelight marches, demonstrations, and vigils. In the fall of 1989, as the regime crumbled, church services in small towns attracted crowds, and while praying for divine intervention, people began to speak out against the government. Following the pattern established in Leipzig and Berlin, village churches held weekly prayer meetings and candlelight marches, and the authorities, as they felt their power undermined, began to back off from confronting the demonstrators (Philipsen, pp. 141–150; Darnton, pp. 222–226). In this way, the churches, the only independent institutions, became the nurseries of dissident organization.

Deviance and Social Control in the Federal Republic

You can see a clear contrast: East Germany was a **collectivist** society that treated individuals as members of groups, but West Germany was an **individualistic** society that saw individuals as autonomous actors, free to join groups or remain private. West Germans belonged to fewer groups than East Germans and the groups they did belong to were under no centralized control. The West German pattern of deviance and social control continues today in the reunified Germany.

Social Groups in an Individualistic Society

As Hall and Hall put it, in western Germany social institutions are compartmentalized. Politically, the nation is divided into states, and the federal government must share power with them. In business, work is divided among departments, which jealously guard their territory. Information is seldom shared freely among work groups (Hall and Hall, pp. 44–45). People keep their friends and their work separate, their school life and social life separate, and their friends and neighbors separate. How they behave in one social group will likely have little bearing on their treatment in another.

Children and School Life. Western German schools were (and are still) quite narrowly focused on academic preparation. Western Germans think schools are for learning, not for character building, team sports, or leadership development, which should be the responsibility of parents, churches, or voluntary groups like the Boy Scouts. School is held only between 8 A.M. and 1 P.M. and is devoted to academic classes. There might be a few classes or clubs in the afternoon, but most students go home for lunch, and then do many hours of homework or play team sports at local sports centers. Few schools have their own playing fields or swimming pools or even libraries or auditoriums where the whole school can assemble. Children often spend a great deal of time with friends or classmates, but their social life is outside the school. Similarly, while schools teach about democracy and the constitution and how the German government works, there are no student government organizations or even debating teams (Ardagh, pp. 241–243).

Women and Group Life. Short school days have had a major effect on women's lives in west Germany. Children don't start school until age 6 or 7 and there are few day-care centers or even kindergartens, and those that exist are privately run and relatively expensive. School, once begun, is only a half-day affair, and there is little after-school care available either. Then, of course, the shops close at 6:30, so someone has to be home to take care of children and shop in the afternoons (Marsh, p. 311). Western German society assumes that it is the responsibility of individual families, not the society or government, to work out this problem. As a result, western German women have been much less likely to work than east German women, and actually less likely to work than women in England or France or the United States.

Under 40 percent of West German women worked in the 1980s, and only a third of these women had children. They brought home only 18 percent of family income. It was the pattern in West Germany for women to work for several years before marriage and childbearing, at which time they left the labor force, reentering it only when their children were grown. As a result, there were few women in professional careers: Only 5 percent of lawyers and 3.4 percent of senior civil servants were women, although 20 percent of doctors were female. In banking, business, and industry, only about 2 percent of all top positions were held by women. Mostly, women found less skilled jobs, primarily in traditionally female occupations like office work and sales, and they earned only about half as much as men. Even women in salaried jobs earned only two-thirds of men's pay. The unemployment rate was about twice as high for women as for men (Ferree, p. 93; Ardagh, pp. 192–194; Nyrop, pp. 123–124).

Responses to Deviance

Western Germans respond to deviance in ways that are both characteristic of parliamentary democracies and characteristically German. Because of the burden of their Nazi past, west Germans are fearful of any government intervention that smacks of totalitarianism. They don't want the government spying on people or controlling private organizations or limiting freedom of speech. But as Germans they value an orderly society and they expect people to conform closely to the law. As we have seen, west Germans take it upon themselves to correct other people's behavior—in the streets, in the neighborhoods, at work. Also, west Germans are notoriously litiginous—that is, they readily litigate, or bring lawsuits against each other. Neighborhood residents will sue a restaurant that stays open too late, or a homeowner who doesn't follow the rules for mowing the grass. At work, employees will use grievance procedures to contest mandatory overtime they think unjustified, or a missed promotion.

> #### Johanna's Story: The Lawsuit
> Johanna Silberschnitt still blushes with embarrassment and anger when she talks about the lawsuit her neighbors brought against her family for excessive noise. They tried, she protests, to observe all the rules about quiet hours and laundry hours and hallway neatness in their apartment house. "But when you have four boys under the age of 10, you have to expect some noise," she remarks. In the end, the courts upheld the Silberschnitts, but "though we won the battle, we lost the war," Johanna says. It was hard to face angry neighbors day after day, and teachers began to look at the older boys as troublemakers. Finally, her in-laws helped them with the down payment and they bought a house in a new development outside town. It's further from the shops and school, Johanna says, but it's worth it. "There is no one living beneath us hearing footsteps and there are a lot more young families in the neighborhood, so people understand."

Political Deviance. Western Germans have a harder time responding to organized political deviance. Activity by skinheads and neo-Nazis has been on the upswing ever since reunification. There are more young men seen in the streets with shaved heads and paramilitary gear, wearing Nazi symbols, and there have been many attacks on foreigners and disabled people. Neo-Nazis have desecrated old Jewish cemeteries, set a synagogue on fire, and firebombed shelters for foreigners seeking political asylum. According to government figures, far-right groups committed 2,285 acts of racial violence in 1992, more than 22 times the level of a decade ago, but still fewer than are committed yearly in Great Britain. There are eighty-two "right-wing extremist organizations and other groupings," according to government intelligence sources, with a total membership of about 22,000, but with probably no more than 1,500 activists (Whitney, Oct. 21, 1993, pp. A1, A10).

There is disagreement among both Germans and outside observers about the seriousness of neo-Nazi violence. The extremist groups remain small, and their political parties have failed to get enough votes to send any representatives to the federal legislature. Most Germans are genuinely horrified by anything smacking of Nazism. In some cases they take individual action, helping a disabled man attacked by skinheads, or throwing a known neo-Nazi out of a bar. In several cities, after neo-Nazi attacks thousands of Germans turned out in candlelight processions to show their opposition to intolerance and anti-Semitism. In the government's view, neo-Nazi groups are an ugly, but relatively minor problem, and while it has increased the security force devoted to keeping them under surveillance, it has not attempted to stamp out their activity, arguing that free speech must be protected. For example, when a gang of 22 neo-Nazis recently threw stones and shouted Nazi slogans at the site of the Buchenwald concentration camp, they were detained by police, but only one was arrested on possible charges of disturbing the peace and making threats (*The New York Times,* July 25, 1994, p. A4; Cowell, p. A4; Whitney, Jan. 19, 1993, p. A4; Ardagh, pp. 504–505).

Erich's Story: The Skinhead

Erich Kessel (age 22) lives in a run-down working-class community on the industrial outskirts of Cologne. His mother works cleaning houses and his father is one of an increasing number of German workers who have been unemployed for years. His father yells at him all the time for leaving his apprenticeship: "You'll be nothing now; nothing, just like me. No one gives a damn for an ordinary worker; even the Ossis *(the east Germans) will spit on you!" Lately Erich has shaved his head, stopped going around the factories looking for regular work, and has been spending much of his time practicing martial arts with his skinhead friends. "It's all those foreigners who are running Germany," he says. "Hitler was right: there's red tide pouring out of the east—Poles and Russians and* Ossis, *taking all the good jobs and stealing our women, breeding a new race of* Untermenschen [inferior people]. *The government is plotting with NATO to let an international government take over Germany. Soon there'll be no more white people."*

Last week Erich and his group surrounded a young Turkish woman on the street downtown. "Hitler would have known what to do with you," they shouted, punching and kicking her. People looked at them aghast, but no one tried to stop them, and by the time the police came they were far away. Last night things didn't go so smoothly. The firebomb they threw into an apartment house filled with Turkish workers exploded magnificently, but as Erich ran from the scene his aging motorcycle refused to start. When the police pulled him off the bike he was still cursing his stupid "Polish" machine. Now he's in jail, charged with attempted murder and very much alone. Even Helga, his girlfriend, turned up only once—and she bluntly told him he was disgusting and she never wanted to see him again!

SOCIAL CHANGE AND THE FUTURE

The story of the *Wende* (German reunification) is a wonderful example of how historic social change actually takes place. Years of quiet organizing by dissident groups suddenly blossomed into exhilarating collective action in the demonstrations that led to the fall of the Berlin Wall. But the pace of change slowed after that, and the discouraging process of institutionalizing a revolution began.

The *Wende* really began with Gorbachev, because he loosened the hold of the Soviet Union upon all its eastern European satellites. When Hungary moved toward democracy and opened its border with Austria, early in 1989, East Germans began fleeing through Hungary to the West. In the first nine months of 1989 alone, 130,000 East Germans defied their government by leaving the country.[3] Because it was unable to stop this flood of emigration, the government's authority was fatally undermined. Gorbachev himself made it clear that Soviet troops would no longer be available to prop up the SED. That emboldened more people to flee and it made the SED seem more vulnerable. In October 1989, SED chief Erich Honecker stepped down and new leaders began to reorganize the party.

Celebrating the fall of the Berlin Wall in 1989, these young German men are intoxicated with the excitement of making history. Emboldened by participating in mass demonstrations, they have actually climbed the Wall. Only days before, they would have been shot by East German police if they had dared to cross the no-man's land which bordered the Wall.

[3]Almost 345,000 people left East Germany by the end of 1989, 2 percent of the country's remaining population. Those who left were mostly young, educated, and skilled, making their loss the more painful (Craig, 1994, p. 36). Many hospitals lost so many staff their operation was crippled.

In November 1989, millions of people demonstrated in East Berlin and Leipzig. They carried banners reading "No More Fear," "Socialism: Who Destroyed Its Meaning?" "Stop Privileges," and "Those Who Don't Move Don't Feel Their Chains." One said only "1789–1989." The crowds roared, "We are the people." After that, events moved quickly. First, the whole ministry resigned, then troops and tanks rolled into the streets of East Berlin, only to be withdrawn; then the whole *Politburo* resigned. Finally, on November 9, an SED spokesman was holding a news conference and someone handed him a handwritten note. He read it off casually, perhaps inaccurately, and reporters announced that the Wall was officially opened! Then Berliners took matters into their own hands. Hundreds of thousands of people from both sides of Berlin converged on the Wall. They argued with the guards, who looked frightened, but didn't shoot, and then suddenly one guard opened a gate. The crowd surged through and suddenly there were thousands of people through the Wall, and then on top of it—dancing, hugging, drinking wine, exchanging flowers, hammering at the Wall, and destroying it with pickaxes. The crowd chanted, "We are ONE people."

Collective Behavior and Social Movements

The fall of the Berlin Wall was one of the great revolutionary moments of the twentieth century, a moment when events move so fast that a crowd, and even individuals in that crowd, hold history in their hands. Just imagine: Those young, frightened border guards could as easily have started shooting as opened the gate. They made history!

Sociologists who study spontaneous history making like this call the phenomenon **collective behavior.** Events on this scale don't happen often, because they require an unusual combination of conditions. First of all, they occur in response to preexisting grievances. People are likely to engage in collective behavior when they are convinced that the authorities won't listen to them any other way. Collective behavior happens most readily in an already existing crisis, when there are structural strains in the society and social controls have weakened. People have a feeling that the possible gains from collective action outweigh the risks that authorities will punish them. Even then, collective action may not occur unless two other prior conditions are present. People need some way to communicate with each other so they know other people share their grievances and will act with them. Then, there is usually some precipitating incident that focuses long-standing complaints.

In Berlin in 1989, demonstrations grew out of years of organizing activity by dissident groups. Dissidents, working mostly through the Protestant churches, organized the growing demonstrations and helped people voice beliefs about the need for change. Then the collapse of the SED precipitated action and many more people spontaneously joined in. In the crowd at the Wall people improvised norms and individual actors played a major role in the actual events.

When the Berlin Wall was opened on November 9, events began to move very quickly. Until then, the dissident movement had focused on demands for democracy—in a separate, socialist East Germany. But the masses of November 9 suddenly looked through the Wall and saw the prosperous West—a society that worked. "We are ONE people," they declared, and the rush to reunification was born. The dissidents who led the movement were horrified. But Helmut Kohl, the chancellor of West Germany, saw a unique opportunity. Hastily, he announced a plan for rapid reunification, figuring that it could take place only while Gorbachev was still in power. In March 1990, East Germans democratically elected a new parliament; by July, the economic union of the two countries was a reality; and on October 3, the two nations were officially joined as one again.

Institutional Change

Germans were euphoric: no one had ever expected Germany to be whole once more, nor had anyone anticipated the end of Soviet domination in the East. But euphoria was short-lived. It soon became clear that in 40 years, West and East had become two very different societies, with contrasting values, different ways of thinking and interacting, as well as two incompatible economic systems. People realized that reunification would be difficult and very expensive. The East required new political institutions: new political parties, a new legal system, and new local governments at every level. It needed newly privatized economic institutions to replace the old state-owned structures. Schools, hospitals, and social welfare institutions had to be reorganized along western lines. And the terrible legacy of environmental damage had to be cleaned up. As institutions changed, East Germans had to reorient themselves to new roles and norms.

Reorganizing the Economy

The course of economic change was set by decisions taken early in the process of reunification. The governments of East and West Germany chose to merge the East into the Federal Republic as rapidly as possible, in part in an effort to stem the tide of emigration which was disruptive to West German society and damaging to the East as well.

The first step toward economic merger was the 1:1 currency union which took effect on July 1, 1990. Once East Germans had deutschmarks to spend, they bought western goods which were cheaper and of better quality. A Trabant had cost 10,000 marks, but a far superior used BMW from the West cost 4,000 marks (Ardagh, p. 431). Without buyers for their goods, without the state subsidies which had kept them afloat, and without guaranteed markets in other Soviet satellite nations (now opening their own borders to western goods), East German factories were driven out of business. Within a year unemployment in the East reached 30 percent.

Privatization. Simultaneously with the currency union, the German government began a process of complete privatization of the East German economy. East German companies would immediately either be sold to private investors or shut down. The government created a new agency, the Public Trust (or *Treuhandanstalt*) to carry out privatization. The Public Trust's job was daunting. As one East German industrialist explained, "No one knew how to transform an economy from socialist central planning to a free market. There was no road map" (Siegfried Schlottig, quoted in Protzman, p. D1).

The *Treuhand* took over more than 13,000 formerly state-owned companies. The agency's work went slowly at first. After a year, only 600 companies had been sold and east Germans had begun to demonstrate against the Kohl government demanding an end to factory closings and better job retraining and replacement plans (Ardagh, pp. 433, 450). In truth, the agency faced enormous obstacles. Many factories were antiquated: They used old equipment and technologies long since discarded in the west. Production caused air and water and soil pollution at levels considered illegal and intolerable in the west. Potential buyers feared becoming responsible for the staggering costs of environmental cleanup. Many factories were overstaffed, so their productivity was low, typically only a third that of western plants. Any buyer would have to spend hundreds of millions of dollars in renovation costs.

By 1995 privatization, however difficult, was almost complete. Perhaps a third of east German companies proved unsaleable and were shut down; others were sold after reorganization by the *Treuhand.* The agency spent $173 billion paying the debts of these companies and another $94 billion in restructuring their operations. They took in $47 billion in sales, leaving a deficit of $170 billion which has been paid by west Germans through increased taxes. Buyers committed themselves to investing a further $112 billion in their new companies. There were 4.1 million people who worked in the companies taken over by the *Treuhand,* but at the end of privatization, only 1.5 million of their jobs still existed (Protzman, pp. D1, D2).

Government Aid. Simultaneously with privatization, the German government began pouring money into eastern Germany: at least $100 billion a year, so far mostly for retraining, industrial restructuring, unemployment benefits, and subsidized work. The subsidies paid for rebuilding the roads, railroads, communications networks, and public buildings. In every major eastern city cranes and bulldozers are still seen everywhere, laying new sewers and power cables, restoring historic churches, and building new roads. This enormous investment is being paid for by a 7.5 percent income tax surcharge on western Germans.

Adopting Western Political Institutions

Superficially, political incorporation of eastern Germany into the Federal Republic proceeded more smoothly than economic reunification. All the old political institutions of the GDR disbanded upon reunification and the East adopted the legal system, constitution, and political institutions of the Federal Republic. The traditional five states of eastern Germany, which had been abolished in the centralizing GDR, were reestablished. The old puppet political parties of the GDR, with two important exceptions, disappeared, and the major West German parties established themselves in the East. One exception was the CDU, then the governing party, which had already existed as an eastern party, and therefore inherited a membership and some organization. The other party that continued in existence was the SED, which purged itself of its top leadership and then continued under a new name, the Party of Democratic Socialism

(PDS). So it did not take long to create all the standard West German political bodies in the former GDR.

On a deeper level, however, the establishment of democratic institutions in eastern Germany remains problematical. After the fall of the Berlin Wall, the dissident organizations that had led the protests struggled to transform themselves into mass democratic parties to lead an independent GDR. For a few months, they met and debated intensely and joined together at the Round Table to negotiate with the departing SED and the West German government. But once it became clear that the two Germanys would reunify, the West German parties moved their operations into the East. They played a dominating role in all the 1990 elections. Don't forget that eastern Germans had no experience with competitive party politics. They were overwhelmed by the TV ads, the posters, the rallies with huge sound systems, the election parties with beer and traditional costumes. The infant dissident parties had no way to compete.

Germany Today: Life in the Berlin Republic

We want the story to have a happy ending: Germany reunified, grateful east Germans enjoying democracy and capitalist affluence; virtuous west Germans proud of the help they gave their eastern brothers and sisters. Unfortunately, a decade after reunification the happy ending has not arrived. Perhaps it will, given sufficient time, but right now, Germany is faced with unanticipated difficulties and conflicts.

The Status of Economic Reunification

One of the most troubling aspects of German life today is the disappointing performance of the east German economy. At the start, Germans had faced economic unification with great optimism. Then–Chancellor Helmut Kohl promised easterners they would see "blooming landscapes" fill the east's gray and polluted land within five years. The height of their optimism has made Germans' disillusionment all the greater.

In some ways, eastern Germans are certainly better off than they were before 1989. Their wages are much higher. Legislation at the time of reunification aimed at equalizing wages and easterners now earn about 80 percent of what westerners earn. They are able to buy consumer goods undreamed of before 1989. They drive shiny BMWs and Mercedes Benz's, instead of the smelly, unsafe Trabants of socialist Germany. They have the most modern telephone system in the world, new roads, shiny new shopping malls. In some cities, like Leipzig, there are restored historic downtown districts filled with upscale restaurants and shops.

But many east Germans feel worse off. They worry terribly about unemployment, which they have never experienced before. They are shocked at the new inequalities present in their society and taken aback by the harsh demands of a capitalist economy. Even the new material abundance seems to them somewhat heartless.

Unemployment is the real root of all the trouble. In government statistics, unemployment in the east is running approximately double unemployment in the west—16–20 percent, compared to 8–10 percent. But there is a lot of disguised unemployment in the east too. Many people over 50 have been encouraged to retire early. Everyone admits there is a whole generation of middle-aged people who will never work again. Then there is government "make-work" and government "retraining." In the obsolete industrial cities along the border with Poland, unemployment runs as high as 35 percent (Andrews, Sept. 10, 1998, p. A12).

A "Hollow Economy." Eastern Germany's economy now has lots of new infrastructure, but too little new production and too few jobs. The new factories that have been built are highly mechanized and employ few workers. For example, Dow Chemical Corporation is rebuilding the toxic old chemical plant at Schkopau. The $7 billion facility will employ only 2,200. The deadly factory it replaces employed 18,000 (Andrews, April 17, 1997, p. D6). But many businesses avoid east Germany, building new factories in Poland or the Czech Republic instead, where wages are much lower. The FDR raised East German wages at the time of reunification, to stop the rush of easterners westward, but now they are paying a very high price for this policy. High wages, including the expensive German benefits package mandated in the welfare state, have slowed economic growth. And the access to western products, which east Germans wanted very much, has also harmed their economy, because local products could not compete against west German products. Now the stories are filled with west German goods and eastern factories are out of business (Nash, July 27, 1995, p. D7). East Germans feel like they are a welfare colony, maintained on the charity of the west, and it angers them very much, because in the past they took pride in their workmanship, their productivity, and their role as the leading socialist economy.

Economic Woes in the West. Western Germans are angry too. Some companies have profitted by buying up bargain-priced eastern enterprises, but by and large, there has been little benefit for the west in the east's dependence. Taxpayers complain of the burden of the 7.5 percent surcharge to help the east, which has continued for longer than most expected. Forty to fifty percent of the typical worker's paycheck is deducted in taxes (Cowell, June 4, 1997, p. A8).

European Unification and the Economy. Germany has been one of the strongest supporters of European unity. This support has reassured Germany's neighbors who were made nervous by German reunification, by the prospect of a larger Germany, once again throwing its weight around Europe. So Germany has a political need for European unification. But in the 1990s, European unification posed big problems for Germany. In order to qualify for inclusion in the European currency union (in order to be part of the Euro conversion), Germany, like other countries, had to reduce its budget deficits, cut back on taxes, and control inflation. And this at a time when German reunification was increasing government spending! What to do? The German government has been caught between two undesirable alternatives: reduce help to the east or cut back on the traditional social spending for German workers, which would mean smaller pensions, later retirement, less insured health care, less money for education, etc. Voters will be angry either way.

Germany in the Global Economy. Germany is also under pressure from global economic competition. Labor costs are exceptionally high: There are high wages, many fringe benefits, long vacations, many holidays, and complex work rules, which all add to the cost of labor. Companies must pay high payroll taxes and high corporate income taxes to contribute to the German welfare state. A Japanese worker costs his or her employer only two-thirds as much as a German worker, and a British worker costs only half as much. A worker in Poland or Romania costs even less. In order to compete, German businesses have been investing abroad, moving production outside Germany to eastern Europe and even merging with American companies. Foreign companies are avoiding Germany too. The result has been high unemployment in Germany (Andrews, Mar. 21, 1998, pp. A1, A3).

German voters want the government to do something about unemployment, but they don't want to accept lower wages, or give up any of their benefits. If the government lowers corporate taxes, it will have less money to pay for the social safety net Germans deem essential and less money to help the east.

Women in the New Germany

Though it had many faults, East German society had one virtue appreciated by its citizens: There were many benefits to help parents, and especially mothers, raise their children while working outside the home. As we have seen, affordable day care was widely available, most children stayed in school for a full day and ate lunch at school, there was generous maternity leave (a year at 80 percent of full pay), and the state enforced and guaranteed child support by absent fathers. Abortions were legal and available through the national health insurance system (Duggan and Folbre, p. 23; Ferree, p. 94). Women were accustomed to marrying young, having children early, and working throughout their childbearing years.

By 1989, 91 percent of East German women of working age were employed, and working women contributed 40 percent of average household income. They held an unusually large percentage of skilled factory jobs and professional jobs. Women were certainly not completely equal to men: They were concentrated in typically "feminine" occupations like education, nursing, and textile production, and they did most of the housework and child care, even when they worked full-time (Dolling, pp. 34–37; Nickel, pp. 50–51: Ferree, pp. 91, 93).

After reunification, eastern German women suddenly found themselves living on the western plan. The cost of day care doubled relative to income, and it is in short supply. Maternity leave now pays only 25 percent of full pay and the state no longer fully guarantees child support. School lets out before lunch and women are expected to be at home waiting for their children. Now two-thirds of unemployed eastern Germans are women. And women now cannot obtain unemployment benefits unless they can prove they already have child care arranged. Finally, abortion is now illegal in eastern Germany, as in western Germany, except in very limited circumstances (Nyrop, p. 123; Ferree, p. 93; Duggan and Folbre, p. 23). (See Table 5.4.)

In the eastern Länder in 1994, 54 percent of married women with children under age 3 were working, and another 26 percent were unemployed but wanted to work. Ninety-five percent of all married mothers in the east worked or wanted to work, while this was true of only 57 percent of those in the west (Federal Statistical Office, Erwerbsbeteiligung von Muttern). East German women have not

TABLE 5.4. Working Women in Germany:
The East German pattern of working mothers and state supported day care
is reflected in percentage of wives with young children who are in the labor force.

	Percent of All Women Employed or Looking for Work Before Reunification 1985	Percent of All Children Under 3 in Day Care Before Reunification 1985	Percent of Married Women with Children Under 3 Employed or Looking for Work After Reunification 1994
Former East Germany	83	80	80
Former West Germany	55	3	44

Sources: Einhorn, Barbara, *Cinderella Goes to Market, Citizenship, Gender and Women's Movements in East Central Europe,* London, Verso Press, 1993
Hohe der Erwerbsbeteiligung der Muter vom Alter jungsten Kindes abhangig, Statistiches Bundesamt, *http://www.Statistik-bund/de/presse/deutsch/pm/p6070031.htm* March 14, 1996

changed their earlier values; they consider paid work to be very important. Now women are one of the groups most disillusioned with reunification. They speculate irritably that the government is trying to push women back into the home to ease unemployment and raise the birthrate.

Cultural Reunification: Building New "Walls"?

> *There is a new joke now in east Germany: " 'We are one people,' says the easterner. 'So are we, says the westerner.' " (Whitney, Jan. 24, 1995, p. A3).*

Institutional changes in the economy and government were quickly accomplished in the former GDR. But cultural reunification is much more difficult to achieve. A decade after reunification Germans worry about "the walls in our heads and hearts (that) have been growing in both parts of Germany." "We have divided more than we have come together," said one east German local official (Cohen, Oct. 25, 1998, p. 6). Eastern Germans feel resentful of westerners, who have been so quick to condemn and discard everything eastern. "What do you expect to achieve by constantly telling 15 million people that everything they did was wrong?" demanded one easterner (Cowell, July 7, 1998, p. A8). It is helpful to contrast east Germany with other former communist countries like the Czech Republic and Poland. People have struggled to adopt market economies in those countries, but they are doing it for themselves and they feel proud of their efforts, while in east Germany, "each new day reminds eastern Germans that they lost the cold war and must defer to the victors" (*The New York Times,* September 1, 1996, p. E8). Many eastern Germans are suddenly nostalgic for their old society: "In the old days we didn't have a crime problem, we didn't have traffic jams, we didn't have trouble finding kindergarten places for our kids, and nobody had to worry about being thrown out of work," said one easterner (Kinzer, Aug. 27, 1994, p. 2).

Many western Germans, in turn, resent the burden of the east, abruptly shouldered before they knew its full weight. They resent paying so much to modernize eastern Germany, and they are particularly infuriated becaused the easterners are self-pitying and angry rather than grateful. They tell stories about passive eastern- ers, unwilling to take responsibility for themselves. The old East Germany was "a cozy, warm, very comfortable place for people who wanted to exist with a mini- mum of effort," one Berliner explained (Koch, p. 26; Cowell, June 4, 1997, p. A8).

Anomie in the Former East Germany

To fully understand the problems of cultural integration in Germany today, we need to turn to the work of a famous French sociologist, the great Emile Durkheim. At the end of the nineteenth century, Durkheim wrote about the harm- ful consequences of rapid change in modern societies. He said that in a period of profound change, such as a time of rapid economic modernization, an economic collapse, or a revolution, old standards of behavior, values, and beliefs become ir- relevant and a state of **anomie** (or normlessness) prevails. Old social controls on individual behavior become ineffective; new ones don't yet exist and people feel directionless and lost. They may expect too much from the changed society and they often become depressed or aggressive. Rates of deviant behavior like suicide, violent crime, and drug and alcohol abuse climb rapidly.

Life in eastern Germany after reunification presents a classic example of anomie. At first, when the Wall came down, there was euphoria. People thought that with Germany reunified, all their problems would be solved. But then every- thing changed. Timothy Garton Ash explains,

> Nowhere in post-Communist Europe has the change in every aspect of life been so sudden and total as in east Germany. Not just the political, economic and legal system but the street signs, the banks, the post offices, the health insurance, the cars, the products in the shops, why even the bread has changed. (Ash, p. 22)

Socialism, a set of ideals which many people respected, even if they thought it had not been achieved, seemed to have been decisively defeated. People were asked to adopt a whole new way of life previously considered reprehensible. They were asked to act as individuals, to put consumer desires first, and to value private en- terprise and profit making. Some people rapidly adapted, but for many others it was as if the world had turned upside down.

Frau Metz's Story: The Teacher

"There couldn't be a worse time to be a teacher," declares Charlotte Metz, a seventh-grade history teacher in the mining town of Cottbus. "I truly don't know what to teach my stu- dents. You know, I really believed in socialism. I taught my students Marxism-Leninism and I though we were building the workers' state. I cried when the Wall came down. But then I saw pictures of the West. I even visited my relatives in Berlin, and it wasn't all poverty and crime and drug addiction as we had been told. But now look what reunifica- tion has done here: the mines are closed and almost all the men are out of work. That would never have happened in the GDR."

"Teach your students both sides," Charlotte's husband interjects. "Let them make up their own minds." "I do. . . I try to," Charlotte replies, "but I can't teach any of it with convic- tion. I don't know what's true anymore or what's the right way to run our country. And there's something worse. My students don't want to know. Yesterday, when I started my lesson on the division of Germany, they put on their earphones. Yes, they actually pulled out their Walkmans and put on their earphones!"

Many eastern Germans describe their state of anomie quite clearly. The Reverend Christian Führer, who was a leader of the dissident movement in Leipzig, explains, "People here feel a real schizophrenia. No one wants to go back to the days of dictatorship, but at the same time we're not really happy with the new system. It's full of challenges for which we are totally unprepared." Even people who are better off economically, Reverend Führer contends, "are worried about what is happening to our society. Brutal competition and the lust for money are destroying our sense of community. Almost everyone feels a level of fear or depression or insecurity" (Kiner, Oct. 14, 1994, p. A14).

Birthrates and Death Rates

Anomie in eastern Germany had chillingly concrete social consequences. Birthrates had been falling gradually in both east and west Germany, but after the fall of the Berlin Wall birthrates in the east fell precipitously. By 1993, there were 60 percent fewer births than there had been in 1989. Rates fell most for married women in the prime childbearing years. Such a sharp decline is almost unprecedented in twentieth-century history, though something similar did happen in Berlin in the last years of World War II. Marriage rates fell to the lowest level in the world today. "Many eastern couples are reluctant to have children, because they are unsure whether they will be able to survive in the newly competitive society," concluded *The New York Times* ("Living, and Dying, in a Barren Land," p. 54; Kinzer, Jan. 25, 1994, p. A3).

Even more disturbing was the sharp rise in death rates in the former GDR. For women between the ages of 25 and 45, the death rate rose by nearly 20 percent between 1989 and 1991, and for men of the same age it rose 30 percent. Most astonishingly, for girls 10 to 14 the death rate rose 70 percent. These increase were not the result of deterioration in health care. Medical care probably improved in the eastern states after reunification, a fact reflected in lower death rates for babies and the elderly. And since longevity had been improving under communism, it was a sharp break with past trends. For men, death rates from cardiovascular disease,

FIGURE 5.1. Falling births in East Germany before and after reunification (1989/1990) 1980 to 1996

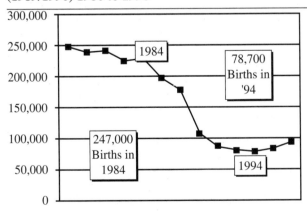

Source: Federal Statistical Office, Germany, "Births in the new Länder and Berlin-East after 1989–90," http://www.statistik-bund.de/presse/englisch/pm/p7291023.htm

injuries, including suicide, and cirrhosis of the liver became particularly high. For women, injuries and suicide stood out. Eastern German men in 1990 were 156 percent more likely to die of injuries or suicide than men in western Germany ("Living, and Dying, in a Barren Land," p. 54).[4]

Political Reunification: The Politics of "Walls"

It surely won't surprise you to learn that the lasting divisions between east and west Germany have found political expression. Easterners, particularly young easterners, have used politics to protest their situation. Their political choices have deepened the split between east and west and reshaped the political landscape of the Berlin Republic. Most worrisome to westerners is the preference of many easterners for what are seen as extremist minor parties of the left and right.

The PDS. The PDS (Party of Democratic Socialism), the successor to the SED, is enjoying a resurgence of support in the eastern Länder (echoing a similar revival of Communist parties in all the former Soviet-bloc nations). In 1990 the PDS captured 11 percent of the eastern vote. Then in 1994 it was up to 19.8 percent, and in 1998, 21 percent. Despite a poor showing in the west, the large eastern vote in 1998 gave the PDS more than 5 percent of the total national vote, qualifying the party for full status as a minority party in parliament. The PDS has done even better in local votes, electing town councillors and mayors and emerging as the strongest local party in east Berlin (Ash, p. 22; Kinzer, June 27, 1994, p. A3; Cowell, July 7, 1998, p. A8; Andrews, Sept. 28, 1998, p. A10; Anderes, Sept. 10. 1998, p. A12).

Parties of the Extreme Right. Some easterners vote for ultraright parties (like the German People's Union and the National Democratic Party) as a protest vote, with no desire to see those parties gain power. But ultraright parties also have serious supporters, many of them young, who are deeply involved in the neo-Nazi movement. While none of the ultraright parties have won enough votes to gain representation in parliament, they are stronger locally. In April 1998, the German People's Union won 12 percent of the vote in Saxony-Anhalt (the eastern state with the highest unemployment rate), with heavy support from young people and the unemployed (Andrews, Sept. 28, 1998, p. A10; Andrews, Sept. 10, 1998, p. A12; Cowell, April 27, 1998, p. A3).

The ultraright parties are all antiforeigner. Campaign posters for the German People's Union in 1998 called for "German Money for German Jobs." Supporters termed foreigners "parasites" who feed on the "*Aryan Volk*," and "*Zecke Verrecke*" (death to the ticks) is one of the slogans of the movement. It may seem strange that antiforeigner sentiment is so strong in a part of Germany where there are in fact very few foreigners. Immigrants are only 1.8 percent of the population in the

[4]Birthrates have recovered somewhat since 1995, but are still only about half their 1989 levels. Death rates have also begun to come down (Federal Statistical Offices, "Population Development and Life Expectancy, 1995–1997).

east, compared to 9 percent in the western states. Foreigners are really **scapegoats** for young east Germans' problems.

As you can see, antiforeign sentiment on the ultraright is often accompanied by neo-Nazi language and imagery. Teenage neo-Nazis shave their heads, dress in paramilitary gear, and call themselves "freedom fighters" battling to establish "national liberation zones." They claim Hitler's values of "industriousness, cleanliness, and racial superiority." The neo-Nazi movement is frightening, but not large. The German government estimates that there are 6,400 neo-Nazis in Germany who actually engage in violence, 3,700 of them in the east (Cowell, Feb. 8, 1998, p. 3).

Young people in the east have been less hesitant to embrace neo-Nazism because they were never taught about the horrors of the Nazi era and they were never expected to take responsibility for it. The socialists and communists who came to power in the east after the division of Germany had been steadfast opponents of Nazism. They tried and jailed and executed many former Nazis and then declared that the guilty had been punished and East Germans no longer had to bear of burden of guilt for the past. Taboos about Nazi rhetoric, dress, and symbols that are very strong in the west have little force in the east (Buruma, pp. 156, 157, 181).

The Election of 1998: A New Era in Mainstream Politics. The big news in German politics is not about the fringe parties; it is an upheaval at the center: the end of the era of Chancellor Helmut Kohl and his party, the Christian Democratic Union (CDU), and the election of the Social Democratic Party (SPD), which governed in 1999 in coalition with the Green Party. Gerhard Schröder, the leader of the Social Democrats, became Germany's new Chancellor.

In 1998 Helmut Kohl had been Chancellor for 16 years. He was 68 years old, the grand old man of German reunification, who had brilliantly steered East Germany out of Soviet control and negotiated European and American consent for reunification. It seemed inconceivable that his legendary political magic could fail. Schröder appealed to two big groups of Germans: people who felt economically threatened in the reunified Germany (and obviously, many of these people were easterners) and younger Germans, who were attracted both to Schröder's SPD and to the Green Party, which still keeps the aura of 1960s rebellion. Together, the SPD and the Greens formed what Germans call a "Red-Green Coalition"—a first in German history.

In many ways Schröder's victory demonstrated the impact of the east on German politics. The vote for the SPD was stronger in the east than in the west. It really showed that the east has had an effect on the culture of the reunified Germany; it has moved Germany left, towards its own socialist heritage. The SPD also made youth an issue in the campaign. Schröder, at 54, presented himself as a "young" candidate, part of a new generation, like Bill Clinton in the United States and Tony Blair in Great Britain. He called himself a *"Spätgeboren,"* someone born too late to bear any of the guilt of the Nazi era and free of the entangling burden of history; the man for a new Germany in the new "Berlin Republic." The Red-Green coalition is, in fact, a younger government, and somewhat more diverse, with more women in parliament and several Turkish legislators (Cohen, Oct. 27, 1998, p. A4).

The Continuing Burden of the Past

It is proving frustratingly difficult for the "new" Berlin Republic to escape the burden of history. Gerhard Schröder's new government found itself immediately embroiled in bitter controversy about the past. The most intense fight began before the 1998 election when a Schröder ally proposed that Germany abandon its plan to build a huge memorial to the victims of the Holocaust in a key Berlin location: right next to the German Parliament building, in the former no-man's land along the Wall, and on the site of Hitler's bunker. Gerhard Schröder concurred, saying Germans should "look ahead without forgetting what happened." The proposal ignited a fiery war of words. Ignatz Bubis, the leader of Germany's Jewish community, was outraged, accusing SPD leaders of a new willingness to "suppress memory." Germans were shaken by the eruption of so much anger and guilt, once again, over whether Germany could be a "normal nation" (Buruma, Dec. 29, 1998, p. A14; Cohen, Nov. 29, 1998, p. 10WK; Cohen, Nov. 10, 1998, p. A16; Cowell, July 26, 1998, p. 13).

Resolving Nazi-Era Claims. Despite, or perhaps because of the bitter battle over the monument, the new Social Democratic government has tried to resolve some continuing issues about German war guilt and German racism. German manufacturers, including Volkswagen, Daimler-Benz, and several chemical companies, now face a battery of American class-action lawsuits on behalf of slave-laborers (many non-Jewish) in Nazi factories. Chancellor Schröder has pressed the industrial corporations to settle up, creating new funds to compensate slave workers, to whom virtually no reparations were ever paid. At the same time, the government has spurred German banks to settle longstanding claims against them for gold stolen from Jews and looted from concentration camp victims during the Nazi era (Andrews and Meier, Dec. 14, 1998, p. A12; Andrews, July 8, 1998, p. A3; Cowell, Aug. 1, 1998, p. A2).

Redefining the Meaning of "German." The first major legislation of the new Social Democratic government was a bold proposal to change Germany's immigration law. The new law spoke to the burden of history because it finally changed the definition of what it means to be a German. Up until 1999, Germany had kept its 1913 law declaring that anyone of German "blood"—whether born in Germany or elsewhere—was German and could automatically claim citizenship. This law always evoked Nazi racial themes and claims of racial superiority. The law also prevented Germany's immigrant population from gaining citizenship. Even the children and grandchildren of immigrants, born in Germany, could not be citizens.

The new law will give automatic citizenship to the German-born children of foreigners, if they have one parent who has been in Germany since age 14. Estimates are that the new law will permit almost 3 million foreign residents—about 43 percent of the total—to became German citizens. It will also lift a burden of guilt from the rest of the Germans (Cohen, Oct. 16, 1998, p. A4).

Germany Faces the Future

In recent decades Germans have worried a lot about whether they are "good" Germans—ashamed of their past, protective of the disadvantaged, careful to maintain "the social peace." They have tried to avoid being "bad" Germans—racist or insensitive, greedy or unjust. Now the future raises a far more radical question: Will they be Germans at all?

Die Deutsche Volk. "Many people have had a rooted image of Germany as a blood community," said Hartmut Esser, German sociologist (Cohen, Oct. 16, 1998, p. A4). Now they must learn to see Germany differently, in a more modern, liberal way, as a community based on citizenship, including people from other parts of the world, people of other races and other religions. It is a shock.

Germany and Europe. "The nation-state in Europe," said Foreign Minister Joschka Fischer, "is now a thing of the past, no more than a virtual reality" (Cohen, Jan. 28, 1999, p. A3). Will Germans lose themselves in Europe? Young Germans are beginning to see themselves as "Europeans"; they speak more English and respond positively to ads written in English. They work abroad in German-owned companies or German-American mergers and soon they will begin doing business in euros, rather than Deutschmarks. Like other European countries, Germany is set to give up control of its monetary policy to a new European Central Bank. More political unification will surely follow (Cohen, Dec. 6, 1998, pp. 1, 14; Cowell, Sept. 23, 1998, p. A6).

Germany and the World Economy. Germany is in the same situation as the other nations in this book: Japan, Mexico, and Egypt. The global economy says "cut": cut wages, cut taxes, cut government spending and deficits, cut government regulation, so profitability will be improved and business will flourish. But Germany, like many other nations, has national traditions at odds with this capitalist imperative. Germans elected the Social Democrats because they wanted to preserve their welfare state, their high labor compensation, strong unions, and relatively equal incomes. Schröder has promised both to preserve the "social market economy" and to make Germany more competitive in the global economy. Will he be able to make good on both promises? Millions of people in Japan and Egypt and Mexico, and all over the world, eagerly await the result.

Thinking Sociologically

1. Describe the values and institutions that made East Germany a socialist society.
2. Germany and Japan are both capitalist societies, but in some ways they are quite different. What differences do you see in their attitudes toward consumerism, leisure, and individualism? How do their economic institutions differ?
3. Do you live in a capitalist society? If so, is its style of capitalism similar or different in any way from Germany's or Japan's?

4. Germany, Japan, and the United States are the world's three biggest capitalist economies. Refer to Table 1.4 and compare how equally or unequally these three societies distribute income to their citizens.
5. In institutional structure, Germany, Japan, and Mexico all are representative democracies. What are some of the differences in the ways their political institutions work?
6. Compare the system of higher education in Germany with the system in your society. What advantages or disadvantages do you see in each?
7. Compare and contrast the ways that East Germany and West Germany defined and responded to deviance.
8. Explain why many people in eastern Germany have experienced anomie since reunification. Can you think of some examples of people experiencing anomie in your own society?
9. Turn to Table 5.3 (p. 266) and compare the percentages of 20- to 24-year-olds attending institutions of postsecondary education in Germany and in the United States. Can you explain why Germans' incomes rival those of Americans even though many fewer Germans attend college or university?

For Further Reading

ARDAGH, JOHN, *Germany and the Germans.* New York: Penguin, 1991.
DARNTON, ROBERT, *Berlin Journal, 1989–1990.* New York: Norton, 1991.
EINHORN, BARBARA, *Cinderella Goes to Market: Citizenship, Gender and Women's Movements in East Central Europe.* London: Verso Press, 1993.
FULBROOK, MARY, *Anatomy of a Dictatorship: Inside the GDR 1949–1989.* New York: Oxford University Press, 1995.
HALL, EDWARD T., AND MILDRED REED HALL, *Understanding Cultural Differences.* Yarmouth, ME: Intercultural Press, 1990.
HAMILTON, STEPHEN F., *Apprenticeship for Adulthood.* New York: Free Press, 1990.
MARCUSE, PETER, *Missing Marx: A Personal and Political Journal of a Year in East Germany, 1989–1990.* New York: Monthly Review Press, 1991.
MARKOVITS, INGA, *Imperfect Justice: An East-West German Diary.* New York: Oxford University Press, 1995.
RUESCHMEYER, MARILYN, AND CHRISTIANE LEMKE, eds., *The Quality of Life in the German Democratic Republic.* Armonk, NY: Sharp, 1989.
STEELE, JONATHAN, *Inside East Germany: The State That Came in from the Cold.* New York: Urizen Books, 1977.

Bibliography

ANDREWS, EDMUND L., "Germans Cut Labor Costs with a Harsh Export: Jobs," *The New York Times,* March 21, 1998, pp. A1, A3.
———, "Volkswagen, in Shift, Will Set Up Fund for Slave Workers," *The New York Times,* July 8, 1998, p. A3.
———, "Gift from Kohl in an Election Year: Temporary Work for East's Jobless," *The New York Times,* Sept. 10, 1998, p. A12.
———, "Former Stronghold Turns Frustrations against Kohl in Voting Booth," *The New York Times,* Sept. 28, 1998, p. A10.
———, AND BARRY MEIER, "Germans Seek Plan to Avoid Suits over Nazi-Era Labor," *The New York Times,* Dec. 14, 1998, p. 12.

ARDAGH, JOHN, *Germany and the Germans.* New York: Penguin, 1991.

ASH, TIMOTHY GARTON, "Kohl's Germany: The Beginning of the End?" *The New York Review,* Dec. 1, 1994, pp. 20–26.

BERGNER, JEFFREY T., *The New Superpowers: Germany, Japan, the U.S. and the New World Order.* New York: St. Martin's Press, 1991.

BURANT, STEPHEN R., ed., *East Germany: A Country Study,* 3d ed., Area Handbook Series. Washington, DC: U.S. Government Printing Office, 1988.

BURUMA, IAN, *The Wages of Guilt: Memories of War in Germany and Japan.* New York: Farrar, Straus & Giroux, 1994.

———, "War Guilt and the Difference between Germany and Japan," *The New York Times,* Dec. 29, 1998, p. A19.

CHILDS, DAVID, *The GDR: Moscow's German Ally.* London: Allen & Unwin, 1983.

COHEN, ROGER, "The Growing Burden of Germany's Unification," *The New York Times,* Mar. 8, 1993, pp. D1, D3.

———, "German Voters End an Era," *The New York Times,* Sept. 28, 1998, pp. A1, A10.

———, "The German 'Volk' Seem Set to Let Outsiders In," *The New York Times,* Oct. 16, 1998, p. A4.

———, "Germany's New Face: Age 22, at Threshold of Change," *The New York Times,* Oct. 25, 1998, p. 6.

———, "New German Parliament Ponders History, Past and Future," *The New York Times,* Oct. 27, 1998, p. A4.

———, "Anniversary Sets Germans to Quarreling on Holocaust," *The New York Times,* Nov. 10, 1998, p. A16.

———, "Germany Searches for 'Normality,' " *The New York Times,* Nov. 29, 1998, p. 10WK.

———, "Berlin Has a Word for Its Ambitions: English," *The New York Times,* Dec. 6, 1998, pp. 1, 14.

———, "Germany's Pragmatic Ex-Radical Thinks Globally." *The New York Times,* Jan. 28, 1999, p. A3.

COWELL, ALAN, "German Paradox: Alongside Healing, New Flames," *The New York Times,* May 8, 1995, p. A4.

———, "Quietly, 22,000 Ex-Soviet News Settle in Germany," *The New York Times,* Sept. 24, 1995, p. 3.

———, "Only Economic Jitters Unite Germans," *The New York Times,* Oct. 3, 1995, p. A10.

———, "It's Young vs. Old in Germany as the Welfare State Fades," *The New York Times,* June 4, 1997, pp. A1, A8.

———, "Neo-Nazis Carving Out Fiefs in Eastern Germany," *The New York Times,* Feb. 8, 1998, p. 3.

———, "Kohl's Party Routed in East; Far Right Enters Assembly," *The New York Times,* April 27, 1998, p. A3.

———, "Gloom in German East May End Kohl's Streak," *The New York Times,* July 7, 1998, pp. A1, A8.

———, "An Opponent of Kohl Puts Taboo Topic into Election," *The New York Times,* July 26, 1998, p. 13.

———, "Biggest German Bank Admits and Regrets Dealing in Nazi Gold," *The New York Times,* Aug. 1, 1998, p. A2.

———, " 'New' Germans Find Escape from Tainted Past," *The New York Times,* Sept. 23, 1998, p. A6.

CRAIG, GORDON A., *The Germans.* New York: Putnam, 1982.

————, "United We Fall," *New York Review of Books,* Jan. 13, 1994, pp. 36–40.

DAHRENDORF, RALF, *Society and Democracy in Germany.* New York: Doubleday Anchor, 1969.

DALTON, RUSSELL J., *Politics in West Germany.* Boston: Scott, Foresman, 1989.

DARNTON, ROBERT, *Berlin Journal, 1989–1990.* New York: Norton, 1991.

DEBARDELEBEN, JOAN, "The Future Has Already Begun," in Marilyn Rueschmeyer and Christiane Lemke, eds., *The Quality of Life in the German Democratic Republic.* Armonk, NY: Sharp, 1989, pp. 144–164.

DOLLING, IRENE, "Culture and Gender," in Marilyn Rueschmeyer and Christiane Lemke, eds., *The Quality of Life in the German Democratic Republic.* Armonk, NY: Sharp, 1989, pp. 22–47.

DUGGAN, LYNN, AND NANCY FOLBRE, "Women and Children Last," *The New York Times,* Jan. 8, 1994, p. 23.

EDWARDS, E. E., *GDR Society and Social Institutions.* New York: St. Martin's Press, 1985.

EINHORN, BARBARA, *Cinderella Goes to Market: Citizenship, Gender and Women's Movements in East Central Europe.* London: Verso Press, 1993.

FEDERAL STATISTICAL OFFICE, GERMANY, "Births in the new Länder und Berlin-East after 1989–90," http://www.statistik-bund.de/presse/englisch/pm/p7291023.htm.

————, "Erwerbsbeteiligung von Müttern, http://www.statistik-bund.de/presse/deutsch/pm/p6070031.htm.

————, "Population Development and Life Expectancy," http://www/Statistik-bund.de/basis/e/popo5.htm.

FERREE, MYRA MARX, "The Rise and Fall of 'Mommy Politics': Feminism and Unification in (East) Germany," *Feminist Studies,* Vol. 19, no. 1 (Spring, 1993), pp. 89–115.

FRIEDRICHS, JURGEN, "Ethnic Segregation in Cologne, Germany 1984–94," *Urban Studies,* Vol. 35, no. 10 (Oct. 1998), pp. 1745–1762.

GANNON, MARTIN J., *Understanding Global Cultures.* London: Sage, 1994.

GERTH, H. H., AND C. WRIGHT MILLS, *From Max Weber: Essays in Sociology.* New York: Oxford University Press, 1958.

GITTER, ROBERT J., AND MARKUS SCHEUER, "US and German Youths: Unemployment and the Transition from School to Work," *Monthly Labor Review* (March 1997), pp. 16–20.

GLAESSNER, GERT-JOACHIM, "Technology Policy and Educational Transformations," in Marilyn Rueschmeyer and Christiane Lemke, eds., *The Quality of Life in the German Democratic Republic.* Armonk, NY: Sharp, 1989, pp. 77–94.

GLOUCHEVITCH, PHILIP, *Juggernaut: The German Way of Business.* New York: Simon & Schuster, 1992.

GOECKEL, ROBERT R., "Church and Society in the GDR," in Marilyn Rueschmeyer and Christiane Lemke, eds., *The Quality of Life in the German Democratic Republic.* Armonk, NY: Sharp, 1989, pp. 210–227.

GRASS, GUNTER, *Two States—One Nation?* New York: Harcourt Brace Jovanovich, 1990.

HALL, EDWARD T., AND MILDRED REED HALL, *Understanding Cultural Differences.* Yarmouth, ME: Intercultural Press, 1990.

HAMILTON, STEPHEN F., *Apprenticeship for Adulthood.* New York: Free Press, 1990.

HANCOCK, M. DONALD, *West Germany: The Politics of Democratic Corporatism.* Chatham, NJ: Chatham House, 1989.

HEILIG, GERHARD, THOMAS BUTTNER, AND WOLFGANG LUTZ, "Germany's Population: Turbulent Past, Uncertain Future," *Population Bulletin,* Vol. 45, no. 4 (Dec. 1990), pp. 1–46.

KELLER, MARYANN, *Collision: GM, Toyota, Volkswagen and the Race to Own the 21st Century.* New York: Doubleday, 1993.

KINZER, STEPHEN, "650 a Baby: Germany to Pay to Stem Decline in Births," *The New York Times,* Jan. 25, 1994, p. A3.

————, "In 'East Germany,' Bad Ol' Days Now Look Good," *The New York Times,* Aug. 27, 1994, p. 2.

————, "A Wall of Resentment Now Divides Germany," *The New York Times,* Oct. 14, 1994, pp. A1, A14.

KIRCH, HENRY, *The German Democratic Republic.* Westview Profile/Nations of Contemporary Europe. Boulder, CO: Westview Press, 1985.

KOCH, BURKHARD, "Post-Totalitarianism in Eastern Germany and German Democracy," *World Affairs,* Vol. 156, no. 1 (Summer, 1993), pp. 26–34.

KOLINSKY, EVA, "Everyday Life Transformed: A Case Study of Leipzig since German Unification," *World Affairs,* Vol. 156, no. 4 (Spring 1994), pp. 159–174.

KRAMER, JANE, "Letter from West Germany," *The New Yorker,* Dec. 19, 1983, pp. 102–121.

LANDUA, DETLEF, "Germany after Unification: Still a Twofold Society," *International Journal of Comparative Sociology,* Vol. 34, no. 1–2 (Jan./Apr. 1993), pp. 75–86.

LAQUEUR, WALTER, *Germany Today.* Boston: Little, Brown, 1985.

LEMKE, CHRISTIANE, "Political Socialization in the 'Micromilieu,' " in Marilyn Rueschmeyer and Christiane Lemke, eds., *The Quality of Life in the German Democratic Republic.* Armonk, NY: Sharp, 1989, pp. 59–73.

LEWIS, FLORA, *Europe: A Tapestry of Nations.* New York: Simon & Schuster, 1987.

"Living, and Dying, in a Barren Land," *The Economist,* Apr. 23, 1994, p. 54.

LONG, ROBERT EMMET, ed., *The Reunification of Germany,* The Reference Shelf. New York: Wilson, 1992.

MARCUSE, PETER, *Missing Marx: A Personal and Political Journal of a Year in East Germany, 1989–1990.* New York: Monthly Review Press, 1991.

MARSH, DAVID, *The Germans: A People at the Crossroads.* New York: St. Martin's Press, 1989.

MARX, KARL, AND FRIEDRICH ENGELS, *Manifesto of the Communist Party.* New York: International Publishers, 1948, 1966.

MERKL, PETER, *Germany: Yesterday and Tomorrow.* New York: Oxford University Press, 1965.

NASH, NATHANIEL C., "A Wall in the Mind," *The New York Times,* July 27, 1995, pp. D1, D7.

NICKEL, HILDEGARD M., "Sex-Role Socialization in Relationships as a Function of the Division of Labor," in Marilyn Rueschmeyer and Christiane Lemke, eds., *The Quality of Life in the German Democratic Republic.* Armonk, NY: Sharp, 1989, pp. 48–58.

NYROP, RICHARD F., ed., *Federal Republic of Germany: A Country Study,* 2d ed., Area Handbook Series. Washington, DC: U.S. Government Printing Office, 1982.

PHILIPSEN, DIRK, *We Were the People: Voices from East Germany's Revolutionary Autumn of 1989.* Durham, NC: Duke University Press, 1993.

"A Profile of the German Education System," *American Educator,* Vol. 18, no. 1 (Spring, 1994), pp. 21–22.

"The Progress of German Unification," *The New York Times,* Sept. 1, 1996, p. E8.

PROTZMAN, FERDINAND, "East Nearly Privatized, Germans Argue the Cost," *The New York Times,* Aug. 12, 1994, pp. D1, D2.

RADEMAEKERS, WILLIAM, "The Oh So Good Life," in Robert Emmet Long, ed., *The Reunification of Germany.* New York: Wilson, 1992, pp. 8–12.

RAMET, PEDRO, "Disaffection and Dissent in East Germany," *World Politics,* Vol. 37, no. 1 (Oct. 1984), pp. 85–111.

RUSSELL, JAMES W., *After the Fifth Sun.* Englewood Cliffs, NJ: Prentice-Hall, 1994.

SCHARF, C. BRADLEY, *Politics and Change in East Germany.* Boulder, CO: Westview Press, 1984.

SHLAES, AMITY, *Germany: The Empire Within.* New York: Farrar, Straus & Giroux, 1991.

STEELE, JONATHAN, *Inside East Germany: The State That Came in from the Cold.* New York: Urizen Books, 1977.

STERN, FRITZ, *Dreams and Delusions: The Drama of German History.* New York: Knopf, 1987.

——, "Freedom and Its Discontents," *Foreign Affairs,* Vol. 72, no. 4 (Sept./Oct. 1993), pp. 108–125.

TURNER, HENRY ASHBY, JR., *The Two Germanies since 1945.* New Haven, CT: Yale University Press, 1987.

UNITED NATIONS, DEPARTMENT OF INTERNATIONAL AFFAIRS, "National Accounts Statistics: Compendium of Income Distribution Statistics," *Statistical Papers,* Series M, No. 79, 1985.

WHITNEY, CRAIG R., Comfortable Germans, Slow to Change (Especially If It Means More Work)," *The New York Times,* Jan. 16, 1995, p. A6.

——, "Germans Five Years Later: Bitter and Still Divided," *The New York Times,* Jan. 24, 1995, p. A3.

WORLD BANK, *World Development Report 1993: Investing in Health.* New York: Oxford University Press, 1993.

Index

About the Author

Catherine Cameron is Professor Emerita in the Behavioral Science Department of the University of LaVerne, LaVerne, California. Born in Canada, she earned a B.A. from McMaster University. After raising a family, she received an M.A. and Ph.D. in sociology from the University of Southern California, with emphases in family sociology and social psychology. She also earned a California license as a marriage and family therapist, and at the University of La Verne, she helped found and direct the master's program in marriage and family therapy.

Dr. Cameron has taught at both the graduate and undergraduate level for 21 years. Although she has not practiced psychotherapy, she found her training invaluable in teaching in the therapy program and also in conducting interviews and survey research. In addition to many articles, She has written two books prior to *Resolving Childhood Trauma*. *The Name Givers* (1983) analyzed the motives and meanings that parents bring to the naming of their children. In 1988, she coauthored *Moving: The Challenge of Change*, which examined the meaning of home to individuals and families, explored why geographic relocation is often traumatic, and showed that effective coping mechanisms can make moving a challenge rather than a catastrophe.

Because Dr. Cameron's research has intrigued the media, she has been frequently interviewed on radio and television and by newspapers, and has lectured in Europe and Asia. Her increasing concern with victimization in society and within the family led to her writing *Resolving Childhood Trauma*. A reviewer has described her as "a concerned yet reasoned voice in the emotionally charged debate about trauma and memory."